CAUSATION IN THE LAW OF THE WORLD TRADE ORGANIZATION

Causation in the Law of the World Trade Organization: An Econometric Approach is for both scholars and practitioners of WTO law with an interest in the causal questions that WTO law raises. Assuming no prior knowledge of causal philosophy or statistical analysis, Catherine Gascoigne discusses the problems in the current approach to assessing causation in the WTO jurisprudence and she then proposes an alternative methodology that draws on causal philosophy and econometric analysis. The book demonstrates how this methodology could be harnessed to make causal determinations for the purpose of implementing trade remedies and also to make out claims of serious prejudice. Additionally, the book argues that the methodology could be helpful for assessing the impact of domestic legislation on policy objectives under the General Exceptions and the Technical Barriers to Trade Agreement. The final chapter draws out the implications of using the methodology in order to calculate the amount of retaliation permissible under the Dispute Settlement Understanding.

CATHERINE GASCOIGNE is a Macquarie Research Fellow at Macquarie Law School, Macquarie University. She earned her PhD in Law at the University of Cambridge, where she studied as both a Gates Cambridge Scholar and a W. M. Tapp Scholar. She won the Society of International Economic Law/Journal of International Economic Law/Oxford University Press Essay Prize (2018/2019), which is awarded to an early career researcher for the best essay on any subject relating to international economic law.

CAMBRIDGE INTERNATIONAL TRADE AND ECONOMIC LAW

Processes of economic regionalisation and globalisation have intensified over the last decades, accompanied by increases in the regulation of international trade and economics at the levels of international, regional and national laws. At the same time, significant challenges have arisen with respect to economic liberalization, rule-based systems of trade and investment, and their political and social impacts. The subject matter of this series is international economic law, in this contemporary context. Its core is the regulation of international trade, investment, finance and cognate areas such as intellectual property and competition policy. The series publishes books on related regulatory areas, in particular human rights, labour, environment and culture, as well as sustainable development. These areas are horizontally interconnected and vertically linked at the international, regional and national levels. The series also includes works on governance, dealing with the structure and operation of international organisations related to the field of international economic law, and the way they interact with other subjects of international and national law. The series aims to include excellent legal doctrinal treatises, as well as cutting-edge interdisciplinary works that engage law and the social sciences and humanities.

Books in the Series

Causation in the Law of the World Trade Organization: An Econometric Approach
Catherine Gascoigne

The European Union and International Investment Law Reform: Between Aspirations and Reality
Ivana Damjanovic

Agricultural Domestic Support under the WTO: Experience and Prospects
Lars Brink and David Orden

Capital Controls and International Economic Law
Bryan Mercurio

The Law and Practice of Global ICT Standardization
Olia Kanevskaia Whitaker

Between Market Economy and State Capitalism: China's State-Owned Enterprises and the World Trading System
Henry S. Gao and Weihuan Zhou

New Asian Regionalism in International Economic Law
Pasha L. Hsieh

Essential Interoperability Standards: Interfacing Intellectual Property and Competition in International Economic Law
Simon Brinsmead

Digital Services in International Trade Law
Ines Willemyns

Law and Politics on Export Restrictions: WTO and Beyond
Chien-Huei Wu

Energy in International Trade Law: Concepts, Regulation and Changing Markets
Anna-Alexandra Marhold

Shareholders' Claims for Reflective Loss in International Investment Law
Lukas Vanhonnaeker

Transparency in the WTO SPS and TBT Agreements: The Real Jewel in the Crown
Marianna B. Karttunen

Preferential Services Liberalization: The Case of the European Union and Federal States
Johanna Jacobsson

Emerging Powers in International Economic Law: Cooperation, Competition and Transformation
Sonia E. Rolland and David M. Trubek

Commitments and Flexibilities in the WTO Agreement on Subsidies and Countervailing Measures
José Guilherme Moreno Caiado

The Return of the Home State to Investor-State Disputes: Bringing Back Diplomatic Protection?
Rodrigo Polanco

Industrial Policy and the World Trade Organization: Between Legal Constraints and Flexibilities
Sherzod Shadikhodjaev

The Public International Law of Trade in Legal Services
David Collins

The Prudential Carve-Out for Financial Services: Rationale and Practice in the GATS and Preferential Trade Agreements
Carlo Maria Cantore

Preferential Services Liberalization: The Case of the European Union and Federal States
Johanna Jacobsson

Judicial Acts and Investment Treaty Arbitration
Berk Demirkol

Distributive Justice and World Trade Law: A Political Theory of International Trade Regulation
Oisin Suttle

Freedom of Transit and Access to Gas Pipeline Networks under WTO Law
Vitalily Pogoretskyy

Reclaiming Development in the World Trading System, 2nd edition
Yong-Shik Lee

Developing Countries and Preferential Services Trade
Charlotte Sieber-Gasser

Establishing Judicial Authority in International Economic Law
Edited by Joanna Jemielniak, Laura Nielsen and Henrik Palmer Olsen

WTO Dispute Settlement and the TRIPS Agreement: Applying Intellectual Property Standards in a Trade Law Framework
Matthew Kennedy

Trade, Investment, Innovation and their Impact on Access to Medicines: An Asian Perspective
Locknie Hsu

The WTO and International Investment Law: Converging Systems
Jürgen Kurtz

The Law, Economics and Politics of International Standardisation
Edited by Panagiotis Delimatsis

Export Restrictions on Critical Minerals and Metals: Testing the Adequacy of WTO Disciplines
Ilaria Espa

Optimal Regulation and the Law of International Trade: The Interface between the Right to Regulate and WTO Law
Boris Rigod

The Social Foundations of World Trade: Norms, Community, and Constitution
Sungjoon Cho

Public Participation and Legitimacy in the WTO
Yves Bonzon

The Challenge of Safeguards in the WTO
Fernando Piérola

General Interests of Host States in International Investment Law
Edited by Giorgio Sacerdoti, with Pia Acconci, Mara Valenti and Anna De Luca

WTO Disciplines on Subsidies and Countervailing Measures: Balancing Policy Space and Legal Constraints
Dominic Coppens

The Law of Development Cooperation: A Comparative Analysis of the World Bank, the EU and Germany
Philipp Dann

Liberalizing International Trade after Doha: Multilateral, Plurilateral, Regional, and Unilateral Initiatives
David A. Gantz

Domestic Judicial Review of Trade Remedies: Experiences of the Most Active WTO Members
Edited by Müslüm Yilmaz

The Relevant Market in International Economic Law: A Comparative Antitrust and GATT Analysis
Christian A. Melischek

International Organizations in WTO Dispute Settlement: How Much Institutional Sensitivity?
Marina Foltea

Public Services and International Trade Liberalization: Human Rights and Gender Implications
Barnali Choudhury

The Law and Politics of WTO Waivers: Stability and Flexibility in Public International Law
Isabel Feichtner

African Regional Trade Agreements as Legal Regimes
James Thuo Gathii

Processes and Production Methods (PPMs) in WTO Law: Interfacing Trade and Social Goals
Christiane R. Conrad

Non-Discrimination in International Trade in Services: 'Likeness' in WTO/GATS
Nicolas F. Diebold

The Law, Economics and Politics of Retaliation in WTO Dispute Settlement
Edited by Chad P. Bown and Joost Pauwelyn

The Multilateralization of International Investment Law
Stephan W. Schill

Trade Policy Flexibility and Enforcement in the WTO: A Law and Economics Analysis
Simon A. B. Schropp

CAUSATION IN THE LAW OF THE WORLD TRADE ORGANIZATION

An Econometric Approach

CATHERINE GASCOIGNE
Macquarie University

CAMBRIDGE
UNIVERSITY PRESS

CAMBRIDGE
UNIVERSITY PRESS

Shaftesbury Road, Cambridge CB2 8EA, United Kingdom

One Liberty Plaza, 20th Floor, New York, NY 10006, USA

477 Williamstown Road, Port Melbourne, VIC 3207, Australia

314–321, 3rd Floor, Plot 3, Splendor Forum, Jasola District Centre, New Delhi – 110025, India

103 Penang Road, #05-06/07, Visioncrest Commercial, Singapore 238467

Cambridge University Press is part of Cambridge University Press & Assessment, a department of the University of Cambridge.

We share the University's mission to contribute to society through the pursuit of education, learning and research at the highest international levels of excellence.

www.cambridge.org
Information on this title: www.cambridge.org/9781316511305

DOI: 10.1017/9781009052146

First published 2023

A catalogue record for this publication is available from the British Library.

A Cataloging-in-Publication data record for this book is available from the Library of Congress

ISBN 978-1-316-51130-5 Hardback

For my parents, John and Kate

CONTENTS

FIGURES

ACKNOWLEDGEMENTS

This book has had a relatively long gestation – beginning as a doctoral thesis at the University of Cambridge and ending during my time as a Research Affiliate at the University of Sydney. Throughout that time, this book has benefitted, both financially and intellectually, from the generosity of many people and institutions that I wish gratefully to acknowledge here.

First and foremost, I would like to thank Professor Lorand Bartels MBE (University of Cambridge), my doctoral supervisor. In particular, I would like to thank him for encouraging me to write on this neglected topic and for guiding me through its development with his characteristic academic rigour, intellectual enthusiasm and wry wit. Additionally, I am greatly indebted to Professor Michael Waibel (University of Vienna) and Professor Jan Wouters (KU Leuven), my doctoral examiners. In addition to providing invaluable advice about how to revise my doctoral thesis for publication, they also generously provided me with introductions to domestic authorities who were able to assist with the domestic approaches discussed in Chapter 2 of this book. Professor David Howarth (University of Cambridge) and my first-year examiner, Professor Alexander (Sandy) Steel (University of Oxford) also provided useful comments on some early drafts of my doctoral thesis that helped to shape its final form.

Additionally, I would like to express my profound gratitude to the Gates Cambridge Trust for supporting my doctoral studies at the University of Cambridge. I am also very thankful for the further financial support of the WM Tapp Studentship from Gonville and Caius College, Cambridge, the Gowrie Scholarship and the Australian Bicentennial Scholarship Award. Finally, I would like to thank the University of Sydney Law School (particularly Professor Chester Brown) for allowing me to be a Research Affiliate during the final stages of completing this book.

Furthermore, I would like to gratefully acknowledge several domestic authorities for the information that they helped to provide regarding the causation and non-attribution analysis discussed in Chapter 2 of the book. In particular, I wish to thank: the United States International Trade Commission, especially Karl von Schriltz, Assistant General Counsel for Import Injury; the United Kingdom Trade Remedies Authority; the Antidumping Commission, Australia; the Directorate-General for Trade of the European Commission; and the Trade and International Team within the Ministry of Business, Innovation and Employment, New Zealand. I also wish to thank the Government of Canada's Trade Law Bureau.

My final, fondest and most profound thanks must go to my family for their tireless support of all of my academic endeavours. First, I would like to thank my parents, John and Kate, to whom this book is dedicated as a token of my appreciation. Lastly, I would like to express my enormous gratitude to my husband, Andrew, as well as my children, Amelia and Alexander, for so graciously accommodating the temporal and material pressures that large academic projects place on family life.

***

It is important to note that, with permission from Cambridge University Press, parts of this book have been published elsewhere. First, a significant part of Chapter 2 has been published as a journal article: Catherine Gascoigne, 'The Determination of Causation in the Application of Trade Remedies' (2021) 20(1) WTR 56. Moreover, select parts of Chapters 3, 4 and 5 appear in the following book chapter: Catherine Gascoigne, '*A Priori* Causal Inferences in the Law of the World Trade Organization' in Kajtar, Cali and Milanovic (eds), *Secondary Rules of Primary Importance in International Law: Attribution, Causality, Evidence and Standards of Review in the Practice of International Courts and Tribunals* (European Society of International Law Series) (OUP 2022).

Finally, the jurisprudence cited in this book was updated to 31 May 2022.

TABLE OF CASES

House of Lords

- *Yorkshire Dale Steamship Co v Minister of War Transport* [1942] AC 691

Permanent Court of International Justice

- *Case Concerning the Factory at Chorzów (Germany v Poland)* (Jurisdiction) (26 July 1927) PCIJ Rep Series A No 9

Supreme Judicial Court of Massachusetts

- *Corey v Havener* (1902) 182 Mass 250, 65 NE 69

United States Court of Appeals for the Federal Circuit

- *Nippon Steel Corp v Int'l Trade Commission*, 345 F.3d 1379, 381 (Fed Cir 2003)

United States Court of International Trade

- *American Spring Wire Corp v United States*, 590 F Supp 1273, 1276 (Ct Int'l Trade 1984)
- *Gilford-Hill Cement Co v United States*, 615 F. Supp 577, 579 (Ct Int'l Trade 1985)

United States International Trade Commission

- USITC, *100- to 150-Seat Large Civil Aircraft from Canada* (701-TA-578 and 731-1368) February 2018

- USITC, *Certain Carbon Steel Products* from Australia, Belgium, Brazil, Canada, Finland, France, Germany, Japan, Korea, Mexico, Netherlands, Poland, Romania, Spain, Sweden, Taiwan and United Kingdom (AA192 1-197 Review) September 2003
- USITC, *Certain Cold-Rolled Steel Products* from Argentina, Brazil, China, Indonesia, Japan, Russia, Slovakia, South Africa, Taiwan, Thailand, Turkey, Venezuela (TA-393-396) July 1999
- USITC, *Certain Crabmeat from Swimming Crabs* (TA-201-71) August 2000
- USITC, *Certain Crabmeat and Certain Seamless Carbon and Alloy Steel Standard, Line and Pressure Pipe* from the Czech Republic, Japan, Mexico, the Republic of South Africa and Romania (731-TA-846-850) October 2017
- USITC, *Forged Steel Fittings from Taiwan* (731-TA-1396) September 2018

United States Supreme Court

- *Castaneda v Partida* 430 US 482 (1977)
- *Hazelwood School District v United States* 433 US 299 (1977)

WTO Article 21.5 Arbitrations

- WTO, *European Communities: Regime for the Importation, Sale and Distribution of Bananas—Recourse to Article 21.5 by the European Communities—Report of the Panel* (12 April 1999) WT/DS27/RW/EEC
- WTO, *European Communities and Certain member States: Measures Affecting Trade in Large Civil Aircraft—Recourse to Article 21.5 of the DSU by the United States—Report of the Appellate Body* (15 May 2018) WT/DS316/AB/RW
- WTO, *European Communities and Certain member States: Measures Affecting Trade in Large Civil Aircraft—Recourse to Article 21.5 of the DSU by the United States—Report of the Panel* (22 September 2016) WT/DS316/RW
- WTO, *United States: Certain Country of Origin Labelling (COOL) Requirements—Recourse to Article 21.5 of the DSU by Canada and Mexico—Report of the Appellate Body* (29 May 2015) WT/DS384/AB/RW; WT/DS386/AB/RW
- WTO, *United States: Certain Country of Origin Labelling (COOL) Requirements—Recourse to Article 21.5 of the DSU by Canada and*

Mexico—Report of the Panel (20 October 2014) WT/DS384/RW; WT/DS386/RW

- WTO, *United States: Countervailing Measures on Certain Hot-Rolled Carbon Steel Flat Products from India—Recourse to Article 21.5 of the DSU by India—Report of the Panel* (15 November 2019) WT/DS436/RW
- WTO, *United States: Investigation of the International Trade Commission in Softwood Lumber from Canada—Recourse to Article 21.5 of the DSU by Canada—Report of the Appellate Body* (13 April 2006) WT/DS277/AB/RW
- WTO, *United States: Measures Concerning the Importation, Marketing and Sale of Tuna and Tuna Products—Recourse to Arbitration by United States under Article 21.5 of the DSU and Second Recourse to Article 21.5 of the DSU by Mexico—Decision by Arbitrations* (14 December 2018) WT/DS381/AB/RW/USA; WT/DS381/AB/RW2
- WTO, *United States: Subsidies on Upland Cotton—Recourse to Article 21.5 of the DSU by Brazil—Report of the Appellate Body* (2 June 2008) WT/DS267/AB/RW
- WTO, *United States: Subsidies on Upland Cotton—Recourse to Article 21.5 of the DSU by Brazil—Report of the Panel* (18 December 2007) WT/DS267/RW

WTO Article 22.6 Arbitrations

- WTO, *Brazil: Export Financing Programme for Aircraft—Recourse to Arbitration by Brazil under Article 22.6 of the DSU and Article 4.11 of the SCM Agreement—Decision by the Arbitrators* (28 August 2000) WT/DS46/ARB
- WTO, *Canada: Export Credits and Loan Guarantees for Regional Aircraft—Recourse to Arbitration by Canada under Article 22.6 of the DSU and Article 4.11 of the SCM Agreement—Decision by the Arbitrators* (17 February 2003) WT/DS222/ARB
- WTO, *European Communities: Measures Concerning Meat and Meat Products (Hormones)—Recourse to Arbitration by the European Communities under Article 22.6—Decision by the Arbitrators* (12 July 1999) WT/DS26/ARB
- WTO, *European Communities: Measures Concerning Meat and Meat Products (Hormones)—Recourse to Arbitration by the European Communities under Article 22.6—Decision by the Arbitrators* (12 July 1999) WT/DS48/ARB

- WTO, *European Communities: Regime for the Importation, Sale and Distribution of Bananas—Recourse to Arbitration by the European Communities under Article 22.6 of the DSU* (9 April 1999) WT/DS27/ARB
- WTO, *European Communities: Regime for the Importation, Sale and Distribution of Bananas—Recourse to Arbitration by European Communities under Article 22.6 of the DSU and Article 4.11of the SCM Agreement—Decision by the Arbitrators* (24 March 2000) WT/DS27/ARB/ECU
- WTO, *European Communities and Certain member States: Measures Affecting Trade in Large Civil Aircraft—Recourse to Arbitration by the European Communities under Article 22.6—Decision by the Arbitrators* (2 October 2019) WT/DS316/ARB
- WTO, *United States: Antidumping Act of 1916—Recourse to Arbitration by the United States under Article 22.6 of the DSU—Decision of the Arbitrators* (24 February 2004) WT/DS136/ARB
- WTO, *United States: Certain Country of Origin Labelling (COOL) Requirements—Recourse to Arbitration by the United States under Article 22.6 of the DSU—Decision by the Arbitrators* (7 December 2015) WT/DS384/ARB; WT/DS386/ARB
- WTO, *United States: Certain Methodologies and Their Application to Anti-Dumping Proceedings Involving China—Recourse to Arbitration by the United States under Article 22.6—Decision by the Arbitrators* (1 November 2019) WT/DS471/ARB
- WTO, *United States: Continued Dumping and Subsidy Offset Act of 2000—Recourse to Arbitration by Brazil under Article 22.6 of the DSU—Decision by the Arbitrators* (31 August 2004) WT/DS217/ARB/BRA
- WTO, *United States: Continued Dumping and Subsidy Offset Act of 2000—Recourse to Arbitration by the United States under Article 22.6 of the DSU—Decision by the Arbitrators* (31 August 2004) WT/DS217/ARB/IND
- WTO, *United States: Continued Dumping and Subsidy Offset Act of 2000—Recourse to Arbitration by the United States under Article 22.6 of the DSU—Decision by the Arbitrators* (31 August 2004) WT/DS217/ARB/JPN
- WTO, *United States: Continued Dumping and Subsidy Offset Act of 2000—Recourse to Arbitration by the United States under Article 22.6 of the DSU—Decision by the Arbitrators* (31 August 2004) WT/DS217/ARB/KOR

- WTO, *United States: Countervailing Duty Measures on Certain Products from China—Recourse to Arbitration by the United States under Article 22.6 DSU—Decision by the Arbitrator* (26 January 2022) WT/DS437/ARB
- WTO, *United States: Measures Affecting the Cross-Border Supply of Gambling and Betting Services—Recourse to Arbitration by the United States Under Article 22.6 of the DSU—Decision by the Arbitrators* (21 December 2007) WT/DS285/ARB
- *United States: Measures Affecting Trade in Large Civil Aircraft (Second Complaint)—Recourse to Arbitration by the United States under Article 22.6—Decision by the Arbitrators* (13 October 2020) WT/DS353/ARB
- WTO, *United States: Measures Concerning the Importation, Marketing and Sale of Tuna and Tuna Products Recourse to Arbitration by the United States under Article 22.6 of the DSU—Decision by the Arbitrators* (25 April 2017) WT/DS381/ARB
- WTO, *United States: Sunset Review of Anti-Dumping Measures on Oil Country Tubular Goods from Argentina—Recourse to Arbitration by Argentina under Article 21.5—Decision by the Arbitrators* (12 April 2007) WT/DS268/AB/RW
- WTO, *United States: Tax Treatment for 'Foreign Sales Corporations'—Recourse to Arbitration by the United States under Article 22.6 of the DSU and Article 4.11 of the SCM Agreement—Decision of the Arbitrators* (30 August 2002) WT/DS108/ARB

WTO Panel and Appellate Body

- WTO, *Argentina: Measures Affecting the Export of Bovine Hides and the Import of Finished Leather—Report of the Panel* (19 December 2000) WT/DS155/R
- WTO, *Argentina: Measures Affecting the Importation of Goods—Report of the Appellate Body* (15 January 2015) WT/DS438/AB/R; WT/DS444/AB/R; WT/DS445/AB/R
- WTO, *Argentina: Measures Relating to Trade in Goods and Services—Report of the Appellate Body* (14 April 2016) WT/DS453/AB/
- WTO, *Argentina: Safeguard Measures on Imports of Footwear—Report of the Appellate Body* (14 December 1999) WT/DS121/AB/R
- WTO, *Argentina: Safeguard Measures on Imports of Footwear—Report of the Panel* (25 June 1999) WT/DS121/R

- WTO, *Australia: Certain Measures Concerning Trademarks, Geographical Indications and Other Plain Packaging Requirements Applicable to Tobacco Products and Packaging—Report of the Appellate Body* (9 June 2020) WT/DS435/AB/R; WT/DS441/AB/R
- WTO, *Australia: Certain Measures Concerning Trademarks, Geographical Indications and Other Plain Packaging Requirements Applicable to Tobacco Products and Packaging—Report of the Panel* (29 June 2020) WT/DS435/R
- WTO, *Australia: Measures Affecting the Importation of Apples from New Zealand—Report of the Appellate Body* (29 November 2010) WT/DS367/AB/R
- WTO, *Australia: Measures Affecting the Importation of Apples from New Zealand—Report of the Panel* (9 August 2010) WT/DS367/R
- WTO, *Brazil: Measures Affecting Imports of Retreaded Tyres—Report of the Appellate Body* (3 December 2007) WT/DS332/AB/R
- WTO, *Brazil: Measures Affecting Imports of Retreaded Tyres—Report of the Panel* (12 June 2007) WT/DS332/R
- WTO, *Canada: Certain Measures Affecting the Automotive Industry—Report of the Panel* (11 February 2000) WT/DS139/R; WT/DS142/R
- WTO, *Canada: Continued Suspension of Obligations in the EC—Hormones Dispute—Report of the Appellate Body* (16 October 2008) WT/DS321/AB/R
- WTO, *China: Countervailing and Anti-Dumping Duties on Grain-Oriented Flat-Rolled Electrical Steel from the United States—Report of the Panel* (15 June 2012) WT/DS414/R
- WTO, *China: Measures Affecting Trading Rights and Distribution Services for Certain Publications and Audiovisual Entertainment Products—Report of the Appellate Body* (21 December 2009) WT/DS363/AB/R
- WTO, *China: Measures Affecting Trading Rights and Distribution Services for Certain Publications and Audiovisual Entertainment Products—Report of the Panel* (12 August 2009) WT/DS363/R
- WTO, *China: Measures Related to the Exportation of Rare Earths, Tungsten, and Molybdenum—Report of the Appellate Body* (7 August 2014) WT/DS/AB431/AB/R; WT/DS/432/AB/R; WT/DS433/AB/R
- WTO, *China: Measures Related to the Exportation of Rare Earths, Tungsten, and Molybdenum—Report of the Panel* (26 March 2014) WT/DS431/R; WT/DS432/R; WT/DS433/R
- WTO, *China: Measures Related to the Exportation of Various Raw Materials—Report of the Appellate Body* (30 January 2012) WT/DS394/AB/R; WT/DS395/AB/R; WT/DS398/AB/R

- WTO, *Colombia: Indicative Prices and Restrictions on Ports of Entry—Report of the Panel* (27 April 2009) WT/DS366/R
- WTO, *Colombia: Measures Relating to the Importation of Textiles, Apparel and Footwear—Report of the Appellate Body* (7 June 2016) WT/DS461/AB/R
- WTO, *Dominican Republic: Measures Affecting the Importation and Internal Sale of Cigarettes—Report of the Panel* (26 November 2004) WT/DS302/R
- WTO, *European Commission: Antidumping Duties on Malleable Cast Iron Tube or Pipe Fittings from Brazil—Report of the Appellate Body* (22 July 2003) WT/DS 219/AB/R
- WTO, *European Commission: Antidumping Duties on Malleable Cast Iron Tube or Pipe Fittings from Brazil—Report of the Panel* (7 March 2003) WT/DS219/R
- WTO, *European Communities: Antidumping Duties on Farmed Salmon from Norway—Report of the Panel* (16 November 2007) WT/DS377/R
- WTO, *European Communities: Countervailing Measures on Dynamic Random Access Memory Chips from Korea—Report of the Panel* (17 June 2005) WT/DS299/R
- WTO, *European Communities and Certain member States: Measures Affecting Trade in Large Civil Aircraft—Report of the Panel* (30 June 2010) WT/DS316/R
- WTO, *European Communities and Its member States: Tariff Treatment of Certain Information Technology Products—Report of the Panel* (16 August 2010) WT/DS375/R; WT/DS376/R; WT/DS377/R
- WTO, *European Communities: Measures Affecting the Approval and Marketing of Biotech Products—Report of the Panel* (29 September 2006) WT/DS291/R; WT/DS292/R; WT/DS293/R
- WTO, *European Communities: Measures Affecting Asbestos and Asbestos-Containing Products—Report of the Appellate Body* (12 March 2001) WT/DS135/AB/R
- WTO, *European Communities: Measures Affecting Asbestos and Asbestos Containing Products—Report of the Panel* (18 September 2000) WT/DS135/R
- WTO, *European Communities: Measures Concerning Meat and Meat Products (Hormones)—Report of the Appellate Body* (16 January 1998) WT/DS26/AB/R; WT/DS48/AB/R
- WTO, *European Communities: Measures Concerning Meat and Meat Products (Hormones)—Report of the Panel* (18 August 1997) WT/DS48/R/CAN

- WTO, *European Communities: Measures Prohibiting the Importation and Marketing of Seal Products—Report of the Appellate Body* (22 May 2014) WT/DS400/AB/R; WT/DS401/AB/R
- WTO, *European Communities: Measures Prohibiting the Importation and Marketing of Seal Products—Report of the Panel* (25 November 2013) WT/DS400/R; WT/DS401/R
- WTO, *European Union: Anti-Dumping Measures on Biodiesel from Indonesia—Report of the Panel* (25 January 2018) WT/DS480/R
- WTO, *European Union: Anti-Dumping Measures on Imports of Certain Fatty Alcohols from Indonesia—Report of the Panel* (16 December 2016) WT/DS442/R
- WTO, *European Union: Countervailing Duties on Certain Polyethylene Terephthalate from Pakistan—Report of the Panel* (6 July 2017) WT/DS486/R
- WTO, *European Union: Countervailing Measures on Certain Polyethylene Terephthalate from Pakistan—Report of the Appellate Body* (16 May 2018) WT/DS486/AB/R
- WTO, *India: Certain Measures Relating to Solar Cells and Solar Modules—Report of the Appellate Body* (24 February 2016) WT/DS456/R
- WTO, *Indonesia: Certain Measures Affecting the Automobile Industry—Report of the Panel* (2 July 1998) WT/DS54/R; WT/DS55/R; WT/DS59/R; WT/DS64/R
- WTO, *Indonesia: Safeguard on Certain Iron or Steel Products—Report of the Panel* (18 August 2017) WT/DS490/R; WT/DS496/R
- WTO, *Japan: Measures Affecting Agricultural Products—Report of the Appellate Body* (19 March 1999) WT/DS76/AB/R
- WTO, *Japan: Measures Affecting the Importation of Apples—Report of the Panel* (15 July 2003) WT/DS245/R
- WTO, *Japan: Taxes on Alcoholic Beverages—Report of the Panel* (11 July 1996) WT/DS8/R; WT/DS10/R; WT/DS11/R
- WTO, *Korea: Measures Affecting Imports of Fresh, Chilled and Frozen Beef—Report of the Appellate Body* (11 December 2000) WT/DS161/R; WT/DS169/R
- WTO, *Korea: Measures Affecting Imports of Fresh, Chilled and Frozen Beef—Report of the Panel* (31 July 2000) WT/DS161/R; WT/DS169/R
- WTO, *Korea: Measures Affecting Trade in Commercial Vessels—Report of the Panel* (7 March 2005) WT/DS273/R
- WTO, *Korea: Taxes on Alcoholic Beverages—Report of the Panel* (17 September 1998) WT/DS75/R; WT/DS84/R

- WTO, *Mexico: Definitive Countervailing Measures on Olive Oil from the European Communities—Report of the Panel* (4 September 2008) WT/DS341/R
- WTO, *Peru: Additional Duty on Imports of Certain Agricultural Products—Report of the Panel* (27 November 2014) WT/DS457/R
- WTO, *Russia: Tariff Treatment of Certain Agricultural and Manufacturing Products—Report of the Panel* (12 August 2016) WT/DS485/R
- WTO, *Thailand: Antidumping Duties on Angles, Shapes and Sections of Iron or Non-Alloy Steel and H-Beams from Poland—Report of the Panel* (28 September 2000) WT/DS122/R
- WTO, *Thailand: Customs and Fiscal Measures on Cigarettes from the Philippines—Report of the Appellate Body* (17 June 2011) WT/DS371/AB/R
- WTO, *Thailand: Customs and Fiscal Measures on Cigarettes from the Philippines—Report of the Panel* (15 November 2010) WT/DS371/R
- WTO, *United States: Anti-Dumping and Countervailing Duties on Ripe Olives from Spain—Report of the Panel* (19 November 2021) WT/DS577/R
- WTO, *United States: Anti-Dumping and Countervailing Measures on Certain Coated Paper from Indonesia—Report of the Panel* (6 December 2017) WT/DS491/R
- WTO, *United States: Antidumping Measures on Certain Hot-Rolled Steel Products from Japan—Report of the Appellate Body* (24 July 2001) WT/DS184/AB/R
- WTO, *United States: Antidumping Measures on Certain Hot-Rolled Steel Products from Japan—Report of the Panel* (28 February 2001) WT/DS184/R
- WTO, *United States: Certain Country of Origin Labelling (COOL) Requirements—Report of the Appellate Body* (29 June 2012) WT/DS384/AB/R; WT/DS386/AB/R
- WTO, *United States: Certain Country of Origin Labelling (COOL) Requirements—Report of the Panel* (18 November 2011) WT/DS384/R; WT/DS386/R
- WTO, *United States: Continued Dumping and Subsidy Offset Act of 2000—Report of the Panel* (16 September 2002) WT/DS217/R; WT/DS234/R
- WTO, *United States: Countervailing and Anti-Dumping Measures on Certain Products from China—Report of the Appellate Body* (22 July 2014) WT/DS449/AB/R

- WTO, *United States: Countervailing Duty Investigation on Dynamic Random Access Memory Semiconductors (DRAMS) from Korea—Report of the Panel* (21 February 2005) WT/DS296
- WTO, *United States: Definitive Safeguard Measures on Imports of Certain Steel Products—Report of the Panel* (11 July 2003) WT/DS248/R; WT/DS249/R; WT/DS251/R; WT/DS252/R; WT/DS253/R; WT/DS254/R; WT/DS258/R; WT/DS259/R
- WTO, *United States: Definitive Safeguard Measures on Imports of Circular Welded Carbon Quality Line Pipe from Korea—Report of the Appellate Body* (15 February 2002) WT/DS202/AB/R
- WTO, *United States: Definitive Safeguard Measures on Imports of Circular Welded Carbon Quality Line Pipe from Korea—Report of the Panel* (29 October 2001) WT/DS202/R
- WTO, *United States: Definitive Safeguard Measures on Imports of Wheat Gluten from the European Communities—Report of the Appellate Body* (22 December 2000) WT/DS166/AB/R
- WTO, *United States: Definitive Safeguard Measures on Imports of Wheat Gluten from the European Communities—Report of the Panel* (31 July 2000) WT/DS166/R
- WTO, *United States: Import Prohibition of Certain Shrimp and Shrimp Products—Report of the Appellate Body* (12 October 1998) WT/DS58/AB/R
- WTO, *United States: Import Prohibition of Certain Shrimp and Shrimp Products—Report of the Panel* (15 May 1998) WT/DS58/R
- WTO, *United States: Measures Affecting the Cross-Border Supply of Gambling and Betting Services—Report of the Appellate Body* (7 April 2005) WT/DS285/AB/R
- WTO, *United States: Measures Affecting the Cross-Border Supply of Gambling and Betting Services—Report of the Panel* (10 November 2004) WT/DS285/R
- WTO, *United States: Measures Affecting Imports of Certain Passenger Vehicle and Light Truck Tyres from China—Report of the Appellate Body* (5 September 2011) WT/DS399/AB/R
- WTO, *United States: Measures Affecting Imports of Certain Passenger Vehicle and Light Truck Tyres from China—Report of the Panel* (13 December 2010) WT/DS399/R
- WTO, *United States: Measures Affecting the Production and Sale of Clove Cigarettes—Report of the Appellate Body* (24 April 2012) WT/DS406/AB/R
- WTO, *United States: Measures Affecting the Production and Sale of Clove Cigarettes—Report of the Panel* (2 September 2011) WT/DS406/R

- WTO, *United States: Measures Affecting Trade in Large Civil Aircraft (Second Complaint)—Report of the Appellate Body* (12 March 2012) WT/DS353/AB/R
- WTO, *United States: Measures Affecting Trade in Large Civil Aircraft (Second Complaint)—Report of the Panel* (31 March 2011) WT/DS353/R
- WTO, *United States: Measures Concerning the Importation, Marketing and Sale of Tuna and Tuna Products—Report of the Appellate Body* (16 May 2012) WT/DS381/AB/R
- WTO, *United States: Safeguard Measures on Imports of Fresh, Chilled or Frozen Lamb Meat from New Zealand and Australia—Report of the Appellate Body* (1 May 2001) WT/DS177/AB/R; WT/DS178/AB/R
- WTO, *United States: Safeguard Measures on Imports of Fresh, Chilled or Frozen Lamb Meat from New Zealand and Australia—Report of the Panel* (21 December 2000) WT/DS177/R; WT/DS178/R
- WTO, *United States: Standards for Reformulated and Conventional Gasoline—Report of the Appellate Body* (29 April 1996) WT/DS2/AB/R
- WTO, *United States: Standards for Reformulated and Conventional Gasoline—Report of the Panel* (29 January 1996) WT/DS2/R
- WTO, *United States: Subsidies on Upland Cotton—Report of the Appellate Body* (3 March 2005) WT/DS267/AB/R
- WTO, *United States: Subsidies on Upland Cotton—Report of the Panel* (8 September 2004) WT/DS267/R
- WTO, *United States: Tariff Measures on Certain Goods from China—Report of the Panel* (15 September 2020) WT/DS543/R

TABLE OF LEGAL INSTRUMENTS

Public International Law Instruments

- *Draft Articles on the Responsibility of States for Internationally Wrongful Acts*, Report of the International Law Commission on the Work of Its Fifty-Third Session, UN GAOR, 56th Sess, Supp No 10, UN Doc A/56/10 (2001)
- International Law Commission, *Draft Articles on Responsibility of States for Internationally Wrongful Acts, with Commentaries*, UN GAOR, 56th Sess, Supp No 10, UN Doc A/56/10 (2001)
- *Vienna Convention on the Law of Treaties* 1155 UNTS 331 (1969) (signed 23 May 1969, entered into force 27 January 1980)

WTO Agreements

- *Agreement on the Application of Sanitary and Phytosanitary Measures*, LT/UR/A-1A/12 (signed 15 April 1994, entered into force 1 January 1995)
- *Agreement on Implementation of Article VI of the General Agreement on Tariffs and Trade 1994*, LT/UR/A-1A/3 (signed 15 April 1994, entered into force 1 January 1995)
- *Agreement on Safeguards*, LT/UR/A-1A/8 (signed 15 April 1994, entered into force 1 January 1995)
- *Agreement on Subsidies and Countervailing Measures*, LT/UR/A-1A/9 (signed 15 April 1994, entered into force 1 January 1995)
- *Agreement on Technical Barriers to Trade*, LT/UR/A-1A/10 (signed 15 April 1994, entered into force 1 January 1995)
- *General Agreement on Tariffs and Trade 1994*, LT/UR/A-1A/1/GATT/1 (signed 15 April 1994, entered into force 1 January 1995)
- *General Agreement on Trade in Services*, LT/UR/A-1B/S/1 (signed 15 April 1994, entered into force 1 January 1995)

- *Ministerial Declaration on Dispute Settlement Pursuant to the Agreement on Implementation of Article VI of the General Agreement on Tariffs and Trade 1994 or Part V of the Agreement on Subsidies and Countervailing Measures*
- *Understanding on Rules and Procedures Governing the Settlement of Disputes*, LT/UR/A-2/DS/U/1 (signed 15 April 1994, entered into force 1 January 1995)

EU Regulations

- Commission Implementing Regulation (EU) 2018/1013 of 17 July 2018, imposing provisional safeguard measures with regard to imports of certain steel products [2018] OJ L181/39
- Commission Implementing Regulation (EU) 2018/1570 of 18 October 2018 terminating the proceedings concerning imports of biodiesel originating in Argentina and Indonesia and repealing Implementing Regulation (EU) No 1194/2013, OJ 2018 L262/40.
- Council Implementing Regulation (EU) No 1194/2013 of 19 November 2013, imposing a definitive antidumping duty and collecting definitively the provisional duty imposed on imports of biodiesel originating in Argentina and Indonesia, OJ 2013 L315/2 [no longer in force]
- Council Regulation (EU) 2015/478 of the European Parliament and of the Council of 11 March 2015 on common rules for imports (codification) OJ L 83/16
- Council Regulation (EC) 2016/1036 on protection against dumped imports from countries not members of the European Union [2016] OJ L176/21
- Council Regulation (EC) 2016/1037 of 30 June 2016 on protection against subsidised imports from countries not members of the European Union [2016] OJ L176/55

Domestic Legislation

- *The Customs Act 1901* (Australia)
- *Special Import Measures Regulations 1984* (Canada)
- *Customs Tariff (Identification, Assessment and Collection of Anti-Dumping Duty on Dumped Articles and for Determination of Injury) Rules, 1995* (India)

- *Trade (Anti-dumping and Countervailing Duties) Act 1988* (New Zealand)
- *The Trade Remedies (Dumping and Subsidisation) (EU Exit) Regulations 2019* (United Kingdom)
- *United States Code, 2006 Edition, Supplement 5, Title 19* (January 3, 2012) 125 Stat. 456, 491, 527, 451, 466, 50 (United States)

Official Documents

- Call for Clarification on Article 3.5 of the AD Agreement: WTO, Negotiating Group on Rules, *Causation: Communication from Egypt*, TN/RL/GEN/140 (6 June 2006) <www.jmcti.org/2000round/com/doha/tn/rl/tn_rl_gen_140.pdf> accessed 30 April 2014
- Communication from the United States, Causation *(AD Agreement 3.5; SCM Agreement Article 15.5)*, TN/RL/GEN/59 (July 13, 2005) <https://docs.wto.org/dol2fe/Pages/SS/directdoc.aspx?filename=Q:/TN/RL/GEN59.pdf&Open=True> accessed 14 May 2014
- Report by the Consultative Board to the Director-General Supachai Panitchpakdi by Peter Sutherland, Jagdish Bhagwati, Kwesi Botchwey, Niall FitzGerald, Koichi Hamada, John H Jackson, Celso Lafer and Thierry de Montbrial, *The Future of the WTO: Introducing Institutional Challenges in the New Millennium* (WTO, 2004) <www.wto.org/english/thewto_e/10anniv_e/future_wto_e.pdf> accessed 28 June 2017
- WTO, Dispute Settlement Body, Minutes of Meeting Held in the Centre William Rappard (16 May 2001) WT/DSB/M/105, 19 June 2001, <www.puntofocal.gov.ar/doc/dsb-m337.pdf> accessed 30 April 2014
- WTO, Negotiating Group on Rules, *Causation (AD Agreement Article 3.5; SCM Agreement Article 15.5): Communication from the United States*, TN/RL/GEN/128 (24 April 2006) <www.jmcti.org/2000round/com/doha/tn/rl/tn_rl_gen_128.pdf> accessed 30 April 2014
- WTO, Negotiating Group on Rules, *General Contribution to the Discussion of the Negotiating Group on Rules on AD Measures, Paper from Brazil; Chile; Colombia; Costa Rica; Hong Kong, China; Israel; Japan; Korea; Norway; Separate Customs Territory of Taiwan, Penghu, Kinmen, and Matsu; Thailand; and Turkey*, TN/RL/W/28 (15 November 2002) <www.meti.go.jp/policy/trade_policy/wto/wto_db/data/ad_gcon0212e.pdf> accessed 30 April 2014

- WTO, Negotiating Group on Rules, Paper by Friends of Antidumping, Antidumping: Illustrative Major Issues, TN/RL/W/6 (26 April 2002) <https://docs.wto.org/dol2fe/Pages/SS/directdoc.aspx?filename=Q:/TN/RL/W6.pdf&Open=True> accessed 4 April 2015
- WTO, Negotiating Group on Rules, Second Submission of India: Antidumping Agreement, TN/RL/W/26 (17 October 2002) <https://docs.wto.org/dol2fe/Pages/SS/directdoc.aspx?filename=Q:/TN/RL/W26.pdf&Open=True> accessed 4 April 2015
- WTO, Negotiating Group on Rules, *Second Submission of Proposals on the Determination of Injury, Paper from Brazil; Chile; Colombia; Costa Rica; Hong Kong, China; Israel; Japan; Korea, Rep. of; Norway; Singapore; Switzerland; the Separate Customs Territory of Taiwan, Penghu, Kinmen and Matsu; and Thailand*, TN/RL/GEN/38 (23 March 2005) <www.pc.gov.au/__data/assets/pdf_file/0015/90204/sub026-attachmentb.pdf> accessed 30 April 2014
- WTO, 'World Trade Report 2005: Exploring the Links between Trade, Standards and the WTO' (2005) <www.wto.org/english/res_e/booksp_e/anrep_e/world_trade_report05_e.pdf> accessed 15 October 2016

ABBREVIATIONS

AB	Appellate Body
AD	antidumping
CAFC	United States Court of Appeals for the Federal Circuit
CVD or CVDs	countervailing duties
DSB	Dispute Settlement Body
DSU	Dispute Settlement Understanding
EC	European Communities
EU	European Union
GATS	General Agreement on Trade in Services
GATT 1994	General Agreement on Tariffs and Trade 1994
INUS	insufficient but necessary part of an unnecessary but sufficient set
LRA	linear regression analysis
NESS	necessary element of a sufficient set
SCM	subsidies and countervailing measures
SST	statistical significance testing
TBT	Technical Barriers to Trade
US	United States
USITC	United States International Trade Commission
VCLT	Vienna Convention on the Law of Treaties
WTO	World Trade Organization

Introduction

Overview of Argument

> There is no question, which on account of its importance, as well as difficulty, has caus'd more disputes both among antient and modern philosophers, than this concerning the efficacy of causes, or that quality which makes them be follow'd by their effects.[1]

Despite the profound difficulty associated with determining causation, the need to do so is nonetheless deeply embedded in all legal systems, and the law of the WTO is no exception. Legal systems are generally interested in the concept of causation for three practical reasons.[2] The first is *attributive* – that is, the law draws on causal principles in order to ascertain whether responsibility should be affixed to an agent on account of his, her or its actions or omissions.[3] The second use is *explanatory*, in the sense that the law attempts to determine how earlier conditions may have led to a later state of affairs.[4] Third and finally, the law requires causation to make *predictions* about the likely future contribution of a condition to a state of affairs.[5]

Whilst most areas of law are primarily interested in causation for its assistance with attributing responsibility to an agent (e.g., negligence law, criminal law and contract law), it will be argued that WTO law draws on causation to assist with each one of the three rationales listed above. It will be seen that Chapters 2, 3 and 5 of this book are interested in causation for its attributive potential, whilst Chapter 4 will draw on

[1] David Hume, *A Treatise of Human Nature* (LA Selby-Bigge ed, 1789) (revised by PH Nidditch, 2nd edn, OUP 1975) Bk I, pt III, s xiv, 156.

[2] Antony Honoré, 'Causation in the Law' *The Stanford Encyclopedia of Philosophy* (Winter edn, 2010) <http://plato.stanford.edu/archives/win2010/entries/causation-law/> accessed 26 September 2015.

[3] ibid.

[4] ibid.

[5] ibid.

causation for its explanatory and predictive capacities. Due to the greater range of reasons for drawing on causation, it follows that causation in WTO law requires a greater arsenal of causal tests than some other areas of law for interrogating causation. As such, this book will employ both non-quantitative causal tests aimed at attributing responsibility (such as the traditional *sine qua non* and weak necessity/strong sufficiency tests) as well as quantitative tests (such as Linear Regression Analysis and the Statistical Significance Test). These causal tests will be detailed in Chapter 1 of this book.

Causation in WTO law is distinctive for a second reason – that is, it involves drawing causal links with respect to something as complex and multifaceted as financial markets and international trade flows. As such, at several points the agreements in WTO law require a fact-finder to separate the causal factor being interrogated from other known factors that may also have contributed to the effect in question. This process of distinguishing the causal factor in question from other known factors is called a non-attribution analysis. WTO law explicitly requires a non-attribution analysis to be undertaken at several points, whilst at others, this book suggests that it may be implied by the nature of the causal analysis in question. The term 'other known factors'[6] will be used throughout this book as an elliptical way of saying 'all those factors that

[6] The term 'other known factors' is used in WTO, *United States: Anti-Dumping Measures on Certain Hot-Rolled Steel Products from Japan—Report of the Appellate Body* (24 July 2001) WT/DS184/AB/R (AB, *US—Hot-Rolled Steel*) [226]. Various other terms are used in the jurisprudence to mean the same thing; for example, 'known factors' is used in WTO, *Mexico: Definitive Countervailing Measures on Olive Oil from the European Communities—Report of the Panel* (4 September 2008) WT/DS341/R [7.297]; WTO, *Thailand: Anti-Dumping Duties on Angles, Shapes and Sections of Iron or Non-Alloy Steel and H-Beams from Poland—Report of the Panel* (28 September 2000) WT/DS122/R (Panel, *Thailand—H-Beams*) [7.273]; WTO, *European Union: Anti-Dumping Measures on Imports of Certain Fatty Alcohols from Indonesia—Report of the Panel* (16 December 2016) WT/DS442/R [7.196]. 'Other factors' is used in WTO, *European Union: Anti-Dumping Measures on Biodiesel from Indonesia—Report of the Panel* (25 January 2018) WT/DS480/R [7.438]; WTO, *Argentina: Safeguard Measures on Imports of Footwear—Report of the Panel* (25 June 1999) WT/DS121/R (Panel, *Argentina—Footwear (EC)*) [8.264]–[8.267]; WTO, *Argentina: Safeguard Measures on Imports of Footwear—Report of the Appellate Body* (14 December 1999) WT/DS121/AB/R (AB, *Argentina—Footwear (EC)*) [134]; WTO, *United States: Safeguard Measures on Imports of Fresh, Chilled or Frozen Lamb Meat from New Zealand and Australia—Report of the Panel* (21 December 2000) WT/DS177/R; WT/DS178/R (Panel, *US—Lamb*) [7.259]–[7.279]; WTO, *United States: Definitive Safeguard Measures on Imports of Certain Steel Products—Report of the Panel* (11 July 2003) WT/DS248/R; WT/DS249/R; WT/DS251/R; WT/DS252/R; WT/DS253/R; WT/DS254/R; WT/DS258/R; WT/DS259/R [10.332]; WTO, *Indonesia: Safeguard on Certain Iron or Steel Products—Report of the Panel* (18 August 2017) WT/

could potentially have contributed to the effect being investigated and that must be excluded by performing a non-attribution analysis'.

In short, those parts of WTO law with which this book is concerned require a causal link to be drawn between factors at the same time that they require a causal link between other factors to be excluded. Accordingly, the terms 'causation' or 'causal link' for the purposes of this book might be understood in the context of the need to establish that an injury, effect or outcome was brought about by a Member's policy and was not caused by any other independent phenomenon that may have occurred at the same time.[7] In this sense, the causation analyses under examination in this book have both positive and negative features. This dual character means that any useful methodology for determining a causal link must be able to reliably discriminate between those factors that were causative vis-à-vis those factors that were immaterial to bringing about an outcome.

This book will discuss nine different parts of WTO law that all have this dual character. The first three, to be discussed in Chapter 2, all relate to trade remedies. The first trade remedy to be discussed is safeguard measures (Articles 2.1 and 4.2(a) and (b) of the *Agreement on Safeguards*[8]), which allow a WTO Member temporarily to protect a domestic industry from an increase in imports of a product if those imports are causing, or threatening to cause, serious injury to that industry. Next, this book will consider antidumping measures (Articles 3.1 and 3.5 of the *Agreement on Implementation of Article VI of the General*

DS490/R; WT/DS496/R [7.5.4.3.1]; WTO, *European Union: Countervailing Measures on Certain Polyethylene Terephthalate from Pakistan—Report of the Appellate Body* (16 May 2018) WT/DS486/AB/R (AB, *EU—PET (Pakistan)*) [5.151]; WTO, *United States: Anti-Dumping and Countervailing Measures on Certain Coated Paper from Indonesia—Report of the Panel* (6 December 2017) WT/DS491/R [7.222]; WTO, *China: Countervailing and Anti-Dumping Duties on Grain-Oriented Flat-Rolled Electrical Steel from the United States—Report of the Panel* (15 June 2012) WT/DS414/R [7.62]. The term 'other known factors' has been chosen because it captures the meaning of both of the other terms used.

[7] This definition draws, to some extent, on the definition of 'causation' in Marion Jansen, Joost Pauwelyn and Theresa Carpenter, 'The Use of Economics in International Trade and Investment Disputes: Complex, Contentious but Oh-So-Important for the Sustainability of Trade and Investment' in Marion Jansen, Joost Pauwelyn and Theresa Carpenter, *The Use of Economics in International Trade and Investment Disputes* (CUP 2017) 5.

[8] *Agreement on Safeguards*, LT/UR/A-1A/8 (signed 15 April 1994, entered into force 1 January 1995) (Safeguards Agreement).

Agreement on Tariffs and Trade 1994[9]), which are measures that a Member may impose on foreign imports that are priced below fair market value and are causing harm to the Member's domestic industry. Third, countervailing duties (Article 15.5 of the *Agreement on Subsidies and Countervailing Measures*[10]) will be discussed – namely, duties that a Member can impose on a foreign Member's exports if the exports have been found to have been subsidised and to have caused injury to domestic producers in the importing country.

Chapter 3 concerns non-attribution and causal link analyses in the context of serious prejudice (Articles 5(c) and 6.3 of the SCM Agreement). Serious prejudice arises where a foreign Member's subsidy causes adverse effects to another Member's trade interests in relation to a particular product in a specified market. Chapter 4 then turns to consider Article XX of the *General Agreement on Tariffs and Trade*,[11] Article XIV of the *General Agreement on Trade in Services*[12] and Article 2.2 of the *Agreement on Technical Barriers to Trade*.[13] These provisions may exempt a Member's measure from the disciplines of the GATT, GATS or the TBT Agreement, respectively, under certain circumstances. Such exemption may take place where a number of criteria are satisfied, only one of which is that a Member's policy measure is found significantly to have contributed to achieving its intended policy objective.

Chapter 5 discusses Article 22.6 of the *Understanding on Rules and Procedures Governing the Settlement of Disputes*[14] and Article 4.10 of the SCM Agreement, which permit a complaining Member to bring retaliatory measures against a responding Member where that responding Member refuses to comply with a DSB ruling. In order to calculate the

[9] *Agreement on Implementation of Article VI of the General Agreement on Tariffs and Trade 1994*, LT/UR/A-1A/3 (signed 15 April 1994, entered into force 1 January 1995) (Antidumping Agreement or AD Agreement).

[10] *Agreement on Subsidies and Countervailing Measures*, LT/UR/A-1A/9 (signed 15 April 1994, entered into force 1 January 1995) (SCM Agreement).

[11] *General Agreement on Tariffs and Trade 1994*, LT/UR/A-1A/1/GATT/1 (signed 15 April 1994, entered into force 1 January 1995) (GATT 1994).

[12] *General Agreement on Trade in Services*, LT/UR/A-1B/S/1 (signed 15 April 1994, entered into force 1 January 1995) (GATS).

[13] *Agreement on Technical Barriers to Trade*, LT/UR/A-1A/10 (signed 15 April 1994, entered into force 1 January 1995) (TBT Agreement).

[14] *Understanding on Rules and Procedures Governing the Settlement of Disputes*, LT/UR/A-2/DS/U/1 (signed 15 April 1994, entered into force 1 January 1995) (DSU).

level of retaliation owed to the complaining Member, the adjudicators must calculate the likely level of nullification and impairment caused, whilst also taking account of other known factors. Chapter 5 argues that non-attribution and causal link analyses might be used to interrogate the relationship between a responding Member's failure to comply with a DSB ruling and the complainant Member's level of nullification and impairment. The jurisprudence has not discussed the need to perform non-attribution and causal link analyses with respect to the areas of law canvassed in Chapters 4 and 5. Nonetheless, Chapters 4 and 5 will argue that the need to do so may be implied by the nature of the causal link analysis in question.

It will be seen in Chapters 3, 4 and 5 that some parts of the current jurisprudence attempt to infer the effects of a cause from an *a priori* judgment about the nature of that cause. To put this another way, the current jurisprudence, at various points, attempts to presume the effect that a cause will have without actually interrogating that effect empirically. This approach, therefore, relies on intuition or a kind of 'common sense' approach to causation. The result is that an unsubstantiated presumption becomes the basis for drawing a causal link. Whilst this tendency manifests in different ways in Chapters 3, 4 and 5, at the root of each of them is a fundamental logical fallacy that not only misunderstands the nature of causation but also results in flawed conclusions. These logical fallacies will be pointed out as and when they occur in each of the chapters that discuss WTO law.

Due to the shortcomings of this intuitive approach in determining causation, this book argues in favour of actually interrogating the empirical effects of an outcome before attempting to derive its causal origins, wherever possible. This book will put forward a methodology for analysing non-attribution and causal links that draws on real-world data and econometric analysis. Econometrics may be defined as 'a special type of economic analysis in which the general theoretical approach – often formulated in explicitly mathematical terms – is combined frequently through the medium of intricate statistical procedures – with empirical measurement of economic phenomena'.[15] The advantage of using an approach that relies on econometric analysis is that it actually interrogates the effects of the causes based on empirical data, instead of

[15] Wassily Leontief, 'Econometrics' in Howard Ellis (ed), *A Survey of Contemporary Economics* (The Blakiston Co 1948) 388 quoted in Gerhard Tintner, 'The Definition of Econometrics' (1953) Econometrica 31, 40.

presuming them. This empirical data, in turn, 'makes for a more accurate outcome', which, in turn, 'enhance[s] the legitimacy of the system'.[16]

Econometric analysis must, of course, be used within the parameters allowed by the customary rules of interpretation of public international law, including Article 31 of the *Vienna Convention on the Law of Treaties* (VCLT).[17] It is suggested that economics and econometrics could be found to fit within the meaning of 'context', 'object and purpose' or 'subsequent practice' (Article 31.1–3 VCLT), 'special meaning . . . if it is established that the parties so intended' (Article 31.4 VCLT) or the phrase, 'supplementary means of interpretation' ('including', but not limited to, 'the circumstances of [the treaty's] conclusion') in Article 32 VCLT.[18]

The methodology developed in this book is derived from paragraph [69] of *US—Wheat Gluten*, in which the AB set out a three-step process for performing a non-attribution and causal link analysis in relation to the Safeguards Agreement.[19] This process is as follows: (1) authorities must separate the injurious effects of increased imports from the injurious effects produced by other known factors; (2) authorities must then attribute to imports the harm they alone have produced before attributing to other known factors the harm that they have occasioned in turn; and (3) finally, authorities should determine whether there is a causal link between imports and 'serious injury or threat thereof'; and if so, whether such a causal link involves a 'genuine and substantial relationship of cause and effect' between these two elements. This three-step methodology will be called the Tripartite Non-attribution/Causal Link Analysis, and its explication and application form the heart of this book. That is, whilst the Tripartite Non-attribution/Causal Link Analysis was developed by the AB in relation to safeguard measures, this book will suggest that it may also usefully be applied to those eight other areas of WTO law that were identified earlier as requiring non-attribution and causal link analyses.

[16] Joost Pauwelyn, 'The Use, Non-use and Abuse of Economics in WTO and Investment Litigation' in Jorge A Huerta-Goldman, Antoine Romaneti and Franz X Stirnimann (eds), *WTO Litigation, Investment Arbitration and Commercial Arbitration* (Kluwer 2013) 171.

[17] *Vienna Convention on the Law of Treaties* 1155 UNTS 331 (1969) (signed 23 May 1969, entered into force 27 January 1980).

[18] Pauwelyn (n 16) 184. Pauwelyn makes this argument only in relation to the use of the term 'economics'. It is suggested that the argument might further be extended specifically to include the term 'econometrics', too.

[19] WTO, *United States: Definitive Safeguard Measures on Imports of Wheat Gluten from the European Communities—Report of the Appellate Body* (22 December 2000) WT/DS166/AB/R (AB, *US—Wheat Gluten*) [69].

Advantages and Disadvantages of an Econometric Approach

One of the chief advantages of the Tripartite Non-attribution/Causal Link Analysis is that it tends to result in a genuine non-attribution analysis. It will be seen that, in the absence of the Tripartite Non-attribution/Causal Link Analysis, fact-finders are not in a position to assess the *interaction* between the causal factor in question (e.g., imports) and other known factors, leading to a causal analysis of dubious reliability. The Tripartite Non-attribution/Causal Link Analysis, on the other hand, performs a non-attribution analysis that allows other known factors to be identified and disaggregated from the causal factor in question.

A second benefit of the Tripartite Non-attribution/Causal Link Analysis is that it brings consistency to the non-attribution and causal link analyses, which, in turn, tends to promote greater legal certainty. Chapter 2 discusses the requirement imposed upon a domestic competent authority to draw a causal link between imports and harm to an industry. Each domestic competent authority is free to devise its own methodology, which has resulted in a lack of consistency and transparency between Members. Similarly, the jurisprudence in Chapter 3 evidences a degree of confusion between cases, particularly with respect to how the non-attribution analysis should be performed. The Tripartite Non-attribution/Causal Link Analysis offers a way of bringing greater clarity and consistency to a finding of serious prejudice. Both Chapters 4 and 5 concern provisions that do not explicitly require non-attribution and causal link analyses; and, as such, the jurisprudence also evidences a degree of inconsistency. This inconsistency could be resolved by having a more formalised approach, in the manner of the Tripartite Non-attribution/Causal Link Analysis. Once again, such a formalised approach would allow Members more easily to predict the way in which their case would be adjudicated.

Having just set out two key advantages of the Tripartite Non-attribution/Causal Link Analysis, it is important to consider some of the pitfalls with using a methodology reliant on econometric analysis. Indeed, these pitfalls are such that, if not managed sufficiently well, the benefits of the Tripartite Non-attribution/Causal Link Analysis discussed earlier become more illusory than real. Specifically, despite their scientific appearance, methodologically unsound econometric models can often suggest correlations between two variables that are statistically related but not, in fact, causally linked.[20]

[20] See, for example, Ted Goertzel, 'Myths of Murder and Multiple Regression' (2002) 26(1) The Skeptical Inquirer 19, 20.

This is because correlations are frequently drawn between two phenomena as a result of temporal ordering. As Moosa observes, however, 'the mere fact that something happens before something else does not mean that the first something causes the second something'.[21] These kinds of correlations are often called 'spurious correlations',[22] which may be defined as 'false indicators of causality, typically arising when an extraneous variable that affects two other variables is omitted'.[23] For example, Vigen has noted farcical correlations between per capita cheese consumption and the number of people who died by becoming tangled in their bedsheets![24] Moreover, incorrect econometric models can actually have the perverse effect of being used to support ideologically driven propositions.[25]

It is suggested that there are, nonetheless, three mechanisms for safeguarding a causal link analysis from the kinds of spurious correlations just described: (1) quality controls surrounding the econometric models used; (2) common sense or intuition about whether correlations appear to make sense; and (3) the contextualising nature of the law itself. Turning to the first, many of the spurious correlations or suspect analyses produced by econometrics are the result of poor methodologies and research standards.[26] Indeed, in the context of econometrics, it is easy for poor methodologies to be 'obscured by a maze of equations',[27] such that 'only other highly trained regression analysts can understand, let alone refute, them'.[28] Notwithstanding the seriousness of these methodological problems, it is arguably overly drastic to dismiss the potential contribution of econometrics to the causation debate entirely. Instead, it is suggested that higher standards or best practice guidelines might be established and followed in relation to the way in which models are selected and applied.[29] In other words, instead of throwing the baby

[21] Imad Moosa, *Econometrics as a Con Art: Exposing the Limitations and Abuses of Econometrics* (Edward Elgar 2017) 170.

[22] See generally Tyler Vigen, *Spurious Correlations* (Hachette Books 2015).

[23] Imad Moosa, 'Blaming Suicide on NASA and Divorce on Margarine: The Hazard of Using Cointegration to Derive Inference on Spurious Correlation' (2017) 49(15) Appl Econ 1483, 1483.

[24] See Tyler Vigen, 'Spurious Correlations' <www.tylervigen.com/spurious-correlations> accessed 14 September 2021.

[25] Moosa, *Econometrics as a Con Art* (n 21) 18.

[26] Michael McAller, Adrian Pagan and Paul Volker, 'What Will Take the Con Out of Econometrics?' (1985) 75(3) Am Econ Rev 293, 306.

[27] Goertzel (n 20) 21.

[28] ibid 23.

[29] McAller, Pagan and Volker (n 26) 306; and Pauwelyn (n 16) 186–87.

out with the bathwater, greater safeguards could be put in place to ensure more accurate and reliable econometric models that are based on sounder assumptions.

Second, many spurious correlations can often be dismissed simply by using common sense. For example, a correlation as spurious as the one involving per capita cheese consumption and the number of people who died by becoming tangled in their bedsheets would easily be discounted once subjected to common sense. In other words, cointegration should not be relied upon to the point that it leads a fact-finder to suspend their common sense and unquestioningly accept spurious relationships between data sets.[30] In this sense, the intuitive or common sense approach to determining causation based on *a priori* judgments that is currently used by the AB need not be seen as completely at odds with econometric analysis. Instead, it is suggested that the optimal approach to determining causation should draw on both schools of thought – namely, econometrics tempered by common sense.

Third, yet another defence against inadvertently accepting spurious correlations comes from the contextualising nature of the law itself. That is, legislation and legal agreements have the effect of delimiting the number of factors, parties and time periods that are relevant to a particular legal issue. For example, in the WTO context, if a domestic competent body were trying to ascertain whether imports caused harm to a domestic industry, this necessarily narrows down the material and temporal factors that might have impacted a domestic industry. This does not mean that a fact-finder might not still draw incorrect causal links, but it does mean that the very wild spurious correlations highlighted by Tyler Vigen earlier are less likely be drawn since they fall outside the limits prescribed by the law.

A second, even more significant problem with econometric analysis relates to the fact that sufficient reliable data is not always available. As the Panel said in *Australia—Apples*, '[i]n the absence of sufficient data, and particularly if numbers are chosen in an arbitrary manner, a quantitative method would only give a misleading impression of objectivity and precision'.[31] The difficulty in collecting sufficient, reliable data is magnified in the case of developing countries, where resources required to

[30] Moosa, 'Blaming Suicide on NASA' (n 23) 1485.

[31] WTO, *Australia: Measures Affecting the Importation of Apples from New Zealand—Report of the Panel* (9 August 2010) WT/DS367/R (Panel, *Australia—Apples*) [7.441].

collect the requisite data may be even more constrained.[32] Where insufficient data is unavailable for econometric models, which are inherently data-intensive, there may be other quantitative methods that can be used that require less data to be inputted. For example, the partial equilibrium model, based on supply and demand conditions,[33] or the 'Cost of Production Test'.[34] Each method has pros and cons, and the method chosen will ultimately depend on the type and quality of data available.

In the event that there is insufficient data even for these other quantitative tests, it may be that fact-finders need to fall back on the AB's non-quantitative approach to inferring the effects of a cause based on *a priori* judgments about the nature of that cause. Self-evidently, this approach is not ideal for all the reasons discussed earlier, and should therefore not be used unless there is no alternative. Moreover, because some of the quantitative approaches rely on drawing correlations, it is still useful to compare the results of these correlations with the AB's more common sense approach based on inference. This is because, as was just discussed, a common sense approach can help to guard against relying on spurious correlations. In this sense, this book does not dismiss the AB's approach to determining causation out of hand, but it is contended that it should be supplemented with a quantitative approach where sufficient data is available to do so.

A third difficulty with the use of econometric analysis in the context of WTO law is that its inherently technical and mathematical nature makes it difficult for lawyers to understand and apply. That is, numerous panel reports reflect a reluctance to engage with economic arguments, and have, at various times, minimised or even dismissed quantitative evidence brought by Members.[35] Given that the WTO legal agreements are

[32] Jai Mah, 'Injury and Causation in the WTO Agreement on Safeguards' (2001) J World Intellect Prop 373, 382. Although Mah's point is made in relation to safeguards, it could be extended to other contexts where data is required to be collected for the purposes of performing econometric analysis.

[33] See generally Kenneth Kelly, 'The Analysis of Causality in Escape Clause Cases' (1988) 37 (2) J Ind Econ 187.

[34] Dukgeun Ahn and William J Moon, 'Alternative Approach to Causation Analysis in Trade Remedy Investigations: "Cost of Production" Test' (2010) 44(5) JWT 1023, 1041–47.

[35] See, for example, WTO, *Japan: Taxes on Alcoholic Beverages—Report of the Panel* (11 July 1996) WT/DS8/R; WT/DS10/R; WT/DS11/R (*Japan—Alcoholic Beverages II*) [6.31]; WTO, *Korea: Taxes on Alcoholic Beverages—Report of the Panel* (17 September 1998) WT/DS75/R; WT/DS84/R (*Korea—Alcoholic Beverages*) [10.44]; WTO, *United States: Subsidies on Upland Cotton—Report of the Panel* (8 September 2004) WT/DS267/R (Panel, *US—Upland Cotton*) [7.1205] and WTO, *European Communities: Measures*

based on economic principles and seem to require econometric analysis to be brought at numerous points,[36] however, it is not possible simply to dismiss the contribution that quantitative evidence can bring to this area of law. Indeed, the AB itself has said that:

> The relative complexity of a model and its parameters is not a reason for a panel to remain agnostic about them. Like other categories of evidence, a panel should reach conclusions with respect to the probative value it accords to economic simulations or models presented to it. This kind of assessment falls within the panel's authority as the initial trier of facts [. . .].[37]

Instead of refusing to engage with the technical elements of econometric models, then, the solution appears to lie in bridging the gap between the technicalities of the law and the technicalities of econometric evidence. To this end, Teh and Yanovich point to the benefits of panellists being provided support from secretariat PhD-level economists, or alternatively, of having panellists with an economics background in addition to a legal one.[38]

Another alternative is that panels can use their power under Article 13.2 of the DSU to seek expert guidance about econometric analysis or quantitative evidence generally. Not only would this allow panellists to ensure that the econometric analysis and quantitative evidence was reviewed by people with expertise in the area, but it could also assist with establishing a forum in which there was a culture of being able to explain complex econometric or quantitative evidence in terms that a lawyer could understand and with which they could engage. That is, as Iacovides and Jansen argue, when working with WTO legal agreements, economists and econometricians need to be able to communicate quantitative evidence using words, rather than formulae or parameters.[39]

Prohibiting the Importation and Marketing of Seal Products—Report of the Panel (25 November 2013) WT/DS400/R; WT/DS401/R (Panel, *EC—Seal Products*) [7.456].

[36] See generally Robert Teh and Alan Yanovich, 'Integrating Economic Analysis into WTO Dispute Settlement Practice: A View from the Trenches' in Jansen, Pauwelyn and Carpenter, *The Use of Economics in International Trade and Investment Disputes* (n 7).

[37] WTO, *United States: Subsidies on Upland Cotton—Recourse to Article 21.5 of the DSU by Brazil—Report of the Appellate Body* (2 June 2008) WT/DS267/AB/RW [357].

[38] Teh and Yanovich (n 36) 37.

[39] Marios C Iacovides and Marion Jansen, 'Lost in Translation: Communication and Interpretation Challenges Related to Economic Evidence in Trade Disputes' in Jansen, Pauwelyn and Carpenter, *The Use of Economics in International Trade and Investment Disputes* (n 7) 191.

In short, the solution to the complexities of applying quantitative evidence to WTO law lies not in dismissing the evidence outright, but rather, in making its terms palatable to lawyers with little expertise in engaging with it.

In sum, the Tripartite Non-attribution/Causation Analysis to be discussed in this book has a number of advantages over the AB's non-quantitative approach. These advantages, however, are subject to the drawbacks that invariably accompany any econometric analysis – namely, the limitations of the model itself, the problems involved in data collection and the difficulties in communicating the technical nature of quantitative evidence to lawyers. To the extent that these drawbacks cannot be adequately overcome, the current approach in the jurisprudence to assessing causation should continue to be used. Where these limitations can be sufficiently managed, however, this book argues that the Tripartite Non-attribution/Causation Analysis offers an alternative approach that brings with it a number of important benefits. These include a genuine non-attribution analysis and a greater level of accuracy, consistency and legal certainty than the current approach in the jurisprudence.

Outline of Chapters

Having set out the outline of this book in the section 'Overview of Argument', it now remains to provide a more detailed overview of the contents of each chapter. Chapter 1 sets out some basic causal theory and concepts that are important for understanding causation and the related concept of non-attribution. It also introduces some causal tests that will be applied in later chapters. In particular, it explains the concepts of necessity and sufficiency as well as non-quantitative causal tests that draw on them – that is, the *sine qua non* test and the weak necessity/strong sufficiency tests, as well as the strengths and weaknesses of those tests. Further, Chapter 1 sets out two quantitative approaches to interrogating causation that will be applied in Chapter 4 of this book – namely, the Statistical Significance Test and Linear Regression Analysis. Chapter 1 does not attempt to provide any kind of comprehensive overview of the theory of causation in the law generally, nor does it detail a fraction of the causal tests that have been developed for interrogating causal links. Its far more modest aim is simply to explain the main causal tests and concepts on which the subsequent chapters will continually draw.

Chapter 2 discusses those provisions that relate to determining causation in relation to safeguard measures, antidumping measures and countervailing duties (collectively, 'trade remedies'). Whilst each of these trade remedies seeks to protect a Member's industry in different ways, each fundamentally requires a Member to show that imports have caused its industry harm. The relevant provisions of each of the agreements explicitly require both non-attribution and causal link analyses to be performed, but the way in which these are conducted is largely left to the discretion of domestic competent authorities. Although there has been a significant amount written about the economic assumptions embedded into the determination of injury in the trade remedies provisions[40] as well as their historical development,[41] these discussions fall outside the purview of Chapter 2. There have been a number of publications that have proposed causal tests to assist with determining injury in respect of each of the trade remedies agreements.[42] Chapter 2 will discuss these proposals, as well as a methodology commonly used by many domestic competent authorities called the 'breaking the causal link' approach before considering some of the drawbacks of this approach. The chapter will finally turn to consider how the Tripartite Non-attribution/Causal Link Analysis that was suggested by the AB in *US—Wheat Gluten* can serve as an alternative approach. The Tripartite Non-attribution/Causal Link Analysis draws on some econometric tests that have

[40] See generally Alan O Sykes, 'The Causation Requirement and "Non-Attribution"' in *The WTO Safeguards Agreement: A Commentary* (OUP 2006); Alan O Sykes, 'The Safeguards Mess: A Critique of WTO Jurisprudence' (2003) 2(3) WTR 261; Fernando Piérola, 'Causal Link' in *The Challenge of Safeguards in the WTO* (CUP 2014); Kelly (n 33); Robert S Pindyck and Julio J Rotemberg, 'Are Imports to Blame? Attribution of Injury under the 1974 Trade Act' (1987) 30 J Law & Econ 101; Alan O Sykes, 'The Economics of Injury in Antidumping Countervailing Duty Investigations' (1996) 16(1) Int Rev Law Econ 5; Ronald A Cass and Michael S Knoll, 'The Economics of "Injury"' in Jagdeep S Bhandari and Alan O Sykes (eds), *Antidumping and Countervailing Duty Cases: A Reply to Professor Sykes, Economic Dimensions in International Law: Comparative and Empirical Perspectives* (CUP 1997); and Richard D Boltuck, 'An Economic Analysis of Dumping' (1987) 21(5) JWT 45.

[41] See generally Simon Lacey, 'Causal Link, Non-Attribution and Contingency Protection in the WTO' (December 2002) Working Paper, 37, <https://ssrn.com/abstract=1135133> accessed 3 November 2017; and James J Nedumpara, *Injury and Causation in Trade Remedy Law: A Study of WTO Law and Country Practices* (Springer 2016).

[42] Nedumpara, *Injury and Causation in Trade Remedy Law* (n 41); David Leys, 'Does a Theory of Causation Exist under the WTO Safeguards Agreement?' (2014) 9(1) GTCJ 10; and Pratik Tayal, 'A New World of Causation in Safeguards: Application of the "But for" Test' (2015) 10(1) GTCJ 355.

been developed largely in the context of trade remedy investigations involving section 201 of the US 1974 Trade Act.[43]

Chapter 3 is concerned with making a determination of serious prejudice under the SCM Agreement. Like a finding of 'injury' under the trade remedies chapter, a determination of serious prejudice explicitly requires both a non-attribution and a causal link analysis. This means that a determination must be made as to whether the market phenomenon is caused by subsidies. To that end, a fact-finder must be careful not to attribute responsibility to subsidies for those things that were, in fact, caused by other known factors. Those provisions relating to non-attribution and the causal link analysis in the context of a serious prejudice finding are less precise than those contained in the trade remedies agreements. As such, the jurisprudence has shown a fair degree of inconsistency in the way in which it has interpreted non-attribution and causal links for the purpose of making a finding of serious prejudice, and sometimes even a fundamental misconception about the nature of causation more broadly. There has been a limited amount of academic commentary about the best approach to use when analysing non-attribution and causal links, which will be discussed in Chapter 3.[44] Ultimately, Chapter 3 will put forward the Tripartite Non-attribution/Causal Link Analysis as a methodology that potentially offers more accuracy and consistency when making determinations about serious prejudice.

Of the four chapters that discuss WTO law, Chapter 4 is the only chapter in this book that is not concerned with some kind of economic harm to a Member's industry. Instead, Chapter 4 relates to the impact of a Member's measure on the achievement of a policy objective under Article XX of the GATT, Article XIV of the GATS and Article 2.2 of the TBT Agreement. The chapter discusses the approach to analysing the impact of a Member's measure in the current jurisprudence, and, to that end, points out some

[43] Gene Grossman, 'Imports as a Cause of Injury: The Case of the US Steel Industry' (1986) 20 J Int Econ 201; Kelly (n 33); Ahn and Moon (n 34); Pindyck and Rotemberg (n 40); Douglas A Irwin, 'Causing Problems? The WTO Review of Causation and Injury Attribution in US Section 201 Cases' (2003) 2(3) WTR 297; David Sharp and Kenneth Zantow, 'Attribution of Injury in the Shrimp Antidumping Case: A Simultaneous Equations Approach' (2005) 6(5) Econ Bull 1; and Thomas J Prusa and David C Sharp, 'Simultaneous Equations in Antidumping Investigations' (2001) 14(1) JFE 63.

[44] Andrew Sapir and Joel P Trachtman, 'Subsidization, Price Suppression, and Expertise: Causation and Precision in Upland Cotton' (2008) 7(1) WTR 183; and see generally, Richard H Steinberg and Timothy E Josling, 'When the Peace Ends: The Vulnerability of EC and US Agricultural Subsidies to WTO Legal Challenge' (2003) 6(2) JIEL 369.

basic conceptual flaws with that approach. As in Chapter 5, and in contrast to Chapters 2 and 3, the non-attribution and causal link requirements are implied, rather than explicit. Nonetheless, it is suggested that assessing the impact of a measure on a policy objective makes little sense without both a non-attribution and causal link analysis. As such, Chapter 4 argues that the Tripartite Non-attribution/Causal Link Analysis could be applied in this context in order to provide the most precise assessment of the contribution of a measure to achieving its policy objective.

Chapter 5 examines the process of calculating retaliatory measures under Article 22.6 of the DSU and Article 4.10 of the SCM Agreement in response to a Member's failure to bring its measure into conformity with a DSB ruling. This chapter examines the current jurisprudence, and suggests that the current procedure demonstrates a misunderstanding of causation. In particular, Chapter 5 suggests that, before the amount of retaliation can be calculated, arbitrators must, as a first step, find a causal link between a Member's failure to bring its measure into conformity with a DSB ruling and the level of nullification or impairment inflicted on an industry. Moreover, this chapter also suggests that arbitrators have neglected meaningfully to consider the need to separate the impact of a Member's failure to bring its measure into conformity with a DSB ruling from other known factors. Accordingly, the non-attribution and causal link analyses that this chapter discusses are not explicitly provided for in the agreements in question. Nonetheless, this chapter suggests that an accurate estimate of the effects of a Member's failure to comply with a DSB ruling does not make sense without them. Once again, this chapter argues that the Tripartite Non-attribution/Causal Link Analysis offers an alternative way of performing these analyses. Having just outlined the causal questions that will be discussed in this book, it remains briefly to address those causal questions that arise in WTO law that will not receive detailed treatment in this book.

Causal Questions That Fall Outside the Scope of This Book

The causal questions that fall outside the scope of this book fall into four main categories – namely, causal questions that: (1) flow from a breach of an obligation to do something specific;[45] (2) relate to prescribed policy

[45] Article X:3 GATT 1994 (n 11) and Article 5(1) of the *Agreement on the Application of Sanitary and Phytosanitary Measures*, LT/UR/A-1A/12 (signed 15 April 1994, entered into force 1 January 1995) (SPS Agreement).

objectives within the SPS Agreement; (3) flow from potential, instead of actual, market impacts;[46] and (4) relate to the nullification or impairment of benefits.[47] Whilst each of these causal questions is just as important as the ones that are the subject of this book, the nature of the causal relationship in these articles does not lend itself to the use of the Tripartite Non-attribution/Causal Link Analysis. As such, this section will briefly consider these articles and the nature of the causal questions that they raise before concluding that the Tripartite Non-attribution/Causal Link Analysis would be an inappropriate methodology for analysing them.

Breach of an Obligation

The first category of causal questions that this section will examine relates to obligations in WTO law to do something specific. In particular, the question of causation arises when determining whether there has been a breach of an obligation.[48] This can be seen in relation to Article X:3 of the GATT 1994 as well as Article 5(1) and Annex A of the SPS Agreement. In these cases, the act or omission of the obligation is the violation.[49]

Article X:3 of the GATT 1994

Article X:3 of the GATT 1994 creates an obligation to guarantee certain minimum standards for transparency and procedural fairness in the administration of trade regulations[50] by ensuring 'that judicial, arbitral, or administrative tribunals or procedures are available for traders to challenge administrative actions relating to customs matters'.[51] Article X:3 of the GATT 1994 provides that Members 'shall maintain, or institute as soon as practicable, judicial arbitral or administrative tribunals or procedures for the purpose, inter alia, of the prompt review and correction of administrative action relating to customs matters'. A violation of Article X:3 GATT 1994 requires a complaining party to demonstrate that

[46] Articles I:1, III:4 and XI GATT 1994 (n 11), Articles XX and XVII GATS (n 12) and Article 2.1 TBT Agreement (n 13).

[47] Article XXIII:1 GATT 1994 (n 11) and Article XXIII:3 GATS (n 12).

[48] Lorand Bartels, 'Procedural Aspects of Shared Responsibility in the WTO Dispute Settlement System' (2013) 4(2) J Int Disput Settl 343, 347.

[49] ibid.

[50] WTO, *Peru: Additional Duty on Imports of Certain Agricultural Products—Report of the Panel* (27 November 2014) WT/DS457/R [7.488].

[51] WTO, *United States: Countervailing and Anti-Dumping Measures on Certain Products from China—Report of the Appellate Body* (22 July 2014) WT/DS449/AB/R [4.109].

there is a causal link between the manner in which 'the responding Member administers the legal instruments of the kind described in Article X:1' and harm to the complaining Member.[52]

Specifically, the way in which the legal instrument is administered must be non-uniform, partial and/or unreasonable.[53] For example, in *Thailand—Cigarettes (Philippines)*, the Panel found that the slow review process of customs valuation determinations resulted in the unreasonable administration of the Thai customs laws under Article X:3(a). The Panel held that:

> The overall length of the administrative process, combined with less-than-prompt actions (for example requesting information from [the importer]) taken by the [Thai Board of Appeals within the Ministry of Finance] (BoA), also tends to show prejudice caused to other Member governments and traders under Article X:3(a). . . . We therefore find that the concerned delays in the BoA review process resulted in the administration of the Thai customs law in an unreasonable manner and are in violation of Article X:3(a) of the GATT 1994.[54]

In other words, the Panel found that there was a causal link between the BoA's unreasonable delay in the administration of the Thai customs law and the harm brought about to other Member governments and traders, thereby violating Article X:3(a) of the GATT 1994. Nonetheless, the causal link analysis required under Article X:3 of the GATT 1994 does not require a non-attribution analysis, and it is therefore not suited to the Tripartite Non-attribution/Causal Link Analysis.

SPS Agreement

Article 5(1) of the SPS Agreement obliges Members to ensure that their sanitary or phytosanitary measures are based on a risk assessment. Specifically, Article 5(1) provides that:

> Members shall ensure that their sanitary or phytosanitary measures are based on an assessment, as appropriate to the circumstances, of the risks to human, animal or plant life or health, taking into account risk assessment techniques developed by the relevant international organizations.

[52] WTO, *Thailand: Customs and Fiscal Measures on Cigarettes from the Philippines—Report of the Panel* (15 November 2010) WT/DS371/R (Panel, *Thailand—Cigarettes (Philippines)*) [7.866].

[53] ibid [7.867].

[54] ibid [7.969].

Whilst on its face Article 5(1) does not appear to raise a causal question, the AB in *EC—Hormones* held that the requirement that an SPS measure be 'based on' a risk assessment was a substantive requirement that 'there be a rational relationship between the measure and the risk assessment'.[55] The AB further held that the requirement of a risk assessment 'was intended as a countervailing factor in respect of the right of Members to set their appropriate level of protection'.[56] In order for an SPS measure to be 'based on' a risk assessment, the SPS measure does not have to 'conform to' the risk assessment.[57] There must, however, be a causal link between the risk assessment and the measure; and the level of causality must reach a threshold that is 'rational'.

To that end, the AB held that, in reviewing the consistency of an SPS measure with Article 5(1) of the SPS Agreement, it must: (1) identify the scientific basis upon which the SPS measure was adopted; (2) verify that the scientific basis comes from a respected and qualified source; (3) determine whether the scientific reasoning is objective and coherent; and (4) determine whether the results of the risk assessment 'sufficiently warrant' the SPS measure at issue.[58] The Panel in *Japan—Apples* considered the term 'sufficient scientific evidence' and found that the term 'sufficient' refers 'not only to the quantity and quality of the evidence as such, but also the "causal link" between the phytosanitary measure at issue and the scientific evidence establishing a phytosanitary risk and justifying the measure'.[59] In sum, the question of causation in Article 5(1) of the SPS Agreement arises when determining whether the risk assessment 'sufficiently warrants' the SPS measure at issue. It is when this causal link cannot be drawn that a violation of Article 5(1) can be found. Again, this causal question does not require a non-attribution analysis, and therefore the Tripartite Non-attribution/Causal Link Analysis is unsuited to this context.

[55] WTO, *European Communities: Measures Concerning Meat and Meat Products (Hormones)—Recourse to Arbitration by the European Communities under Article 22.6—Decision by the Arbitrators* (12 July 1999) WT/DS26/ARB (*EC—Hormones (Recourse to Arbitration—Article 22.6)*) [193].

[56] ibid [177].

[57] ibid [193].

[58] WTO, *Canada: Continued Suspension of Obligations in the EC—Hormones Dispute—Report of the Appellate Body* (16 October 2008) WT/DS321/AB/R (AB, *Canada—Continued Suspension*) [591].

[59] WTO, *Japan: Measures Affecting the Importation of Apples—Report of the Panel* (15 July 2003) WT/DS245/R (Panel, *Japan—Apples*) [8.82].

Sanitary or Phytosanitary Measures to Relate to Prescribed Policy Objectives

The SPS Agreement seeks to balance a Member's right to adopt or enforce measures necessary to protect human, animal or plant life or health against the requirement that such measures are 'not applied in a manner which would constitute a means of arbitrary or unjustifiable discrimination between Members where the same conditions prevail or a disguised restriction in international trade'.[60] One of the ways in which the SPS Agreement strikes this balance is to require a causal link between sanitary or phytosanitary measures and prescribed policy objectives. Three provisions of the SPS Agreement contain such a causal requirement: (1) Article 2(2); (2) Article 3(1); and (3) Annex A(1).

Turning to Article 2(2) of the SPS Agreement, first, this provision provides that:

> Members shall ensure that any sanitary or phytosanitary measure is applied only to the extent necessary to protect human, animal or plant life or health, is based on scientific principles and is not maintained without sufficient scientific evidence, except as provided for in paragraph 7 of Article 5.[61]

The AB in *Japan—Agricultural Products II* agreed with the Panel in the same case that the obligation in Article 2(2) of the SPS Agreement 'requires that there be a rational or objective relationship between the SPS measure and the scientific evidence'.[62] The AB said in the same case that:

[60] Recital 1 of the SPS Agreement (n 45) provides: Reaffirming that no Member should be prevented from adopting or enforcing measures necessary to protect human, animal or plant life or health, subject to the requirement that these measures are not applied in a manner which would constitute a means of arbitrary or unjustifiable discrimination between Members where the same conditions prevail or a disguised restriction on international trade.

[61] Article 5(7) of the SPS Agreement (n 45) provides: In cases where relevant scientific evidence is insufficient, a Member may provisionally adopt sanitary or phytosanitary measures on the basis of available pertinent information, including that from the relevant international organizations as well as from sanitary or phytosanitary measures applied by other Members. In such circumstances, Members shall seek to obtain the additional information necessary for a more objective assessment of risk and review the sanitary or phytosanitary measure accordingly within a reasonable period of time.

[62] WTO, *Japan: Measures Affecting Agricultural Products—Report of the Appellate Body* (19 March 1999) WT/DS76/AB/R, 277 (AB, *Japan—Agricultural Products II*) [84].

> [w]hether there is a rational relationship between an SPS measure and the scientific evidence is to be determined on a case-by-case basis and will depend upon the particular circumstances of the case, including the characteristics of the measure at issue and the quality and quantity of the scientific evidence.[63]

In sum, the requirement that the relationship between an SPS measure and the scientific evidence be 'rational' in nature makes is essentially a causal relationship. The causal nature of the relationship can be seen through the failure to make it out in the *Japan—Apples* case. In that case, the Panel found that the phytosanitary measure at issue in the case was 'disproportionate to the risk identified on the basis of the scientific evidence available';[64] and accordingly, the causal link between the measure and the scientific evidence was not made out. The causal relationship in Article 2(2) of the SPS Agreement does not, however, require a non-attribution analysis, thereby rendering the use of the Tripartite Non-attribution/Causation Analysis unnecessary.

Second, Article 3(1) of the SPS Agreement requires a link between sanitary and phytosanitary measures and international standards, guidelines or recommendations, where they exist. Specifically, Article 3(1) of the SPS Agreement provides as follows:

> To harmonize sanitary and phytosanitary measures on as wide a basis as possible, Members shall base their sanitary or phytosanitary measures on international standards, guidelines or recommendations, where they exist, except as otherwise provided for in this Agreement, and in particular in paragraph 3.

In *EC—Hormones*, the AB held that '[a] thing is commonly said to be "based on" another thing when the former "stands" or is "founded" or "built" upon or "is supported by" the latter'.[65] The Panel in that case found that 'for a sanitary measure to be based on an international standard in accordance with Article 3.1, that measure needs to reflect the same level of sanitary protection as the standard'.[66] In other words, in

[63] ibid.

[64] Panel, *Japan—Apples* (n 59) [8.198].

[65] WTO, *European Communities: Measures Concerning Meat and Meat Products (Hormones)—Report of the Appellate Body* (16 January 1998) WT/DS26/AB/R; WT/DS48/AB/R (AB, *EC—Hormones*) [163].

[66] WTO, *European Communities: Measures Concerning Meat and Meat Products (Hormones)—Report of the Panel* (18 August 1997) WT/DS48/R/CAN (Panel, *EC—Hormones*) [8.76].

order to determine whether a sanitary measure is based on an international standard, a comparison needs to be made between the level of protection reflected in the EC measure in dispute and the international standard in question. The causal question is therefore whether there is a sufficiently proximate relationship between the level of protection provided by the sanitary measure and the level of protection offered by the international standard. To put it another way, an international standard reflects a specific level of sanitary protection and, to the extent that a sanitary measure implies a different level, that measure could not be said to be based on the international standard.[67] Yet again, Article 3(1) of the SPS Agreement does not necessitate conducting a non-attribution analysis, and therefore the Tripartite Non-attribution/Causation Analysis is unnecessary here.

Finally, Annex A(1) of the SPS Agreement contains two causal requirements that have the effect of circumscribing the policy objectives to which sanitary or phytosanitary measures may relate. Annex A(1) provides as follows:

1. Sanitary or phytosanitary measure – Any measure applied:
   (a) to protect animal or plant life or health within the territory of the Member from risks arising from the entry, establishment or spread of pests, diseases, disease-carrying organisms or disease-causing organisms;
   (b) to protect human or animal life or health within the territory of the Member from risks arising from additives, contaminants, toxins or disease-causing organisms in foods, beverages or feedstuffs;
   (c) to protect human life or health within the territory of the Member from risks arising from diseases carried by animals, plants or products thereof, or from the entry, establishment or spread of pests; or
   (d) to prevent or limit other damage within the territory of the Member from the entry, establishment or spread of pests.

Sanitary or phytosanitary measures include all relevant laws, decrees, regulations, requirements and procedures, including inter alia, end product criteria; processes and production methods; testing, inspection, certification and approval procedures; quarantine treatments, including relevant requirements associated with the transport of animals or plants, or with the materials necessary for their survival during transport;

[67] ibid [8.75].

provisions on relevant statistical methods, sampling procedures and methods of risk assessment; and packaging and labelling requirements directly related to food safety.

The AB held in *Australia—Apples* that Annex A(1) establishes a required link between the measure and the protected interest.[68] Specifically, the AB held that the word 'applied' indicates the application of the measure. This, therefore, suggests that the relationship between the measure and one of the objectives listed in Annex A(1) must be manifest in the measure itself or from the circumstances related to the application of the measure.[69] The AB in *Australia—Apples* went on to say that, '[w]hether a measure is "applied ... to protect" in the case of Annex A (1)(a) must be ascertained not only from the objectives of the measure as expressed by the responding party, but also from the text and structure of the relevant measure, its surrounding regulatory context, and the way in which it is designed and applied'.[70] The AB went on to say that an analysis of these circumstances 'must reveal a clear and objective relationship between that measure and the specific purposes enumerated in Annex A(1)(a)'.[71] If such a relationship cannot be made out, the measure would be found to fall outside the scope of Annex A(1), and therefore the SPS Agreement would not apply to it.[72]

The second causal question arising from the SPS Agreement relates to the phrase 'risks arising from' in subparagraphs (a), (b) and (c) of Annex A(1) and the phrase 'other damage ... from' in subparagraph (d) of Annex A(1). The Panel in *EC—Approval and Marketing of Biotech Products* interpreted the term 'risks arising from' in subparagraph (a) as meaning 'to occur as a result of',[73] thereby suggesting a causal analysis. In other words, there must be a causal link between the object to be protected (e.g., animal or plant life) and the risk (e.g., from the entry, establishment or spread of pests, diseases, disease-carrying organisms or

[68] WTO, *Australia: Measures Affecting the Importation of Apples from New Zealand—Report of the Appellate Body* (29 November 2010) WT/DS367/AB/R (AB, *Australia—Apples*) [172].

[69] ibid.

[70] ibid [173].

[71] ibid.

[72] Compare WTO, *European Communities: Measures Affecting the Approval and Marketing of Biotech Products—Report of the Panel* (29 September 2006) WT/DS291/R; WT/DS292/R; WT/DS293/R (Panel, *EC—Approval and Marketing of Biotech Products*) [7.389]–[7.391].

[73] ibid [7.224].

disease-causing organisms). The Panel in *EC—Approval and Marketing of Biotech Products* gave a broad interpretation to the term 'arising from' in the context of Annex A (1)(a), as it noted that the phrase had an unqualified character.[74] That is, the phrase is sufficiently broad to include risks that may only potentially arise in the future.[75] In this sense, the phrase not only covers risks that are of immediate concern, but also those that are more indirect and remote in time. As Gruszczynski argues, '[i]n practical terms, this means that the required causality between the entry, establishment, or spread of pests, diseases, disease-carrying organisms, or disease-causing organisms, and risk to animal and plant life and health is not very demanding'.[76]

Similarly, the Panel in *EC—Approval and Marketing of Biotech Products* gave a broad interpretation to the phrase 'other damage … from' in Annex A(1)(d).[77] Specifically, the Panel found that, because the term 'other damage' is 'broad and unqualified', this suggests that it was intended to cover 'a residual category of damage' which 'is not limited to environmental damage'.[78] The Panel further said that the category of 'other damage' in Annex A(1)(d) could include damage to property, including infrastructure and economic damage.[79]

The *Canada—Continued Suspension* case considered the question of whether the causal link between the object to be protected and the risk it seeks to protect against can be severed by intervening factors. Specifically, the AB considered whether the EC needed to isolate the contribution made by residues of oestradiol-17β in meat from cattle treated with the hormone for growth promotion from other contributing factors. The AB said that:

> In order to meet the requirements of Article 5.1 and Annex A of the *SPS Agreement*, it was sufficient for the European Communities to demonstrate that the additional human exposure to residues of oestradiol-17β in meat from treated cattle is one of the factors contributing to the possible adverse health effects. The European Communities was not required to isolate the contribution made by residues of oestradiol-17β in meat from cattle treated with the hormone for growth promotion from the contributions made by other sources. Where multiple factors may contribute to a particular risk, a

[74] ibid [7.226].
[75] ibid [7.225].
[76] Lukasz Gruszczynski, *Regulating Health and Environmental Risks under WTO Law: A Critical Analysis of the SPS Agreement* (OUP 2010) 54.
[77] Panel, *EC—Approval and Marketing of Biotech Products* (n 72) [7.209].
[78] ibid.
[79] ibid [7.370].

> risk assessor is not required to differentiate the individual contribution made by each factor. Article 5.1 requires that SPS measures be based on a risk assessment 'as appropriate to the circumstances', which suggests that the scientific inquiry involved in a risk assessment must take due account of particular methodological difficulties posed by the nature and characteristics of the particular substance and risk being evaluated. However that does not excuse the risk assessor from evaluating whether there is a connection between the particular substance being evaluated and the possibility that adverse health effects may arise.[80]

In other words, the EC was required to establish that there was a causal link between the possibility of adverse health effects and specific hormone residues. It was sufficient, however, to show that such residue was one of a number of factors contributing to the overall level of risk. To put it another way, a risk assessor is not required to conduct a kind of non-attribution analysis in order to identify the relative causal contributions made by each factor in a set of factors that form the risk. This lack of a necessity to perform a non-attribution requirement in the context of Annex A(1) reflects the methodological difficulties associated with isolating the contribution of one substance vis-à-vis another source in the context of addressing a risk. As Gruszczynski observes, the 'low threshold makes the whole assessment process much easier'.[81]

This lack of a requirement to perform a non-attribution analysis distinguishes Annex A(1) from the provisions that are the subject of this book – namely, those that require causal factors to be separated from those factors that were immaterial to an outcome. Accordingly, the Tripartite Non-attribution/Causal Link Analysis would not be appropriate to use in the context of Article A(1) of the SPS Agreement.

Potential Market Impacts

The third category of causal questions beyond the scope of this book relates to potential market impacts. These include Articles I:1,[82]

[80] AB, *Canada—Continued Suspension* (n 58) [562]; footnotes omitted.

[81] Gruszczynski (n 76) 124.

[82] Article I:1 of the GATT 1994 (n 11) provides that:

> any advantage, favour, privilege or immunity granted by any contracting party to any product originating in or destined for any other country shall be accorded immediately and unconditionally to the like product originating in or destined for the territories of all other contracting parties.

II:1(a),[83] III:4[84] and XI:1[85] of the GATT 1994, Articles II[86] and XVII[87] of the GATS and Article 2.1[88] of the TBT Agreement (collectively, 'potential market impacts provisions'). The potential market impacts provisions protect expectations of equal competitive opportunities for the trade of goods and services, rather than actual trade flows.[89] As such, the jurisprudence has emphasised that the potential market impacts provisions

[83] Article II:1(a) GATT 1994 (n 11) provides that:

> Each contracting party shall accord to the commerce of the other contracting parties treatment no less favourable than that provided for in the appropriate Part of the appropriate Schedule annexed to this Agreement.

[84] Article III:4 GATT 1994 (n 11) provides that:

> [t]he products of the territory of any contracting party imported into the territory of any other contracting party shall be accorded treatment no less favourable than that accorded to like products of national origin in respect of all laws, regulations and requirements affecting their internal sale, offering for sale, purchase, transportation, distribution or use.

[85] Article XI:1 GATT 1994 (n 11) provides that:

> No prohibitions or restrictions other than duties, taxes or other charges, whether made effective through quotas, import or export licences or other measures, shall be instituted or maintained by any contracting party on the importation of any product of the territory of any other contracting party or on the exportation or sale for export of any product destined for the territory of any other contracting party.

[86] Article II:1 of the GATS (n 12) provides that:

> With respect to any measure covered by this Agreement, each Member shall accord immediately and unconditionally to services and service suppliers of any other Member treatment no less favourable than that it accords to like services and service suppliers of any other country.

[87] Article XVII of the GATS (n 12) provides that:

> In the sectors inscribed in its Schedule, and subject to any conditions and qualifications set out therein, each Member shall accord to services and service suppliers of any other Member, in respect of all measures affecting the supply of services, treatment no less favourable than that it accords to its own like services and service suppliers.

[88] Article 2.1 of the TBT Agreement (n 13) provides that:

> Members shall ensure that in respect of technical regulations, products imported from the territory of any Member shall be accorded treatment no less favourable than that accorded to like products of national origin and to like products originating in any other country.

[89] Article I:1 GATT 1994 (n 11): WTO, *European Communities: Measures Prohibiting the Importation and Marketing of Seal Products—Report of the Appellate Body* (22 May 2014) WT/DS400/AB/R; WT/DS401/AB/R (AB, *EC—Seal Products*) [5.90]; Article II:1(a)

do not require a Member to provide the actual trade effects of a specific measure,[90] in the form of empirical data so as to perform the causal analysis. Instead, the jurisprudence examines the causal question relating to the potential market impacts provisions by looking at the design, structure and expected operation of the measure.[91] The fact that these

GATT 1994 (n 11): WTO, *European Communities and Its Member States: Tariff Treatment of Certain Information Technology Products—Report of the Panel* (16 August 2010) WT/DS375/R; WT/DS376/R; WT/DS377/R [7.757]. See also: WTO, *Russia: Tariff Treatment of Certain Agricultural and Manufacturing Products—Report of the Panel* (12 August 2016) WT/DS485/R (Panel, *Russia—Tariff Treatment*) [7.18]; Article III:4 GATT 1994 (n 11): WTO, *Korea: Measures Affecting Imports of Fresh, Chilled and Frozen Beef—Report of the Panel* (31 July 2000) WT/DS161/R; WT/DS169/R (Panel, *Korea—Various Measures on Beef*) [625]; Article XI:1 GATT 1994 (n 11): WTO, *Argentina: Measures Affecting the Export of Bovine Hides and the Import of Finished Leather—Report of the Panel* (19 December 2000) WT/DS155/R (Panel, *Argentina—Hides and Leather*) [11.20]; Article II:1 GATS (n 12): WTO, *European Communities: Regime for the Importation, Sale and Distribution of Bananas—Recourse to Article 21.5 by the European Communities* (12 April 1999) WT/DS27/RW/EEC [6.150]; Article XVII:1 GATS (n 12): WTO, *Canada: Certain Measures Affecting the Automotive Industry—Report of the Panel* (11 February 2000) WT/DS139/R; WT/DS142/R (Panel, *Canada—Autos*) [10.303]; Article 2.1 TBT Agreement (n 13): WTO, *United States: Certain Country of Origin Labelling (COOL) Requirements—Report of the Appellate Body* (29 June 2012) WT/DS384/AB/R; WT/DS386/AB/R (AB, *US—COOL*) [270]. In the case of Article 2.1 TBT Agreement (n 13), in addition to making an inquiry as to whether a technical regulation had a detrimental impact on competitive opportunities for the group of imported vis-à-vis the group of domestic like products, a panel must further determine whether the detrimental impact on imports 'stems exclusively from a legitimate regulatory distinction rather than reflecting discrimination against the group of imported products': WTO, *United States: Measures Affecting the Production and Sale of Clove Cigarettes—Report of the Appellate Body* (24 April 2012) WT/DS406/AB/R (AB, *US—Clove Cigarettes*) [182].

90 Article I:1 GATT 1994 (n 11): Panel, *EC—Seal Products* (n 35) [7.597]; Article II:1(a) GATT 1994 (n 11): Panel, *Russia—Tariff Treatment* (n 89) [7.20]; Article III:4 GATT 1994 (n 11): Panel, *Korea—Various Measures on Beef* (n 89) [495]; Article XI:1 GATT 1994 (n 11): Panel, *Argentina—Hides and Leather* (n 89) [11.20]; Article II:1 GATS (n 12): WTO, *Argentina: Measures Relating to Trade in Goods and Services—Report of the Appellate Body* (14 April 2016) WT/DS453/AB/R/Add 1 (AB, *Argentina—Financial Services*) [6.111]; Article XVII:1 GATS (n 12): Panel, *Canada—Autos* (n 89) [10.303]; Article 2.1 TBT Agreement (n 13): AB, *US—COOL* (n 89) [325].

91 Article I:1 GATT 1994 (n 11): Panel, *EC—Seal Products* (n 35) [7.597]; Article III:4 GATT 1994 (n 11): Panel, *Korea—Various Measures on Beef* (n 89) [495]; Article XI:1 GATT 1994 (n 11): WTO, *Argentina: Measures Affecting the Importation of Goods—Report of the Appellate Body* (15 January 2015) WT/DS438/AB/R; WT/DS444/AB/R; WT/DS445/AB/R (AB, *Argentina—Import Measures*) [5.217] (referring to WTO, *China: Measures Related to the Exportation of Various Raw Materials—Report of the Appellate Body* (30 January 2012) WT/DS394/AB/R; WT/DS395/AB/R; WT/DS398/AB/R (AB, *China—Raw Materials*) [319]–[320]); Article II:1 GATS (n 12): AB, *Argentina—Financial Services* (n

provisions examine *potential* market impacts, rather than *actual* market impacts, means that they are unsuited to the Tripartite Non-attribution/ Causal Link Analysis, which is concerned with real-world effects.

Nullification or Impairment of Benefits

Article XXIII:1 of the GATT 1994[92] and Article XXIII:3 of the GATS[93] technically raise a causal question in relation to meeting the conditions for a WTO Panel to have jurisdiction in a matter. Bartels provides two reasons why causation is a non-issue under Article XXIII:1 of the GATT 1994, and his reasoning may be extended to Article XXIII:3 of the GATS. First, both provisions are subjective, in the sense that they only require that the WTO Member 'considers' that a measure of another WTO Member has 'nullified or impaired' benefits accruing to it. This subjective element of the provisions means that, in practice, there is no need to test the objective truth of the causal question.[94] The second reason why the causation element of the provisions is rarely tested is because, in violation cases, nullification or impairment of benefits is presumed, and therefore

90) [6.127]. This test has not yet been extended to Article II:1 GATT 1994 (n 11) or Article XVII:1 GATS (n 12) in the jurisprudence; Article 2.1 TBT Agreement (n 13): AB, *US—COOL* (n 89) [269] (quoting WTO, *Thailand: Customs and Fiscal Measures on Cigarettes from the Philippines—Report of the Appellate Body* (17 June 2011) WT/DS371/AB/R [130]).

92 Article XXIII:1 GATT 1994 (n 11) provides that:

> If any contracting party should consider that any benefit accruing to it directly or indirectly under this Agreement is being nullified or impaired or that the attainment of any objective of the Agreement is being impeded . . . the contracting party may, with a view to the satisfactory adjustment of the matter, make written representations or proposals to the other contracting party or parties which it considers to be concerned.

93 Article XVII:1 GATS (n 12) provides that:

> If any Member considers that any benefit it could reasonably have expected to accrue to it under a specific commitment of another Member under Part III of this Agreement is being nullified or impaired as a result of the application of any measure which does not conflict with the provisions of this Agreement, it may have recourse to the DSU. If the measure is determined by the DSB to have nullified or impaired such a benefit, the Member affected shall be entitled to a mutually satisfactory adjustment on the basis of paragraph 2 of Article XXI, which may include the modification or withdrawal of the measure.

94 Bartels, 'Procedural Aspects of Shared Responsibility' (n 48) 348.

no causal analysis is required.[95] For both these reasons, a Tripartite Non-attribution/Causal Link Analysis is unsuited to this causal context.

Conclusion

This section has considered those provisions of WTO law that raise causal questions but nonetheless fall outside the scope of this book. These provisions fall into four categories – causal questions that flow from: (1) a breach of an obligation to do something specific (Article X:3 of the GATT 1994 and Article 5(1) and Annex A of the SPS Agreement); (2) prescribed policy objectives within the SPS Agreement; (3) potential, instead of actual, market impacts (Articles I:1,[96] II:1(a),[97] III:4[98] and XI:1[99] of the GATT 1994, Articles II[100] and XVII[101] of the GATS and

[95] ibid.

[96] Article I:1 of the GATT 1994 (n 11) provides that:

> any advantage, favour, privilege or immunity granted by any contracting party to any product originating in or destined for any other country shall be accorded immediately and unconditionally to the like product originating in or destined for the territories of all other contracting parties.

[97] Article II:1(a) GATT 1994 (n 11) provides that:

> Each contracting party shall accord to the commerce of the other contracting parties treatment no less favourable than that provided for in the appropriate Part of the appropriate Schedule annexed to this Agreement.

[98] Article III:4 GATT 1994 (n 11) provides that:

> [t]he products of the territory of any contracting party imported into the territory of any other contracting party shall be accorded treatment no less favourable than that accorded to like products of national origin in respect of all laws, regulations and requirements affecting their internal sale, offering for sale, purchase, transportation, distribution or use.

[99] Article XI:1 GATT 1994 (n 11) provides that:

> No prohibitions or restrictions other than duties, taxes or other charges, whether made effective through quotas, import or export licences or other measures, shall be instituted or maintained by any contracting party on the importation of any product of the territory of any other contracting party or on the exportation or sale for export of any product destined for the territory of any other contracting party.

[100] Article II:1 of the GATS (n 12) provides that:

> With respect to any measure covered by this Agreement, each Member shall accord immediately and unconditionally to services and service suppliers of any other Member treatment no less favourable than that it accords to like services and service suppliers of any other country.

[101] Article XVII of the GATS (n 12) provides that:

Article 2.1[102] of the TBT Agreement); and (4) the nullification or impairment of benefits (Article XXIII:1 of the GATT 1994 and Article XXIII:3 of the GATS).

The kind of causal analysis that each of the aforementioned provisions requires clearly does not fit with the Tripartite Non-attribution/Causal Link Analysis. Specifically, the aforementioned provisions do not require: (1) the collection of any real-world data; or (2) a causal factor to be disaggregated from a cluster of other potential causal factors, in the manner of a non-attribution analysis. Accordingly, whilst the causal analysis that each requires is no less important than the provisions that are the subject of this book, they remain outside its scope.

Sources and Methodology

Despite the importance and difficulty of analysing non-attribution and causal links in WTO law, it has not attracted the amount of academic commentary that it arguably deserves. There has not been any literature to date on what this book has called the Tripartite Non-attribution/Causal Link Analysis. Indeed, there does not appear to be any commentary recognising the potential significance of the three-step process at all.

Moreover, given that the non-attribution and causal link analyses in Chapters 4 and 5 are implicit, there has been no commentary on conducting non-attribution and causal link analyses in those contexts whatsoever. There has been some discussion of non-attribution and causal link analyses in respect of trade remedies, which will be considered in Chapter 2. A small amount of consideration has also been given to causation in respect of serious prejudice, which will be canvassed in Chapter 3. Overall, however, the subject has attracted remarkably little comment, and therefore this book will draw on relatively few secondary sources. Instead, this book overwhelmingly draws upon the international

> In the sectors inscribed in its Schedule, and subject to any conditions and qualifications set out therein, each Member shall accord to services and service suppliers of any other Member, in respect of all measures affecting the supply of services, treatment no less favourable than that it accords to its own like services and service suppliers.

[102] Article 2.1 of the TBT Agreement (n 13) provides that:

> Members shall ensure that in respect of technical regulations, products imported from the territory of any Member shall be accorded treatment no less favourable than that accorded to like products of national origin and to like products originating in any other country.

treaties and the jurisprudence. In Chapter 2, it also draws on some limited domestic law and jurisprudence as a means of understanding the causal threshold required for a determination of injury in relation to trade remedies.

This book is primarily concerned with adapting and applying the Tripartite Non-attribution/Causal Link Analysis to the nine parts of WTO law that were identified earlier. It has been seen that Chapter 1 sets out the causal theories and tests that will be critical to understanding the rest of the book. Chapters 2–5 begin with an examination of the state of the current jurisprudence before preceding to argue how the Tripartite Non-attribution/Causal Link Analysis offers an alternative approach to analysing non-attribution and causal links in WTO law. That said, the precise form that the Tripartite Non-attribution/Causal Link Analysis takes will differ in each chapter, depending on the nature of the causal questions that each chapter raises. In this sense, the Tripartite Non-attribution/Causal Link Analysis acts as a kind of scaffolding, whilst the precise details of what must occur at each of the three steps and what kinds of causal tests must be applied varies between chapters.

Limitations of This Book

There are two points at which this book draws on quantitative tests. The first is in relation to the second step of the Tripartite Non-attribution/ Causal Link Analysis, which requires econometric tests to be undertaken at the Disentanglement Stage of the non-attribution analysis. The need to draw on econometric tests at this point of the Tripartite Non-attribution/ Causal Link Analysis recurs in four out of the five chapters. In particular, econometric tests are required to quantify the impact of one factor vis-à-vis other known factors. This book cites some existing research about the econometric tests that have been developed for separating the impact of imports vis-à-vis other known factors. It is, however, beyond the scope of this book to provide any analysis of the best econometric approach or to suggest alternative econometric approaches. Moreover, the Panels that might be tasked with applying the Tripartite Non-attribution/Causal Link Analysis can draw on a group of experts under Article 13.2 of the DSU to assist with designing econometric tests that are most appropriate for the disentanglement exercise in question.

The second set of quantitative tests that this book discusses is in relation to interpolating the future effect of a measure on a policy objective in relation to Article XX of the GATT, Article XIV of the

GATS or Article 2.2 of the TBT Agreement in Chapter 4. That is, it will be argued in Chapter 4 that, to the extent that a Panel must examine the future effects of a measure on a policy objective, there are quantitative tests that can be drawn upon to assist with predicting future impact based on small amounts of present data. Chapter 4 looks at the way in which the Statistical Significance Test and Linear Regression Analysis can assist with these predictions. It is possible that other factual scenarios may require different quantitative tests. In this sense, the discussion of the use of the SST and LRA is a guide only; and again, future Panels may be required to seek expert advice from econometricians about the most appropriate quantitative tests for this particular scenario under Article 13.2 of the DSU.

1

Causal Theory

1.1 Introduction

This chapter will detail the main causal concepts and tests that will be applied in Chapters 2–5 of this book. To this end, it is helpful to begin with a concrete, factual scenario that raises causal questions, to which this chapter will constantly return in its exposition of the way in which the causal tests operate. This factual scenario is as follows:

> Adam is burning some excess wood and kindling in his back garden inside a large drum. Adam is supervising the burning, but is distracted for a minute by his wife, Beatrice. During this moment of distraction, a bird collects a smouldering stick in its beak and flies away. The bird drops the smouldering stick in the unkempt garden of one of Adam's neighbours and continues to fly away. The smouldering stick catches fire, and the fire quickly spreads and burns down the house of Adam's neighbours before the fire brigade has time to come and extinguish the flames. Who or what caused the house of Adam's neighbours to burn down?

The way in which a fact-finder goes about assessing causation in the aforementioned factual scenario – or indeed, in any factual scenario – depends very much on the purpose that such a causal explanation is required to serve within the practical projects of the law.[1] It was seen in the Introduction that the law generally draws on causation for three purposes – (1) so as to attribute responsibility to an agent; (2) to explain how earlier conditions may have led to a later state of affairs; and (3) to make predictions about the likely future contribution of a condition to a state of affairs.[2] In this sense, unlike a causal philosopher, who may

[1] Guido Calabresi, 'Concerning Cause and the Law of Torts' (1975–76) 43 U Chi L Rev 69, 107.

[2] Antony Honoré, 'Causation in the Law', *The Stanford Encyclopedia of Philosophy* (Winter edn, 2010) <http://plato.stanford.edu/archives/win2010/entries/causation-law/> accessed 26 September 2015.

regard causation as a 'context-free project',[3] lawyers are interested in causation to the extent that it advances their own practical objectives. Despite this difference in the motivations for studying causation, the law has borrowed extensively from philosophy in developing causal tests that are accepted by decision-makers and legal theorists alike.

Returning to the example of Adam and the fire, if a lawyer is trying to sue Adam under negligence law, he or she would emphasise those facts associated with Adam's lack of care in his supervisory duties as the cause of the harm. Adam's defence lawyer might, instead, place more weight on the unkempt state of the garden of Adam's neighbours. In other words, the purpose of suing Adam in negligence law is *attributive*, as the lawyers seek to attribute responsibility for the injury to a particular party.

Whilst almost all negligence cases are attributive in purpose,[4] it will be seen in subsequent chapters that WTO law is concerned with all three of these objectives – attributive, explanatory and predictive. It is for this reason that it is necessary to consider both retrospective and prospective causal tests. Accordingly, this chapter will detail causal tests that examine both past and predicted future causal contributions with the view to determining responsibility.

Having just said that causation can be explained in a manner that fits with the practical purposes of the law, it does not follow that this book means to suggest that causation is in some way ontologically barren or that it has no core essence.[5] The idea that causation is bereft of any essential nature has been argued by some contemporary causal philosophers, such as Nancy Cartwright and Peter Godfrey-Smith. They see causation not as a unified concept with a distinct essence, but rather as one that takes on different forms in different systems.[6] This fundamental philosophical question about whether causation contains a true essence

[3] Jane Stapleton, 'Causation in the Law' in Helen Beebee, Christopher Hitchcock and Peter Menzies (eds), *The Oxford Handbook of Causation* (OUP 2009) 750.

[4] Peter Cane, *Responsibility in Law and Morality* (OUP 1950) 116.

[5] See, for example, John Mackie and Immanuel Kant, who defend the notion that causation has a core essence: John L Mackie, *The Cement of the Universe* (OUP 1974) especially 270–96; and see generally Immanuel Kant, *Prolegomena to Any Future Metaphysics That Will Be Able to Come Forward as Science: With Selections from the Critique of Pure Reason* (Gary Hatfield tr and ed, CUP 1997) especially s 17; Immanuel Kant, *Critique of Pure Reason* (Paul Guyer and Allen W Wood tr and ed, CUP 1998) pt II, Div I, Bk I, ch I.

[6] See generally Nancy Cartwright, 'One Word, Many Things' (2002) 71(5) Phil Sci 805; Nancy Cartwright, *The Dappled World: A Study of the Boundaries of Science* (CUP 1999); and Peter Godfrey-Smith, 'Causal Pluralism' in Beebee, Hitchcock and Menzies (n 3); and Daniel M Hausman, 'Essay Review: Physical Causation' (2002) 33 Stud Hist Philos 717.

and the form that this might take is one on which this book remains agnostic. In sum, by arguing for the idea that causation is manipulated in a manner that suits the practical projects of the law, this book is making an epistemological claim about how causation is best *revealed* in different contexts. It is not, however, making an ontological claim about the *essence* of the concept of causation itself.

Consistent with traditional explanations of causal theory, this chapter divides its discussion into two main sections. The first, known as 'cause-in-fact' theories of causation, will be discussed in Section 1.2, whilst the second, known as 'cause-in-law' theories of causation, will be the subject of Section 1.3. Whilst some theorists, such as Michael Moore, posit a 'singularist' theory of causation that does away with the binary between cause-in-fact and cause-in-law,[7] it is useful to maintain the binary in this chapter for the purposes of promoting greater clarity.

Turning first to Section 1.2, this section will discuss some causal tests used to establish the factual basis of causation. This includes two popular non-quantitative causal tests. The first is the *sine qua non* test. The second involves tests that will be termed 'weak necessity/strong sufficiency tests', because of the different weights that they place on the qualities of necessity and sufficiency. Section 1.2 will also set out some of the limits to the use of the *sine qua non* test, since this causal test has frequently been used as a kind of default causal test in common law systems,[8] even by the Appellate Body (AB) in adjudicating WTO law.[9] It will also illustrate some of the ways in which the weak necessity/strong sufficiency tests are superior to the *sine qua non* test, whilst still acknowledging that the *sine qua non* test has some important merits. Section 1.2 will also set out the main features of two econometric tests that will be applied in Chapter 4. The first econometric approach draws upon the Statistical Significance Test, a mathematical approach used to determine the probability that two variables are in a causal relationship. The second

[7] See generally Michael S Moore, *Causation and Responsibility: An Essay in Law, Morals, and Metaphysics* (OUP 2009) chapter 20.

[8] Calabresi (n 1) 85; John D Rue, 'Returning to the Roots of Bramble Bush: The "But for" Test Regains Primacy in Causal Analysis in the American Law Institute's Proposed Restatement (Third) of Torts' (2003) 71(6) Fordham L Rev 2679, 2684.

[9] See, for example, the current causation test used for Serious Prejudice: Chapter 3, Section 3.6; and the causation test used to determine whether a responding Member's failure to comply with a DSB ruling caused the complaining Member's nullification and impairment: Chapter 5, Section 5.3.

is Linear Regression Analysis, which will be used to model the causal relationship between a dependent and an independent variable.

Section 1.3 will then turn to consider so-called cause-in-law theories. To that end, it will first explain what is meant by 'cause-in-law' before turning to consider why these theories are necessary for the purposes of attributing responsibility to a causal agent. Section 1.3 will then explain why cause-in-law theories need not be drawn upon in this book. This is due to the nature of the non-attribution step in the Tripartite Non-attribution/Causal Link Analysis and the way in which this step uses quantitative methods to attribute responsibility to causal factors, thereby reducing the dependence on non-quantitative cause-in-law theories.

It is important to emphasise that this chapter does not attempt to provide a comprehensive account of the philosophy of causation in the law generally, nor does it aim to cover all features of the non-quantitative or quantitative approaches to causation specifically. Instead, the scope of this chapter is narrower. Its ambit is dictated by the ultimate relevance of the causal theories and principles to the arguments that will be made in subsequent chapters. As such, only those causal principles or tests that will be discussed or applied in subsequent chapters are represented here.

The fact that this chapter only sets out those causal tests and theories that are relevant to the remainder of the book has another important consequence that is particularly regrettable. That is, it is unfortunate that this chapter will only discuss causal tests and causal theorists from the Anglo-American causal philosophical tradition. Whilst there have been many useful contributions to the field of causal philosophy from other jurisdictions,[10] it is a source of regret that these have not been represented in this book. Again, this is simply because this chapter captures only those causal tests and theories that were considered most useful in the chapters that follow. This chapter now turns to consider those causal tests and theories in more detail.

[10] See, for example, Karl Engisch, *Die Kausalität als Merkmal der strafrechtlichen Tatbestände* (Tübingen 1931); Francesco Antolisei, *Il Rapporto di Causalità nel Diritto Penale* (Padua 1934); Franz Leonhard, *Die Kausalität als Erklärung durch Ergänzun* (W Schmitz 1946); Wilhelm Lexis, *Zur theorie der massenerscheinungen in der menschlichen gesellschaft* (W Schmitz 1877); Albert Michotte, *La Perception de la causalité* (Louvain 1954); Hans Stoll, *Kausalzusammenhang und Normzweck im Deliktsrecht* (Tubingen 1968); and Friedrich Adolf Trendelenburg, *Logische Untersuchungen* (S Hirzel 1870).

1.2 Cause-in-Fact Causal Theory

Cause-in-fact causal theory is concerned with interrogating the factual components of causation.[11] To this end, it draws on both quantitative and non-quantitative approaches. It is to the latter that this section now turns.

1.2.1 Some Non-quantitative Approaches to Determining Causation

The non-quantitative approach to causation involves making a determination about causation based on the quality of the connection between a causal factor and an outcome. That is, the connection between a causal factor and an outcome may take on a particular form or nature – such as a necessary or sufficient connection with the ensuing outcome. In order to illustrate these forms of necessary and sufficient connection, this section will adapt Mackie's famous example involving slot machines.[12]

Suppose that there are two chocolate machines that produce chocolate in response to the insertion of a one-pound coin. The first machine (Machine One) is designed to produce chocolate if a person inserts a one-pound coin. Machine One usually produces chocolate in response to a person inserting a one-pound coin; but, due to a technical fault, occasionally Machine One fails to produce the chocolate despite the entry of a one-pound coin. It can thus be said that a necessary condition for Machine One to produce chocolate is the insertion of a one-pound coin, because the first machine *never* delivers a chocolate *unless* a one-pound coin is inserted. This means that it is impossible to get chocolate without inserting a one-pound coin – though it is possible to insert a one-pound coin and not get chocolate. In this sense, entry of the coin is *necessary but not sufficient* for the production of chocolate in all cases. Taking this specific example and extrapolating more broadly, a necessary condition for an effect may be defined, then, as a condition that must be satisfied in order for that effect to be brought about.

[11] Michael Moore, 'Causation in the Law', *The Stanford Encyclopedia of Philosophy* (Fall 2019) <https://plato.stanford.edu/entries/causation-law/> accessed 10 August 2021.

[12] This book will not enter into the debate about whether two of Mackie's three chocolate machines are 'indeterministic', since this is beyond the scope of this book: see Mackie, *The Cement of the Universe* (n 5) 40–41; compare Tony Honoré, 'Necessary and Sufficient Conditions in Tort Law' in David G Owen (ed), *The Philosophical Foundations of Tort Law* (OUP 1997) 381; and Richard W Wright, 'The NESS Account of Natural Causation: A Response to Criticisms' in Benedikt Kahmen and Markus Stepanians (eds), *Critical Essays on Causation and Responsibility* (Walter de Gruyter 2013) 48–50.

The second machine (Machine Two) is also designed to produce chocolate if a person inserts a one-pound coin. Due to a different technical fault than the one that affects Machine One, Machine Two will always produce chocolate when a one-pound coin is inserted, but occasionally it will also produce chocolate when a one-pound coin has *not* been inserted. In this scenario, inserting a coin into the machine is *sufficient but not necessary* for the production of chocolate in all cases. That is, the one-pound coin is *sufficient* because, if a person inserts a one-pound coin into Machine Two, they can be assured that this will definitely result in chocolate being produced, but it is not *necessary* because Machine Two will occasionally produce chocolate without the insertion of a one-pound coin. In view of this example, it is possible to define a sufficient condition for an effect as a condition that, if satisfied, guarantees that effect. With this understanding of necessary and sufficient conditions, this section turns to discuss the two most important non-quantitative causal tests that have drawn on them.

Counterfactuals and the *Sine Qua Non* Test

In order to understand how counterfactual theory works in practice, it is helpful to begin with a practical example. To take the factual scenario with which this chapter opened, a counterfactual way of explaining causation in this scenario would be to say that *but for* Beatrice distracting Adam from supervising the burning of the wood, Adam would have shooed away the bird that went on to take the smouldering kindling. In other words, a counterfactual approach to providing a causal explanation for an outcome involves isolating one factor that 'made a difference' to that outcome.[13] In this case, the fact that Beatrice distracted Adam made a difference to the outcome that followed, because it was the point from which all of the events leading up to the burning down of the house of Adam's neighbours followed. To put this in more technical language, it could be said that the event of the house burning down counterfactually depended on Beatrice distracting Adam from supervising the burning wood and kindling. This counterfactual explanation might be represented diagrammatically as in Figure 1.1.

In sum, the *sine qua non* test involves asking, 'But for X, would Y have occurred?' which is a means of interrogating whether Y counterfactually depended on X. If it is likely that Y would have occurred regardless of X,

[13] Moore, *Causation and Responsibility* (n 7) 84.

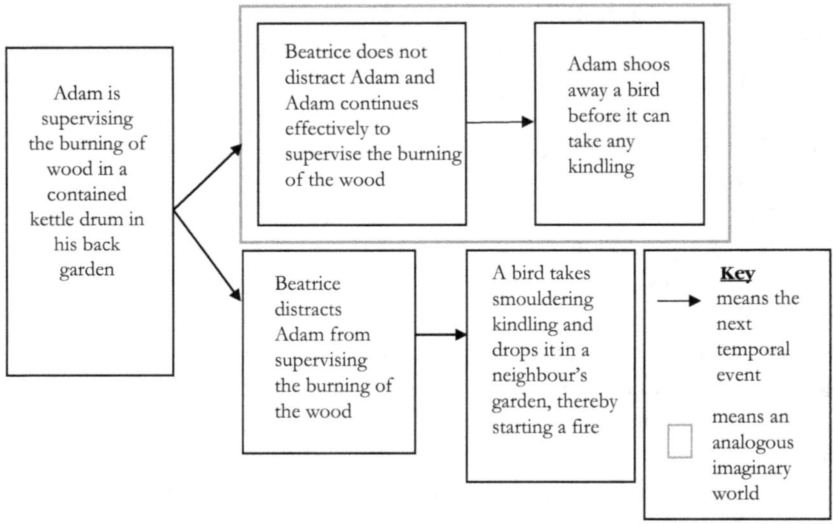

Figure 1.1 The application of the *sine qua non* test to the factual scenario of Beatrice distracting Adam from supervising the burning wood

it is unlikely that X is the cause or one of the causes of Y. If, on the other hand, Y would not have occurred in the absence of X, it may be concluded that X is the cause or one of the causes of Y.[14] Accordingly, X is what made a difference to Y, and in this sense, X must be *necessary* for Y. It follows that the counterfactual account of causation privileges Hume's idea of 'necessary connexion' as the most important relation between cause and effect.[15]

14 One of David Hume's definitions of causation is as follows: an object, followed by another, and where all the objects similar to the first are followed by objects similar to the second. Or, in other words, where, if the first object had not been, the second never had existed: David Hume, *An Enquiry Concerning Human Understanding* (LA Selby-Bigge ed, 3rd edn, OUP 1975) s VII, pt II, 76–77 (emphasis original). There is some controversy surrounding whether Hume's definition here refers to two different approaches to causation, or only one. See generally, for example, JA Robinson, 'Hume's Two Definitions of "Cause"' (1962) 12(47) Phil Q 162. Certainly, David Lewis was of the view that 'Hume defined causation twice over': David Lewis, 'Causation' (1973) 70 J Phil 556. Lewis claimed that Hume's second definition, 'if the first object had not been, the second never had existed' formed the foundation of the counterfactual theory, whereas his first definition was foundational to the 'regularity' theory: Lewis, 'Causation' 556.

15 David Hume, *A Treatise of Human Nature* (LA Selby-Bigge ed, 1789; revised by PH Nidditch, 2nd edn, OUP 1975) Bk I, pt III, s II, 77.

If conducting an experiment, a fact-finder would be in a position precisely to identify which factor made the difference to the outcome by repeating experiments with controlled variations. That is, the fact-finder might include a factor in one experiment and then exclude it in another so as to identify clearly which factor made the difference. This kind of experimental method is not possible when attempting to isolate which factor was necessary to bringing about an injury in the law.[16] As such, in order to try to discover which factor was material to producing injury in the law, a fact-finder would construct an analogous imaginary world using the *sine qua non* test, in which all conditions remain the same, except for the condition whose material difference is being tested.[17] This idea can be seen in Figure 1.1.

David Lewis, in his development of a counterfactual approach to causation, takes the idea of analogising the actual world with other possible worlds much further.[18] His theory not only requires analogising one possible imaginary world, as is a requirement of the *sine qua non* test, but rather, analogising many possible imaginary worlds. Nonetheless, Lewis' possible worlds approach is beyond the scope of this book because it is unsuited to the projects of the law. Specifically, Lewis' possible worlds theory is interested in the metaphysics of causation for its own sake; and, as such, to test his hypothesis would involve an extremely complex series of analogous possible worlds that would be difficult or even impossible to apply in the context of a courtroom. That is, testing Lewis' theory would involve setting up a control in the real world, the results from which would then need to be compared with the results of the hypothetical world. As setting up these controls is difficult or even impossible, from a practical viewpoint, it is unlikely that Lewis' hypothetical world theory could be verified in the requisite way.

Unlike Lewis' possible worlds theory, the *sine qua non* test, which is also grounded in counterfactualism, has been widely applied by common law courts, partly because it is the most intuitive of causal tests to 'the ordinary man'.[19] A further benefit of the test is that it is heuristically simple when compared to the weak necessity/strong sufficiency tests to

[16] Gregory Messenger, 'The Development of International Law and the Role of Causal Language' (2016) 36(1) Ox J Legal Stud 110, 114.

[17] Mackie, *The Cement of the Universe* (n 5) 56.

[18] See generally David Lewis, *Counterfactuals* (Blackwell 1973) and David Lewis, *On the Plurality of Worlds* (Blackwell 1986).

[19] *Yorkshire Dale Steamship Co v Minister of War Transport* [1942] AC 691 (HL) 703 per Lord Macmillan.

be discussed later, because it does not require establishing a 'set' of conditions in order to analyse causation. Nonetheless, the *sine qua non* test as a means of interrogating causation has important limitations that make it unsuitable in some circumstances. It is to these limitations and various theorists' attempts to overcome them that this chapter now turns.

Criticisms of the *Sine Qua Non* Test

'Over-Inclusiveness' of the Sine Qua Non *Test* Despite the important benefits of the *sine qua non* test, it also has some significant limitations. Some critics of the *sine qua non* test object to what they perceive as its 'over-inclusiveness'.[20] This is because the test can be misapplied to support the attribution of causal responsibility to fairly trivial causal factors in scenarios involving cumulative causal contributions. For example, it is contrary to common sense to find that simply because Beatrice distracted Adam from supervising the burning of wood, Beatrice caused the neighbours' house to burn down. This, however, is an important consequence of the fact that the *sine qua non* test only uses the quality of 'necessity' to interrogate cause.

To some extent, this 'over-inclusiveness' problem may partially be resolved by repeating the *sine qua non* test any number of times in order to reveal multiple simultaneous causal factors. For example, the *sine qua non* test could be repeated to reveal the following other factors: *but for* the fact that a bird picked up some smouldering kindling; or *but for* the fact that the wood was not being burnt in a sealed environment where birds could not get at it; or *but for* the fact that Adam did not ask someone else to supervise the burning of the wood for the period when he stopped supervising and so forth. However, the difficulty with the *sine qua non* test is that, once all of these necessary factors have been revealed, the test has no ability to identify which (if any) of the resulting multiple necessary conditions is ultimately *sufficient* for bringing about the injury. This is because the test has no sufficiency criterion to assist in determining which of the necessary factors should be attributed with causal responsibility. Accordingly, the *sine qua non* test must be used with extreme caution to find the responsible cause in cases involving cumulative causal factors.

'Under-Inclusiveness' of the Sine Qua Non *Test* Having just said that the *sine qua non* test is worrisome for its 'over-inclusiveness', more

[20] Moore, *Causation and Responsibility* (n 7) 85.

worrisome still is the potential for the test to be *under*-inclusive.[21] Like all counterfactual tests,[22] the *sine qua non* test is unable to deal reliably with cases of 'duplicative' or 'pre-emptive' over-determination. To take each of these terms in turn, duplicative over-determination cases are those that involve multiple causes that duplicate the injury.[23] For example, to tweak the facts of the case of Adam and the incineration of his neighbours' house, imagine that, just as the bird dropped the smouldering kindling in the neighbours' garden, the neighbours left a candle unattended in a bedroom, which would have caused the house to burn down anyway. Under these revised facts, the neighbours' house would have burnt down because of *both* the fire started by the smouldering kindling in the back garden *as well as* the fire started by the unattended candle in the bedroom.

The *sine qua non* test produces false conclusions when analysing this type of factual scenario involving duplicative over-determination. This is because, if one factor had not brought about the injury, the other factor would have brought it about instead. That is, *neither* the fire in the bedroom *nor* the fire in the back garden is *necessary* to have burnt down the neighbours' house, since, if one of these factors was not there, the second factor would have caused the house to burn down regardless. As neither factor is *necessary* to burn down the house in this sense, the *sine qua non* test finds that *neither* factor caused the house to burn down. This result is manifestly unacceptable from the perspective of a lawyer seeking to attribute an agent with responsibility for the fire.

Similarly, the reliability of the *sine qua non* test further falters in the face of pre-emptive over-determination cases. Pre-emptive over-determination cases are those that involve two sets of factors that would, theoretically, each be minimally sufficient to bring about the harm, but the first actual sufficient set of factors occurs prior to the alternative hypothetically sufficient set. For example, to alter the facts again, this would involve the bird dropping the smouldering stick in the neighbours' back garden (at, say, 3.02 p.m.) and then the unattended candle starting a fire in the bedroom (at, say, 3.08 p.m.), where the effect is that the neighbours' house is incinerated. In this sense, the fire started by the smouldering stick in the back garden pre-empts the fire started by the unattended candle. Once again, the *sine qua non* test produces a false

[21] ibid 86.

[22] LA Paul, 'Counterfactual Theories' in Beebee, Hitchcock and Menzies (n 3) 172–82.

[23] Richard W Wright, 'Causation in Tort Law' (1985) 73(6) California L Rev 1735, 1791–92.

conclusion when analysing this kind of factual scenario. According to the *sine qua non* analysis, neither factor was necessary to cause the house to burn down, because if the first factor had not occurred, then the second factor would have brought about the same injury six minutes later. In this sense, neither factor is *necessary* for the house to have burnt down, and therefore, neither factor is causally responsible for the destruction of the house. As with the analysis of duplicative over-determination, this conclusion is nonsensical, and highlights that the *sine qua non* test is similarly limited in dealing with cases involving pre-emptive over-determination.

From a legal perspective, where attributing responsibility for causing injury is paramount, the inability of the *sine qua non* test to reach correct conclusions in cases of duplicative and pre-emptive over-determination is indeed problematic. Several causation scholars have sought to find conceptual solutions to this limitation.[24] These solutions have been more successful in the case of pre-emptive over-determination than duplicative over-determination. When confronted with duplicative over-determination cases, Mackie claims that it could only confidently be said that the cause for duplicative over-determined cases is the 'cluster of events',[25] the vagueness of which has been criticised.[26] Moreover, where Mackie attempts to interrogate further as to which factor in the cluster 'really caused' the injury, he concedes that, if no further information can be furnished to discriminate between the two identical factors that occasioned harm, 'this question has no answer' from the perspective of the *sine qua non* test.[27] It is conceded that cases of duplicative over-determination are fairly rare outside causal philosophy textbooks. Nonetheless, the unacceptable conclusion that the *sine qua non* test

[24] Such proposed solutions have included, for example, detailing the precise manner of the occurrence (Rollin M Perkins, *Criminal Law* (2nd edn, Foundation Press 1969) 689; Mackie, *The Cement of the Universe* (n 5) 44–47; detailing the precise manner of the injury (Arno C Becht and Frank W Miller, *The Test of Factual Causation in Negligence and Strict Liability Cases* (Washington University Studies 1961); excluding hypothetical facts (Glanville Williams, 'Causation in the Law' (1961) 19 Camb LJ 62, 63–65, 69); aggregating potential multiple causes (William Lloyd Prosser et al., *Prosser and Keeton on the Law of Torts* (5th edn, West Publishing 1984) 17); the substantial factor test (Jeremiah Smith, 'Legal Cause in Actions in Tort' (1911–12) 25 Harvard L Rev 103, 103–28, 223–52, 303–27, 309–21).

[25] Mackie, *The Cement of the Universe* (n 5) 47.

[26] See, for example, HLA Hart and Tony Honoré, *Causation in the Law* (2nd edn, OUP 1985) xli.

[27] Mackie, *The Cement of the Universe* (n 5) 47.

produces in respect of duplicative over-determination, in particular, means that it cannot be relied upon to analyse all causal scenarios.

The Hypothetical World Problem In addition to its over- and its under-inclusiveness, there is a third difficulty that besets the use of the *sine qua non* test. This stems from the fact that the *sine qua non* test relies fundamentally on comparing and contrasting a set of facts or events in the real world with an imagined hypothetical world.[28] This inherently comparative approach means that it is very difficult effectively to compare the facts and events of the real world with a hypothetical world whose features are only imagined and therefore indeterminate.[29] In particular, it is impossible directly to observe or gather evidence in relation to the hypothetical world.[30] Accordingly, in order to make the comparison between the real and imagined world sufficiently determinate, it is necessary to make a set of assumptions about how the imagined world would operate.[31] This book has called the methodological problems associated with this difficult comparison the *hypothetical world problem*; and it is to this problem that this book will continually revert.

The difficulties associated with the hypothetical world problem can be demonstrated with a practical example. To this end, it is helpful to return to the example of Adam and Beatrice, which involves comparing the real world in which Adam is distracted with an imagined, hypothetical world, in which the fact-finder must assume that Adam is not distracted by something or someone else in this hypothetical world. It may be possible that Beatrice does not distract Adam in the analogous, imaginary world, but it is also possible that Adam is distracted instead by a spider crawling up his leg or some chest pain or the cricket score on his portable radio. In other words, the assumptions that a fact-finder is required to make in order to compare the real world with an imagined, hypothetical world may not necessarily be sound.

Some theorists have argued that this apparent conceptual difficulty associated with the *sine qua non* test is not insurmountable, since the comparison with the imagined hypothetical world may be performed with the view simply to revealing which factor 'made a difference' to the outcome.[32] On this analysis, then, the only comparison that needs to take

[28] Jonathan Schaffer, 'Contrastive Causation in the Law' (2010) 16 Leg Theory 259, 261.
[29] Moore, *Causation and Responsibility* (n 7) 85.
[30] Richard Scheines, 'Causation, Truth and the Law' (2008) 73(2) Brooklyn L Rev 625, 638.
[31] Moore, *Causation and Responsibility* (n 7) 85.
[32] Schaffer (n 28) 285.

place is a comparison between the factor that was necessary to cause the outcome with the absence of this factor. For example, Adam's distracted state would be compared with a possible world where he was not distracted. At first sight, this proposal appears to be a panacea; but, in practice, it is impossible to know whether changing one feature of the hypothetical world would also significantly impact other features of that same world to the point that the comparison is unworkable.

This is particularly the case with complex systems, such as economic systems, with which WTO law is concerned. For instance, to take an example that will be developed in Chapter 2 of this book, if a fact-finder were to interrogate whether an injury would have occurred but for a Member's increased imports, it is impossible to know which other features of that Member's economy would also change in the absence of these increased imports, and what potential impact these changed economic features might have on the question. In the absence of increased imports, for example, it is possible that there would have been excessive demand and insufficient supply of a particular good, thereby pushing up the price of the good and distorting the market. In this way, changing one economic feature of the hypothetical world generally brings about a cluster of other changes that make the comparison very difficult. Accordingly, in addition to the two other reasons set out above, the *sine qua non* test must be used with caution in relation to comparing complex systems. Given these significant conceptual difficulties with the *sine qua non* test, it is necessary to turn to an alternative non-quantitative test that was specifically designed to overcome these difficulties.

The Weak Necessity/Strong Sufficiency Tests

In contrast to the *sine qua non* analysis, the weak necessity/strong sufficiency test conceives of causation in terms of clusters of factors that, when aggregated, bring about an outcome. For example, the weak necessity/strong sufficiency test would analyse the factual scenario involving the incineration of the house of Adam's neighbours by finding that the fact that Beatrice distracted Adam from supervising the wood being burnt was only *one* necessary factor in a *set* of factors which, when all taken together, were collectively sufficient to cause the house to burn down. This contrast between the *sine qua non* test analysis and the weak necessity/strong sufficiency test analysis may be seen from the contrast between Figures 1.2 and 1.3.

There are three important contrasts between the *sine qua non* test and the weak necessity/strong sufficiency test that can be identified from

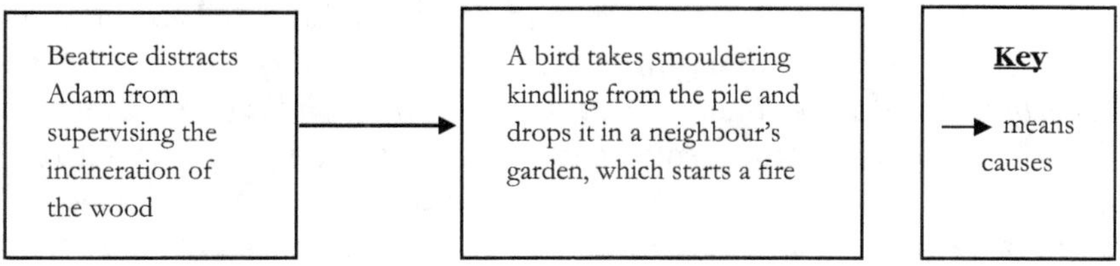

Figure 1.2 Representation of the one factor cause in the *sine qua non* analysis

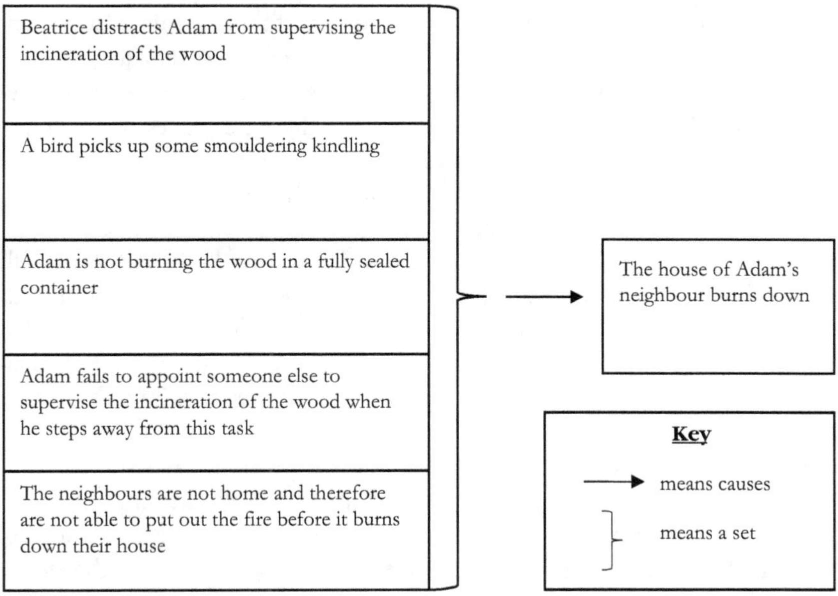

Figure 1.3 Representation of the importance of the set in the weak necessity/strong sufficiency test

comparing Figures 1.2 and 1.3. First, unlike the *sine qua non* test, the weak necessity/strong sufficiency test conceives of a cause in terms of a *set* of factors, rather than as a single factor.[33] Second, and following on from the first point, the criterion of necessity is weaker in the weak necessity/strong sufficiency test than it is in the *sine qua non* test. That

[33] The weak necessity/strong sufficiency test owes a debt to the causal account of JS Mill, particularly Mill's insight that '[t]he cause [. . .] philosophically speaking, is the sum total of the conditions, positive and negative taken together': JS Mill, *A System of Logic Ratiocinative and Inductive* (JM Robson ed, Routledge 1973) Bk III, ch V, s 3.

is, the *sine qua non* test requires a condition to be *strongly* necessary for the occurrence of the injury, in the sense that *the injury would not have been brought about without the existence of that condition.* In contrast, the weak necessity/strong sufficiency tests rely upon a *weaker* idea of necessity. That is, a condition must only be necessary to the sufficiency of a *set*, rather than to the injury itself. To put this another way, if a *set* of conditions is a cause of the injury, then that set is made up of the *minimum* number of conditions that makes the set sufficient to have produced the injury. In this sense, the quality of necessity is subordinated to the quality of sufficiency. It is important to bear this distinction between strong and weak necessity in mind throughout this section.

The third important difference between the *sine qua non* test and the weak necessity/strong sufficiency test is that the latter relies on the idea that each member of a sufficient set has a relationship with the injury that is ascertainable by general laws.[34] That is, the weak necessity/strong sufficiency test relies on the idea that any causal statement 'X causes Y' not only implies that X is causally connected with Y but also that all causal facts or events relevantly resembling X are also causally connected with causal facts or events that relevantly resemble Y.[35] For example, striking this particular match ignites this particular flame, but it also reveals the more general causal relationship between striking matches and igniting flames. In contrast, the *sine qua non* test relies on the counterfactual approach to causation, and therefore, it does not rely on general laws in forming causal relationships. Instead, the *sine qua non* test is focused simply on the specific factual scenario in question and the way in which each necessary factor counterfactually depends on the event that preceded it.

A key feature of the weak necessity/strong sufficiency test that follows from these points of difference is that the weak necessity/strong sufficiency

[34] Hart and Honoré (n 26) 111. It was seen in the context of understanding counterfactuals that one of Hume's definitions of causation is as follows: *an object, followed by another, and where all the objects similar to the first are followed by objects similar to the second*: Hume, *An Enquiry Concerning Human Understanding* (n 14), s VII, pt II, 76. Whilst Hume's restatement of this sentence went on to inspire Lewis' approach to counterfactuals, this sentence by itself has been widely interpreted as a summation of Hume's 'regularity' account of causation. Hume's 'regularity' account of causation is, in essence, that 'every singular causal statement [is] an instance of one or more general propositions asserting invariable sequence, and that causal connection consisted solely in this': Hart and Honoré (n 26) 11.

[35] Tom L Beauchamp and Alexander Rosenberg, *Hume and the Problem of Causation* (OUP 1981) 24.

test can resolve the problem of duplicative and pre-emptive over-determination that was shown to be a fundamental flaw in the use of the *sine qua non* test. To take the case of duplicative over-determination first, it is worth reiterating that duplicative over-determination cases involve multiple causal sets that duplicate the injury. The weak necessity/strong sufficiency test is able to interrogate whether each set of circumstances is made up of necessary elements that are collectively sufficient to have caused the harm in question. Under this approach, unlike the *sine qua non* test, therefore, it is immaterial that neither set is *necessary* for the harm, since the key question is whether the set is made up of necessary elements that are collectively *sufficient* for the harm. As it is possible to have multiple sets of circumstances that are sufficient for the harm,[36] it is also possible under the weak necessity/strong sufficiency test to have multiple causes.[37]

To illustrate the analysis of duplicative over-determination under the weak necessity/strong sufficiency test, it is helpful to revert to the case of the neighbours' burning house. To return to the revised facts of the duplicative over-determination case set out previously, imagine that the neighbours' unattended candle started a fire in one of the bedrooms of their house at exactly the same time that the bird dropped the smouldering kindling in their back garden. Under this new set of facts, there are two sets of factors that are sufficient to bring about the injury to the neighbours' house – that is, (1) there is a set of factors associated with the unattended candle in the bedroom starting a fire; and (2) there is a set of factors involving the smouldering kindling in the back garden. According to the weak necessity/strong sufficiency test, *each* set of factors is sufficient in and of itself for the neighbours' house to burn down. Accordingly, under this analysis, *both* sets of factors would be held causally responsible for the injury – in contrast to the *sine qua non* analysis, where it was seen that

[36] As well as drawing on Mill's insights about the complexity of causation, the weak necessity/strong sufficiency test also draws on Mill's ideas about the potential for there to be a plurality of causes. That is, Hume maintained that 'the same effect never arises but from the same cause': Hume, *An Enquiry Concerning Human Understanding* (n 14) Bk I, s XV, pt III, 173. Mill's account departs from Hume in this sense, not only by suggesting that an effect may have been produced by multiple factors, but also that an outcome may potentially be produced my multiple *sets* of factors: Mill (n 33) Bk III, ch X, s 1. See also Hart and Honoré (n 26) 19–20.

[37] The weak necessity/strong sufficiency account departs from Hume's idea here and adopts JS Mill's notion instead that an effect may have been brought about by multiple causes: Mill (n 33) Bk III, ch X, s 1.

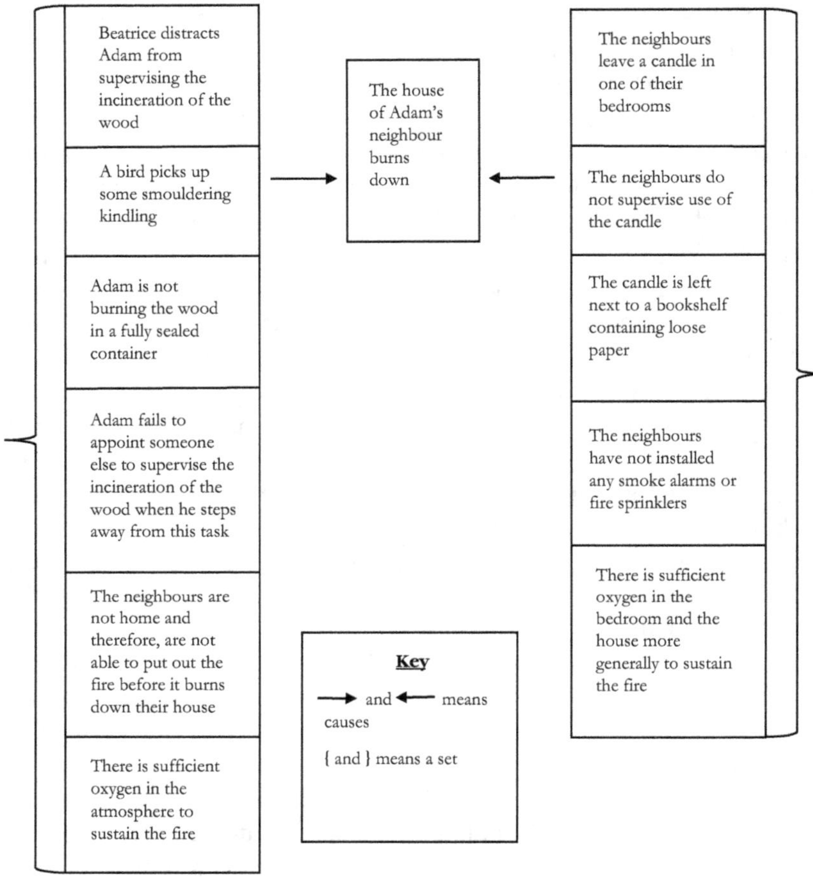

Figure 1.4 The weak necessity/strong sufficiency analysis of duplicative over-determination

neither would be found to be a cause. This result under the weak necessity/strong sufficiency test is far more in keeping with common sense as well as moral intuitions of responsibility than the *sine qua non* analysis of duplicative over-determination. The weak necessity/strong sufficiency analysis of duplicative over-determination may be seen diagrammatically in Figure 1.4.

In a similar vein, the weak necessity/strong sufficiency test can also resolve the difficulties that the *sine qua non* test has with pre-emptive over-determination. To demonstrate, it is necessary to change the details of the factual scenario concerning Adam and the smouldering kindling. Contrary to the facts in the previous paragraph, imagine that the bird drops the smouldering kindling in the garden of Adam's neighbours six minutes *before* the unsupervised candle in the neighbours' bedroom starts a fire. Under these new facts, there are still the same two sets of factors that are each sufficient to bring about the injury to the neighbours' house, as under the duplicative over-determination example. That is, (1) there is a set of factors associated with the unattended candle in the bedroom starting a fire; and (2) there is a set of factors involving the smouldering kindling in the back garden. However, whereas under the duplicative over-determination example, each set of factors is equally causally responsible, in this case involving pre-emptive over-determination, the first set of factors is sufficient *on its own* to be causally responsible for the injury to the neighbours' house. This is because the first set of factors brought about the injury before the second set of factors even materialised. Therefore, whilst the second set of factors involving the unsupervised candle would have been sufficient to have caused the injury to the neighbours' house, its effects were already pre-empted by the first set. Accordingly, only the first set of factors is causally responsible. The weak necessity/strong sufficiency analysis of pre-emptive over-determination may be seen diagrammatically in Figure 1.5.

There have been a number of different forms of the weak necessity/strong sufficiency test. The first, known as the 'causally relevant factor' account, was developed by Hart and Honoré.[38] Hart and Honoré's test was primarily aimed at resolving the difficulty of over-determination,[39] which it did successfully. Nonetheless, other theorists saw potential to expand the basic premise of the test. In particular, Richard Wright, otherwise a proponent of Hart and Honoré's 'causally relevant factor' test,[40] criticised the inability of the 'causally relevant factor' account to deal with cases of duplicative over-determination involving multiple contributory factors.[41] These are cases involving multiple causal sets that duplicate the injury where one or more of the sets is insufficient on its own to cause the injury, but become sufficient when combined with one or more other sets of factors. It is convenient to call these types of cases *contributory duplicative over-determination cases.*

[38] Hart and Honoré (n 26) 113.
[39] ibid 113–14.
[40] Wright, 'Causation in Tort Law' (n 23) 1788.
[41] ibid 1791–92.

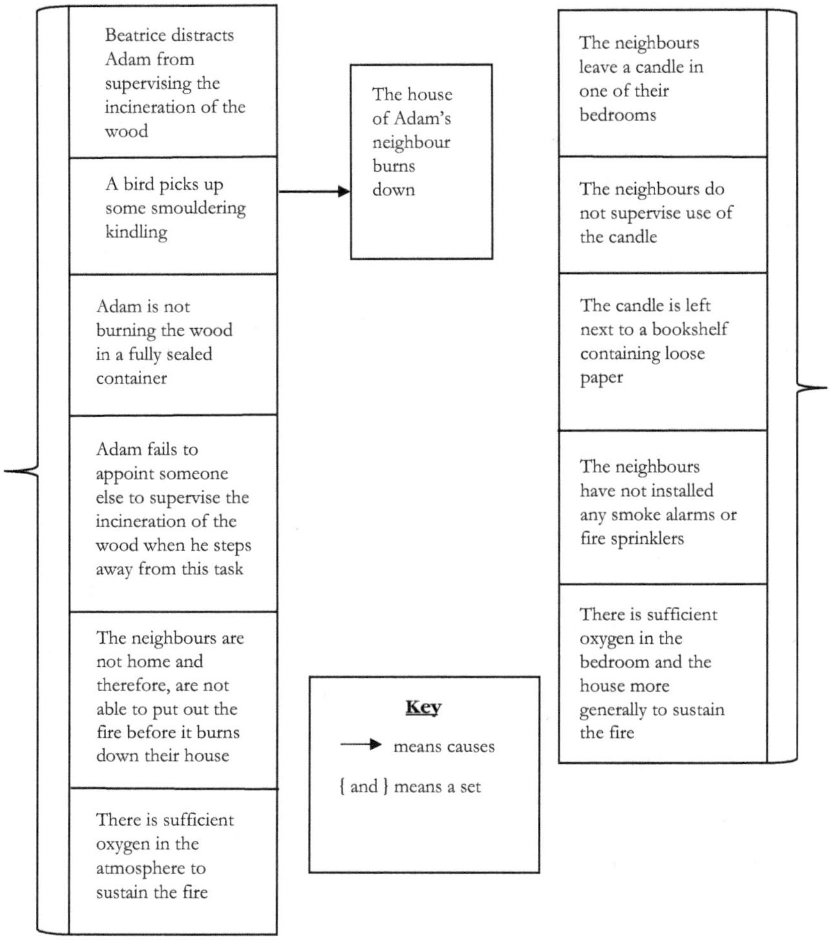

Figure 1.5 The weak necessity/strong sufficiency analysis of pre-emptive over-determination

To illustrate, imagine that the unattended candle in the bedroom of the neighbours' house catches fire, but that, in this scenario, the fire only engulfs the bedroom before it is fused with a second fire that was started by the bird dropping the smouldering kindling in the back garden. In short, there is a small fire that only burns a fraction of the house, and it is joined by a large fire that is capable of burning down the whole house on its own. According to Hart and Honoré's 'causally relevant factor' test, each fire would only be considered as causally responsible for burning down the neighbours' house if it was independently sufficient to have

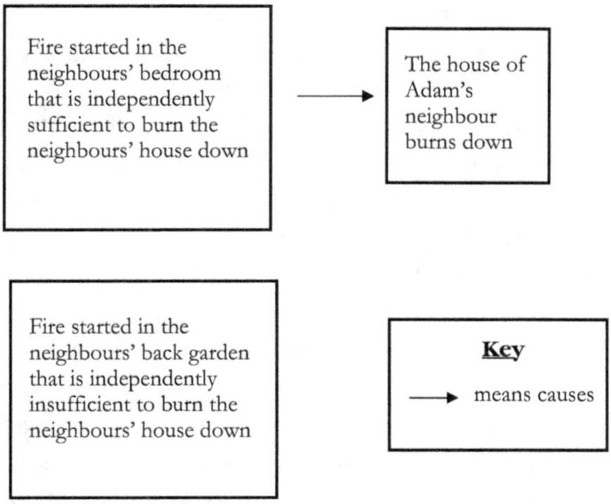

Figure 1.6 Hart and Honoré's 'causally relevant factor' analysis of contributory duplicative over-determination cases

done so.[42] Concomitantly, under Hart and Honoré's analysis, only the large fire would be deemed causally responsible for the destruction of the neighbours' house, whereas the small fire would not be considered causative. Hart and Honoré's 'causally relevant factor' analysis may be seen diagrammatically as in Figure 1.6.

Wright disagrees with Hart and Honoré's analysis of what has here been called contributory duplicative over-determination cases. According to Wright, the 'causally relevant factor' account is too restrictive, in that it requires each set to be sufficient independently of the other causal set.[43] Instead, Wright puts forward a revised version of the weak necessity/strong sufficiency test called the Necessary Element of a Sufficient Set (NESS) test.

Unlike the 'causally relevant factor' test, the NESS test is able to deal with situations involving one or more insufficient sets of factors that merge with a sufficient set, in order, potentially, to create more than one cause. To illustrate this revised version, if the fire that was started in the back garden is independently sufficient to cause damage to Adam's neighbours' house, then, self-evidently, it is a cause of the destruction. Wright's contribution is that, if the fire that started in the bedroom was insufficient independently to burn down the neighbours' entire house,

[42] Hart and Honoré (n 26) 123–25, 206–07, 235–39, 245, 249.

[43] Wright, 'Causation in Tort Law' (n 23) 1791–92.

but nonetheless *becomes* sufficient when fused with the fire started in the back garden, the fire that started in the bedroom should be considered an additional cause at the moment of that fusion.[44] To frame Wright's point in more general terms, causes can be made up of sets that are independently sufficient to cause injury as well as sets that are independently insufficient but *become* sufficient when joined with those other contributory factors that make the set ultimately sufficient.

The logic embedded in Wright's NESS test, he points out, has been used in case law, as where a plaintiff brought a nuisance claim against a set of motorcycles in the case of *Corey v Havener*.[45] In that case, it was not possible to found a nuisance claim based on the noise generated by one motorcycle independently of the others, though it was possible to reach the necessary nuisance threshold where the noise of all of the motorcycles was aggregated. Wright's treatment of contributory duplicative over-determination cases will be drawn upon in the discussion of the Apportionment Analysis in Chapter 2. Wright's contribution to this causal question can be seen diagrammatically in Figure 1.7.

John Mackie, too, put forward a version of the weak necessity/strong sufficiency test that preceded Wright's NESS test, which can also be used reliably to analyse cases of duplicative over-determination, pre-emptive over-determination and contributory duplicative over-determination. Mackie said that a conjunction of conditions may be seen as 'an *insufficient* but *non-redundant* part of an *unnecessary* but *sufficient* condition' or 'INUS' condition.[46] To demonstrate this formulation, Mackie also uses the example of a fire that breaks out in part of a house that is extinguished before the house is completely destroyed.[47] When analysed, experts attribute the cause of the fire to an electrical short-circuit. Mackie explains, however, that it would be incorrect to say that the short-circuit was actually a necessary and sufficient condition of the fire. Instead, he explains that, prior to the fire, there were actually a set of conditions, some of which were positive (such as the presence of flammable material) and some negative (such as the absence of a fire sprinkler to extinguish the flame), all of which combined with the short-circuit to create a complex condition that was sufficient for the house to catch alight.[48] In this way,

[44] ibid 1793.
[45] (1902) 182 Mass 250, 65 NE 69, discussed in Wright, 'Causation in Tort Law' (n 23) 1792.
[46] Mackie, *The Cement of the Universe* (n 5) 62 (emphasis original).
[47] JL Mackie, 'Causes and Conditions' (1965) 2 Am Phil Q 245, 245–64, 245.
[48] ibid.

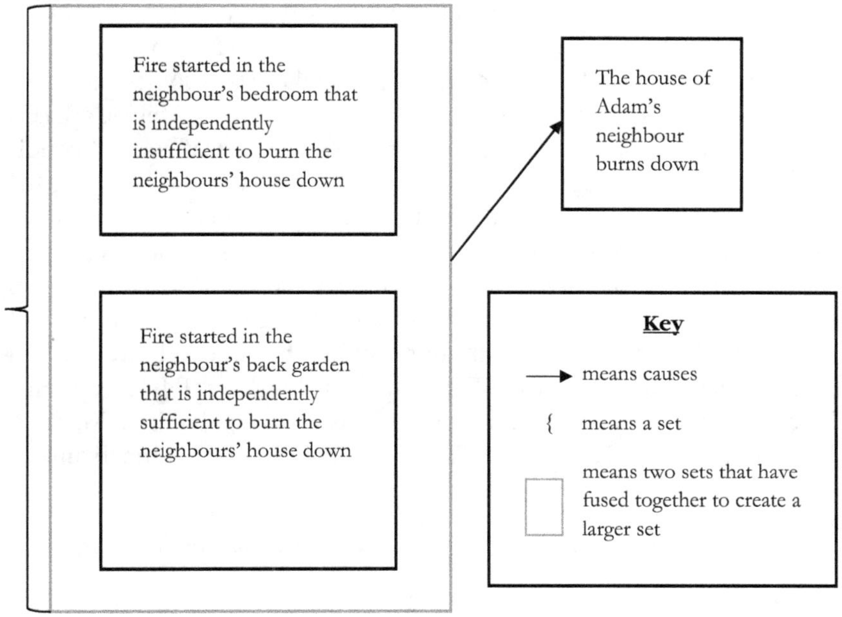

Figure 1.7 Wright's NESS analysis of contributory duplicative over-determination cases

then, Mackie describes the short-circuit as an 'insufficient but necessary part of a condition which is itself unnecessary but sufficient' for the fire.[49]

To break this down, first, the short-circuit is *insufficient* or 'I' because other positive and negative factors are required to start the fire. It is non-redundant or 'N' in the sense that it is necessary to a set of conditions that is sufficient to start the fire. Second, the set is *unnecessary* or 'U' for the ignition of the fire because the existence of the short-circuit does not guarantee the fire. (That is, the fire could have been ignited by something other than the short-circuit – for example, an unattended candle in a bedroom.) Finally, the cluster is *sufficient* or 'S' in the sense that, if the set of factors were to occur, a fire would result.

As with Wright's NESS test, Mackie's INUS test can similarly handle cases of contributory duplicative over-determination. To illustrate, it is helpful to return to the example of the house that is burnt down and, upon investigation, it is found that: (1) the fire that started in the back

[49] ibid.

garden is independently sufficient to have caused the damage; and (2) the fire started in the bedroom was insufficient independently to have caused damage to the neighbours' house, but nonetheless becomes sufficient when fused with the fire from the back garden. Using Mackie's INUS analysis, each fire is an insufficient but necessary part of a set of conditions that is unnecessary but is sufficient for the effect. That is, on the INUS analysis, it is immaterial that there is more than one sufficient set because there is no requirement that the set be necessary and sufficient for the effect.[50] Although there are some philosophical discrepancies between Wright's NESS test and Mackie's INUS test,[51] these are not significant for the purposes of this book. This book, however, will preferentially use Wright's NESS test over Mackie's INUS test only because the NESS test is conceptually easier to apply than Mackie's INUS test,[52] as the latter can be somewhat conceptually cumbersome.

1.2.2 Some Quantitative Approaches to Determining Causation

Introduction

So far, this chapter has examined non-quantitative approaches to interrogating causation – based on the qualities of necessity and/or sufficiency. This book will also use two quantitative tests to interrogate causation. These include the Statistical Significance Test as well as Linear Regression Analysis. The first test measures the probability that the effect was brought about by random chance alone; while the second measures the probability that one variable had a causal effect on another variable. These tests provide the fact-finder with an indication of the level of confidence that one variable has a causal relationship with another variable. These quantitative tests will be used in Chapter 4 of this book.

Linear Regression Analysis

Regression analysis is 'a way of predicting an outcome variable from one predictor variable (simple regression) or several predictor variables (multiple regression)'.[53] Linear Regression Analysis, or LRA, is performed by fitting a statistical model to data in the form of a straight line.[54] It is

[50] Moore, *Causation and Responsibility* (n 7) 416.
[51] See Wright, 'The NESS Account of Natural Causation' (n 12) 17–18.
[52] Judea Pearl, *Causality, Models, Reasoning, and Inference* (CUP 2000) 314.
[53] Andy Field, Jeremy Miles and Zoë Field, *Discovering Statistics Using R* (Sage 2012) 246.
[54] ibid.

Table 1.1 *Number of houses burnt down in Sylvania from 2012–2017*

Year	Number of Houses Burnt Down in Sylvania
2012	42
2013	40
2014	36
2015	29
2016	28
2017	8

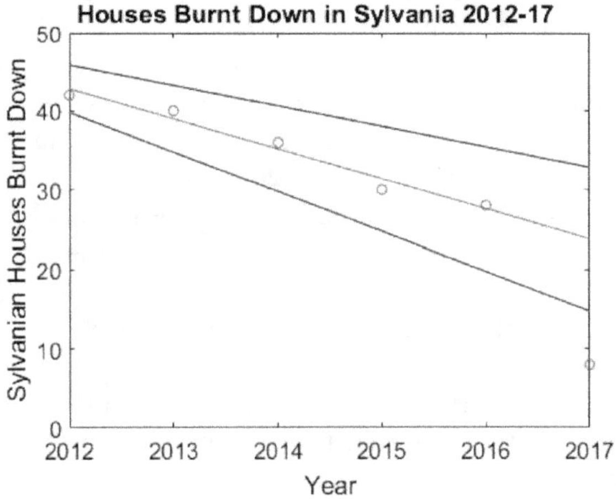

Figure 1.8 Graph of the number of houses burnt down in Sylvania from 2012–17

helpful to explain the utility of the regression analysis with the practical example that has punctuated this chapter. Imagine that the neighbourhood next to Adam's (called Sylvania) has also been having problems with residential fires. Sylvania Council hears about the impact of the Residential Fire Regulation in Adam's neighbourhood, and it decides to introduce the same regulation in Sylvania in 2016. One year after Sylvania's introduction of the Residential Fire Regulation, the Sylvania Council has noticed a drop in the number of fires in its neighbourhood and would also like to know whether the Residential Fire Regulation is responsible for the drop. Sylvania collects the data provided in Table 1.1.

This data can be graphed as shown in Figure 1.8.

The assumptions for this Linear Regression Analysis are as follows:

- any uncertainties arising from other known factors in the data are the same for each value point on the graph;
- the uncertainties arising from other known factors for each value point must be independent of each other; and
- a linear fit to the data is the simplest model for the data.

The middle line is a 'least-square fit line' or 'regression line', which means that it is the line that is 'closest' to fitting all of the value points.[55] This means that it is the line that best optimises or 'fits' with the value points. The purpose of this is to demonstrate where the value point for 2017 would be if the Residential Fire Regulation had no influence on the number of houses in Sylvania that were burnt down. That is, it would be expected that the value point for 2017 would correspond to the extrapolated line in Figure 1.8. Here, we are therefore not only comparing the number of houses burnt down to the average number of houses burnt in recent years, but we are also considering long-term trends in the data, such as a slow decline in the number of houses burnt down during the period 2012–16. It can be seen from the aforementioned graph that, following Sylvania's Residential Fire Regulation in 2017, the value point is markedly lower than where the extrapolated line would suggest. This departure from the trajectory of the extrapolated line indicates that the number of houses burnt down after Sylvania's introduction of the Residential Fire Regulation is fewer than would be expected.

The light grey and dark grey lines on either side of the 'least-square fit lines' indicate the range of statistical significance. As before, we can formulate two hypotheses:

- a *null hypothesis*, which provides that there is no causal relationship between the Residential Fire Regulation and the reduction in the number of houses burnt down in Sylvania; and
- an *alternative hypothesis*, which is that the Residential Fire Regulation contributed to a reduction in the number of houses burnt down in Sylvania.

The significance value (represented as α) will be set at 5 per cent or 0.05 – though it may be recalled that the significance value may potentially be set at any value. Where a Member's data falls within the statistical significance

[55] Xin Yan and Xiao Gang Su, *Linear Regression Analysis: Theory and Computing* (World Scientific 2009) 11–12.

lines, it must be said that the drop in data values is not considered statistically significant for the purpose of this model. Accordingly, for this reason, the null hypothesis must be accepted.

The benefits of using a quantitative approach to analysing the aforementioned data are considerable. First, using a Linear Regression Analysis allows the fact-finder to see graphically the difference between the extrapolated least-square fit line and the data after the introduction of the Residential Fire Regulation. This difference represents the likely number of houses that would have been burnt down were it not for Sylvania Council's decision to introduce the Residential Fire Regulation. In this sense, an extrapolation of the trajectory of the least-square fit line serves as a kind of graphical equivalent to the non-quantitative *sine qua non* test, in the sense that one can see graphically what the likely data is 'but for' the intervention of the measure. Moreover, adopting a quantitative approach has the additional benefit of applying the Statistical Significance Test to the data so that the probability that the Residential Fire Regulation caused the drop in the number of houses can be determined with greater accuracy. The Statistical Significance Test also enables the fact-finder to determine when it is reasonable to search for an alternative confounding factor that may have also contributed to the decline in the incineration of houses.

The Statistical Significance Test

The Statistical Significance Test, or SST, is used to determine the probability that the relationship between two variables is simply due to random chance.[56] In order to demonstrate the operation of the SST, this section will start with a practical example. Imagine that, in addition to the house of Adam's neighbours, a number of other houses have been burnt down in Adam's local neighbourhood as a result of other residents negligently burning things on their property. Accordingly, the local Council introduces the Residential Fire Regulation, which makes it illegal to burn things on any property in the area, except where the resident has a permit from the Council and has attended adequate fire safety training. A year after the Council introduces this regulation, they find that the number of fires in the local area has fallen sharply. The Council would like to determine whether the Residential Fire Regulation contributed to reducing fires in the local area or if the drop in fires is simply due to random chance.

[56] Kevin R Murphy, Brett Myors and Allen Wolach, *Statistical Power Analysis: A Simple and General Model for Traditional and Modern Hypothesis Tests* (4th edn, Routledge 2014) 2–3.

The SST interrogates whether the null hypothesis should be rejected or retained. The null hypothesis is a default position that there is no relationship between the independent and dependent variables.[57] The null hypothesis may be rejected if the p-value is less than the significance level (represented as α).[58] The p-value is the probability of observing a causal relationship between the two variables given that the null hypothesis is true.[59] The significance or α level is the probability of rejecting the null hypothesis when the null hypothesis is nonetheless true.[60] The 'alternative hypothesis', in contrast to the null hypothesis, provides a statement that one variable has a causative effect on another variable.[61] As is customary, the null hypothesis in this example will be set at 5 per cent (that is, 0.05).[62] This means that if the result of the SST is less than 5 per cent, the null hypothesis should be rejected.[63]

To apply the SST to the present case, the following assumptions can be made:

- each house that burns down does so independently (e.g., the fire started in one house does not cause a series of houses in a row to burn down); and
- each house is sampled in a uniformly random way.

With these assumptions in view, imagine that the local Council had collected the following data:

- during the ten years prior to the introduction of the Residential Fire Regulation, 12 properties out of every 1,000 properties sampled was burnt down every year, meaning that 1.2 per cent of properties was incinerated; and
- one year after the introduction of the Residential Fire Regulation, 3 properties (k) out of the 1,000 properties (n) sampled were burnt down, which makes the percentage of properties that were incinerated 0.3 per cent.

[57] Perry R Hinton, *Statistics Explained* (3rd edn, Routledge 2014) 33.

[58] Geoff Cumming and Robert Calin-Jageman, *Introduction to the New Statistics: Estimation, Open Science, and Beyond* (Routledge 2017) 129.

[59] ibid.

[60] Hinton (n 57) 35.

[61] Murphy, Myors and Wolach (n 56) 5.

[62] Hinton (n 57) 83.

[63] ibid 80.

Based on this data, it is possible to formulate hypotheses about the causal relationship between the Residential Fire Regulation and the reduction in the number of houses burnt down. It is customary to formulate both a 'null hypothesis' and an 'alternative hypothesis' before conducting the SST. The null hypothesis and alternative hypothesis as applied to the Council's Residential Fire Regulation might be stated as follows:

- The *null hypothesis*, based on the data provided, is that there is no relationship between the introduction of the Residential Fire Regulation and the reduction in the number of properties burnt down. This means that, even after the introduction of the Residential Fire Regulation, the probability of a house being burnt down within the sample size per year is $p = 1.2\%$.
- The *alternative hypothesis* based on the data provided is that the Residential Fire Regulation contributes to a reduction in properties burnt down.

The null hypothesis and alternative hypothesis are represented in the graph set out at Figure 1.9. If the number of houses incinerated falls within the area shaded dark grey then the null hypothesis is to be considered true. If, on the other hand, the number of houses incinerated falls within the area shaded light grey, then the alternative hypothesis must be held to be true, as in Figure 1.9.

The expectation value (η) is the size of the sample multiplied by the probability that a house will be burnt down. Under the null hypothesis, the expectation value is 12 for a sample size of 1,000. This can be expressed mathematically as follows: Expectation value $(\eta) = n * p = 12$.

Based on the data, the Council wants to calculate the probability that the number of properties burnt down per 1,000 properties sampled (n) is less than or equal to 3 if the probability for each house to burn down is

$$p = 1.2\%.$$

In statistical terms, this can be written as follows:

$$P(x \leq 3 | p = 1.2\%).$$

The probability of exactly x houses being burnt down can be calculated using the binomial distribution:

$$P(x) = \binom{x}{x} p^x (1 - p)^{n-x}.$$

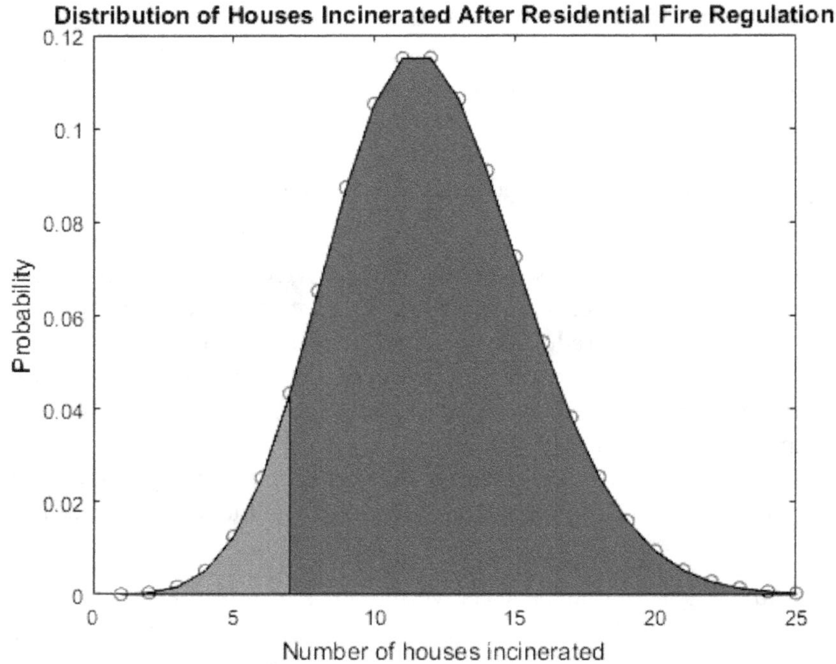

Key
Dark grey – Probability of null hypothesis being true
Light grey – Probability of null hypothesis being false

Figure 1.9 Binomial distribution of the probability of the number of houses incinerated based on the null hypothesis

The probability of getting less than or equal to 3 properties burnt down per 1,000 properties sampled without the policy intervention may be calculated as follows:

$$P(x \leq 3|p = 1.2\%) = \sum_{a=0}^{3} P(x = a) = \sum_{a=0}^{3} \binom{n}{a} p^a (1-p)^{n-a}$$
$$= \sum_{a=0}^{3} \binom{1,000}{a} 0.012^a 0.988^{1,000-a} = 0.2\%.$$

Given that 0.2 per cent is less than 5 per cent, the null hypothesis must be rejected. In other words, it is highly unlikely that the relationship between the Residential Fire Regulation and the reduction in the number of local houses burnt down is due to random chance.

1.3 Cause-in-Law Causal Theory

So far, this chapter has discussed the way in which a causal link might be demonstrated between a causal factor and an outcome by using a selection of quantitative or non-quantitative methods. On this question, there has been some degree of common interest amongst lawyers and philosophers. This current section, however, is of less interest to philosophers than it is to lawyers, since it is chiefly concerned with considering how the causal tests discussed in Section 1.2.2 might be applied in a manner that fulfils the primary objectives of the law – namely, attributing responsibility to a causal agent.

In this section, the term 'the cause' will be used as an elliptical way of saying 'the (responsible) cause' or the cause that is attributed with responsibility for the outcome in question. This is to be contrasted with Section 1.2.2, which discussed the way in which 'the cause' is really a number of facts or events, both positive and negative, that collectively form 'the cause' once aggregated together. This section, however, is more concerned with isolating which of the facts or events in this cluster should be attributed with responsibility for the particular outcome in question.

The most difficult question regarding the attribution of responsibility is the way in which it should be delimited. The question of imposing limits on the attribution of responsibility is sometimes termed the question of 'proximate causation' or 'cause-in-law'. The way in which the limits to responsibility are set is very important because, if an injury is explained in terms of the facts or events that preceded it, there are potentially an infinite number of facts or events stretching back into the past that were necessary for bringing about subsequent events. This idea might be demonstrated by taking an absurd example that builds upon the case study with which this chapter opened. That is, it could be argued that, were it not for Beatrice's mother giving birth to Beatrice, Beatrice would never have been alive to distract Adam from the burning of wood and kindling in the drum. According to this logic, it is Beatrice's mother who should be attributed with responsibility for the fire.

Similarly, were limits not set on the attribution of responsibility, responsibility could also expand forward indefinitely into the future.

For example, returning to the case study once again, imagine that Adam's neighbours' house is burnt down and Adam's neighbours use the insurance money to build a new and much-improved house. This house is then eventually sold for a larger profit than it would have been were it not for the fact that the neighbours were forced to rebuild it after the fire. With the additional profit that Adam's neighbours procured, they were then able to buy a small investment property, which, in turn, made an unexpectedly large profit when sold. In this sense, the fact that Adam's neighbours' house was burnt down had an unexpected financial gain for the neighbours' family that continued well into the future.

Far-fetched as these examples might seem, the causal analysis within them is actually technically correct. That is, potentially causative events can expand both backwards and forwards through time – prompting Glanville Williams famously to term this infinite regress of necessity as the 'cone'[64] of causation, as the search goes from a narrow point and broadens out through time. If causally relevant conditions could automatically ground responsibility for every outcome they brought about, then it follows that responsibility for injury could similarly have the potential to expand backwards and forwards indefinitely. Indeed, the examples used in this section appear unsettling, not because their causal analysis is incorrect, but because they showcase what would happen if limits were not placed around the attribution of responsibility. There is general consensus, then, that responsibility for causing harm must be restricted in some way by policy or other normative considerations. The more difficult question is what these considerations should be and at what point in the process of legal reasoning they should be assessed.

Almost all of the causal theory pertaining to the cause-in-law debate has been written in relation to the law of torts. Certainly, none of it has directly considered the law of the WTO. Nonetheless, the debate is still an important one to consider for the purpose of this book because it is just as crucial to consider how responsibility should be delimited when attributing it to WTO Members. In the WTO context, as in other legal contexts, the anxieties pertaining to the infinite regress of causation are mitigated to some extent by the nature of the covered agreements themselves. That is, the covered agreements serve to delimit the potential causal events and the number of Members that are relevant to the question at hand, in the same way as a piece of domestic legislation might delimit the potential causal events and number of parties to an action.

[64] Glanville Williams, *Joint Torts and Contributory Negligence* (Stevens 1951) 239.

Nonetheless it is suggested that this book does not need to enter into a detailed treatment of cause-in-law and the methods by which responsibility for causing harm might be delimited in the WTO law context because of the nature of the Tripartite Non-attribution/Causal Link Analysis model itself. Specifically, the nature of the Tripartite Non-attribution/Causal Link Analysis is that it uses quantitative methods to isolate causal factors and attribute them with responsibility. This reliance on quantitative methods means that it is not necessary to delimit responsibility by relying on traditional cause-in-law doctrines, such as 'harm-within-the-risk'[65] and foreseeability.[66] In order to understand the way in which the Tripartite Non-attribution/Causal Link Analysis attributes responsibility in this way, it is first necessary to understand the different steps of the process, particularly the second step concerned with non-attribution.

It may be recalled from the introduction that the Tripartite Non-attribution/Causal Link Analysis involved three stages of analysis: (1) authorities must separate the injurious effects of increased imports from the injurious effects produced by other known factors; (2) authorities must then attribute to imports the harm they alone have produced before attributing to other known factors the harm that they have occasioned in turn; and (3) finally, authorities should determine whether there is a causal link between imports and 'serious injury or threat thereof'; and if so, whether such a causal link involves a 'genuine and substantial relationship of cause and effect' between these two elements. These three steps might be seen diagrammatically in Figure 1.10.

As can be seen from Figure 1.10, the second step of this Non-attribution/Causal Link Analysis is the non-attribution analysis step. It requires authorities to use econometric tests in order to apportion responsibility for injury to, say, imports vis-à-vis other known factors. So, for example, as can be seen in Figure 1.10, Sub-Injury A might be found to have been caused by 70 per cent imports vis-à-vis 30 per cent other known factors; Sub-Injury B, to have been caused by 50 per cent imports and so forth. It is only those sub-injuries that are sufficiently the product of imports as to

[65] Harm-within-the-risk theorists argue that the causal explanation for a chain of events should be framed in terms of that aspect of the defendant's negligent conduct that placed the plaintiff at risk. See generally Robert Keeton, *Legal Cause in the Law of Torts* (Ohio State UP 1963).

[66] The foreseeability test asks whether it was foreseeable to a defendant at the time that she acted that her act would cause the harm that it went on to cause. See generally Leon Green, 'The *Wagon Mound No. 2*: Foreseeability Revised' (1967) 2 Utah LR 197.

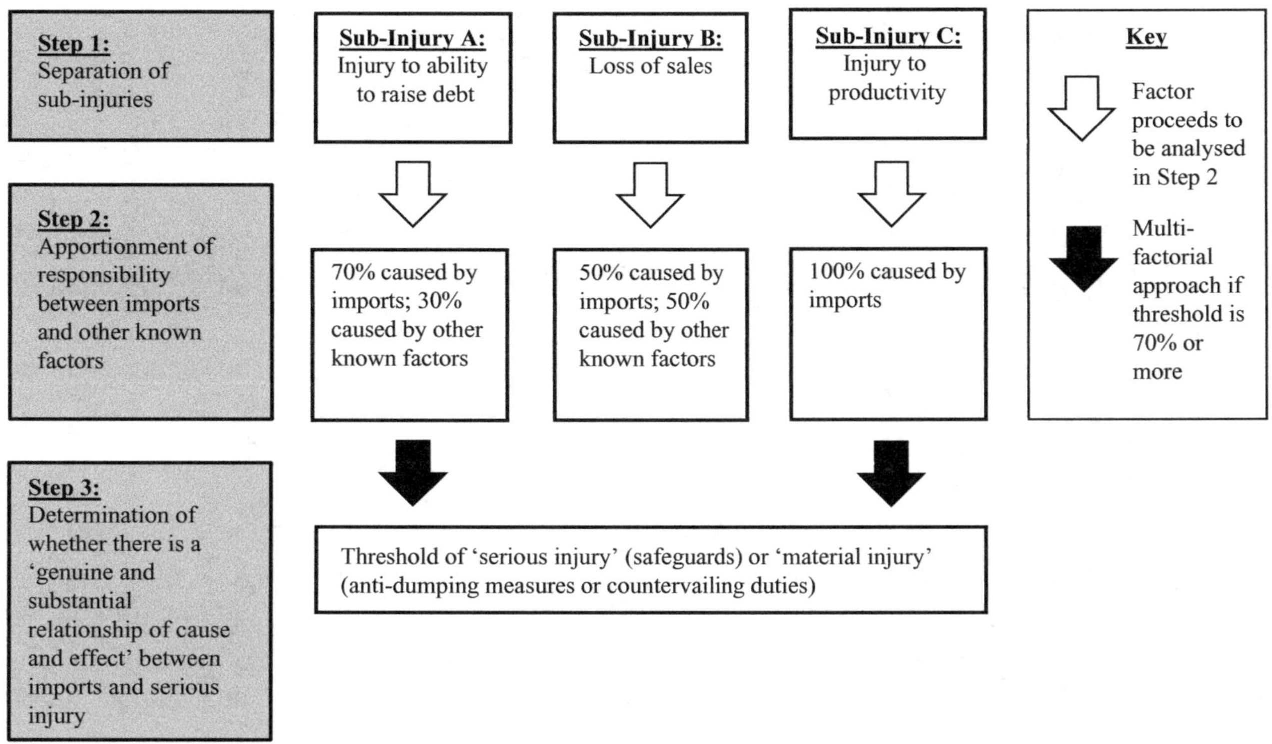

Figure 1.10 Overview of the three steps of the Tripartite Non-attribution/Causal Link Analysis

reach a prescribed threshold that go on to be included in Step Three of the Non-attribution/Causal Link Analysis. To illustrate, using Figure 1.10 again, if the prescribed threshold were to be set at 70 per cent, only Sub-Injury A and Sub-Injury C would pass the threshold and be included in Step Three.

The very raison d'être of the non-attribution step, then, is to identify those factors that contributed to the injury and apportion each with responsibility based on quantitative methods. For this reason, when the Non-attribution/Causal Link Analysis is used, it is not necessary to use non-quantitative cause-in-law tests in order to delimit responsibility for injury. Instead, if a Sub-Injury is identified as being sufficiently the product of one causal factor as to reach a nominated threshold, then it becomes identified as 'the cause'. The real policy question therefore is at what point the nominated threshold should be set. That is, at what point should policymakers deem that the causal factor might be said to be the responsible cause of the Sub-Injury – should it be, for example, set at 80 per cent, 85 per cent or 88 per cent? Self-evidently, the higher the threshold is set, the less likely that imports will be found to be the responsible cause.

In sum, the difficulty associated with identifying the responsible cause is as much of an issue in the causal questions that this book examines as it is any other context. Nonetheless, instead of relying on traditional cause-in-law doctrines, the Non-attribution/Causal Link Analysis deals with delimiting responsibility for an outcome by setting a quantitative threshold, beyond which a causal factor is taken to be responsible for the injury. To put it another way, the nature of the non-attribution step and its role in the Non-attribution/Causal Link Analysis essentially transfers the question of delimiting responsibility from a non-quantitative question to a quantitative one. It is for this reason that it is not necessary for this book to give detailed treatment to the traditional cause-in-law doctrines and their role in delimiting responsibility.

1.4 Conclusion

This chapter has canvassed some of the most important aspects of causal theory insofar as they are relevant for the rest of this book. Turning to cause-in-fact theories first, the causal approaches canvassed in this chapter are tailored to suit different aspects of interrogating causation. It is argued that the causal questions embedded into WTO law require non-quantitative and quantitative forms of causal analysis. The two non-quantitative tests that have been discussed in this chapter are the *sine qua non* test and the weak necessity/strong sufficiency test. The *sine qua non* test is a heuristically simple tool that can quickly identify whether a particular injury would have come about in the absence of the specific causal agent. It has been seen, however, that the *sine qua non* test has a number of limitations that make it ill-suited to particular causal contexts. The weak necessity/strong sufficiency test is in many ways a panacea to the problems that beset the *sine qua non* test. Nonetheless, the weak necessity/strong sufficiency test is less heuristically simple than the *sine qua non* test because it requires the fact-finder to establish a set. Both the *sine qua non* test and the weak necessity/strong sufficiency test, then, have different strengths and limitations, and their use should be guided by the nature of the particular causal problem at hand.

In addition to these non-quantitative causal tests, it will be argued that some of the causal questions raised in WTO law are better interrogated using quantitative causal tests. The quantitative tests can demonstrate with more precision than non-quantitative causal tests what difference a particular phenomenon made to an outcome. That is, whilst both the *sine qua non* test and the weak necessity/strong sufficiency test can isolate what made a difference to a result, they cannot say precisely *how much* of a difference the phenomenon made. The SST is particularly suited to making this assessment, as it can determine the probability that the effect of a particular phenomenon occurred by random chance. Second, whereas the non-quantitative tests are mainly directed at interrogating causation retrospectively, quantitative tests are more suited to predicting future causation, since they can make extrapolations based on a past data set. For example, the Linear Regression Analysis can be used to show the likely future trajectory of a phenomenon based on the previous value points. This is particularly useful when a fact-finder must make a decision about future effects, as will be discussed in Chapter 4.

Additionally, this chapter discussed briefly what is meant by cause-in-law theories of causation and why they are necessary. The chapter explained that it is not necessary for this book to cover cause-in-law theories of causation in great depth because the non-attribution step in the Non-attribution/Causal Link Analysis attributes responsibility to causal factors through the use of quantitative methods. Specifically, it was seen that, by attributing responsibility to causal factors and nominating a threshold above which causal factors are deemed to be 'responsible', it is unnecessary to incorporate non-quantitative cause-in-law theories into the model.

Given that determining causation is inherently difficult and requires a significant amount of specialised knowledge, this chapter has provided some theoretical background to interrogating causation and delimiting responsibility for causing an outcome. The next four chapters will each analyse the current approach in the jurisprudence to interrogating causation and will also propose alternative approaches that draw heavily on the theories and causal tests that were explained in this chapter.

2

Trade Remedies*

2.1 Introduction

WTO law offers three forms of remedies to protect a domestic industry against the injurious effects of imports: safeguard measures,[1] antidumping measures[2] and countervailing duties[3] (collectively, 'trade remedies'). Safeguard measures temporarily restrict imports of a product so as to protect a specific domestic industry from an increase in imports of any product that is causing, or threatening to cause, serious injury to the industry.[4] Antidumping measures, on the other hand, are introduced as a means of counteracting the injurious effects of products that are sold to another Member at 'less than the normal value of the product'.[5] Finally, countervailing duties are introduced so as to protect a domestic industry from exporters or producers whose products benefit from a government subsidy that causes or threatens to cause injury to the industry in the importing country.[6]

Due to the distorting effects of trade remedies, their use is subject to the satisfaction of stringent criteria. While the relevant criteria of the trade remedies agreements will be detailed later, each has two key requirements at their heart that must be fulfilled in order for the trade

* An abbreviated version of this chapter has been published as Catherine E. Gascoigne, 'The Determination of Causation in the Application of Trade Remedies' (2021) 20(1) WTR 56.

1 *Agreement on Safeguards*, LT/UR/A-1A/8 (signed 15 April 1994, entered into force 1 January 1995) (Safeguards Agreement).

2 *Agreement on Implementation of Article VI of the General Agreement on Tariffs and Trade 1994*, LT/UR/A-1A/3 (signed 15 April 1994, entered into force 1 January 1995) (Antidumping Agreement or AD Agreement).

3 *Agreement on Subsidies and Countervailing Measures*, LT/UR/A-1A/9 (signed 15 April 1994, entered into force 1 January 1995) (SCM Agreement).

4 Article 2.1 of the Safeguards Agreement (n 1).

5 Article VI:1 of the *General Agreement on Tariffs and Trade 1994*, LT/UR/A-1A/1/GATT/1 (signed 15 April 1994, entered into force 1 January 1995) (GATT 1994). See generally Richard D Boltuck, 'An Economic Analysis of Dumping' (1987) 21(5) JWT 45.

6 SCM Agreement (n 3) Article 15.5.

remedies to be legally implemented. The first is a requirement to determine that it is the imports that have caused the injury to the domestic industry (the causal link limb). The second is to ensure that the injury to a Member's domestic industry was not caused by other known factors (the non-attribution limb). Importantly, each of these analyses is performed by a Member's domestic competent authority. It is only if the analysis that is performed by the domestic competent authority is challenged by another Member that a WTO Panel or the AB would be required to review the analysis of the domestic competent authority.

Despite the obvious benefits of having clear guidance about how the causal link and non-attribution limbs are to be interpreted, both the jurisprudence and academic commentary evidence a degree of confusion. Indeed, Members have called for clarification in respect of the relevant provisions of all of the trade remedies agreements.[7] Moreover, in the Doha Ministerial Declaration, WTO Members agreed to undertake:

[7] See generally James J Nedumpara, *Injury and Causation in Trade Remedy Law: A Study of WTO Law and Country Practices* (Springer 2016) ch 6; Jorge Miranda, 'Causal Link and Non-Attribution as Interpreted in WTO Trade Remedy Disputes' (2010) 44(4) JWT 729; and Devin Sikes, 'The Need for New Causation Standards in Antidumping, Countervailing Duty and Safeguard Actions' (2010) 7(1) Manch J Int Econ Law 39, 39. In respect of the Safeguards Agreement, see the call for clarification on Article 4.2 of the Safeguards Agreement: WTO, Dispute Settlement Body, Minutes of Meeting Held in the Centre William Rappard (16 May 2001) WT/DSB/M/105, 19 June 2001, <www.puntofocal.gov.ar/doc/dsb-m337.pdf> accessed 30 April 2014, [46], per Japan and [49] per Hong Kong, China. See also Simon Lacey, 'Causal Link, Non-Attribution and Contingency Protection in the WTO' (December 2002) Working Paper, 37, <https://ssrn.com/abstract=1135133> accessed 3 November 2017; Chad P Bown, 'Why Are Safeguards under the WTO So Unpopular?' (2002) 47 WTR 47; In respect of the AD Agreement and Article 15.5 of the SCM Agreement, see Negotiating Group on Rules, Paper by Friends of Antidumping, Antidumping: Illustrative Major Issues, TN/RL/W/6 (26 April 2002); WTO, Negotiating Group on Rules, Second Submission of India: Antidumping Agreement, TN/RL/W/26 (17 October 2002); Call for Clarification on Article 3.5 of the AD Agreement: WTO, Negotiating Group on Rules, *Causation: Communication from Egypt*, TN/RL/GEN/140 (6 June 2006) <www.jmcti.org/2000round/com/doha/tn/rl/tn_rl_gen_140.pdf> accessed 30 April 2014; WTO, Negotiating Group on Rules, *General Contribution to the Discussion of the Negotiating Group on Rules on AD Measures, Paper from Brazil; Chile; Colombia; Costa Rica; Hong Kong, China; Israel; Japan; Korea; Norway; Separate Customs Territory of Taiwan, Penghu, Kinmen, and Matsu; Thailand; and Turkey*, TN/RL/W/28 (15 November 2002) <www.meti.go.jp/policy/trade_policy/wto/wto_db/data/ad_gcon0212e.pdf> accessed 30 April 2014; WTO, Negotiating Group on Rules, *Second Submission of Proposals on the Determination of Injury, Paper from Brazil; Chile; Colombia; Costa Rica; Hong Kong, China; Israel; Japan; Korea, Rep. of; Norway; Singapore; Switzerland; the Separate Customs Territory of Taiwan, Penghu, Kinmen and Matsu; and Thailand*, TN/RL/GEN/38 (23 March 2005) <www.pc.gov.au/__data/assets/pdf_file/0015/90204/sub026-attachmentb.pdf> accessed 30 April 2014; WTO, Negotiating Group on Rules,

> negotiations aimed at clarifying and improving disciplines under the Agreements on Implementation of Article VI of the GATT 1994 and on Subsidies and Countervailing Measures, while preserving the basic concepts, principles and effectiveness of these Agreements and their instruments and objectives, and taking into account the needs of developing and least-developed participants.[8]

This confusion has two fundamental sources. First, many commentators query the economic assumptions that are embedded in the drafting of Article 4.2 of the Safeguards Agreement, Article 3.5 of the Antidumping Agreement and Article 15.5 of the SCM Agreement ('the provisions'). In particular, the provisions are drafted so as to reflect the premise that imports are a source of injury to a domestic industry. Several commentators, however, have noted that imports are a function of consumer tastes and habits; and therefore, that it is more accurate to say that it is a change in consumer tastes and habits via imports that cause injury.[9] This economic debate is beyond the scope of this chapter. Moreover, any discussion of the jurisprudence relating to findings of temporal and other sources of correlation between imports and other injurious factors is also beyond the scope of this chapter, since this jurisprudence essentially relates to the same economic debate.[10]

Causation (AD Agreement Article 3.5; SCM Agreement Article 15.5): Communication from the United States, TN/RL/GEN/128 (24 April 2006) <www.jmcti.org/2000round/com/doha/tn/rl/tn_rl_gen_128.pdf> accessed 30 April 2014; in respect of Article 15.5 of the SCM Agreement, see ibid, TN/RL/GEN/128; Communication from the United States, Identification of Additional Issues under the Antidumping and Subsidies Agreements, TN/RL/W/98 (6 May 2003); Communication from the United States, Causation (*AD Agreement 3.5; SCM Agreement Article 15.5*), TN/RL/GEN/59 (13 July 2005); Marc Benitah, *The Law of Subsidies under the GATT/WTO System* (Kluwer 2001) 281–304 and Marc Benitah, 'From Economic Complexity to Legal Indeterminacy: Causality between Subsidy and Injury' (1999) 33(1) JWT 87.

[8] WTO, Ministerial Declaration (14 November 2001) WT/MIN (01)/DEC/1, 41 ILM 746 (2002) (Doha Declaration).

[9] For this view, see generally Alan O Sykes, 'The Causation Requirement and "Non-Attribution"' in *The WTO Safeguards Agreement: A Commentary* (OUP 2006); Alan O Sykes, 'The Safeguards Mess: A Critique of WTO Jurisprudence' (2003) 2(3) WTR 261; Fernando Piérola, 'Causal Link' in *The Challenge of Safeguards in the WTO* (CUP 2014); Kenneth Kelly, 'The Analysis of Causality in Escape Clause Cases' (1988) 37(2) J Ind Econ 187; Robert S Pindyck and Julio J Rotemberg, 'Are Imports to Blame? Attribution of Injury under the 1974 Trade Act' (1987) 30 J Law & Econ 101; and Ronald A Cass and Michael S Knoll, 'The Economics of "Injury"' in Jagdeep S Bhandari and Alan O Sykes (eds), *Antidumping and Countervailing Duty Cases: A Reply to Professor Sykes, Economic Dimensions in International Law: Comparative and Empirical Perspectives* (CUP 1997); and Boltuck (n 5).

[10] For a general overview of the jurisprudence related to temporal and other sources of correlation between imports and other injurious factors, see generally Miranda (n 7).

This chapter instead concerns itself with the secondary source of confusion raised by the provisions. This relates to the lack of a clear and consistent methodology for domestic competent authorities to use in order to: (a) separate the effects of imports from other injurious factors; and (b) determine whether the injurious effects of the imports are sufficient to reach the requisite injury threshold, as is required by the provisions. In adopting this focus, the chapter starts from the basic assumption that the economic premise embedded in the provisions of the trade remedies agreements is justified – namely, that imports are causal. In the alternative, this chapter argues that, even if the provisions are indeed 'economically fallacious',[11] a fact-finder is still required to follow the guidance in the jurisprudence as to how they are to be interpreted until such time as the provisions are either redrafted (which seems unlikely) or the jurisprudence signals a radically new interpretation.

This chapter begins by setting out the provisions and examining the relevant jurisprudence relating to the provisions. The chapter will then turn, in Section 2.6, to consider the way in which some domestic competent authorities have used the 'breaking the causal link approach' to perform the non-attribution and causal link analyses. This involves making an assessment as to whether there is a causal link between imports and market injury before turning to consider whether such a causal link has been broken based on the non-quantitative features of injurious factors other than imports. Despite the fact that both the Panel in *EU—PET (Pakistan)* and the AB found that use of the 'breaking the causal link' methodology was not inconsistent with the causal link and non-attribution requirements of Article 15.5 of the SCM Agreement,[12] this chapter will raise some difficulties with this approach. It will, moreover, consider how an alternative approach that involves econometric analysis based on guidance put forward by the AB in *US—Wheat Gluten* may resolve some of these difficulties.

Despite the different economic rationales for each of the trade remedies, the relevant Panels and the AB have demonstrated a willingness to draw analogies between the provisions, due to similarities in their

[11] Sykes, 'The Causation Requirement' (n 9) 191.

[12] WTO, *European Union: Countervailing Duties on Certain Polyethylene Terephthalate from Pakistan—Report of the Panel* (6 July 2017) WT/DS486/R (Panel, *EU—PET (Pakistan)*) [7.127]; WTO, *European Union: Countervailing Measures on Certain Polyethylene Terephthalate from Pakistan—Report of the Appellate Body* (16 May 2018) WT/DS486/AB/R (AB, *EU—PET (Pakistan)*) [5.227]–[5.230].

drafting. This chapter will continue this willingness, as it contends that the non-attribution and causal link limbs that are embedded in the provisions should be approached using the same three-step process that will be detailed later, with different permutations to account for their diverse economic rationales. Drawing on the AB's willingness to find interpretive parallels between the provisions, Section 2.7 of this chapter largely considers the non-attribution and causal link requirements of the provisions together. The different economic policies underlying each of the three agreements are nonetheless reflected in the different thresholds that form part of the causation analysis.

It is argued that the heart of the difficulty with the provisions in question is that they are focused on finding causation between factors at the same time as they are focused on excluding causation between factors. It follows from this dual character that any useful causal test must be able to reliably discriminate between those factors that were relevant to bringing about harm to a Member's domestic industry and those factors that were immaterial to producing such injury. The chapter concludes by reflecting upon how such interpretative choices ultimately have policy implications for the WTO's aspirations to maintain a 'level playing field' amongst its Members.[13]

2.2 The Meaning of a 'Genuine and Substantial Relationship of Cause and Effect'

In *US—Wheat Gluten*, the AB said that the causal standard for determining whether imports caused serious injury in the safeguards context was 'a genuine and substantial relationship of cause and effect'.[14] The AB applied the same causal standard in the context of countervailing measures.[15] The AB has not yet had an opportunity to examine the anti-dumping causation standard in detail, but it did criticise a Panel for failing to 'examine whether the [United States International Trade Commission (USITC)] identified and explained the positive evidence establishing a genuine and substantial relationship of cause and effect

[13] Consultative Board to the Director-General Supachai Panitchpakdi by Peter Sutherland, Jagdish Bhagwati, Kwesi Botchwey, Niall FitzGerald, Koichi Hamada, John H Jackson, Celso Lafer and Thierry de Montbrial, *The Future of the WTO: Introducing Institutional Challenges in the New Millennium* (WTO 2004) 15.

[14] WTO, *United States: Definitive Safeguard Measures on Imports of Wheat Gluten from the European Communities—Report of the Appellate Body* (22 December 2000) WT/DS166/AB/R (AB, *US—Wheat Gluten*) [69].

[15] AB, *EU—PET (Pakistan)* (n 12) [5.178].

between imports and threat of injury'.[16] The causal standard of a 'genuine and substantial relationship of cause and effect' has also been applied in the context of serious prejudice under the SCM Agreement.[17]

Having found that the 'genuine and substantial relationship of cause and effect' standard applies to the provisions, it remains to consider: (1) the meaning of this standard; and (2) whether this causal standard has any implications for the determination of the causal link in the application of trade remedies. In examining the meaning of the term, 'genuine and substantial relationship of cause and effect', this article will look at how the term has been interpreted in the serious prejudice jurisprudence, where the AB in *US—Large Civil Aircraft (2nd Complaint)* considered the meaning of the term in some depth. In so doing, it is important to note, as the AB did in *US—Upland Cotton*,[18] that the non-attribution and causal link requirements in the trade remedies context 'apply in different contexts and with different purposes' than the causal link and non-attribution requirements in the serious prejudice context, and '[t]herefore, they must not be automatically transposed'.[19] Nonetheless, the jurisprudence that relates to the serious prejudice context can still be useful in helping to understand the meaning of that causal standard in the context of trade remedies.

In the context of serious prejudice, the AB in *US—Large Civil Aircraft (2nd Complaint)* considered that the term 'genuine and substantial relationship of cause and effect' means that:

> When tasked with determining whether the causal link in question meets the requisite standard of a 'genuine and substantial' causal relationship, a Panel will often be confronted with multiple factors that may have contributed, to varying degrees, to that effect. Indeed, in some circumstances, it may transpire that factors other than the subsidy at issue have caused a particular market effect. Yet the mere presence of other causes that contribute to a particular market effect does not, in itself, preclude the subsidy from being found to be a 'genuine and substantial' cause of that effect. Thus, as part of its assessment of the causal nexus between the subsidy at issue and the effect(s) that it is alleged to have had, a Panel must seek to understand the interactions

[16] WTO, *United States: Investigation of the International Trade Commission in Softwood Lumber from Canada (Recourse to Article 21.5 of the DSU by Canada)—Report of the Appellate Body* (13 April 2006) WT/DS277/AB/RW [132]. To this end, it also cited AB, *US—Wheat Gluten* (n 14) [69].

[17] WTO, *United States: Subsidies on Upland Cotton—Report of the Appellate Body* (3 March 2005) WT/DS267/AB/R (AB, *US—Upland Cotton*) [438] quoting AB, *US—Wheat Gluten* (n 14) [69].

[18] ibid.

[19] ibid.

> between the subsidy at issue and the various other known factors, and make an assessment of their connections to, as well as the relative importance of the subsidy and of the other factors in bringing about, the relevant effects. In order to find that the subsidy is a genuine and substantial cause, a Panel need not determine it to be the *sole* cause of that effect, or even that it is the *only* substantial cause of that effect. A Panel must, however, take care to ensure that it does not attribute the effects of those other known factors to the subsidies at issue, and that the other known factors do not dilute the causal link between those subsidies and the alleged adverse effects such that it is not possible to characterize that link as a genuine and substantial relationship of cause and effect. The subsidy at issue may be found to exhibit the requisite causal link notwithstanding the existence of other causes that contribute to producing the relevant market phenomena if, having given proper consideration to all other relevant contributing factors and their effects, the Panel is satisfied that the contribution of the subsidy has been demonstrated to rise to that of a genuine and substantial cause.[20]

With this survey of the meaning of 'genuine and substantial relationship of cause and effect' in view, it is clear that the causal standard relates to something less than 100 per cent import-induced injury. That is, the causal standard has some tolerance for other known factors. Before seeking to interrogate the nature of the causal standard, it is important first to consider the meaning of 'injury' in the context of trade remedies.

2.3 The Meaning of 'Injury' in the Trade Remedies Context

It has just been seen that the legality of implementing a trade remedy depends on whether a Member can demonstrate that there is a 'genuine and substantial relationship of cause and effect' between imports and injury to an industry. This section is concerned with understanding what is meant by 'injury' in the trade remedies context.

In the safeguards context, 'serious injury' to an industry is defined in the Safeguards Agreement as 'a significant overall impairment in the position of a domestic industry'.[21] Horn and Mavroidis call this 'a mundane, almost tautological definition'.[22] Turning to the antidumping

[20] WTO, *United States: Measures Affecting Trade in Large Civil Aircraft (Second Complaint)—Report of the Appellate Body* (12 March 2012) WT/DS353/AB/R (AB, *US—Large Civil Aircraft (2nd complaint)*) [914] (emphasis original; footnotes omitted).

[21] Safeguards Agreement (n 1) Article 4(1)(a).

[22] Heinrik Horn and Petros C Mavroidis, '*US – Lamb: United States – Safeguard Measures on Imports of Fresh, Chilled or Frozen Lamb Meat from New Zealand and Australia: What Should be Required of a Safeguard Investigation?*' (2003) 2(3) WTR 395, 411.

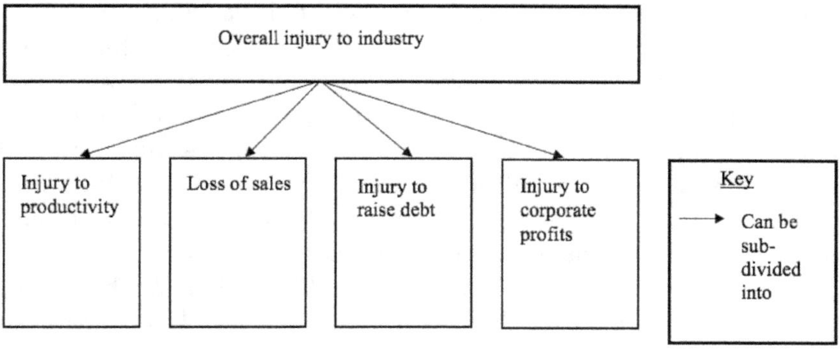

Figure 2.1 Example of how an 'overall' injury to industry might be divided into sub-injuries

context, 'injury' is defined as 'material injury to a domestic industry, threat of material injury to a domestic industry or material retardation of the establishment of such an industry'.[23] The agreement does not define the term 'material'. It does, however, require that a determination of injury be based on positive evidence and involve an objective examination of: (i) the volume of dumped imports and the effect of the dumped imports on prices in the domestic market for like products; and (ii) the consequent impact of the dumped imports on domestic producers of the like product.[24] Finally, in relation to countervailing duties, 'injury' is defined in the SCM Agreement in the same way as 'injury' is defined in the Antidumping Agreement – namely, 'material injury to a domestic industry, threat of material injury to a domestic industry or material retardation of the establishment of such an industry'.[25]

It is worth emphasising that these definitions conceive of 'injury' as a general harm to an industry. This general or 'overall' harm to an industry is manifested in many ways – for example, injury to an industry manifests in an inability to raise debt, an injury to consumer demand, an injury to productivity and so on. This chapter will call these manifestations or indicia of an overall harm 'sub-injuries', as they are smaller, more specific injuries that are a subset of the overall harm to an industry. Sub-injuries are additive, in the sense that they may be aggregated together to total the 'overall' harm. This idea may be seen in Figure 2.1.

[23] Antidumping Agreement (n 2) n 9.
[24] Antidumping Agreement (n 2) Article 3.1.
[25] SCM Agreement (n 3) n 45.

It is conceded that it is somewhat artificial to balkanise the indicia of injury to an industry in the clinical fashion suggested by 'sub-injuries'. That is, in reality there is a significant degree of overlap between sub-injuries. For example, injury to an industry's productivity will obviously impact an industry's cash flow, and this, in turn, will self-evidently affect an industry's ability to raise debt and so forth. Nonetheless, it is suggested that the exercise of sub-dividing the overall injury into smaller sub-injuries is useful for the process of performing the econometric analysis at Step Two of the Tripartite Non-attribution/Causal Link Analysis to be discussed in Section 2.7. To this end, it is suggested that data be collected about the nature of the 'sub-injuries' as they are at a particular moment in time.

The advantage of breaking down the analysis of injury to an industry into 'sub-injuries' – instead of examining the 'overall' injury in one step – is that an analysis that is broken down into its component parts is more likely to be fine-grained in nature, thereby increasing its likelihood of accuracy and robustness. Conversely, analysing the 'overall' injury in one step is likely to be deficient in detail and of questionable accuracy. The notion of injury and 'sub-injuries' will be returned to in Section 2.7. Before this, it remains to consider the factors involved in drawing the causal link between imports and injury.

2.4 The 'Multi-factorial' Approach

The first time that a Panel was required[26] to consider whether a domestic competent authority had satisfactorily demonstrated the causal link between increased imports and 'serious injury or threat thereof' was in *US—Wheat Gluten*,[27] in the context of safeguards. In that case, the *US—Wheat Gluten* Panel held that a WTO Member must 'demonstrate that

[26] Although causation under the Safeguards Agreement (n 1) was first considered in WTO, *Argentina: Safeguard Measures on Imports of Footwear—Report of the Panel* (25 June 1999) WT/DS121/R (Panel, *Argentina—Footwear (EC)*) [8.237]–[8.246], the Panel was not technically required to consider it. As the AB observed, the Panel had found no increased imports and no serious injury or threat thereof, and therefore it was 'surpris[ing]' that the Panel went on to consider causation in that Panel report: WTO, *Argentina: Safeguard Measures on Imports of Footwear—Report of the Appellate Body* (14 December 1999) WT/DS121/AB/R (AB, *Argentina—Footwear (EC)*) [145].

[27] WTO, *United States: Definitive Safeguard Measures on Imports of Wheat Gluten from the European Communities—Report of the Panel* (31 July 2000) WT/DS166/R (Panel, *US—Wheat Gluten*).

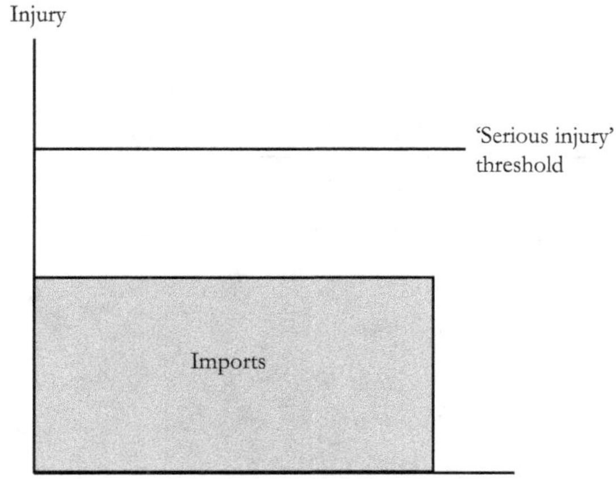

Figure 2.2 Graphic illustration of the 'sufficiency of imports approach'

the increased imports [...] *in and of themselves*, cause *serious injury.*'[28] The *US—Wheat Gluten* Panel then went on to say that this does not mean that other known factors could not exist in a situation of serious injury, but simply that increased imports must be sufficient in and of themselves to reach the threshold of 'serious injury'.[29]

This idea that increased imports would be the sole reason to introduce safeguards will be referred to, throughout this chapter, as the 'sufficiency of imports approach'. To illustrate the 'sufficiency of imports approach', it is helpful to think of the injury threshold as a kind of horizontal line along a y-axis. Depending on the nature of the imports, the imports will either reach this horizontal line or not. This may be seen in Figure 2.2, which demonstrates a situation in which the injury from imports does not reach the level of 'serious injury'. Please note that the notion of 'sub-injuries' has been dispensed with in order to simplify the diagram in Figure 2.2.

The *US—Wheat Gluten* Panel reflects the sufficiency of imports approach. That is, the Panel acknowledges that other known factors may have contributed to the injury in question, but it contends that imports must be sufficient *in and of themselves* to reach the threshold of

[28] ibid [8.138] (emphasis original).
[29] ibid.

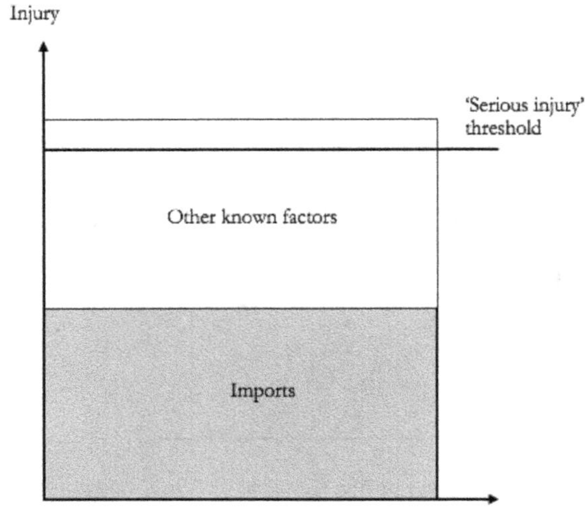

Figure 2.3 Graphic illustration of the 'multi-factorial approach'

'serious injury or threat thereof'. The *US—Lamb* Panel substantially repeated the sufficiency of imports approach in its report.[30]

The AB in *US—Wheat Gluten* disagreed with the sufficiency of imports approach, leading it to overturn both the non-attribution and causal link analyses of the *US—Wheat Gluten* and *US—Lamb* Panel reports. Specifically, the AB in *US—Wheat Gluten* said that 'the language of Article 4.2(b), as a whole, suggests that "the causal link" between increased imports and serious injury may exist, *even though other factors are also contributing "at the same time", to the situation of the domestic industry*'.[31] It is convenient to call this approach by the short-form, 'multi-factorial approach'. An illustration of the multi-factorial approach may be seen graphically in Figure 2.3 (again, the idea of 'sub-injuries' has been dispensed with in order to simplify the diagram).

A comparison of Figures 2.2 and 2.3 confirms that it is easier to reach the 'serious injury' threshold when the multi-factorial approach is used than when the sufficiency of imports approach is used. This is because, under the multi-factorial approach, *both* imports *and* other known factors might be combined together to reach the 'serious injury'

[30] WTO, *United States: Safeguard Measures on Imports of Fresh, Chilled or Frozen Lamb Meat from New Zealand and Australia—Report of the Panel* (21 December 2000) WT/DS177/R; WT/DS178/R (Panel, *US—Lamb*) [7.238].

[31] AB, *US—Wheat Gluten* (n 14) [67] (emphasis original).

threshold. The sufficiency of imports approach, however, would require that the 'serious injury' threshold is reached using imports *alone*. It follows from this that a causal link is more easily made out using the multi-factorial approach. The multi-factorial approach was subsequently upheld in later safeguards jurisprudence.[32]

The applicability of the multi-factorial approach to the antidumping context was confirmed by the Panel in *US—Hot Rolled Steel*[33] and the need to perform a non-attribution analysis in relation to antidumping was also affirmed by the AB in the same case.[34] The multi-factorial approach and non-attribution requirement have been applied in subsequent antidumping jurisprudence.[35] Similarly, the AB confirmed the use of the 'multi-factorial approach'[36] and the non-attribution analysis[37] in the countervailing duties context in *EU—PET (Pakistan)*. Again, subsequent countervailing duties jurisprudence has continued to apply the multi-factorial approach and to perform a non-attribution analysis.[38] In short, the jurisprudence in relation to the use of all three of the trade remedies would seem to require the use of the multi-factorial approach and a non-attribution analysis that separates and distinguishes the causal contributions of imports vis-à-vis other known factors.

The multi-factorial approach and the non-attribution analysis developed in the aforementioned jurisprudence are consistent with the way in which the AB defined the term 'genuine and substantial

[32] See, for example, WTO, *United States: Safeguard Measures on Imports of Fresh, Chilled or Frozen Lamb Meat from New Zealand and Australia—Report of the Appellate Body* (1 May 2001) WT/DS177/AB/R; WT/DS178/AB/R (AB, *US—Lamb*) [170].

[33] WTO, *United States: Antidumping Measures on Certain Hot-Rolled Steel Products from Japan—Report of the Panel* (28 February 2001) WT/DS184/R (Panel, *US—Hot-Rolled Steel*) [7.258]–[7.261].

[34] WTO, *United States: Anti-Dumping Measures on Certain Hot-Rolled Steel Products from Japan—Report of the Appellate Body* (24 July 2001) WT/DS184/AB/R (AB, *US—Hot-Rolled Steel*) [226]–[227].

[35] See, for example, WTO, *European Commission: Antidumping Duties on Malleable Cast Iron Tube or Pipe Fittings from Brazil—Report of the Panel* (7 March 2003) WT/DS219/R (Panel, *EC—Tube or Pipe Fittings*); and WTO, *European Commission: Antidumping Duties on Malleable Cast Iron Tube or Pipe Fittings from Brazil—Report of the Appellate Body* (22 July 2003) WT/DS 219/AB/R (AB, *EC—Tube or Pipe Fittings*).

[36] AB, *EU—PET (Pakistan)* (n 12) [5.175].

[37] ibid [5.171].

[38] See, for example, WTO, *United States: Countervailing Measures on Certain Hot-Rolled Carbon Steel Flat Products from India—Recourse to Article 21.5 of the DSU by India—Report of the Panel* (15 November 2019) WT/DS436/RW (*US—Carbon Steel (India)*); WTO, *United States: Anti-Dumping and Countervailing Duties on Ripe Olives from Spain—Report of the Panel* (19 November 2021) WT/DS577/R (*US—Ripe Olives from Spain*).

relationship of cause and effect' in *US—Large Civil Aircraft (2nd complaint)*. That is, it will be recalled from the passage quoted in Section 2.3 that the AB said in that case that '[t]he subsidy at issue may be found to exhibit the requisite causal link notwithstanding the existence of other causes', but that a Panel must 'ensure that it does not attribute the effects of those other known factors to the subsidies at issue'.[39] Notwithstanding the fact that the *US—Large Civil Aircraft (2nd complaint)* was concerned with subsidies instead of imports, the multi-factorial approach and the non-attribution analysis square precisely with the definition of a 'genuine and substantial relationship of cause and effect'.

The choice of whether to use the sufficiency of imports approach or the multi-factorial approach has profound policy implications. First, a direct consequence of the multi-factorial approach is that, if the injury threshold is easier to reach using the multi-factorial approach, this means, in turn, that trade measures (and their concomitant trade-distortive effects) will be easier to justify than when the sufficiency of imports approach is used. A second consequence of the use of the multi-factorial approach is that domestic competent authorities must find some way of separating and distinguishing the harms caused by increased imports from those caused by other known factors.[40] The purpose of this process is to assist with carrying out the non-attribution analysis – namely, ensuring that harm caused by other known factors is not falsely attributed to the harm produced by imports.[41] It is therefore important to consider the role of the non-attribution analysis in determining a 'genuine and substantial relationship of cause and effect', which is the subject of Section 2.5.

2.5 The Role of the Non-attribution Analysis in the Face of the Multi-factorial Approach

Having seen that the AB has consistently found in favour of the multi-factorial approach, this chapter now turns to consider the apparent

[39] AB, *US—Large Civil Aircraft (2nd complaint)* (n 20) [914] (emphasis original; footnotes omitted).

[40] AB, *US—Wheat Gluten* (n 14) [68]. This process was reaffirmed in AB, *US—Lamb* (n 32) [167]–[168]; WTO, *United States: Definitive Safeguard Measures on Imports of Circular Welded Carbon Quality Line Pipe from Korea—Report of the Appellate Body* (15 February 2002) WT/DS202/AB/R (AB, *US—Line Pipe*) [215].

[41] AB, *US—Wheat Gluten* (n 14) [69]; AB, *US—Lamb* (n 32) [179]–[180].

incompatibility between the multi-factorial approach and a non-attribution analysis. That is, on the one hand, it has just been seen that the multi-factorial approach requires that the causal contribution of imports be *combined* with the causal contribution of other known factors; and, on the other hand, a non-attribution analysis is aimed at *separating* imports from other known factors. A number of scholars have commented on this ostensible contradiction.

Irwin, for example, writing in the safeguards context, has said that '[n]on-attribution requires the authorities to separate and distinguish the sources of injury but otherwise plays no substantive role in the proceedings and cannot affect the end result'.[42] Similarly, Sapir and Trachtman have said that:

> The AB's position on non-attribution in the safeguards setting has always been incoherent: the AB believes that separation is required, but cannot articulate a purpose for separation given that (in its view) there is no need to determine that the increased imports (in that context) are sufficient on their own to cause serious injury.[43]

Also writing in the safeguards context, Sykes has said that '[i]f increased imports need not suffice to cause serious injury [...] but must simply have made some contribution to injury, what is the point of the non-attribution requirement?'[44] Finally, writing in the antidumping context, Mavroidis et al. also contend on what seems to have been the same assumption that:

> While there is an obligation to separate and distinguish the nature and extent of the injury caused by other factors, it appears that the [AB] holds the view that there is no need to somehow quantify and deduct the injury caused by other factors from the injury caused by the dumped imports to determine whether the dumped imports alone were sufficient to cause material injury. What the goal of separating and distinguishing these other factors' effects then is, remains an open question.[45]

Despite this ongoing concern in the literature, it is suggested that a non-attribution analysis is only at odds with the multi-factorial approach if

[42] Douglas A Irwin, 'Causing Problems? The WTO Review of Causation and Injury Attribution in US Section 201 Cases' (2003) 2(3) WTR 297, 309.

[43] Andrew Sapir and Joel P Trachtman, 'Subsidization, Price Suppression, and Expertise: Causation and Precision in Upland Cotton' (2008) 7(1) WTR 183, 199.

[44] Sykes, 'The Causation Requirement' (n 9) 179.

[45] Petros C Mavroidis, Patrick A Messerlin and M Wauters, *The Law and Economics of Contingent Protection in the WTO* (Edward Elgar 2008) 122 (footnotes omitted).

injury to the industry must be caused by 100 per cent imports. One way of resolving this inconsistency is to infer that the threshold of import-induced sub-injury is actually less than 100 per cent. That is, it might be inferred that there is some tolerance for those sub-injuries to industry that were the product of a *combination* of imports and other known factors. Indeed, the idea that a threshold that is lower than 100 per cent import-induced may also be inferred from the AB's insistence on a multi-factorial approach. It is worth repeating that the AB has said that 'the language in the first sentence of Article 4.2(b) does *not* suggest that increased imports be *the sole* cause of the serious injury, or that "*other* factors" causing injury must be excluded from the determination of serious injury'.[46] Moreover, it is worth recalling that the AB in *US—Large Civil Aircraft (2nd complaint)* said that 'a panel need not determine [a subsidy] to be the *sole* cause of that effect, or even that it is the *only* substantial cause of that effect' in order to find a 'genuine and substantial relationship of cause and effect'.[47]

It surely follows from the AB's statements that the test for non-attribution must be something that is less than 100 per cent import-induced, though the AB has not explicitly stated what this threshold is. This tolerance for some level of causal contribution by other known factors reflects a more realistic view of harm to industry. That is, it is unrealistic that harm to industry would purely and solely be caused by imports alone. Instead, it is logical that those sub-injuries inflicted on an industry would be the result of a combination of injurious effects inflicted by both imports and other known factors. Moreover, different factors tend to interact within an economy – for example, a recession may affect consumer demand for a product, which in turn, lessens demand for foreign imports of a product. This interaction within an economy means that the effect of imports and other known factors cannot be separated with the clinical precision that the 'sufficiency of imports' approach would suggest. Accordingly, the multi-factorial approach reflects a far more realistic view of how an economy operates in practice.

Indeed, the idea that injury to an industry need not be 100 per cent caused by imports is also reflected in domestic legislation. Under EU and US law, there is no requirement that imports must be 100 per cent responsible for injury to an industry before safeguards, antidumping

[46] AB, *US—Wheat Gluten* (n 14) [67] (emphasis original).

[47] AB, *US—Large Civil Aircraft (2nd Complaint)* (n 20) [914] (emphasis original; footnotes omitted).

duties and countervailing measures may be legally applied. For example, in the EU safeguards context, Articles 15 and 16 of Regulation 2015/478[48] provide that, in order for the EU to implement safeguard measures, it must be established that the serious injury sustained by Union producers is caused by the increased quantities of imports. Nonetheless, the increased imports do not need to be solely responsible for the injury, in the sense that there is some tolerance for other known factors.[49] In the US safeguards context, section 201 of the *Trade Act of 1974* provides that the injury or threatened injury must be 'serious' and that the increased imports must be a 'substantial cause' of the serious injury or threat thereof. The term 'substantial cause' is defined in subsection 201(4) as 'a cause which is important and not less than any other cause'. To put it another way, in the US safeguards context, there is no requirement that injury to industry be caused by imports alone.

In the EU antidumping context, it is sufficient to make an injury determination when the volume and/or price levels of the dumped imports indicate that dumping is having a material impact on the Union industry, even though there may be other sources of injury to the Union industry than dumping.[50] Similarly, under US domestic law, the phrase 'by reason of' in 19 USC §1674 and §1673d(b)(1) has been interpreted as requiring a causal nexus between dumped imports and injury.[51] The United States Court of Appeals for the Federal Circuit said that, with respect to making a determination in relation to antidumping measures, '[a]s long as its effects are not merely incidental, tangential, or trivial, the foreign product sold at less than fair value meets the causation requirement'.[52]

Finally, in respect of EU countervailing duties, Article 8(5) of Regulation 2016/1037[53] requires a demonstration that the injury is the result of the subsidised imports. Article 8(5) provides that such a

[48] Council Regulation (EC) 2015/478 of the European Parliament and of the Council of 11 March 2015 on common rules for imports (codification) OJ L83/16.

[49] Van Bael & Bellis, *EU Anti-Dumping and Other Trade Defence Instruments* (6th edn, Wolters Kluwer 2019) 677.

[50] Council Regulation (EC) 2016/1036 on protection against dumped imports from countries not members of the European Union [2016] OJ L 176/21 (Regulation 2016/1036 dumped imports) Articles 3(1), 3(6) and 3(7). See also Van Bael & Bellis (n 49) 254.

[51] *Gilford-Hill Cement Co v United States*, 615 F Supp 577, 579 (Ct Int'l Trade 1985); *American Spring Wire Corp v United States*, 590 F Supp 1273, 1276 (Ct Int'l Trade 1984).

[52] *Nippon Steel Corp v Int'l Trade Commission*, 345 F.3d 1379 (Fed Cir 2003).

[53] Council Regulation (EC) 2016/1037 of 30 June 2016 on protection against subsidised imports from countries not members of the European Union [2016] OJ L176/55 (Regulation 2016/1037 subsidised imports).

demonstration of a causal link 'shall entail demonstrating that the volume and/or price levels identified [...] are responsible for an impact on the Union industry [...] and that that impact exists to a degree which enables it to be classified as material'. Likewise, turning to the United States' countervailing measures context, the United States' countervailing duty legislation provides that countervailing duties may be imposed where an industry is materially injured 'by reason of imports'.[54] The USITC does not need to determine whether subsidised imports are the principal cause of material injury – rather, only that the subsidised imports contributed to the injury.[55]

In sum, in the context of the EU and the United States, the causal standard in respect of each of the trade remedies demonstrates a degree of tolerance for the input of other known factors to bringing about injury. That is, there is no requirement that, in order for trade remedies to be implemented, the injury sustained to the industry must be 100 per cent the product of imports. This chapter now turns further to consider the dominant approach used by domestic competent authorities (including the EU and the United States) in order to draw the causal link between imports and injury in the face of other known factors – namely, an approach known as 'breaking the causal link'.

2.6 Breaking the Causal Link

2.6.1 Popularity of the 'Breaking the Causal Link' Approach with Domestic Competent Authorities

The 'breaking the causal link' approach,[56] commonly used by domestic competent authorities, essentially relies on three steps when drawing a causal link between imports and domestic injury. The first step involves a domestic competent authority making a provisional assessment as to whether there is a causal link between imports and the domestic injury based on examining correlations between movements in imports and

54 *United States Code, 2006 Edition, Supplement 5, Title 19* (3 January 2012) 125 Stat 456, 491, 527, 451, 466, 50 (19 US Code) s1671(a)(2)).

55 ER Easton and WE Perry, 'Countervailing Duty Investigations' in CR Johnston Jr (ed and comp), *Law and Practice of United States Regulation of International Trade* (Oceana Publications 1989) 44.

56 The term 'breaking the causal link' is used to describe this approach throughout the Panel and AB decisions in *European Union: Countervailing Duties on Certain Polyethylene Terephthalate from Pakistan*. See generally, Panel, *EU—PET* (n 12) and AB, *EU—PET* (n 12).

injury factors.[57] The second step then involves the domestic competent authority turning to consider whether any other known factors could have broken this causal link. In light of its consideration of the impact of other known factors, the fact-finder determines, as a final step, whether the causal link between imports and injury is still in place, or whether it has, in fact, been 'broken' by the impact of other known factors. Implicit in the 'breaking the causal link' approach is that the point at which the causal link is 'broken' is the point at which the percentage of other known factors exceeds its permitted ceiling, and, concomitantly, that imports fall short of reaching their injury threshold. In other words, the 'breaking the causal link' approach also relies on a multi-factorial approach.

In many ways, the 'breaking the causal link' approach has similarities with the three-step approach to establishing a causal link that was described by the Panel in *Argentina—Footwear (EC)*,[58] a case that was published about eighteen months prior to the Appellate Body decision in *US—Wheat Gluten*. That is, the Panel in *Argentina—Footwear (EC)* set out three steps to assessing causation in the context of safeguards as follows:

> Applying our standard of review, we will consider whether Argentina's causation analysis meets these requirements on the basis of (i) whether an upward trend in imports coincides with downward trends in the injury factors, and if not, whether a reasoned explanation is provided as to why nevertheless the data show causation; (ii) whether the conditions of competition in the Argentine footwear market between imported and domestic footwear as analysed demonstrate, on the basis of objective evidence, a causal link of the imports to any injury; and (iii) whether other relevant factors have been analysed and whether it is established that injury caused by factors other than imports has not been attributed to imports.[59]

The first two steps outlined by the Panel in *Argentina—Footwear (EC)* dovetail with the first step of the 'breaking the causal link' approach,

[57] The AB in *Argentina—Footwear (EC)* said that an analysis of correlations involves focusing on 'the *relationship* between *movements* in imports (volume and market share) and the *movements* in injury factors' (emphasis original): AB, *Argentina—Footwear (EC)* (n 26) [144]. The AB also said that correlation 'cannot by itself prove causation', and that, in the absence of such correlation, an affirmative causation finding might still be made, provided that a 'compelling analysis is present': AB, *Argentina—Footwear (EC)* (n 26) [144].

[58] Panel, *Argentina—Footwear (EC)* (n 26).

[59] ibid [8.229]. The AB in *Argentina—Footwear (EC)* (n 26) said that they saw 'no error in its interpretation of the causation requirements': [145].

whilst the third step, concerned with non-attribution, set out by the Panel in *Argentina—Footwear (EC)* overlaps with the second non-attribution step of the 'breaking the causal link' approach. The final step of the 'breaking the causal link' approach essentially involves an assessment of whether the provisional causal link is still in place once the non-attribution analysis is performed. In sum, whilst it has not been explicitly recognised, the 'breaking the causal link' has some jurisprudential basis to it from the *Argentina—Footwear (EC)* Panel case.

The EU has relied extensively on the 'breaking the causal link' approach in its trade remedies investigations. For example, in Commission Implementing Regulation (EU) 2018/1013 of 17 July 2018,[60] the Commission made a preliminary determination that there was a causal link between the increase of steel imports and a threat of serious injury to the EU.[61] It then went on to examine other known factors that might have broken the causal link – including global overcapacity[62] and imports from the European Economic Area.[63] The Commission determined that these other known factors were insufficient to have broken the causal link between steel imports and injury to the EU, and accordingly, provisional safeguard measures were implemented.[64]

In contrast, in Council Implementing Regulation (EU) No 1194/2013 of 19 November 2013, the Commission made a preliminary determination that there was a causal link between the dumped imports of biodiesel from Argentina and the injury suffered by the Union industry.[65] This conclusion, however, was revisited by the Commission in Commission Implementing Regulation (EU) 2018/1570 of 18 October 2018.[66] In the latter case, the Commission found that during the

[60] Commission Implementing Regulation (EU) 2018/1013 of 17 July 2018, imposing provisional safeguard measures with regard to imports of certain steel products [2018] OJ 2018 L 181/39 (70)–(81).

[61] ibid (70)–(77).

[62] ibid (79).

[63] ibid (80).

[64] ibid (96).

[65] Council Implementing Regulation (EU) No 1194/2013 of 19 November 2013, imposing a definitive anti-dumping duty and collecting definitively the provisional duty imposed on imports of biodiesel originating in Argentina and Indonesia, OJ 2013 L 315/2, Recital 189 [no longer in force].

[66] Commission Implementing Regulation (EU) 2018/1570 of 18 October 2018 terminating the proceedings concerning imports of biodiesel originating in Argentina and Indonesia and repealing Implementing Regulation (EU) No 1194/2013, OJ 2018 L 262/40 (82)–(95).

investigation period, almost half of all imports into the Union came from Indonesia at a price lower than either Union or Argentinian prices.[67] Moreover, the exponential increase of import volumes from Indonesia as well as their market share significantly contributed to the material injury to the Union industry.[68] Finally, the Commission found that the Union industry was at overcapacity and that the Union had inflicted some injuries on itself.[69] Accordingly, the Commission concluded that it could not establish that there was 'a genuine and substantial causal relationship between the dumped imports from Argentina and the material injury suffered by the Union industry'.[70] It is implicit in the reasoning of *Commission Implementing Regulation (EU) 2018/1570 of 18 October 2018*[71] that the point at which the causal link between the dumping of Argentinian biodiesel and the injury to the Union industry occurred was the point at which the other known factors exceeded the maximum threshold (and, by implication, that the dumping of Argentinian biodiesel fell short of the threshold).

Turning now to the US context, the 'breaking the causal link' approach can be seen in the USITC case, *Forged Steel Fittings from Taiwan*.[72] In that case, the Commission examined whether the US industry was materially injured by dumped imports of forged steel fittings from Taiwan. The Commission examined the volume and market share data available and concluded that '[t]he relatively smaller nonsubject import volume and market share was not likely to apply the substantial pressure on the domestic prices that the larger volume of subject imports exerted'.[73] The Commission also looked at other economic factors,[74] but ultimately concluded that 'there was significant underselling of the domestic like product by cumulated subject imports and that

[67] ibid (83).
[68] ibid (83).
[69] ibid (84).
[70] ibid (85).
[71] ibid (82)–(95).
[72] Investigation Nos 731-TA-1396 (September 2018) Publication 4823.
[73] *Forged Steel Fittings from Taiwan* (731-TA-1396) September 2018, 31.
[74] ibid 17.

low-priced cumulated subject imports suppressed prices of the domestic like product to a significant degree'.[75] In sum, the Commission found that there was a causal link between the subject imports and the injury to domestic industry and that this causal link was not broken by the other known factors.

The *Forged Steel Fittings from Taiwan* case may be contrasted with the *100- to 150-Seat Large Civil Aircraft from Canada*.[76] In that case, the USITC examined volume and market share data that led it to conclude that a provisional causal link between imports and domestic injury could not be made out. Specifically, the Commission found that the subject import prices were 'not likely to have a significant depressing or suppressing effect on domestic prices or to increase demand for further imports'.[77] Whilst the Commission went on to consider other economic factors that were relevant to the industry,[78] given that there was no provisional finding of a causal link, these economic factors did not affect or 'break' the ultimate conclusion that the industry was 'not threatened with material injury by reason of imports of 100- to 150-seat LCA from Canada . . .'.[79] In other words, the injury caused by imports failed to reach the prescribed threshold.

The 'breaking the causal link' approach is also widely used by other domestic competent authorities, including Australia, Canada, India, New Zealand and the United Kingdom.[80] That is, each of these domestic competent authorities is required by domestic legislation to determine whether there is a causal link between imports and domestic injury based on examining correlations between movements in imports and injury

[75] ibid 26.
[76] USITC, *100- to 150-Seat Large Civil Aircraft from Canada* (701-TA-578 and 731-1368) February 2018.
[77] ibid 47.
[78] ibid 19–22.
[79] ibid 48.
[80] This selection of domestic competent authorities was largely the product of the fact that they provide public access to the relevant laws and decisions in English. It is regrettable that more domestic competent authorities were unable to be included, due to limitations in public access to documents in English.

factors.[81] Each of these Members also has domestic legislation that directs them to perform a non-attribution analysis before making a conclusion as to the legality of the implementation of the trade

[81] *Australia: Customs Act 1901*, sub-s 269TAE(1): in determining whether there has been material injury to industry, the Minister may have regard to: (a) the quantity of goods of that kind that, during a particular period, have been or are likely to be exported to Australia from the country of export; and (b) any increase or likely increase, during a particular period, in the quantity of goods of that kind exported to Australia from the country of export; and (c) any change or likely change, during a particular period, in the proportion that: (i) the quantity of goods of that kind exported to Australia from the country of export and sold or consumed in Australia; or (ii) the quantity of goods of that kind, or like goods, produced or manufactured in the Australian industry and sold or consumed in Australia; bears to the quantity of goods of that kind, or like goods, sold or consumed in Australia; and (d) the export price that has been or is likely to be paid by importers for goods of that kind exported to Australia from the country of export; and (e) the difference between: (i) the price that has been or is likely to be paid for goods of that kind, or like goods, produced or manufactured in the Australian industry and sold in Australia; and (ii) the price that has been or is likely to be paid for goods of that kind exported to Australia from the country of export and sold in Australia; and (f) the effect that the exportation of goods of that kind to Australia from the country of export in those circumstances has had or is likely to have on the price paid for goods of that kind, or like goods, produced or manufactured in the Australian industry and sold in Australia; and (g) any effect that the exportation of goods of that kind to Australia from the country of export in those circumstances has had or is likely to have on the relevant economic factors in relation to the Australian industry.

Canada: Special Import Measures Regulations 1984, para 37.1(1) and (2) set out indicia of a dumping or subsidies that have caused injury or are threatening to cause injury. Specifically, para 37.1(1) provides that the following factors may be considered in determining whether the dumping or subsidising of goods has caused injury or retardation: (a) the volume of the dumped or subsidised goods and, in particular, whether there has been a significant increase in the volume of imports of the dumped or subsidised goods, either in absolute terms or relative to the production or consumption of like goods; (b) the effect of the dumped or subsidised goods on the price of like goods and, in particular, whether the dumped or subsidised goods have significantly (i) undercut the price of like goods, (ii) depressed the price of like goods, or (iii) suppressed the price of like goods by preventing the price increases for those like goods that would otherwise likely have occurred; (c) the resulting impact of the dumped or subsidised goods on the state of the domestic industry and, in particular, all relevant economic factors and indices that have a bearing on the state of the domestic industry, including (i) any actual or potential decline in output, sales, market share, profits, productivity, return on investments or the utilisation of industrial capacity, (ii) any actual or potential negative effects on cash flow, inventories, employment, wages, growth or the ability to raise capital, (ii.1) the magnitude of the margin of dumping or amount of subsidy in respect of the dumped or subsidised goods, and (iii) in the case of agricultural goods, including any goods that are agricultural goods or commodities by virtue of an Act of Parliament or of the legislature of a province, that are subsidised, any increased burden on a government support programme; and (d) any other factor that is relevant in the circumstances. Para 37.2 sets out factors to consider in determining whether the dumping or subsidising of goods is threatening to cause injury: (a) the nature of the subsidy in question and the effects it is likely to have on trade; (b) whether there has been a significant rate of increase of dumped or subsidised goods imported into Canada, which rate of increase indicates a likelihood of substantially increased imports into Canada of the dumped or

remedies.[82] As a result, these domestic competent authorities consider a series of other known factors before concluding whether the other known factors affect the causal link finding. Their conclusions are based on the

subsidised goods; (c) whether there is sufficient freely disposable capacity, or an imminent, substantial increase in the capacity of an exporter, that indicates a likelihood of a substantial increase of dumped or subsidised goods, taking into account the availability of other export markets to absorb any increase; (d) the potential for product shifting where production facilities that can be used to produce the goods are currently being used to produce other goods; (e) whether the goods are entering the domestic market at prices that are likely to have a significant depressing or suppressing effect on the price of like goods and are likely to increase demand for further imports of the goods; (f) inventories of the goods; (g) the actual and potential negative effects on existing development and production efforts, including efforts to produce a derivative or more advanced version of like goods; (g.1) the magnitude of the margin of dumping or amount of subsidy in respect of the dumped or subsidised goods; (g.2) evidence of the imposition of anti-dumping or countervailing measures by the authorities of a country other than Canada in respect of goods of the same description or in respect of similar goods; and (h) any other factor that is relevant in the circumstances.

India: Customs Tariff (Identification, Assessment and Collection of Anti-Dumping Duty on Dumped Articles and for Determination of Injury) Rules, 1995, Annexure II and Rule 11 (2): The designated authority shall determine the injury to domestic industry, threat of injury to domestic industry, material retardation to establishment of domestic industry and a causal link between dumped imports and injury, taking into account all relevant facts, including the volume of dumped imports, their effect on price in the domestic market for like articles and the consequent effect of such imports on domestic producers of such articles and in accordance with the principles set out in Annexure II to these rules. (3) The designated authority may, in exceptional cases, give a finding as to the existence of injury even where a substantial portion of the domestic industry is not injured, if – (i) there is a concentration of dumped imports into an isolated market, and (ii) the dumped articles are causing injury to the producers of all or almost all of the production within such market.

New Zealand: Trade (Anti-dumping and Countervailing Duties) Act 1988, sub-s 8(1) provides that, when determining injury to industry, the chief executive shall have regard to: (a) the volume of imports of the dumped or subsidised goods; (b) the effect of the dumped or subsidised goods on prices in New Zealand for like goods; and (c) the consequent impact of the dumped or subsidised goods on the relevant New Zealand industry.

UK: The Trade Remedies (Dumping and Subsidisation) (EU Exit) Regulations 2019, sub-s 30(2) provides that, in order to determine whether a UK industry is suffering or has suffered injury, the Trade Regulatory Authority must consider: (a) the volume of the dumped goods or subsidised imports during the injury period; (b) the effect of the dumped goods or subsidised imports on prices of the like goods in the United Kingdom during the injury period; (c) the consequent impact of the dumped goods or subsidised imports on a UK industry during the injury period; and (d) any other factors it considers relevant.

82 *Australia: The Customs Act 1901*, sub-s 269TAE(2A) provides that, for the purposes of a non-attribution analysis, the Minister must consider whether any injury to an industry is being caused or threatened by a factor other than the exportation of those goods.

Canada: Special Import Measures Regulations 1984, para 37.1(3)(b) provides that the Tribunal must consider 'whether any factors other than dumping or subsidizing of the subject goods are threatening to cause injury'.

India: The Customs Tariff (Identification, Assessment and Collection of Anti-Dumping Duty on Dumped Articles and for Determination of Injury) Rules, 1995, Annexure II (v).

use of non-quantitative criteria alone – that is, none of them uses empirical data to determine the impact of the other known factors on the industry or the interaction between the other known factors and injury factors. Moreover, none of the domestic competent authorities have indicated whether there is any quantitative threshold at which the provisional causal link between dumping or subsidies and injury to industry is 'broken'. Instead, once again, whether the causal link is broken is based on non-transparent and non-quantitative criteria.

2.6.2 *The Appellate Body's Assessment of the 'Breaking the Causal Link' Approach*

The validity of the 'breaking the causal link' approach as a means of determining a causal link between imports and injury came before the WTO in the *EU—PET (Pakistan)* case. In that case, Pakistan challenged the EU Commission's use of the 'breaking the causal link' approach as a means of satisfying the requirements of Article 15.5 of the SCM Agreement. It is not necessary to canvass the specific arguments of Pakistan and the EU in that case here. It is sufficient to note that both the Panel and the AB found that the EU's use of the 'breaking the causal link' methodology was not inconsistent with the causal link and non-attribution requirements of Article 15.5 of the SCM Agreement.[83]

Specifically, the AB agreed with the Panel that a domestic competent authority is permitted to make an initial determination of a causal link prior to performing a non-attribution analysis and then, as a final step, reach a conclusion about the nature of the causal relationship between imports and injury.[84] Moreover, the AB reiterated that Article 15.5 SCM Agreement does not lay down a particular methodology, and therefore a

New Zealand: Trade (Anti-dumping and Countervailing Duties) Act 1988, sub-s 8(2)(e) provides that the chief executive shall have regard to factors other than the dumped or subsidised goods that have injured, or are injuring, the industry.

UK: The Trade Remedies (Dumping and Subsidisation) (EU Exit) Regulations 2019, s 35 provides that, for the purposes of making a determination about the injurious effects of dumped goods or subsidised imports, the UKTRA must ensure that no other known factors 'have caused or are causing injury to a UK industry'.

[83] Panel, *EU—PET (Pakistan)* (n 12) [7.127]; AB, *EU—PET (Pakistan)* (n 12) [5.227]–[5.230].

[84] AB, *EU—PET (Pakistan)* (n 12) [5.180].

domestic competent authority was free to choose its own.[85] The 'core question' for the AB in conducting its review was simply whether the domestic competent authority objectively determined that the imports were a 'genuine and substantial' cause of the domestic injury, having taken into account the injurious effects of other known factors.[86]

Despite the Panel and AB's endorsement of the 'breaking the causal link' approach, it is suggested that the approach has a number of problems with it. Specifically, economic theory posits that injury to an industry is a function of multiple economic factors that interact and simultaneously affect each other.[87] In particular, imports are themselves endogenous to other known factors;[88] and therefore, the EU Commission's conception of imports and other known factors as entirely separate from each other results in an inaccurate economic model. Indeed, the idea that the level of harm to an industry is affected by the interaction between imports and other known factors is likely to be the raison d'être for the AB's preference for the 'multi-factorial approach' over the 'sufficiency of imports' approach. That is, the 'multi-factorial approach' reflects a more realistic model of how an economy truly operates.

The failure to take account of the way in which multiple factors interact with each other within an economy manifests in the flawed way in which the Commission identified the impact of other known factors. That is, Pakistan argued that when the Commission assessed whether other known factors broke the provisional link, it examined the effect of each other known factor individually. In doing so, Pakistan argued that the Commission was essentially examining the effect of one other known factor vis-à-vis the combination of the provisional causal link together with the remaining other known factors.[89] To put Pakistan's argument another way, by 'assessing separately the effect of each [other known] factor on a variable that is a function of a number of factors might result in a bias known as "omitted variable bias" and might preclude identifying the true impact of either of the [other known] factors'.[90]

85 ibid [5.172].

86 ibid [5.178].

87 Horn and Mavroidis (n 22) 416.

88 Gene Grossman, 'Imports as a Cause of Injury: The Case of the US Steel Industry' (1986) 20 J Int Econ 201, 207.

89 AB, *EU—PET (Pakistan)* (n 12) [5.200].

90 Arevik Gnutzmann-Mkrtchyan and Isabelle Van Damme, 'Expired Measures, Excess Duty Drawbacks and Causation: The Appellate Body Report in *EU-PET (Pakistan)*' (2020) 19 WTR 232, 247.

The AB rejected Pakistan's argument, seemingly without fully understanding it. That is, the AB said that 'the Commission took into account all the injurious effects of the other [known] factors compared to the strength of the initial "causal link" between the subsidized imports and the injury when it reached its final conclusion that the subsidized imports had "caused" material injury to the EU industry'.[91] Pakistan's argument, however, was not that the Commission did not consider the impact of the other known factors. Instead, Pakistan's argument was that, by only examining the *individual* impact of each other known factor, the Commission may not have correctly identified the full impact of each other known factor and its ability to *interact* with the broader economy. Indeed, the AB's misunderstanding of Pakistan's argument is somewhat curious here, since it has acknowledged the point in the context of causation in serious prejudice. That is, in *US—Large Civil Aircraft (2nd complaint)*, the AB said that when multiple factors have contributed to an adverse effect, 'a panel must seek to understand the interactions' between the subsidies at issue and the other known factors.[92] It is suggested that understanding the interaction between multiple factors in the trade remedies context is just as important as in the context of serious prejudice.

A second and related objection that Pakistan raised about the 'breaking the causal link' approach is that the methodology 'precluded the Commission from properly separating and distinguishing the effects of those factors', as is required when performing a non-attribution analysis.[93] That is, because economic factors simultaneously interact with each other, it is impossible to distinguish the effects of these factors when assessed individually. For example, the Commission found that, although the economic downturn contributed to the domestic industry's injury, subsidised imports worsened the impact of the economic downturn.[94] As Gnutzmann-Mkrtchyan and Van Damme observe, however, the Commission's approach 'did not consider the possibility of reverse causality, namely that the economic downturn affected the competitiveness of the domestic industry, pushing domestic prices up and creating endogenous demand for lower-priced imports'.[95] To put this another way,

[91] AB, *EU—PET (Pakistan)* (n 12) [5.208].
[92] AB, *US—Large Civil Aircraft (2nd complaint)* (n 20) [914] and [1206].
[93] AB, *EU—PET (Pakistan)* (n 12) [5.186].
[94] Provisional Determination (Panel Exhibit PAK-1), recital 254 quoted in AB, *EU—PET (Pakistan)* (n 12) [5.194].
[95] Gnutzmann-Mkrtchyan and Van Damme (n 90) 232–48.

assessing the effect of one other known factor individually in the manner described above means that a fact-finder cannot fully separate and distinguish the effect of one other known factor vis-à-vis another. This critique of domestic competent authorities and their failure to conduct a simultaneous causal analysis has also been made by Horn and Mavroidis in relation to the USITC's analysis in *US—Lamb*[96] and Mitchell and Prusa in relation to the analysis of the Ministry of Commerce of the People's Republic of China in *China—Autos*.[97] Nonetheless, the AB found that Pakistan's argument on this point was 'not clear';[98] and it addressed Pakistan's argument as if it pertained to the use of the term 'break', and therefore rejected the claim on the same grounds as Pakistan's first argument.[99] In sum, by failing to appreciate the *interaction* between causal factors in an economy and their potential for reverse causality, the 'breaking the causal link' approach leads to a non-attribution analysis of dubious reliability.

A third difficulty with the 'breaking the causal link' approach is that the point at which the provisional causal link between imports and injury is 'broken' appears to be somewhat arbitrary. That is, without the use of a nominated quantitative threshold to determine the point at which other known factors have exceeded their permitted ceiling, domestic competent authorities use a non-quantitative approach. Whilst it may be that keeping the prescribed threshold somewhat vague in this manner gives domestic competent authorities a degree of flexibility in their adjudications, such flexibility comes at the cost of legal certainty for Members. That is, in the absence of any quantitative threshold, it is very difficult for a Member to know what degree of tolerance will be given to other known factors.

It is suggested that the non-attribution and causal link analysis proposed by the AB in *US—Wheat Gluten* (albeit in the safeguards context) sets out a possible alternative approach that can achieve a more reliable non-attribution analysis. Pakistan raised the *US—Wheat Gluten* three-step approach before the Panel in *EU—PET (Pakistan)*, noting that it was at odds with the 'breaking the causal link' approach.[100] The Panel in

[96] Horn and Mavroidis (n 22) 303–25.

[97] Andrew D. Mitchell and Thomas J. Prusa, 'China – Autos: Haven't We Danced This Dance Before?' (2016) 15:2 WTR 303–25.

[98] AB, *EU—PET (Pakistan)* (n 12) [5.221].

[99] ibid.

[100] Panel, *EU—PET (Pakistan)* (n 12) [7.108].

EU—PET (Pakistan) rejected the idea that the AB's report in *US—Wheat Gluten* prescribes a specific methodology to which Members must adhere.[101] To this end, it quoted the AB in *US—Lamb*, who said that the 'three steps' identified in *US—Wheat Gluten* 'simply describe *a* logical process for complying with the obligations relating to causation', and 'are not legal "tests" mandated by the text of the Agreement on Safeguards'.[102] Nonetheless, whilst not mandatory, the three-step process set out in *US—Wheat Gluten* arguably provides a potential solution to the problems identified in the 'breaking the causal link' approach discussed earlier.

The AB in *US—Wheat Gluten* said that the non-attribution and causal link analysis should involve: (1) distinguishing the injurious effects of imports from the injurious effects caused by other known factors; (2) attributing the level of injury caused by imports on the one hand vis-à-vis other known factors; and (3) as a final step, determining whether a causal link exists between imports and injury to industry, 'and whether this causal link involves a genuine and substantial relationship of cause and effect between those two elements'.[103] Although the *US—Wheat Gluten* case was concerned with safeguards, it is suggested that the conceptual basis underlying the causal link and non-attribution analysis is the same for antidumping and countervailing measures.

Indeed, in *US—Hot-Rolled Steel*, the AB developed a five-step methodology for establishing a causal link for the purposes of implementing antidumping duties. Specifically, it said in relation to Article 3.5 of the *Antidumping Agreement* that:

> This provision requires investigating authorities, as part of their causation analysis, first, to examine all 'known factors', 'other than dumped imports', which are causing injury to the domestic industry 'at the same time' as dumped imports. Second, investigating authorities must ensure that injuries which are caused to the domestic industry by known factors, other than dumped imports, are not 'attributed to the dumped imports.' (emphasis added)[104]

In sum, this methodology for determining a causal link in relation to antidumping duties may be summarised as follows: (1) identify the factors that potentially cause injury to the industry; (2) verify whether

[101] ibid [7.116].
[102] ibid [7.115].
[103] ibid.
[104] AB, *US—Hot-Rolled Steel* (n 34) [222].

these factors operate simultaneously; (3) examine these factors to determine if they have an injurious effect; (4) distinguish between the effects of imports vis-à-vis other known factors; and (5) ensure that the effects of other known factors are not attributed to the effect of imports.

Prima facie, these five steps might seem different to the Tripartite Non-attribution/Causal Link Analysis. Upon closer inspection, however, it is clear that these five steps are just a more expansive version of the first two steps of the Tripartite Non-attribution/Causal Link Analysis. To put it another way, the first step of the Tripartite Non-attribution/Causal Link Analysis implies the first four steps set out by the AB in *US—Hot-Rolled Steel*, whilst the second step of the Tripartite Non-attribution/ Causal Link Analysis and the fifth step of the *US—Hot-Rolled Steel* case are essentially the same. The only real difference is that the third step of the Tripartite Non-attribution/Causal Link Analysis provides for a causal standard that must be reached, whilst the AB in *US—Hot-Rolled Steel* prescribes no such standard in relation to antidumping duties.

In sum, the AB's methodology in *US—Hot-Rolled Steel* demonstrates that the conceptual basis behind determining a causal link between imports and injury is essentially the same in relation to safeguards and antidumping duties. Moreover, given the similarity between the treatment of antidumping duties and countervailing measures, it is highly likely that the methodology in *US—Hot-Rolled Steel* would also be applied with respect to countervailing measures.[105] As such, this chapter will continue to put forward the Tripartite Non-attribution/Causal Link Analysis as the methodology that captures the essential requirements for making out a causal link for the purposes of all three types of trade remedies. It is therefore to a closer examination of the Tripartite Non-attribution/Causal Link Analysis that this chapter now turns.

[105] *Ministerial Declaration on Dispute Settlement Pursuant to the Agreement on Implementation of Article VI of the General Agreement on Tariffs and Trade 1994 or Part V of the Agreement on Subsidies and Countervailing Measures* recognises 'the need for the consistent resolution of disputes arising from antidumping and countervailing duty measures': *The Declaration on Dispute Settlement Pursuant to the Agreement on Implementation of Article VI of the General Agreement on Tariffs and Trade 1994 or Part V of the Agreement on Subsidies and Countervailing Measures*, <www.wto.org/english/docs_e/legal_e/41-dadp3_e.htm> accessed 23 October 2017 (*Declaration on Art VI of the GATT 1994 or Pt V of the SCM*). This need for consistency in interpretation between the two agreements was also recognised by the Panel in WTO, *United States: Countervailing Duty Investigation on Dynamic Random Access Memory Semiconductors (DRAMS) from Korea—Report of the Panel* (21 February 2005) WT/DS296 (Panel, *US—Countervailing Duty Investigation on DRAMs*) [7.351].

2.7 The Tripartite Non-attribution/Causal Link Analysis

2.7.1 The First Step of the Tripartite Non-attribution/Causal Link Analysis

A domestic competent authority must begin the Tripartite Non-attribution/Causal Link Analysis by separating the sub-injuries to the Member's domestic industry, as per the AB's guidance in *US—Wheat Gluten*. This step is necessary regardless of whether a domestic competent authority is investigating safeguards, antidumping measures or countervailing duties. It is helpful to illustrate how a Member might go about separating sub-injuries by setting out a concrete example. Imagine that one Member (Ruritania) claimed that its cotton industry had been injured as a result of another Member's (Laurania) dumped goods. Using the Tripartite Non-attribution/Causal Link Analysis, a domestic competent authority would begin by identifying and separating out the sub-injuries inflicted on Ruritania's cotton industry. For instance the sub-injuries might include injury to Ruritania's: (1) ability to raise debt; (2) consumer demand; (3) productivity; and (4) cash flow and so on.[106] These sub-injuries are examples only – there will be different sub-injuries in each case; and there may well also be more or less than four in number.

This separation of sub-injuries may be seen diagrammatically in Step One of Figure 2.4. It is important to clarify that whilst this diagram depicts each of these sub-injuries to be of equal size spatially, in reality, each sub-injury might well be of greater or lesser significance to the ultimate finding of 'serious injury or threat thereof'. To this end, a panel or the AB may well decide to accord more weight to one sub-injury vis-à-vis another.

2.7.2 The Second Step of the Tripartite Non-attribution/Causal Link Analysis

Introduction

The second step of the Tripartite Non-attribution/Causal Link Analysis is by far the most difficult of the three steps for three reasons: (1) it involves three causal link analyses; (2) it requires the respective percentage

[106] Further examples of sub-injuries in the safeguards context may be seen, for example, in: 19 US Code (n 54) s 2252(c)(1) and Regulation 2015/478 imports (n 48) Article 9(1)(c). In the antidumping context, see Regulation 2016/1036 dumped imports (n 50) Article 3 (5). In the context of countervailing measures, see the SCM Agreement (n 3) Article 15.4 and Regulation 2016/1037 subsidised imports (n 53) Article 8(4).

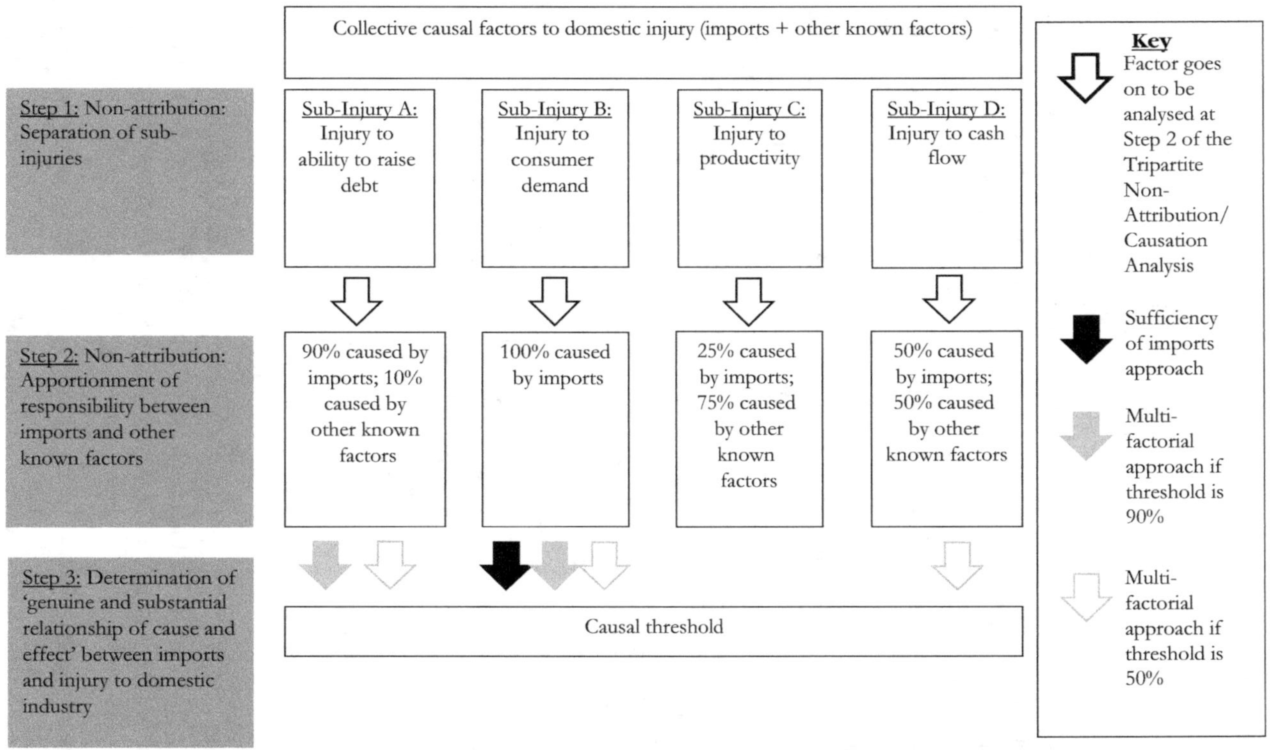

Figure 2.4 Overview of Steps One, Two and Three of the Tripartite Non-attribution/Causation Analysis: Non-attribution and causation analysis under Articles 4.2 of the Safeguards Agreement, 3.5 of the Antidumping Agreement and 15.5 of the SCM Agreement

contributions to a sub-injury to be apportioned between imports on the one hand and other known factors on the other; and (3) it is argued that a threshold for satisfying causation under the second causal link test is required, but the level of this threshold is as yet unknown.

The second step in the Tripartite Non-attribution/Causal Link Analysis involves analysing whether a sub-injury that is necessary to the ultimate finding of injury was caused by imports and/or other known factors, or some combination thereof. This will be called the 'Apportionment Analysis'. The Apportionment Analysis has two parts to it. The first part involves identifying the other known factors that may have contributed to the injury using a causation analysis. This will be called the 'Identification of other known factors stage'. The second involves disentangling the injury caused by imports from the injury caused by other known factors. This is the second causation analysis and will be called the 'Disentanglement stage'. Once the Apportionment Analysis is complete, the next question is whether a specific sub-injury is sufficiently attributable to imports alone that it can pass the non-attribution limb and qualify for the final causation analysis. This third causation test will be called the 'Qualification Analysis'. Each of these three causation analyses will now be examined in turn.

A diagrammatic overview of the Tripartite Non-attribution/Causal Link Analysis as it is applied to safeguards, antidumping measures and countervailing duties is set out at Figure 2.4. It is contended that the methods proposed in the Tripartite Non-attribution/Causal Link Analysis are identical for safeguards, antidumping measures and countervailing duties. The only difference between each of the measures is the causation threshold applied at the stage of the Qualification Analysis at Step Two, to be discussed later.

Apportionment Analysis As Step Two in Figure 2.4 illustrates, it is theoretically possible that sub-injuries will fall into three categories of causal responsibility: (1) some sub-injuries may have been caused exclusively by imports; (2) yet others, exclusively by other known factors; and (3) finally, by some kind of combination of imports and other known factors. It is contended that a sub-injury cannot be over-determined[107] by imports on the one hand and other known factors on the other hand.[108]

[107] See Chapter 1 for a description of over-determination.

[108] Compare James J Nedumpara, 'Causation in Trade Remedy Actions: Problems with the "But For" Test' (2015) 10(11) GTCJ 402, 405.

This is because a sub-injury is not an all-or-nothing phenomenon, such as a fire that does or does not get ignited, as in the example given in Chapter 1 of this book. Instead, a sub-injury is a *continuous* phenomenon, which would only be *intensified* where both imports and other known factors were each sufficient to cause harm. For example, if it were found that imports were 50 per cent causally responsible for a sub-injury and other known factors were also 50 per cent causally responsible, it does not make sense to say that the sub-injury was over-determined. Instead, the sub-injury has simply received inputs from both sources.

Identification of Other Known Factors Stage Most of the scholarly literature on the Apportionment Analysis has focused on the Disentanglement Stage, with little discussion at all being had about the 'Identification of other known factors stage'. This is perhaps because the Disentanglement Stage is the more conceptually difficult of the two stages. Nonetheless, it is suggested that the 'Identification of other known factors stage' also merits consideration. The identification stage is simply concerned with the question of whether it seems likely that other known factors contributed in some way to the sub-injury at all. At the identification stage, it is not necessary to know whether other known factors really did contribute to a sub-injury, or to what extent – as this is interrogated more deeply at the 'Disentanglement Stage'. At this point, it is sufficient simply for the fact-finder to identify those other known factors that appear to have made a contribution.

In the safeguards context, the domestic competent authority must satisfy itself that all the other known factors have been identified for the purpose of performing the non-attribution analysis. That is, the domestic competent authority cannot rely on the findings of the interested parties; but instead, where the domestic competent authority believes that other known factors must be identified, it must investigate.[109] In contrast, in the antidumping and countervailing duty context, it seems that the domestic competent authority does not have the same requirement actively to investigate other known factors on its own initiative, except where it is aware of a factor that is not apparent to the parties. That is, the Panel in *Thailand—H-Beams* held that:

> We consider that other 'known' factors would include those causal factors that are clearly raised before the investigating authorities by interested

[109] AB, *US—Wheat Gluten* (n 14) [52]–[56].

> parties in the course of an AD investigation. We are of the view that there is no express requirement in Article 3.5 AD that investigating authorities seek out and examine in each case *on their own initiative* the effects of *all* possible factors other than imports that may be causing injury to the domestic industry under investigation. Of course, they would certainly not be precluded from doing so if they chose to. We note that there may be cases where, at the time of the investigation, a certain factor may be 'known' to the investigating authorities without being known to the interested parties. In such a case, an issue might arise as to whether the authorities would be compelled to examine such a known factor that is affecting the state of the domestic industry.[110]

This conclusion was not reviewed by the AB. In a related vein, the Panel in *EC—Salmon (Norway)* found that if a domestic competent authority has prior knowledge of certain causal factors, such knowledge may 'play a part' in the non-attribution analysis.[111] Whilst there have not been any statements about the requirement to investigate other known factors with regard to the imposition of countervailing duties, it is likely that any future Panel would follow the position in respect of the Antidumping Agreement. This is because the WTO strives for consistency of interpretation between the Antidumping Agreement and Article 15.5 of the SCM Agreement. In particular, the *Ministerial Declaration on Dispute Settlement Pursuant to the Agreement on Implementation of Article VI of the General Agreement on Tariffs and Trade 1994 or Part V of the Agreement on Subsidies and Countervailing Measures* recognises 'the need for the consistent resolution of disputes arising from antidumping and countervailing duty measures'.[112] This need for consistency in interpretation between the two agreements was also recognised by the Panel in *US—Countervailing Duty Investigation on DRAMs*.[113] Indeed, Nedumpara concludes with respect to the antidumping and countervailing duties jurisprudence that, 'despite their almost separate and wholly unconnected evolution and existence, the injury and causality requirements of antidumping and countervailing duties investigations have nearly merged and look almost indistinguishable now'.[114]

[110] WTO, *Thailand: Anti-Dumping Duties on Angles, Shapes and Sections of Iron or Non-Alloy Steel and H-Beams from Poland—Report of the Panel* (28 September 2000) WT/DS122/R (Panel, *Thailand—H-Beams*) [7.273] (emphasis original; footnotes omitted).

[111] WTO, *European Communities: Antidumping Duties on Farmed Salmon from Norway—Report of the Panel* (16 November 2007) WT/DS377/R [7.667].

[112] *Declaration on Art VI of the GATT 1994 or Pt V of the SCM* (n 105) .

[113] Panel, *US—Countervailing Duty Investigation on DRAMs* (n 105) [7.351].

[114] Nedumpara, *Injury and Causation in Trade Remedy Law* (n 7) 54.

Both the 'Identification of other known factors stage' and the 'Disentanglement stage' involve causation analyses, since both are fundamentally directed at interrogating the extent to which imports and other known factors contributed to the sub-injuries. If these other known factors are found likely to have had some impact on the sub-injury identified earlier (e.g., injury to productivity), they will then be considered in the Disentanglement Stage. It is suggested that a non-quantitative causal test will suffice for the identification stage. The question becomes, then, which non-quantitative causal test is most appropriate for completing the identification stage.

Before turning to consider how each of the non-quantitative causal tests might be applied in this context, it is helpful to return to the concrete example of Ruritania, which alleges that its cotton industry has been injured by Laurania's dumped goods. Imagine that Laurania has brought proceedings against Ruritania in the WTO because Laurania alleges that Ruritania has illegally introduced antidumping measures against it. Ruritania contends that its antidumping measures are legal because its domestic competent authority has determined that there was a causal link between Laurania's dumped cotton goods and 'serious injury or threat thereof' to Ruritania's domestic cotton industry. Laurania then alleges that Ruritania's injured cotton industry is not due to imports, but rather, due to Ruritania's own internal circumstances, such as dissatisfaction amongst cotton factory workers and a major fire and earthquake. Ruritania's domestic competent authority must then provide its internal report to the WTO Panel so that the WTO Panel can make a determination as to whether the introduction of the safeguard measures was legal.

In reviewing the report, the WTO Panel must be satisfied that Ruritania considered the injurious effects of the other known factors on the cotton industry. Above all, the WTO Panel must be satisfied that Ruritania's other known factors were not sufficient to negate the 'genuine and substantial relationship of cause and effect' between imports and 'serious injury or threat thereof' to Ruritania's cotton industry. The way in which Ruritania's domestic competent authority might go about conducting these non-attribution and causal link analyses is the subject of this section. Although this worked example considers the process of demonstrating the legality of introducing antidumping measures, the process for a domestic competent authority to demonstrate the legality of introducing a safeguard or countervailing measure would be identical, except in relation to the threshold to be discussed later.

Imagine that the following other known factors were identified as having had a possible impact on Ruritania's injured cotton industry: (1) a one-day labour strike amongst the cotton factory workers; (2) an outbreak of *salmonella* in the local water supply; (3) an earthquake that destroyed the majority of the cotton factories which were located in a particular area of the same city; and (4) a growing cotton industry in a nearby country that is actively recruiting former cotton factory workers from Ruritania and offering them better conditions. The question is which non-quantitative causal test will best identify any other known factors – or indeed, any such factors at this stage of the analysis.

The *Sine Qua Non* Test

A fact-finder using the *sine qua non* test[115] would ask, '*But for* the existence of this particular other known factor, would the sub-injury have occurred?' When applied to the four other known factors identified earlier, it is unlikely that the *salmonella* outbreak would be found to be necessary to the resulting sub-injury. The labour strike is likely to have played some very small causal role, and is therefore likely to be included in the disentanglement stage, since the *sine qua non* test does not distinguish between factors that are definitely necessary and those that are only marginally so. It is likely that both the earthquake and the increased competition for workers from the foreign cotton industry would be found to be necessary. For a diagrammatic representation of this example, see Figure 2.5.

The fact that the *sine qua non* test is over-inclusive – and would therefore include other known factors that were technically necessary but ultimately insignificant in producing the sub-injury – is not fatal to its use here. This is because those factors that were technically necessary but ultimately immaterial would be discarded from consideration in the Qualification Analysis stage of non-attribution, which will be discussed later. The fact that the *sine qua non* test cannot deal with cases of over-determination is also not problematic in this case because, as has been discussed previously, a sub-injury cannot be over-determined in the same manner as an all-or-nothing phenomenon, such as a fire. One potential objection to the use of the *sine qua non* test in this context is the intractable 'hypothetical world problem'.[116] That is, in order for a fact-finder to know the extent to which any other known factor caused the

[115] For a description of the *sine qua non* test, see Chapter 1.

[116] For an explanation of the 'hypothetical world problem', see Chapter 1.

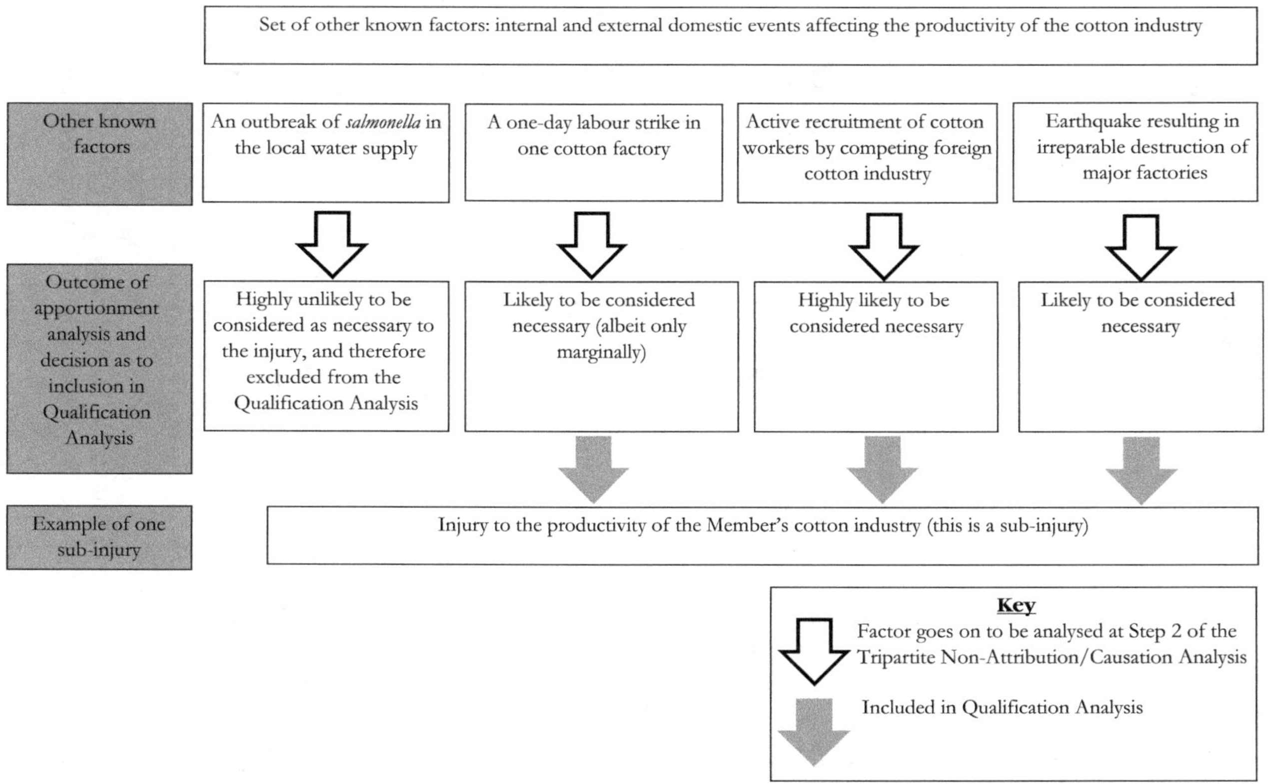

Figure 2.5 Step Two of the Tripartite Non-attribution/Causal Link Analysis: Example of applied apportionment causal link test: Application of the *sine qua non* test

sub-injury, that fact-finder must be able to imagine a hypothetical world in which that other known factor did not exist. For example, in order to appreciate whether a Member's earthquake causally contributed to the sub-injury, a fact-finder must be able to imagine a hypothetical world in which such an earthquake did not take place and then consider whether it was the earthquake that made the difference to the sub-injury. This 'hypothetical world problem' is not fatal to the use of the *sine qua non* test in this context, but it does mean that the *sine qua non* test must be approached with some caution.

Hart & Honoré's 'Causal Factor Test'

Alternatively, the weak necessity/strong sufficiency test might be used to assist in identifying other known factors. This involves a fact-finder looking at the data and asking, 'Are these other known factors necessary to a set that is minimally sufficient for producing the sub-injury?' In answering this question, it is again likely that the labour strike and *salmonella* outbreak would not be found to be necessary to a minimally sufficient set. Whilst the labour strike may have played some small causal role, it is likely to be excluded from the set because the set must be *minimally* sufficient to cause the sub-injury. That is, as few causal factors as possible must be included in the calculation of sufficiency.[117] This represents a difference from the *sine qua non* test. Nonetheless, it is likely that both the earthquake and the increased competition for workers from the foreign cotton industry would be found to be necessary for a set of factors that is minimally sufficient to cause injury to the productivity of the cotton industry (i.e., a sub-injury). For a diagrammatic representation of Hart and Honoré's causal factor test to this example, see Figure 2.6.

Wright's NESS Test

When deciding which of the weak necessity/strong sufficiency tests is the most suited to performing the identification of other known factors stage, it is important to consider the possibility that factors that are individually insufficient to bring about harm may be sufficient to cause injury once aggregated. That is, in the antidumping context, the AB in *EC—Tube or Pipe Fittings* said that, although not necessary in every case, there may be circumstances in which a domestic competent authority might need to consider the *collective effect* of other known factors in bringing about

[117] See Chapter 1 for an explanation of the importance of making a set minimally sufficient.

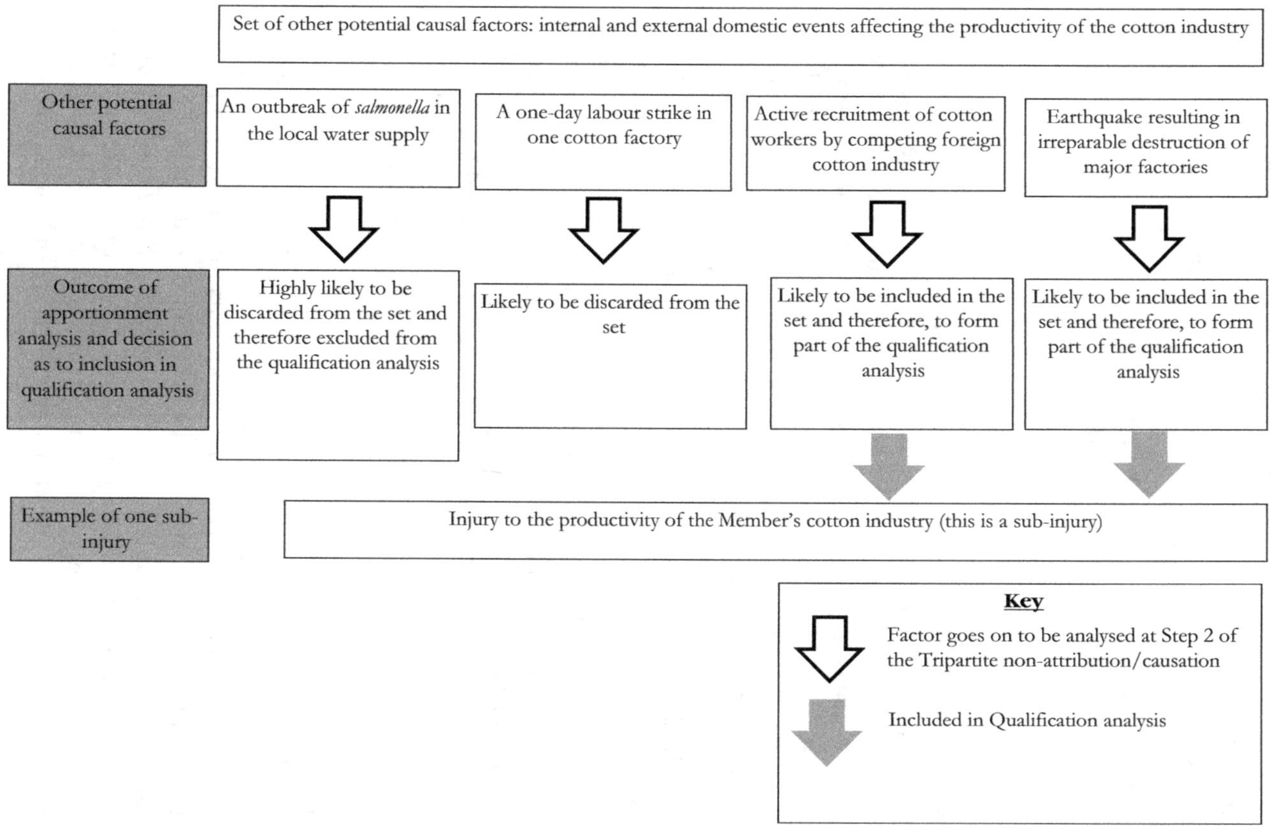

Figure 2.6 Step Two of the Tripartite Non-attribution/Causal Link Analysis: Example of applied apportionment causal link test: Hart and Honoré's 'Causal Factor Test'

harm.[118] Further supporting the idea of the possible need for collective assessment of other known factors, the *EC—Tube or Pipe Fittings* Panel also said that it was:

> certainly aware of the theoretical possibility that a causation methodology which separates and distinguishes between individual injury factors may not accommodate the possibility that multiple 'insignificant factors' might *collectively* constitute a significant cause of injury such as to sever the link between dumped imports and injury.[119]

This idea was echoed by the AB in the countervailing duties context in the *EU—PET (Pakistan)* case, where it said that:

> . . . in a situation where multiple other known factors, taken together, have a significant impact on the state of the domestic industry – while the impact of each of them in isolation may be only insignificant – an investigating authority may be required to assess whether the effects of all of these factors, collectively, are so significant that the subsidized imports cannot be characterized as a 'genuine and substantial' cause of the injury.[120]

This requirement, although only a 'theoretical possibility', and not explicitly addressed in the safeguards context, nonetheless suggests that domestic competent authorities and other authorities involved in the investigation process must be cognisant of the possibility that some independently insufficient other known factors might become sufficient when amalgamated with others. This 'theoretical possibility', more than any other, restricts the field of potential causal tests in this setting. This is because it requires a test that can aggregate multiple individual causal factors that are individually insufficient to have caused injury, but may reach the threshold of sufficiency once so aggregated.

No causal test can fulfil the potential requirements of the AB in *EC—Tube or Pipe Fittings* so well as Richard Wright's NESS test. That is, it may be recalled from Section 1.2.1 of Chapter 1 that the focus of Hart and Honoré's 'causally relevant factor' test is on whether an *individual* causal factor within a set is necessary and sufficient to cause a sub-injury *on its own*. It might be further recalled that Wright perceived this potential blind spot and corrected it at the outset in his revised

118 AB, *EC—Tube or Pipe Fittings* (n 35) [192].

119 Panel, *EC—Tube or Pipe Fittings* (n 35) [7.369] (emphasis original). See also, Panel, *EC—Tube or Pipe Fittings* (n 35) [7.388].

120 AB, *EU—PET (Pakistan)* (n 12) [5.176].

NESS test in order to take account of contributory duplicative overdetermination cases.[121] For this reason, Wright's NESS test is specifically designed to be able to amass individual insufficient causal factors into a set and then consider the sufficiency of that set to the sub-injury accordingly. Therefore, in order to take account of this theoretical possibility, it is suggested that Wright's NESS test is the most appropriate for performing the identification of other known factors stage.

It might be countered that the collective assessment of other known factors has only been raised as a potential issue in the antidumping and countervailing duties context, and has not yet been considered in the safeguards context. It might further be contended that it follows from this that the application of Wright's revised NESS test should only be considered for Article 3.5 of the Antidumping Agreement, and Article 15.5 of the SCM Agreement but not Article 4.2 of the Safeguards Agreement. This may be a possibility; but given that the *US—Hot Rolled Steel* and *US—Tyres (China)* Panel and the AB have been willing in their reasoning to draw analogies between the three provisions on account of their similar drafting, it would be prudent to draw on a causal test that can adapt to the potential for safeguards jurisprudence to move in this direction.

Applying Wright's NESS test to the cotton example at hand, if the factory workers' one-day strike mentioned earlier is combined with other known factors that are also individually insufficient, these may, once aggregated, become a set that is minimally sufficient to cause an injury. This is the scenario anticipated by the *EC—Tube or Pipe Fittings* Panel and the AB. For example, the workers' strike might be combined with other individually insufficient factors, such as excessively high absenteeism across all cotton factories in the industry, mass resignations from one particular factory and the malicious destruction of important equipment from a group of disgruntled workers in another factory. While none of these factors is individually sufficient to cause injury to the productivity of Member B's cotton industry, they may well be collectively sufficient to do so. This example is represented diagrammatically by the addition of the black arrow in Figure 2.7. Figure 2.8, which immediately follows Figure 2.7, diagrammatically represents the phenomenon of factors that are individually insufficient being pooled together to form a factor that is collectively sufficient to form part of a set.

[121] Richard W Wright, 'Causation in Tort Law' (1985) 73(6) California L Rev 1735, 1791–92. See Chapter 1.

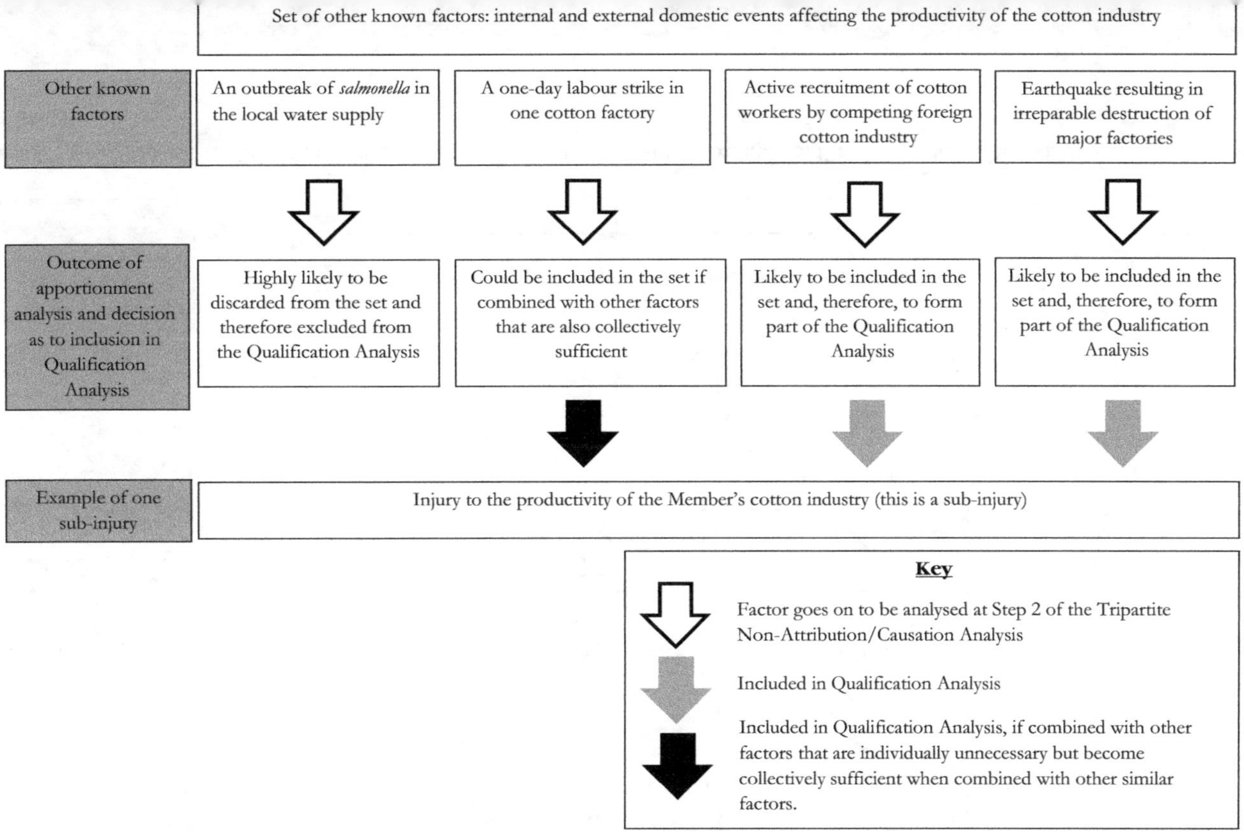

Figure 2.7 Step Two of the Tripartite Non-attribution/Causal Link Analysis: Example of applied apportionment causal link test: Richard Wright's NESS test

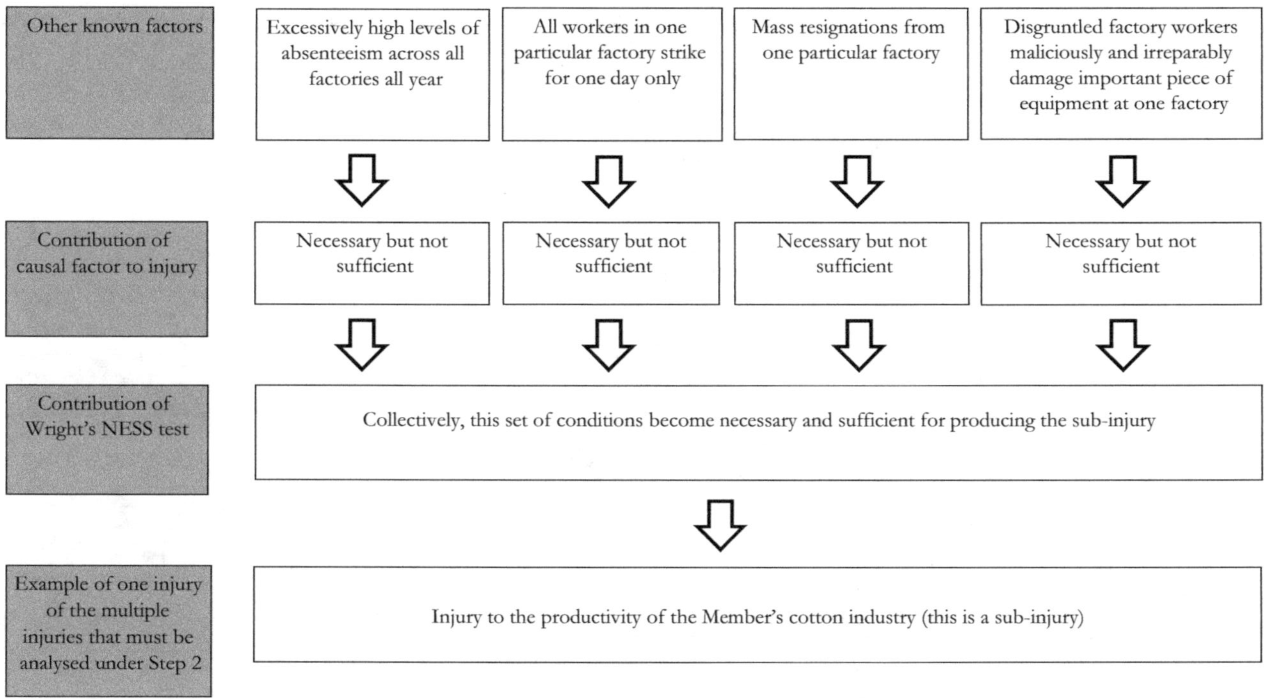

Figure 2.8 Step Two of the Tripartite Non-attribution/Causal Link Analysis: example of the aggregation of individually insufficient factors under Wright's NESS test

Conclusion

This survey of non-quantitative causal tests has demonstrated that the more inclusive approach facilitated by Wright's NESS analysis means that more other known factors will be identified at this stage than if Hart and Honoré's 'Causal Factor Test' or the *sine qua non* test were used. To see this difference diagrammatically, it is helpful to compare Figures 2.5 and 2.6. It can also be seen from comparing the operation of the *sine qua non* test with Wright's NESS test that the *sine qua non* test is as inclusive as Wright's NESS test. To see this diagrammatically, compare Figures 2.5 and 2.7. Although both the *sine qua non* test and Wright's NESS test obtained the same result, they did so using different methodologies. That is, the *sine qua non* test included factors that are technically necessary but only marginally so, whereas Wright's NESS test obtained the result by allowing a collection of individually insufficient factors to be aggregated to form a collectively sufficient factor. The final result is that, whilst the technically necessary factor would reach the Qualification Analysis stage, it would be quickly dismissed as marginal at that stage. Conversely, the collectively sufficient factors under Wright's NESS test may well pass the Qualification Analysis stage, since they are, once aggregated, far more substantial.

In sum, Wright's NESS test is the most inclusive of the three non-quantitative causal tests. The fact that the NESS test includes more other known factors in its analysis means that it is more likely that causal responsibility for injury will be apportioned to other known factors rather than imports at the next Disentanglement stage. Concomitantly, it may be more difficult under Wright's NESS test to attribute causal responsibility for injury to imports alone. In practice, a Member's domestic competent authority has an incentive to try to attribute as much causal responsibility to imports as possible. This is because the Member's domestic competent authority would be trying to justify the legality of its trade remedies by demonstrating that they are a response to the injury caused by imports. It follows from this that it is extremely unlikely that any Member's domestic competent authority would *voluntarily choose* to use Wright's NESS test to identify other known factors. Instead, it is likely that Hart and Honoré's test would be used because it is the least inclusive of the three non-quantitative causal tests canvassed here. Whichever causal factor test is used, the end result of performing the identification stage is to have a list of other known factors that appear likely to have contributed to various sub-injuries and that will need to be disentangled from imports at the next stage of the Tripartite Non-attribution/Causal Link Analysis, to which this chapter now turns.

Disentanglement Stage With the other known factors having been identified in the previous stage, it remains to canvas those methods by which the injurious effects of the other known factors might be disentangled from the injurious effects of imports. The purpose of the disentanglement stage is that the sub-injuries will be classified into the three categories of causal responsibility identified previously – namely, (1) some sub-injuries may have been caused exclusively by imports; (2) yet others, exclusively by other known factors; and finally, (3) by a combination of imports and other known factors.

The AB has emphasised that there is no prescribed methodology for determining causation for the purposes of introducing safeguards, anti-dumping measures and countervailing duties.[122] Therefore, domestic competent authorities have some discretion about the methodology that they choose for disentangling the injurious effects of imports from other known factors. Nonetheless, in the dumping context, the AB said in *US—Hot Rolled Steel* that the AB would require 'a satisfactory explanation of the nature and extent of the injurious effects of the other factors, as distinguished from the injurious effects of the dumped imports'.[123] As Ahn and Moon observe, the implication of this statement is that a quantitative test must be used in order to perform the disentanglement exercise.[124] To this end, the use of the word 'extent' is particularly significant. Moreover, the Panel in EC – Countervailing Measures on DRAM Chips held that, in the countervailing measures context, an effort must be made 'to quantify the impact of other known factors, relative to subsidized imports'.[125] Whilst these statements were made in the anti-dumping and countervailing measures contexts, given the similarity in drafting between the provisions, it would be prudent for domestic competent authorities also to use quantitative causal tests as a means of disentangling imports from other known factors in the safeguards contexts.

Nedampura notes that it is worth considering that many WTO Members would lack the capacity to use the sophisticated econometric

[122] In the safeguards context, see AB, *US—Lamb* (n 32) [181]; in the AD context, see AB, *US—Hot-Rolled Steel* (n 34) [224]; and in the countervailing measures, see Panel, *US—Countervailing Duty Investigation on DRAMs* (n 105) [7.405].

[123] AB, *US—Hot-Rolled Steel* (n 34) [223].

[124] Dukgeun Ahn and William J Moon, 'Alternative Approach to Causation Analysis in Trade Remedy Investigations: "Cost of Production" Test' (2010) 44(5) JWT 1023, 1031.

[125] WTO, *European Communities: Countervailing Measures on Dynamic Random Access Memory Chips from Korea—Report of the Panel* (17 June 2005) WT/DS299/R (Panel, *EC—Countervailing Measures on DRAM Chips*) [7.405] (emphasis original).

tools necessary for performing a quantitative analysis.[126] This is an important point, but it is suggested that resource constraints should not be an obstacle to using what appears to be the most intuitive and compelling interpretation of the provisions. Instead, these considerations serve more to reinforce the importance of the WTO continuing to provide resources and support to those Members who need it in order to bring dispute settlement claims.[127]

A number of quantitative causal tests have already been developed and applied in order to quantify the effects of imports, and in some cases, disentangle them from the injurious effects of other known factors. The USITC has used a number of methods for determining the impact of imports vis-à-vis other known factors on the domestic industry in the context of safeguards and antidumping measures.[128] The first major approach was the 'Comparative Analysis of the Domestic Industry's Condition' model, which was then refined into the 'Commercial Policy Analysis System' (COMPAS). COMPAS makes its calculation based on six parameters that the analysis must 'guesstimate'[129] – namely, the aggregate US market elasticity of demand for the relevant product, the domestic producers' supply elasticity, the fair-traded import supply elasticity, the substitution of domestic product for subject imports, the substitution of a domestic product for fairly traded imports and the substitution of subject imports for fairly traded imports. The COMPAS model takes these inputs and calculates the effect of the imports on the domestic market.

In this sense, the COMPAS model makes no attempt to disentangle the effect of imports on the domestic market from the effect of other known

[126] Nedumpara, *Injury and Causation in Trade Remedy Law* (n 7) 6.

[127] For an overview of efforts being made to better include developing countries in the WTO dispute settlement system, see generally Chad P Bown, *Self-Enforcing Trade: Developing Countries and WTO Dispute Settlement* (Brookings Institution Press 2009).

[128] For an overview of the five most common approaches used by the USITC in reaching material injury determinations in antidumping investigations, see Seth Kapla, 'Injury and Causation in USITC Antidumping Determinations: Five Recent Approaches,' in PKM Tharakan (ed), *Policy Implications of Antidumping Measures* (Elsevier Science Publishers 1991). For an overview of approaches taken in relation to separating imports from other known factors in antidumping and safeguards investigations, see JP Durling and MP McCullough, 'Teaching Old Laws New Tricks: The Legal Obligation of Non-Attribution and the Need for Economic Rigour in Injury Analyses under US Trade Law,' in EK Choi and J Hartigan (eds), *Handbook of International Trade, Volume II* (OUP 2005).

[129] Thomas J Prusa and David C Sharp, 'Simultaneous Equations in Antidumping Investigations' (2001) 14(1) JFE 63, 67; and Durling and McCullough (n 128) 80.

factors.[130] This failure to disentangle the causes of injury is inconsistent with the requirements of the relevant covered agreements. Indeed, the AB has found the method to be inconsistent with the covered agreements on several occasions.[131] Given that it fails in this fundamental respect, any result brought about by this methodology is at risk of being found to be non-compliant with the covered agreements. Accordingly, it is suggested that the COMPAS model should be abandoned as a methodology for disentangling the injurious effects of imports vis-à-vis other known factors for the purpose of assessing the legality of trade remedies.

Following a series of decisions from the AB that found the COMPAS methodology to be unsuitable, the USITC has adopted a number of econometric models to separate harm caused by imports from harm caused by other known factors. The econometric approach identifies those factors that affect supply and demand and then analyses and quantifies each of those effects.[132] The details and operation of the quantitative models that have been used by the USITC for safeguards[133] and antidumping[134] investigations have been set out elsewhere, and therefore will not be replicated here.[135] Econometric models based on the use of simultaneous equations have proved particularly useful and have been applied in a series of USITC investigations.[136] Unlike the

130 S Kaplan, 'Injury and Causation in USITC AD Determinations: Five Recent Approaches' in Tharakan (n 128) 49; ME Morke and HE Kruth, 'Determining Whether Dumped or Subsidised Imports Injure Domestic Injuries' (1989) 7 Contemp Pol Issues 78 and Durling and McCullough (n 128) 80.

131 In the Safeguards context, see AB, *US—Wheat Gluten* (n 14) [91]; AB, *US—Lamb* (n 32) [184]–[88]; WTO, *United States: Definitive Safeguard Measures on Imports of Circular Welded Carbon Quality Line Pipe from Korea—Report of the Panel* (29 October 2001) WT/DS202/R [7.283]–[7.290]; AB, *US—Line Pipe* (n 40) [218]–[22]. In the AD context, see the AB, *US—Hot-Rolled Steel* (n 34) [227]–[236].

132 For a discussion of the way in which inferences can be drawn from economic modelling in antidumping, countervailing duty and safeguard investigations, see generally James J Fetzer, 'Inference for Econometric Modeling in Antidumping, Countervailing Duty and Safeguard Investigations' (2009) 8(4) WTR 545.

133 In the Safeguards context, see Pindyck and Rotemberg (n 9).

134 In the Antidumping context, see Grossman (n 88); Prusa and Sharp (n 129); and David Sharp and Kenneth Zantow, 'Attribution of Injury in the Shrimp Antidumping Case: A Simultaneous Equations Approach' (2005) 6(5) Econ Bull 1.

135 An overview for non-economists can be found in Durling and McCullough (n 128).

136 See, in the Antidumping context, for example, *Certain Cold-Rolled Steel Products* from Argentina, Brazil, China, Indonesia, Japan, Russia, Slovakia, South Africa, Taiwan, Thailand, Turkey, Venezuela (TA-393-396); *Certain Crabmeat and Certain Seamless Carbon and Alloy Steel Standard, Line and Pressure Pipe* from the Czech Republic, Japan,

COMPAS methodology, these tests actually do attempt to separate those harms caused by imports from those caused by other known factors. These econometric tests do not show causation as such, but they do show correlation.[137] Various Panels and the AB have made statements to the effect that correlation is not decisive of causation, but that it is strongly indicative of it.[138] Moreover, the econometric tests endeavour to demonstrate correlation between a number of economic factors, rather than simply one factor, in order to give a better sense of the state of the market. Therefore, econometric tests that suggest correlation are still important in this analysis.[139]

These econometric models are very data-intensive, and cannot be relied upon in the absence of sufficient data.[140] Accordingly, where insufficient data is available to perform these econometric models, the USITC has tended to revert to its reliance on the use of the COMPAS methodology.[141] It has already been seen, however, that not only is the COMPAS methodology inaccurate, but that, more fundamentally, its failure to disentangle imports from other known factors has led the AB to find that it does not fulfil the legal requirements of the relevant covered agreements. Accordingly, it is suggested that the COMPAS methodology should be abandoned, even where there is insufficient data to perform econometric tests. Instead, there are a number of other methods that might be used in the alternative to the econometric

Mexico, the Republic of South Africa and Romania (731-TA-846-850); *Certain Crabmeat from Swimming Crabs* (TA-201-71); and *Certain Carbon Steel Products* from Australia, Belgium, Brazil, Canada, Finland, France, Germany, Japan, Korea, Mexico, Netherlands, Poland, Romania, Spain, Sweden, Taiwan, and United Kingdom (AA192 1-197 Review).

137 Sykes argues that, in the safeguards context, it is only possible to show correlation and not causation because increased imports do not *cause* 'serious injury' to the domestic industry; rather, they are simply correlated with it: AO Sykes, *The WTO Safeguards Agreement* (n 9) 164–66. As was stated in the introduction to this chapter (Section 2.1), this chapter will not enter into a discussion of the economic merits of the provisions, as its focus is instead on the legal causal tests required to interrogate the provisions.

138 Panel, *Argentina—Footwear (EC)* (n 26) [8.229]; AB, *Argentina—Footwear (EC)* (n 26) [145]; WTO, *United States: Measures Affecting Imports of Certain Passenger Vehicle and Light Truck Tyres from China—Report of the Panel* (13 December 2010) WT/DS399/R) [7.234].

139 For criticisms of relying on correlation as evidence of causation, see, in particular, Sykes, 'The Safeguards Mess' (n 9) 269–70; Sykes, 'The Causation Requirement' (n 9) 161–74; and see generally Sikes (n 7).

140 Prusa and Sharp (n 129) 77; and Durling and McCullough (n 128) 80.

141 Durling and McCullough (n 128) 80.

approach that are less data-intensive. One alternative is the partial equilibrium model, which is based on supply and demand conditions in the market and has been advocated for by Kelly[142] and refined by Irwin.[143] The 'Cost of Production Test' put forward by Ahn and Moon merits further investigation as a second alternative.[144] Each method has pros and cons, and the method chosen will ultimately depend on the type and quality of data available.

Whichever method is used, the point of the disentanglement exercise is to apportion responsibility for the identified sub-injuries as follows: (a) 100 per cent to imports; (b) 100 per cent to other known factors; or (c) a percentage that represents that causal responsibility is shared by a combination of imports and other known factors. With this breakdown of the possible apportionment of responsibility in view, it remains to progress to the second part of the Tripartite Non-attribution/Causal Link Analysis – namely, the Qualification Analysis.

Qualification Analysis Once the apportionment of responsibility for individual sub-injuries is complete, it remains for domestic competent authorities to perform a Qualification Analysis as the last element of Step Two of the Tripartite Non-attribution/Causal Link Analysis. For a diagrammatic representation of Step Two, see Figure 2.4. The purpose of the Qualification Analysis is for the domestic competent authority to decide whether a specific sub-injury is sufficiently attributable to imports alone that it can pass the non-attribution limb and qualify for final causal link analysis under Step Three. To put it another way, if it is clear from the Apportionment Analysis that causal responsibility for a sub-injury exceeds the permitted threshold for other known factors, that sub-injury would *not* go on to be considered in the causal link analysis at the tertiary stage. For example, if harm to Member B's cotton industry productivity is found to have been caused by 75 per cent other known factors and 25 per cent imports and the threshold is set at 50 per cent imports, the sub-injury of productivity will not be included in Step Three.[145] This example can be seen diagrammatically at Sub-Injury C, Figure 2.4.

[142] Kelly (n 9).
[143] Irwin (n 42).
[144] Ahn and Moon (n 124) 1041–47.
[145] The only way in which the injury to productivity could be included in the Step Three analysis is if the threshold under the multi-factorial approach is as low at 25 per cent, which is unlikely. The discussion of thresholds is directly below.

The Qualification Analysis is the point at which the distinction between the sufficiency of imports approach and the multi-factorial approach becomes critical. Under the Safeguard Panels' sufficiency of imports approach, only sub-injuries that were caused by imports alone would qualify for consideration under Step Three of the Tripartite Non-attribution/Causal Link Analysis. Accordingly, those sub-injuries that were partially or entirely caused by other known factors would be excluded at this second stage of the non-attribution analysis from further consideration. As may be seen from the fully black arrow in Step Two of Figure 2.4, the fact that only sub-injuries caused exclusively by imports may be included in the causal link analysis means that there are potentially far fewer inputs into the final causal link analysis at Step Three. It follows from this that, under the sufficiency of imports approach, it is more difficult to reach the threshold of 'serious injury or threat thereof' and make out the concomitant causal link of a 'genuine and substantial relationship of cause and effect' between imports and 'serious injury or threat thereof' to domestic industry.

The way in which non-attribution should be conducted under the multi-factorial approach is less clear than under the sufficiency of imports approach. If the non-attribution test excludes all sub-injuries from further analysis unless they were produced by 100 per cent imports, it would follow that: (1) the AB's multi-factorial approach would produce the same result as the sufficiency of imports approach; and (2) the second stage of the Tripartite Non-attribution/Causal Link Analysis would be otiose, as would domestic competent authorities' efforts to apportion responsibility for a sub-injury between imports and other known factors.

Nonetheless, it was established in Section 2.5 that the multi-factorial approach only makes sense if it is inferred that the threshold of import-induced sub-injuries is lower than 100 per cent. In other words, under the multi-factorial approach, sub-injuries caused by a *combination* of imports and other known factors may still be included in the final causal link analysis under Step Three. If, for example, the threshold for the non-attribution test is 90 per cent, then those sub-injuries that were produced by 90 per cent imports and 10 per cent other known factors or less would not be discarded by the non-attribution analysis (see Sub-Injury A in Figure 2.4). If, on the other hand, the threshold for the non-attribution test is 50 per cent, then those sub-injuries that were produced by 50 per cent imports and 50 per cent other known factors or less would not be discarded (see Sub-Injury D, Figure 2.4). Self-evidently, the lower the threshold in the non-attribution test, the more sub-injuries would go on to be included in the causal link analysis under the tertiary step. Moreover, the more sub-injuries that are included in the causal link analysis, the greater the likelihood, in turn, that the threshold of 'serious injury or threat thereof' would be reached and the causal link between imports and injury would be made out. From the perspective of the domestic competent authority trying to make out this causal link, then, the lower the threshold, the easier it is to demonstrate causation. The easier it is to determine causation, the easier it is, in turn, to justify the use of trade remedies.

Turning now to the threshold for antidumping measures and countervailing duties, it is suggested that the process for analysing causation should be identical to that which was described with respect to safeguards, except that the threshold used at the Qualification Analysis stage would be lower. Again, although the AB has not provided an indication of what this threshold should be, it was seen above that the CAFC has suggested a standard that represents a helpful starting point. That is, the CAFC said that, with respect to making a determination in relation to antidumping measures, that, '[a]s long as its effects are not merely incidental, tangential, or trivial, the foreign product sold at less than fair value meets the causation requirement'.[146] Whilst it is difficult to translate this into numerical terms, it is likely that, if this definition were accepted by the AB, the sub-injuries that have been found to have been caused by at least 20 per cent dumped imports would pass the Qualification Analysis stage. This much lower threshold reflects the fact that antidumping measures are generally less trade-restrictive than safeguard measures.[147] Having examined the first two steps of the Tripartite Non-attribution/Causal Link Analysis for analysing the non-attribution and causal link requirements of the provisions, it remains now to turn to the third step.

2.7.3 *The Third Step of the Tripartite Non-attribution/Causal Link Analysis*

The AB has offered little guidance as to how this last step should be undertaken. Under the Safeguards Agreement, it seems to involve two components: (1) the domestic competent authority should determine whether there is a causal link between imports and 'serious injury or

[146] *Nippon Steel Corp v USITC* (n 52).
[147] Mavroidis, Messerlin and Wauters (n 45) 465–66.

threat thereof'; and (2) if such a link exists, domestic competent authorities ought to determine whether such a causal link involves a 'genuine and substantial relationship of cause and effect'.[148] Again, whilst this language only pertains to the Safeguards Agreement, the Antidumping Agreement and Part V of the SCM Agreement also require that some causal link between imports and injury is found.[149]

Despite the lack of guidance from the AB and domestic competent authorities alike, it remains to set out how Step Three of the Tripartite Non-attribution/Causal Link Analysis might be performed with what little information is at hand. That is, once the domestic competent authority has aggregated all of the sub-injuries, it must then decide whether there is a causal link between imports and 'serious injury or threat thereof'. Self-evidently, the more significant the sub-injuries that qualify for inclusion at this step are, the more likely that a causal link between imports and 'serious injury or threat thereof' will be made out; and the more likely, in turn, that such a causal link will be found to be a 'genuine and substantial relationship of cause and effect'. It is for this reason that the interpretative choices made in Step Two of the Tripartite Non-attribution/Causal Link Analysis are so critical. Specifically, (1) the multi-factorial approach as opposed to the sufficiency of imports approach; and (2) the lower threshold under the multi-factorial approach both have the effect of increasing the number of sub-injuries that qualify for analysis in Step Three.

After having made these necessary interpretative choices, it remains to turn to the question of what is the most appropriate causal test for determining whether a causal link exists between imports and 'serious injury or threat thereof'. Leys and Tayal have each separately proposed that the *sine qua non* test is the most appropriate for determining causation in the safeguard context.[150] Narayanan also argues in favour of a *sine qua non* test in the context of an allegation of material injury in the dumping context.[151] Nedumpara contends that the *sine qua non* test

[148] AB, *US—Wheat Gluten* (n 14) [69].

[149] AD Agreement (n 2) Article 3.5.

[150] David Leys, 'Does a Theory of Causation Exist under the WTO Safeguards Agreement?' (2014) 9(1) GTCJ 10; and Pratik Tayal, 'A New World of Causation in Safeguards: Application of the "But for" Test' (2015) 10(1) GTCJ 355. Nedumpara criticises the use of the *sine qua non* test in this context, but for different reasons than that which has been suggested here: Nedumpara, 'Causation in Trade Remedy Actions' (n 108) 402.

[151] Prakash Narayanan, 'Injury Investigations in "Material Retardation" Antidumping Cases' (2004) 25(1) Nw J Int'l L & Bus 37, 59.

might be appropriate in circumstances where increased imports/dumped or subsidised imports are the most probable cause of injury.[152] To perform the *sine qua non* test in light of the steps that have been proposed before, this would involve: (1) aggregating all the sub-injuries to which increased imports had contributed; (2) looking solely at the contribution of the imports; and (3) asking 'but for the increased imports, would the Member's domestic economy have suffered from "serious injury or threat thereof"?'

It is argued that use of the *sine qua non* test is fundamentally flawed in this context. It has been seen that the *sine qua non* test relies solely on the quality of *necessity*. It is worth recalling the meaning of necessity as it was explained in the context of the chocolate machines in Chapter 1 – namely, a necessary condition for an effect may be defined as a condition that must be satisfied in order for that effect to be brought about.[153] In other words, the *sine qua non* test would involve interrogating whether the sub-injuries were a pre-condition for bringing about the finding of 'serious injury or threat thereof'. In reality, however, it is obvious that the sub-injuries are necessary for such a finding. Indeed, it is impossible to make a finding of overall injury *without* the inclusion of sub-injuries. Accordingly, if the *sine qua non* test were used in this context, it is difficult to see a circumstance where the *sine qua non* test would *not* find that the sub-injuries were necessary for the finding of 'serious injury or threat thereof'. In short, use of the *sine qua non* test in this context is redundant.

Instead, the causal inquiry must be one that involves the criterion of *sufficiency*. In this vein, it is helpful to recall the meaning of a sufficient condition developed in Chapter 1 – that is, a sufficient condition is one that, if satisfied, guarantees the effect.[154] It is suggested that this is a more appropriate causal criterion for determining whether the sub-injuries are sufficiently numerous and serious to amount to a finding of 'serious injury or threat thereof'. In other words, the inquiry interrogates whether, once the injurious effects of the other known factors are separated, the injurious effects of the imports are sufficient as a set to have caused the sub-injuries.

This book has discussed three causal tests that use a sufficiency criterion: (1) Hart and Honoré's 'causal factor test'; (2) Wright's NESS test;

[152] Nedumpara, *Injury and Causation in Trade Remedy Law* (n 7) 106.
[153] See Chapter 1.
[154] See Chapter 1.

and (3) Mackie's INUS test. Ahn and Moon contend that Mackie's INUS test is the ideal causal test to use in making a determination as to whether the imports are sufficiently serious to amount to a finding of 'serious injury or threat thereof'.[155] Ahn and Moon are correct that a causal test that involves the criterion of sufficiency is important here; but it is suggested that Hart and Honoré's 'causal factor test' or Wright's NESS test would be equally appropriate in this context. Whichever one of these three causal tests is used, each has the ability to interrogate whether an identified sub-injury is a necessary element of a set of sub-injuries that is collectively sufficient to bring about a finding of 'serious injury or threat thereof'. The process of aggregating sub-injuries using a weak necessity/strong sufficiency test may be seen in Figure 2.9.

The rest of this chapter will use Wright's NESS test to complete the analysis simply because it is conceptually easier to apply, but it does so on the understanding that Hart and Honoré's 'causal factor test' or Mackie's INUS test could also be used. The application of the NESS test to the causation analysis in the safeguards context may be illustrated by returning to the example of the cotton industry and the introduction of safeguards as set out in Figure 2.4. If the multi-factorial approach were used, and a 90 per cent threshold applied at the Qualification Analysis stage, two sub-injuries would be considered at Step Three. On the other hand, if the multi-factorial approach were used, and a 50 per cent threshold were adopted at the Qualification Analysis stage, three sub-injuries would be included in the analysis at Step Three. These alternative analyses and the effect of the different thresholds may be seen in Step Two of Figure 2.4. Due to the trade-distorting quality of safeguards, it is suggested that the threshold should be closer to 90 per cent than 50 per cent; but, without more specific guidance from the AB, it is difficult to offer a more precise figure. Whichever figure is used, the decision-maker would be required to look at those sub-injuries that had qualified for the third stage of the Tripartite Non-attribution/Causal Link Analysis and ask whether each sub-injury was necessary to a set of sub-injuries that was, in turn, sufficient to cause 'serious injury or threat thereof'.

If the domestic competent authority does find a causal link, the final stage involves a determination as to whether the causal link represents a 'genuine and substantial relationship of cause and effect'. Unfortunately, this wording does not offer much in the way of concrete guidance as to

[155] Ahn and Moon (n 124) 1049–51.

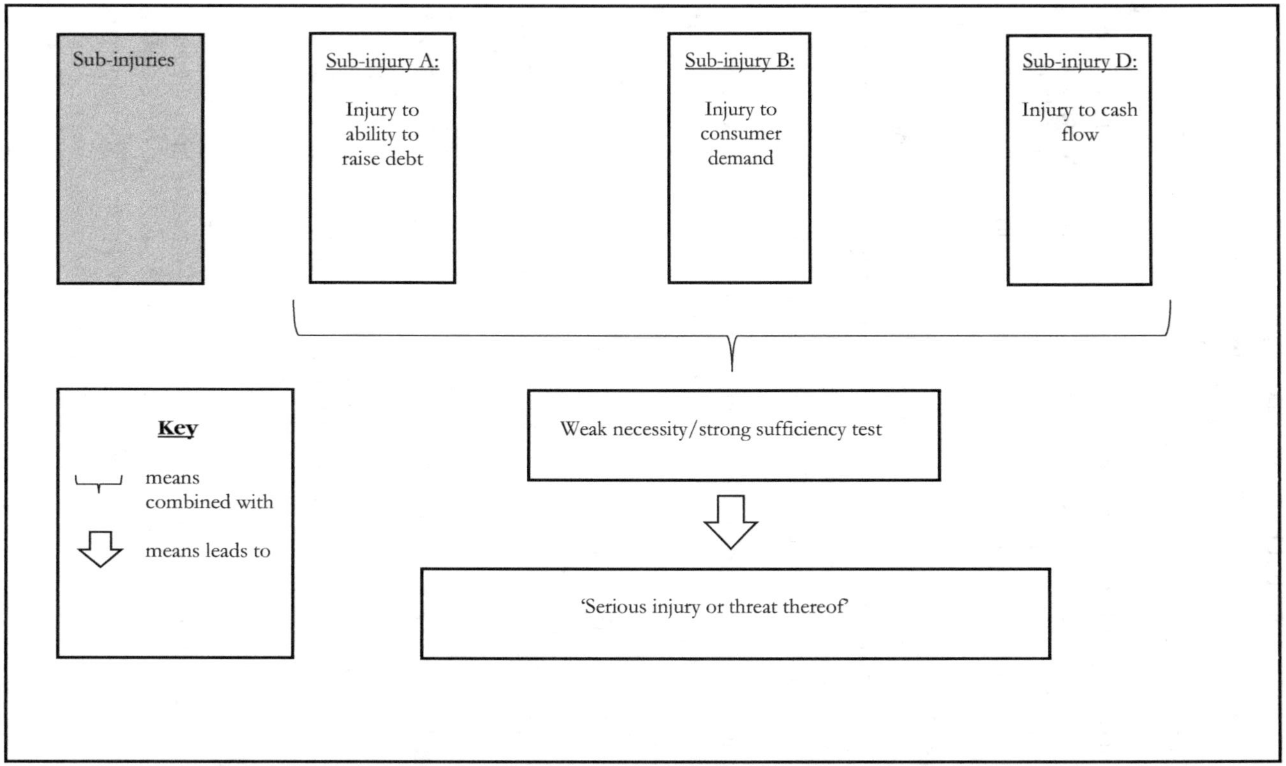

Figure 2.9 Step Three of the Tripartite Non-attribution/Causal Link Analysis: Causal Link Analysis

how the causal relationship between imports and injury should be demonstrated.[156] Nonetheless, it is contended that it is of a higher threshold than the causation standard used in the Qualification Analysis.

Returning to the case of Member B's cotton industry, then, it seems highly likely that, if three sub-injuries are included in the final analysis, the causal link between imports and 'serious injury or threat thereof' would be found to be a 'genuine and substantial relationship of cause and effect'. If only two sub-injuries are included in the final analysis, it is still likely that a domestic competent authority's finding of a 'genuine and substantial relationship of cause and effect' would be held to be reasonable, though this would be a more borderline case. It is for cases such as these that more guidance from the AB would be helpful.

2.8 Conclusion

Each of the trade remedies agreements require a Member to demonstrate that another Member's imports have caused injury to the domestic market before the relevant trade remedies might be implemented. To that end, they require a Member to conduct both a non-attribution as well as a causal link analysis, so as to ensure that other known factors are separated from the impact of imports when determining causation. Other than these two requirements, the trade remedies agreements offer little guidance as to how to perform these causation requirements.

The jurisprudence offers some additional guidance, but still leaves much to the discretion of domestic competent authorities. It was seen in Section 2.6 that the dominant approach used by domestic competent authorities is the 'breaking the causal link' approach, which involves making a provisional determination as to causation before assessing whether any other known factors 'break' that causal link. It was argued that this approach has a number of flaws to it, which might be resolved by using the three-step process set out in paragraph [69] of *US—Wheat Gluten*, which this book has taken up and termed 'The Tripartite Non-attribution/Causal Link Analysis'.

This chapter has sought to propose a methodology for negotiating the difficult causal questions embedded in the provisions of the trade remedies agreements. In doing so, this chapter has noted that there are various interpretative choices that the AB has signalled should be made

[156] Lacey (n 7) 26.

in Step Two of the Tripartite Non-attribution/Causal Link Analysis that affect the quantity of sub-injuries likely to qualify for the third step – the causal link analysis. The first interpretive choice is the 'sufficiency of imports approach' vis-à-vis the 'multi-factorial approach', and the second is the threshold that is permissible for sub-injuries to pass the Qualification Analysis at Step Two of the Tripartite Non-attribution/Causal Link Analysis. As the worked example of Member B's cotton industry demonstrated, these choices significantly influence the ease or difficulty with which a Member can legally demonstrate causation and introduce safeguards, antidumping measures and countervailing duties. This chapter has settled upon Wright's NESS test as the best test for determining causation at the identification of other known factors stage in Step Two as well as the causation stage in Step Three – though, in the latter stage, any weak necessity/strong sufficiency test could be used.

From a policy perspective, the interpretative choices used, as well as the causal thresholds selected, are crucial. This is because safeguard, antidumping measures and countervailing duties are inherently trade-restrictive. It therefore follows that, if methods are selected that make it too easy to draw the causal link between imports and injury, such trade-restrictive measures may be too easy to implement. This would, in turn, have implications for eroding the principle of non-discrimination between trading partners, which is at odds with the WTO's aspirations for a 'level playing field'.[157]

[157] *The Future of the WTO* (n 13) 15.

3

Serious Prejudice

3.1 Introduction

The SCM Agreement provides, inter alia, for the disciplines surrounding the use of subsidies and the use of countervailing duties to offset injury occasioned by subsidised imports. The non-attribution and causal link requirements embedded into the disciplines that concern the use of countervailing duties were discussed in Chapter 2, and so will not be revisited again in this chapter. Instead, this chapter is concerned with the causal considerations involved in making out that a subsidy is actionable under the SCM Agreement. That is, Article 5 of the SCM Agreement sets out three forms of 'adverse effects' that are potentially the result of subsidies and, if demonstrated, are actionable. So far, with the exception of two cases, all claims alleging 'adverse effects' as a result of a subsidy have been brought in relation to the third of the listed potential adverse effects – namely, serious prejudice, set out at Article 5(c) of the SCM Agreement.[1] As a result, the focus of this chapter is confined to a consideration of the causal requirements involved in a determination of serious prejudice.

According to Article 5(c) of the SCM Agreement, a Member should not, through its subsidies, cause serious prejudice to the interests of another Member. The term 'serious prejudice' is not defined in Article 5, but Article 6.3 sets out the circumstances in which serious prejudice 'may' be held to apply. In seeking to interpret the term 'serious prejudice',

[1] First, in WTO, *United States: Continued Dumping and Subsidy Offset Act of 2000—Report of the Panel* (16 September 2002) WT/DS217/R; WT/DS234/R, the panel considered Mexico's claim under Article 5(b) of the SCM Agreement, but found against Mexico. Second, in WTO, *European Communities and Certain member States: Measures Affecting Trade in Large Civil Aircraft—Report of the Panel* (30 June 2010) WT/DS316/R (Panel, *EC and Certain member States—Large Civil Aircraft*), the panel considered the United States' claim within the meaning of Article 5(a) of the SCM Agreement, but found against the United States. As these cases do not relate to serious prejudice under Article 5(c) of the SCM Agreement, they are beyond the scope of this chapter.

the Panel in *Korea—Commercial Vessels* held that serious prejudice is a different concept from injury.[2] That is, according to the Panel in that case, serious prejudice is not so much concerned with the condition of a Member's particular domestic injury, as with the 'negative effects on a Member's trade interests in respect of a product caused by another Member's subsidization'.[3] The Panel therefore concluded that:

> Serious prejudice to a Member's interests, in the sense of *SCM* Article 5 (c), consists of adverse effects on that Member's trade in a particular product in a specified market, resulting from subsidization by another Member. That is, the situations listed in Article 6.3(a) – (d) in themselves constitute serious prejudice.

In *US—Upland Cotton*, the United States argued before the Panel that the use of the word 'may' in the chapeau of Article 6.3 indicates that serious prejudice may or may not exist, even if the circumstances enumerated in Article 6.3 are made out.[4] The Panel rejected the United States' argument, however, and found that a demonstration of at least one of the situations listed in Article 6.3 is a necessary basis to conclude that serious prejudice exists.[5] In other words, making out one or more of those effects-based phenomena is sufficient for a finding of serious prejudice.

There are some similarities between a determination of serious prejudice under the SCM Agreement and a determination of 'injury' under the trade remedy agreements, which was discussed in Chapter 2. In particular, like a finding of 'injury' under the trade remedy agreements, a determination of serious prejudice requires both a non-attribution analysis and a causal link analysis. This means that a fact-finder must make a determination as to whether the market phenomenon is caused by subsidies; and, to that end, must be careful not to attribute blame to subsidies for those things that were, in fact, caused by other known factors. Nonetheless, Articles 5 and 6.3 'do not contain the more elaborate and precise "causation" and non-attribution language which is

[2] WTO, *Korea: Measures Affecting Trade in Commercial Vessels—Report of the Panel* (7 March 2005) WT/DS273/R (Panel, *Korea—Commercial Vessels*) [7.578].

[3] ibid.

[4] WTO, *United States: Subsidies on Upland Cotton—Report of the Panel* (8 September 2004) WT/DS267/R (Panel, *US—Upland Cotton*) [7.1369].

[5] ibid [7.1380]. See also WTO, *Indonesia: Certain Measures Affecting the Automobile Industry—Report of the Panel* (2 July 1998) WT/DS54/R; WT/DS55/R; WT/DS59/R; WT/DS64/R (Panel, *Indonesia—Autos*) [14.238] where the Panel also equated a finding of one or more of the effects-based phenomena listed in Article 6.3 with a finding of serious prejudice.

contained in the trade remedy [agreements]'.[6] The Panel and the AB in *US—Upland Cotton* have interpreted this less directive language in Articles 5 and 6.3 as an indication that there is greater discretion with regard to how to conduct the non-attribution and causal link analyses contained in those provisions.[7]

Another significant difference between determining injury under the trade remedy agreements vis-à-vis serious prejudice under Articles 5 and 6.3 of the SCM Agreement is that the latter is performed by a Panel or the AB, as opposed to a domestic competent authority. It follows from this that the Panel and the AB have more control regarding the processes by which the non-attribution and causal link analyses are performed with respect to a finding of serious prejudice than they do with respect to a finding of 'injury' under the trade remedy agreements.[8] One of the consequences of the degree of discretion that the Panels and the AB have in relation to determinations of serious prejudice is that there is a certain amount of variation in the jurisprudence in relation to how the non-attribution and causal link analyses are performed.

This chapter will argue for a more consistent approach to conducting the non-attribution and causal link analyses for the purposes of determining serious prejudice. One source of variation in the jurisprudence with respect to how the non-attribution and causal link analyses are performed under Articles 5 and 6.3 of the SCM Agreement relates to whether the causal relationship between the subsidy/ies and the market phenomenon is drawn in one step (the unitary approach) or two steps (the bifurcated approach). The chapter that follows argues strongly in favour of the bifurcated approach. Another source of variation in the jurisprudence relates to the role of the causation analysis. Whilst each of the cases use some form of counterfactual analysis, the particular form this takes varies between cases. Moreover, some cases employ an implicit weak necessity/strong sufficiency test in the way in which they collect the effects of subsidies together, whilst others do not. The

[6] Panel, *US—Upland Cotton* (n 4) [7.1343].

[7] WTO, *United States: Subsidies on Upland Cotton—Report of the Appellate Body* (3 March 2005) WT/DS267/AB/R (AB, *US—Upland Cotton*) [436].

[8] An exception to this is where the Panel and AB are required to perform a *de novo* review of a domestic authority's finding of 'injury' under the trade remedy agreements.

Tripartite Non-attribution/Causal Link Analysis is put forward as a possible alternative approach to more accurately and consistently interrogate the relationship between subsidies and the relevant market phenomenon, where sufficient data and an appropriate econometric model are available. Before turning to consider how such non-attribution and causal link analyses ought to be performed for the purposes of making a serious prejudice analysis, this chapter will turn to consider the kinds of market phenomena that might be considered in relation to a finding of serious prejudice.

3.2 The Nature of a Market Phenomenon in Relation to a Finding of Serious Prejudice

Due to the importance of the provisions to this chapter, the relevant parts of Article 5 as well as Article 6.3 of the SCM Agreement will be set out here below:

> ***Article 5: Adverse Effects***
> No Member should cause, through the use of any subsidy referred to in paragraphs 1 and 2 of Article 1, adverse effects to the interest of other Members, i.e.:
>
> [...]
>
> (c) serious prejudice to the interests of another Member.[13]
>
> [...]
>
> [13] The term 'serious prejudice to the interests of another Member' is used in this Agreement in the same sense as it is used in paragraph 1 of Article XVI of GATT 1994, and includes threat of serious prejudice.
>
> ***Article 6: Serious Prejudice***
> 6.3 Serious prejudice in the sense of paragraph (c) of Article 5 may arise in any case where one or several of the following apply:
>
> (a) the effect of the subsidy is to displace or impede the imports of a like product of another Member into the market of the subsidising Member;
> (b) the effect of the subsidy is to displace or impede the exports of a like product of another Member from a third country market;
> (c) the effect of the subsidy is a significant price undercutting by the subsidized product as compared with the price of a like product of another Member in the same market or significant price suppression, price depression or lost sales in the same market;

(d) the effect of the subsidy is an increase in the world market share of the subsidizing Member in a particular subsidized primary product or commodity as compared to the average share it had during the previous period of three years and this increase follows a consistent trend over a period when subsidies have been granted.[9]

This chapter now turns to consider the kinds of market phenomena that might be considered in relation to a finding of serious prejudice under the aforementioned provisions.

3.2.1 Articles 6.3(a) and (b): Displacement and Impedance

It has just been seen that Article 6.3(a) of the SCM Agreement provides that one of the manifestations of serious prejudice is where 'the effect of the subsidy is to displace or impede the imports of a like product of another Member into the market of the subsidising Member'. The Panel in *Indonesia—Autos* found that 'displacement relates to a situation where sales volume has declined, while impedance relates to a situation where sales which otherwise would have occurred were impeded'.[10] The Panel in *EC and certain member States—Large Civil Aircraft* held that it generally agreed that 'this distinction between displacement and impedance is inherent in the ordinary meaning of the terms'.[11]

The Panel in *EC and certain member States—Large Civil Aircraft* said that there is nothing in the text of Article 6.3(a) or (b) that requires that evidence be brought in a particular form.[12] The jurisprudence has consistently examined market share data as a way of determining whether displacement or impedance has occurred.[13] In *EC and certain member States—Large Civil Aircraft*, the Panel found that market share data alone was sufficient to demonstrate displacement, but not impedance.[14] The Panel in that case said that making out an impedance claim requires a Panel to be satisfied that sales that would otherwise have taken place were obstructed.[15]

[9] Footnote 17 to Article 6.3(d) is not necessary for the purposes of this chapter and has therefore been omitted.
[10] Panel, *Indonesia—Autos* (n 5) [14.218].
[11] Panel, *EC and Certain member States—Large Civil Aircraft* (n 1) [7.1738].
[12] ibid [7.1751].
[13] Panel, *Indonesia—Autos* (n 5) [14.211]; Panel, *Korea—Commercial Vessels* (n 2) [7.555]; and Panel, *EC and Certain member States—Large Civil Aircraft* (n 1) [7.1739].
[14] Panel, *EC and Certain member States—Large Civil Aircraft* (n 1) [7.1739].
[15] ibid.

In *EC and certain member States—Large Civil Aircraft*, the Panel said that, on the basis of the data presented, it was clear that Boeing's share of LCA deliveries to the EC market declined over the period in question, while EC's Airbus share of that market increased in the same period.[16] The Panel then found that the EC's subsidies enabled Airbus to develop and launch LCA as and when it did.[17] The Panel said that this alone was sufficient evidence to support a displacement claim but that the 'United States had failed to demonstrate that the effect of the subsidies in dispute was to impede United States' imports into the EC market, and United States' exports from the markets of certain third countries, during the period 2001–2006'.[18]

In sum, in order to make out a finding of displacement under Articles 6.3(a) and (b), a Panel must consider: (1) whether the complainant's market share in a particular market has declined; and (2) whether such a decline was the effect of subsidies, as opposed to other known factors. In respect of impedance, on the other hand, a Panel must consider: (1) whether the market data shows that another Member's imports or exports of a like product have been impeded from entry into the market; and (2) whether such impeded entry was caused by the subsidy/ies (and not other known factors).

3.2.2 Article 6.3(c): Significant Price Suppression or Price Depression

The text of Part III of the SCM Agreement does not provide a definition or any interpretive guidance regarding the meaning of price suppression or price depression as those terms are used in Article 6.3(c).[19] Nonetheless, turning to price depression first, the Panel in *US—Upland Cotton* defined price depression as 'the situation where "prices" are pressed down, or reduced'.[20] The question of price depression was considered by the Panel in *EC and certain member States—Large Civil Aircraft*. In that case, the Panel looked at the market data presented to it, which indicated that price depression had occurred in three of the four

[16] ibid [7.1758].
[17] ibid [7.2025].
[18] Panel, *EC and Certain member States—Large Civil Aircraft* (n 1) [7.2027].
[19] Panel, *US—Upland Cotton* (n 4) [7.1275] and Panel, *Korea—Commercial Vessels* (n 2) [7.533].
[20] Panel, *US—Upland Cotton* (n 4) [7.1277].

Boeing LCA models over the period 2001–06.[21] On the basis of this data, the Panel made a finding of price depression.

Like price depression, price suppression is not defined in the SCM Agreement. Nonetheless, the Panel in *US—Upland Cotton* defined 'price suppression' as a situation in which:

> 'prices' – in terms of the 'amount of money set for sale of upland cotton' or the 'value or worth' of upland cotton – either are prevented or inhibited from rising (i.e., they do not increase when they otherwise would have) or they do actually increase, but the increase is less than it otherwise would have been.[22]

As the Panel found in *Korea—Commercial Vessels*, it is not difficult to establish that the price of a particular product has decreased, remained flat or increased only slightly.[23] It is much more difficult to demonstrate that prices should not have decreased or that they should have increased by more than they did.[24]

The AB in *US—Upland Cotton (Article 21.5)* elaborated on the differences between price suppression and price depression as follows:

> At a conceptual level, we see some differences between the concepts of 'price depression' and 'price suppression' as defined in the original proceedings. While price depression is a directly observable phenomenon, price suppression is not. Falling prices can be observed; by contrast, price suppression concerns whether prices are less than they would otherwise have been in consequence of various factors, in this case, the subsidies. The identification of price suppression, therefore, presupposes a comparison of an observable factual situation (prices) with a counterfactual situation (what prices would have been) where one has to determine whether, in the absence of the subsidies (or some other controlling phenomenon), prices would have increased or would have increased more than they actually did.[25]

[21] Panel, *EC and Certain member States—Large Civil Aircraft* (n 1) [7.1854].

[22] Panel, *US—Upland Cotton* (n 4) [7.1276]. The Panel in *Korea—Commercial Vessels* (n 2) put it more simply when it said that '"price suppression" refers to the situation where prices have not increased when, or have increased less than, they otherwise would have': [7.533].

[23] Panel, *Korea—Commercial Vessels* (n 2) [7.536].

[24] ibid.

[25] WTO, *United States: Subsidies on Upland Cotton—Recourse to Article 21.5 of the DSU by Brazil—Report of the Appellate Body* (2 June 2018) WT/DS267/AB/RW (AB, *US—Upland Cotton (Article 21.5—Brazil)*) [351].

This comparison between the observable world and a hypothetical world can be seen in the reasoning of the Panel in *EC and certain member States—Large Civil Aircraft*, which dealt with the question of whether price suppression had occurred, amongst other market phenomena. In that case, the Panel found that price suppression in world market prices for Boeing LCA had occurred in three out of the four Boeing LCA models between 2001 and 2006, based on a comparison of actual indexed prices with the United States Aircraft Manufacturers Producer Price Index.[26] In its reasoning, the Panel effectively compared the current success of Airbus LCA with a hypothetical world in which the Airbus LCA had not had subsidies. It concluded that the LA/MSF subsidies:

> shift[ed] a significant portion of the risk of launching an aircraft from the manufacturer to the governments supplying the funding [...] Based on our review of the development of successive models of Airbus LCA, we conclude that Airbus' ability to launch, develop, and introduce to the market, each of its LCA models was dependent on subsidised LCA/MSF.[27]

Despite this finding, the Panel nonetheless found that the subsidies had not actually caused the price suppression.[28]

The Panel's reasoning behind its failure to find price suppression is that, based on the evidence before it, it could not draw any firm conclusions as to whether price suppression had occurred. Specifically, the Stiglitz/Greenwald statement raised two possible hypothetical scenarios, and the Panel did not know how to choose which of the two was more likely.[29] In other words, the Panel was experiencing the difficulties associated with resolving the 'hypothetical world problem' – a perennial problem associated with counterfactual analyses that was discussed in Chapter 1[30] and which recurs throughout this book.

In sum, like a displacement finding in Article 6.3(a), price depression in Article 6.3(c) may be made out in absolute terms. Specifically, as the AB in *US—Upland Cotton (Article 21.5)* said, findings of price depression may be directly observed,[31] as may findings of displacement. To make a

[26] Panel, *EC and certain member States—Large Civil Aircraft* (n 1) [7.1860].
[27] ibid [7.1949].
[28] ibid [7.2026].
[29] ibid [7.1995].
[30] Chapter 1, Section 1.2.2.
[31] AB, *US—Upland Cotton (Article 21.5—Brazil)* (n 25) [351].

finding of price depression, therefore, a Panel must find: (1) that prices for a particular product are 'pressed down'; and (2) that such depression is the result of subsidies and not other known factors. A finding of price suppression in Article 6.3(c), on the other hand, involves determining: (1) whether the data indicates that prices are less than they would be if the subsidies were not in place; and (2) whether subsidies – as opposed to other known factors – are causally responsible for this suppression of prices. In making a determination as to price suppression, it seems difficult to avoid setting up a parallel hypothetical world in which subsidies did not occur with which to compare the real world. In this sense, the 'hypothetical world problem' would seem to be inextricably linked with a price suppression determination. The jurisprudence has tended to move straight from a comparison of the real world with a hypothetical world containing no subsidies to then making a determination as to price suppression. It is argued, however, that an intermediate non-attribution step is required in order to attempt to ensure that the data is not distorted by other known factors.

3.2.3 Article 6.3(d): Increase in Market Share

Finally, under Article 6.3(d), a subsidy has an adverse effect if: (1) it increases the world market share of the subsidising Member with respect to primary products or commodities as compared to the average share it had during the previous three years; and (2) this trend has been consistent since subsidies were first initiated. The Panel in *US—Upland Cotton* held that the phrase 'world market share' in Article 6.3(d) 'refers to a share of the world market supplied by the subsidizing Member of the product concerned'.[32]

3.3 Jurisprudence Concerning Non-attribution and Causal Link Analysis in Respect of a Serious Prejudice Analysis

Article 6.3 is silent with respect to the procedure to be followed in order to make out a claim of serious prejudice.[33] Moreover, Article 6.3 does not

[32] Panel, *US—Upland Cotton* (n 4) [7.1464].

[33] Panel, *EC and Certain member States—Large Civil Aircraft* (n 1) [7.1731].

use the word 'cause'. Nonetheless, the Panel in *US—Upland Cotton* interpreted the word 'effect' in Article 6.3(c) as meaning that a causal link must be established between the subsidy and the significant price suppression.[34] This interpretation was confirmed by the AB,[35] which, quoting *US—Wheat Gluten* from the safeguards context, held that the causal threshold to be reached is one of a 'genuine and substantial relationship of cause and effect' between the subsidy and the market phenomenon.[36] The meaning of a 'genuine and substantial relationship of cause and effect' was already discussed in more detail in Chapter 2 in relation to the causal standard under trade remedies. Therefore, it is sufficiently simply to reiterate the most important part of the standard articulated by the AB in *US—Large Civil Aircraft*:

> In order to find that the subsidy is a genuine and substantial cause, a Panel need not determine it to be the sole cause of that effect, or even that it is the only substantial cause of that effect. A Panel must, however, take care to ensure that it does not attribute the effects of those other known factors to the subsidies at issue, and that the other known factors do not dilute the causal link between those subsidies and the alleged adverse effects such that it is not possible to characterize that link as a genuine and substantial relationship of cause and effect. The subsidy at issue may be found to exhibit the requisite causal link notwithstanding the existence of other causes that contribute to producing the relevant market phenomena if, having given proper consideration to all other relevant contributing factors and their effects, the Panel is satisfied that the contribution of the subsidy has been demonstrated to rise to that of a genuine and substantial cause.[37]

The AB in *US—Tyres (China)* also held that the 'genuine and substantial' causal link standard 'implies a higher degree of causality than subject

[34] Panel, *US—Upland Cotton* (n 4) [7.1343]–[7.1344]; Similarly, the Panel in *Korea—Commercial Vessels* held that 'we view these terms [price suppression or price depression] as implicitly including a certain built-in concept of causation': Panel, *Korea—Commercial Vessels* (n 2) [7.534].

[35] AB, *US—Upland Cotton* (n 7) [435].

[36] ibid [438] quoting WTO, *United States: Definitive Safeguard Measures on Imports of Wheat Gluten from the European Communities—Report of the Appellate Body* (22 December 2000) WT/DS166/AB/R (AB, *US—Wheat Gluten*) [69].

[37] WTO, *United States: Measures Affecting Trade in Large Civil Aircraft (Second Complaint)—Report of the Appellate Body* (12 March 2012) WT/DS353/AB/R (AB, *US—Large Civil Aircraft (2nd complaint)*) [914].

imports being merely "a cause" of the requisite level of injury to the domestic industry'.[38] Finally, the AB has confirmed that the 'genuine and substantial relationship of cause and effect' standard applies in respect of all forms of serious prejudice under Article 6.3.[39]

One important factor in making out the causal link between a subsidy and a market phenomenon is the way in which the product market of the subsidising Member is defined for the purposes of the litigation. That is, the product market involves assessing the 'the *competitive relationship* between specific products' with the view to determining 'the extent to which a complainant has brought its case with respect to the correct product markets'.[40] Specifically, the tighter the market definition, the easier it will be to demonstrate causation; and conversely, the looser the market definition, the more difficult it will be to make out causation.[41]

Moreover, the Panel in *US—Upland Cotton* further held that determining 'the effect of the subsidy' within the meaning of Article 6.3(c) 'necessarily calls for an examination of United States subsidies, within the context of other possible causal factors, to ensure an appropriate attribution of causality'[42] – that is, a non-attribution analysis. The Panel in *US—Large Civil Aircraft (2nd complaint)* held that there is no requirement to perform the non-attribution analysis as a step that is separate from the causal link analysis.[43] Instead, it is permissible to perform the non-attribution analysis at the same time as determining a causal link.[44]

[38] WTO, *United States: Measures Affecting Imports of Certain Passenger Vehicle and Light Truck Tyres from China—Report of the Appellate Body* (5 September 2011) WT/DS399/AB/R (AB, *US—Tyres (China)*) [181].

[39] WTO, *EC and certain member States: Measures Affecting Trade in Large Civil Aircraft—Report of the Appellate Body* (18 May 2011) WT/DS316/AB/R (AB, *EC and certain member States—Large Civil Aircraft*) [1232].

[40] WTO, *European Communities and Certain member States: Measures Affecting Trade in Large Civil Aircraft—Recourse to Article 21.5 of the DSU by the United States—Report of the Panel* (22 September 2016) WT/DS316/RW (Panel, *EC and Certain member States—Large Civil Aircraft (Article 21.5—US)*) [6.1160].

[41] WTO, *European Communities and Certain member States: Measures Affecting Trade in Large Civil Aircraft—Recourse to Article 21.5 of the DSU by the United States—Report of the Appellate Body* (15 May 2018) WT/DS316/AB/RW [5.489].

[42] Panel, *US—Upland Cotton* (n 4) [7.1344].

[43] WTO, *United States: Measures Affecting Trade in Large Civil Aircraft (2nd complaint)—Report of the Panel* (31 March 2011) WT/DS353/R (Panel, *US—Large Civil Aircraft (2nd complaint)*) [7.1660].

[44] ibid.

The AB in *US—Upland Cotton* upheld this approach.[45] The AB in *EC and certain member States—Large Civil Aircraft* confirmed that the same standard of causation and non-attribution that applied to Article 6.3(c) also applies to Articles 6.3(a) and (b).[46] The AB in *US—Upland Cotton* drew analogies between the Panel's approach and the non-attribution and causal link requirements in the Safeguards and Antidumping agreements.[47] Specifically, the AB said that the procedures for determining non-attribution and a causal link cannot be 'automatically transposed' from the Safeguards and Antidumping agreements. Nonetheless, it said that 'they may suggest ways of assessing whether the effect of a subsidy is significant price suppression rather than it being the effect of other factors'.[48] Whilst the jurisprudence is consistent with respect to the need for a non-attribution and causal link analysis, it diverges with respect to the process by which the cause and effect of a subsidy ought to be determined, which is the subject of Section 3.4.

3.4 The Unitary vis-à-vis the Bifurcated Process for Determining the Cause and Effect of a Market Phenomenon

There is a cleavage in the jurisprudence regarding whether the cause and effect of a subsidy should be determined together in one step (the unitary approach) or in two steps (the bifurcated approach). Both approaches are essentially aimed at interrogating: (1) whether a particular market phenomenon exists (e.g., a decline in market share or the impedance of a Member's imports or exports of a competitive product into the market); and (2) whether the market phenomenon was the effect of a subsidy/ies or other known factors.

Under the 'unitary approach', the particular market phenomenon identified in the subparagraphs of Article 6.3 and the causal relationship between the market phenomenon and the challenged subsidies are both analysed together.[49] For example, an analysis of whether 'price suppression' has taken place is conducted at the same time as an analysis of what caused the price suppression. In contrast, the bifurcated approach involves, first, an analysis of the market phenomenon and then an examination of the causal

[45] AB, *US—Upland Cotton* (n 7) [437].
[46] AB, *EC and certain member States—Large Civil Aircraft* (n 39) [1232].
[47] AB, *US—Upland Cotton* (n 7) [438].
[48] ibid.
[49] AB, *EC and certain member States—Large Civil Aircraft* (n 39) [1107].

link between the potential causes and the market phenomenon.[50] The bifurcated approach was used by the Panel in *US—Upland Cotton*.[51] In that case, the Panel considered: (1) whether there was price suppression in the world market for upland cotton and whether this price suppression was significant; and (2) whether a causal relationship existed between the significant price suppression and certain price-contingent subsidies.[52] The bifurcated approach may also be seen in the reasoning of the Panel in *EC and certain member States—Large Civil Aircraft*.[53]

The AB has indicated that the unitary approach is the preferred approach, saying that 'at least in respect of identifying price suppression and its causes [the unitary approach] has a sound conceptual foundation'.[54] The AB does not further elaborate on its basis for finding that the unitary approach has a 'sound conceptual foundation'. The unitary approach was used by the Panel in *Korea—Commercial Vessels*[55] and the AB in *US—Upland Cotton*,[56] where they considered that the term 'suppression' contains some sort of inherent causation requirement. Moreover, these cases also reflect the belief that the factors that were necessary for a determination of the existence of price suppression were also relevant to the question of what caused the price suppression. In this sense, the very way in which they define the term 'suppression' suggests that it is impossible to separate the existence of such suppression from its cause. For example, the AB in *US—Upland Cotton* held that:

> The ordinary meaning of the transitive verb 'suppress' implies the existence of a subject (the challenged subsidies) and an object (in this case, prices in the world market for upland cotton). This suggests that it would be difficult to make a judgement on significant price *suppression* without taking into account the effect of the subsidies.[57]

The Panel in *Korea—Commercial Vessels* held that the text of Article 6.3(c) implies a *sine qua non* or 'but for' approach to causation in respect of price suppression/price depression.[58] The *sine qua non* test appears to

[50] ibid. The AB in *US—Upland Cotton* said that they saw 'no legal error in this approach': AB, *US—Upland Cotton* (n 7) [431].
[51] Panel, *US—Upland Cotton* (n 4) [7.1275]–[7.1363].
[52] ibid.
[53] Panel, *EC and Certain member States—Large Civil Aircraft* (n 1) [7.1731].
[54] AB, *US—Upland Cotton (Article 21.5—Brazil)* (n 25) [354].
[55] Panel, *Korea—Commercial Vessels* (n 2) [7.534].
[56] AB, *US—Upland Cotton* (n 7) [433].
[57] ibid.
[58] Panel, *Korea—Commercial Vessels* (n 2) [7.612].

go hand in hand with the unitary approach, in the sense that the unitary approach relies on a counterfactual analysis. The use of the *sine qua non* test in relation to Article 6.3(c) was repeated by the Panel in *US—Upland Cotton (Article 21.5—Brazil)*,[59] which was upheld by the AB[60] as well as the Panel in *US—Large Civil Aircraft (2nd complaint)*.[61] The *sine qua non* test has also been used in the jurisprudence in relation to Article 6.3(a).[62] The AB in *US—Large Civil Aircraft (2nd complaint)* held that the counterfactual reasoning may be either non-quantitative or quantitative, or a combination of the two, depending on the case at hand.[63] The suitability of the *sine qua non* test as the causal test to interrogate the link between subsidies and the market phenomenon will be evaluated in Section 3.6. This section will instead evaluate the suitability of the unitary approach to determining the cause of a phenomenon.

It is suggested that the unitary approach is fundamentally flawed as a methodology for interrogating the link between subsidies and a market phenomenon for two reasons. First, at the most basic conceptual level, the unitary approach involves identifying the effect of the subsidy (i.e., the market phenomenon, such as price suppression) at the same time that it seeks to establish its cause (i.e., the subsidies). In this sense, under the unitary approach, the nature of the effect of the subsidy is not fully established at the time that the fact-finder is seeking to understand its cause. To put this in symbolic terms, whilst causal tests generally ask, 'Did C cause E?', the unitary approach asks, 'What is E? And is it the effect of C?' This form of questioning represents a logical error in two respects. First, the unitary approach falsely assumes that an effect may be knowable *a priori* simply through analysing its cause. Second and relatedly, it is premised on the false assumption that cause and effect are not entirely distinct concepts. Again, this is a false assumption, since the one cause may produce a plurality of possible effects; and the effect is not knowable until it has been fully realised. Indeed, Hume said:

> The mind can never possibly find the effect in the supposed cause, by the most accurate scrutiny and examination. For the effect is totally different

[59] WTO, *United States: Subsidies on Upland Cotton—Recourse to Article 21.5 of the DSU by Brazil—Report of the Panel* (18 December 2007) WT/DS267/RW (Panel, *US—Upland Cotton (Article 21.5—Brazil)*) [10.146].

[60] AB, *US—Upland Cotton (Article 21.5—Brazil)* (n 25) [370].

[61] Panel, *US—Large Civil Aircraft (2nd complaint)* (n 43) [7.1788], [7.1791] and [7.1794].

[62] Panel, *Indonesia—Autos* (n 5) [14.218].

[63] AB, *US—Large Civil Aircraft (2nd complaint)* (n 37) [1019].

> from the cause, and consequently can never be discovered in it. Motion in the second Billiard-ball is a quite distinct event from motion in the first; nor is there anything in the one to suggest the smallest hint of the other. [. . .] In a word, then, every effect is a distinct event from its cause. It could not, therefore, be discovered in the cause, and the first invention or conception of it, a priori, must be entirely arbitrary. And even after it is suggested, the conjunction of it with the cause must appear equally arbitrary, since there are always many other effects, which, to reason, must seem fully as consistent and natural.[64]

This quotation was taken from a larger passage in which Hume was observing the importance of experience in helping observers to make causal links between factors. Nonetheless, Hume's point about the impossibility of inferring an effect simply from examining its supposed cause is a sound one. It follows from Hume's point that the effect-based phenomenon (i.e., the effect) must be identified *prior* to any analysis of its cause (i.e., the subsidy/subsidies or the other known factors).

It also follows from the basic conceptual misunderstanding of causation that the unitary approach to causation results in circular reasoning. That is, the unitary approach requires a fact-finder to address the question of whether a market phenomenon is in existence before addressing 'the effect of the subsidy'. Essentially, then, this requires contending that a market phenomenon was brought about as a result of subsidies, and then using this conclusion to support a finding of causation between a subsidy and its effect. The United States made this point in its appellant's submissions in *US—Upland Cotton*.[65] It is suggested, therefore, that the unitary approach does not have the 'sound conceptual foundation'[66] asserted by the AB in *US—Upland Cotton (Article 21.5—Brazil)*.

The second reason that the unitary approach is flawed is that it does not allow for a genuine and rigorous non-attribution analysis to be undertaken. That is, it has been seen that the jurisprudence in respect of cases concerning serious prejudice requires that a non-attribution analysis be performed in order to ensure that any factors that played no causative role in bringing about a market phenomenon are excluded

[64] David Hume, *An Enquiry Concerning Human Understanding* (LA Selby-Bigge ed, 3rd edn, OUP 1975) s IV, pt I, 29.

[65] United States' appellant's submission, para 230 quoted in AB, *US—Upland Cotton* (n 7) [430].

[66] AB, *US—Upland Cotton (Article 21.5—Brazil)* (n 25) [354].

from the causal link analysis.[67] The unitary approach, however, leaves no scope for conducting a rigorous non-attribution analysis. This is because the very method of defining the market phenomenon is dependent upon subsidies being the cause. To put it another way, the nature of the market phenomenon is defined in terms of the effect of subsidies. Accordingly, it becomes impossible to then decide in light of a non-attribution analysis that the subsidies played no causative role and that the market phenomenon was caused by some other known factor – for example, a decline in world demand for that particular product instead. In this sense, there is no way to reconcile the unitary approach with a meaningful non-attribution analysis. It follows that it is difficult, in turn, to reconcile the unitary approach with statements made in the jurisprudence about the importance of conducting a non-attribution analysis.

In sum, the unitary approach is inappropriate for determining the cause and effect of a market phenomenon for the purposes of Article 6.3 of the SCM Agreement and should arguably be abandoned. It is suggested that the bifurcated approach is superior as it is the only approach that reflects a coherent vision of causation. This bifurcated approach should first identify the existence of the market phenomenon set out at Article 6.3; and then address, as a second step, whether there is a causal link between the subsidy/ies and the market phenomenon and that the link is not attenuated by other known factors. The rest of this chapter is dedicated to considering the precise process by which this bifurcated process should be conducted.

3.5 Non-attribution: The First Two Steps of the Tripartite Process

3.5.1 Introduction

Under the bifurcated approach, once the market data is analysed, the second step in the process of determining whether a market phenomenon has occurred involves a non-attribution and causal link analysis. It was seen in Section 3.3 that the AB has said that the procedures for determining non-attribution and a causal link in the context of the Safeguards and Antidumping agreements might be used to 'suggest ways' of approaching the determination of serious prejudice in the context of the SCM Agreement. Nonetheless, the AB has not gone so far as explicitly to put forward the methodology for analysing non-attribution

[67] AB, *US—Upland Cotton* (n 7) [438]; Panel, *US—Upland Cotton* (n 4) [7.1344].

and a causal link that was laid down by the AB in *US—Wheat Gluten* – namely, what this book has called 'the Tripartite Non-attribution/Causal Link Analysis'. It is contended, however, that the Tripartite Non-attribution/Causal Link Analysis might offer an alternative approach for assessing the non-attribution and causal link for the purposes of making a determination of serious prejudice under the SCM Agreement.

To this end, it is worth recalling that the Tripartite Non-attribution/Causal Link Analysis involves three analytical steps.[68] These steps will be set out as follows, with each tailored to a finding of serious prejudice: (1) authorities must identify and separate the types of injurious effects of subsidies vis-à-vis the injurious effects of other known factors; (2) authorities must then attribute to imports the harm they alone have produced before attributing to other known factors the harm that they have occasioned in turn; and (3) finally, authorities should determine whether there is a causal link between subsidies and a market phenomenon, leading to a finding of serious prejudice; and if so, whether such a causal link involves a 'genuine and substantial relationship of cause and effect' between these two elements.[69] The first two steps relate to the non-attribution limb, while the third step pertains to the causal link analysis.[70]

The Panels and the AB have provided little guidance about the way in which a causal link should be drawn between a subsidy and a market distortion for the purposes of making a determination as to serious prejudice. The Panel in *US—Upland Cotton* nonetheless held that the causal link must be a 'genuine and substantial relationship of cause and effect'.[71] To this extent, then, the same causal standard attaches to a finding of serious prejudice as is required for applying safeguards, anti-dumping measures and countervailing duties.

Since the Tripartite Non-attribution/Causal Link Analysis is somewhat abstract in nature, the worked hypothetical example of a Member's cotton industry will again be used throughout Sections 3.5 and 3.6 of this chapter in order to make the discussion more concrete. To that end, imagine that Ruritania has brought proceedings against Laurania in the WTO because Ruritania alleges that the subsidies introduced by Laurania to its cotton industry have caused Ruritania's cotton industry to suffer serious prejudice.

68 AB, *US—Wheat Gluten* (n 36) [69].
69 ibid.
70 ibid.
71 AB, *US—Upland Cotton* (n 7) [438] quoting AB, *US—Wheat Gluten* (n 36) [69].

3.5.2 *The First Step of the Non-attribution Process*

It will be recalled that the first step of the non-attribution process involves identifying the *type* of effects inflicted on the affected industry. Taking the example of the cotton industry, a fact-finder would be required to separate all of the injurious effects to the cotton industry into smaller effects. This chapter will call these 'sub-effects'. For the purposes of a serious prejudice determination, sub-effects to a cotton industry might include, for example, (1) displacement of imports of cotton within the meaning of Article 6.3(a); (2) displacement of exports of cotton within the meaning of Article 6.3(b); and (3) significant lost cotton sales within the meaning of Article 6.3(c) of the SCM Agreement. There may well be more sub-effects than those that have been identified here and in Figure 3.1. A representation of the separation of the sub-effects of subsidies can be seen in Step One of Figure 3.1. It is important to clarify that, whilst Figure 3.1 depicts each of the sub-effects of the subsidies as being of equal size spatially, in reality, each sub-effect might well be of greater or lesser significance to the ultimate finding of serious prejudice.

3.5.3 *The Second Step of the Non-attribution Process*

Introduction

The second step of the non-attribution process is essentially directed at determining whether the nominated sub-effects were caused by subsidies or other known factors and the respective quantitative contribution of each to the sub-effects. The AB has acknowledged that the sub-effects on a particular industry might be brought about by the 'interaction'[72] between subsidies and other known factors. Accordingly, it is possible that some sub-effects on an industry may have been caused by: (1) exclusively other known factors; (2) exclusively subsidies; or (3) a combination of subsidies and other known factors. Once the injurious sub-effects of the subsidies have been separated from the other known factors, it remains in the second step of the non-attribution process: (1) to apportion causal responsibility for the sub-effects between subsidies on the one hand and other known factors on the other; and (2) to determine which factors would qualify for inclusion in the final causal link analysis. This section will first review the current approach in the jurisprudence to

[72] AB, *US—Large Civil Aircraft (2nd complaint)* (n 37) [914] and [1206].

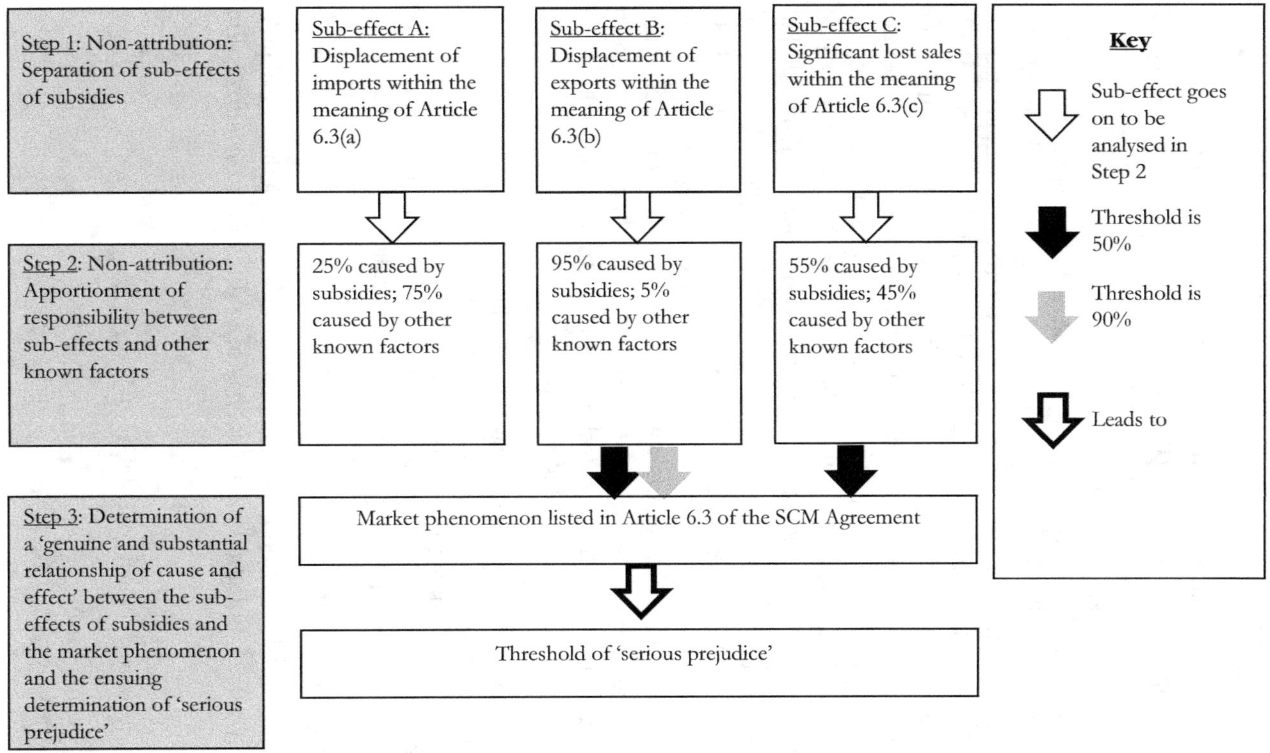

Figure 3.1 Overview of Steps One, Two and Three of the Tripartite Non-attribution/Causal Link Analysis: Non-attribution and causal link analysis under Article 6.3 of the SCM Agreement

the disentanglement exercise before turning to argue that a quantitative approach may be an alternative, where sufficient data and a viable econometric model is available.

The current approach in the jurisprudence will be considered first. The dominant approach in the jurisprudence is to make a preliminary finding of a causal link between subsidies and adverse effects on an industry before deciding whether any other known factors attenuate that causal link. In other words, the dominant approach in the jurisprudence is the 'breaking the causal link' approach that was discussed in Section 2.6 of Chapter 2. For example, in *US—Upland Cotton*, the Panel examined the other known factors raised by the United States in order to make a determination as to whether it was likely that those other known factors attenuated or negated the causal link between the United States' subsidies and a finding of price suppression under Article 6.3(c).[73] The Panel in *US—Upland Cotton* looked at the following other known factors that were raised by the United States after the Panel had established that there was a 'genuine and substantial causal link' between the United States' mandatory price-contingent subsidies and price suppression: (1) softening demand for cotton;[74] (2) the United States' exchange rate adjustments which affect textile trade flows;[75] (3) the strong US dollar since the mid-1990s;[76] (4) Chinese subsidies which have pushed down prices;[77] and (5) the effect of technological factors of upland cotton production.[78] The Panel concluded that:

> Although some of these factors may have contributed to lower, and even suppressed, world upland cotton prices during MY 1999–2002, they do not attenuate the genuine and substantial causal link that we have found between the United States mandatory price-contingent subsidies at issue and the significant price suppression. Nor do they reduce the effect of the mandatory price-contingent subsidies to a level which cannot be considered 'significant'.[79]

As was observed in Section 2.6 of Chapter 2, this 'breaking the causal link' approach has its limitations. First, as has been discussed, the correlation

[73] Panel, *US—Upland Cotton* (n 4) [7.1357]–[7.1362].
[74] ibid [7.1358].
[75] ibid [7.1359].
[76] ibid [7.1360].
[77] ibid [7.1361].
[78] ibid [7.1362].
[79] ibid [7.1363].

between the introduction of a subsidy to an industry and adverse effects may not always be reliable. Second, the process of determining whether other known factors have negated or 'broken' the causal link between subsidies and adverse effects is somewhat arbitrary. For example, in *Korea—Commercial Vessels*, the Panel found that it would:

> bear in mind the need to take into account the effects of identified factors other than the subsidies, to determine whether such factors would attenuate any affirmative causal link that we may find, or render insignificant any price suppression or price depression effect of the subsidy that we may find.[80]

It is unclear what 'bear[ing] in mind the need to take into account' other known factors means, nor precisely how this works in practice. This imprecision means that there is a lack of legal certainty for Members as to how the causal link between subsidies and adverse effects might be adjudicated. The third difficulty with the 'breaking the causal link' approach in this context, as was the case with trade remedies in Chapter 2, is that the approach does not allow for the fact that subsidies and other known factors might interact in the creation of an effect on an industry, or, in this case, serious prejudice. Indeed, it may be recalled from the introduction to this section that the AB has conceded that the sub-effects on a particular industry might be brought about by the 'interaction'[81] between subsidies and other known factors. Nonetheless, the AB upheld the conclusions of the Panel in *US—Upland Cotton*.[82] This is despite the fact that neither the Panel nor the AB had made clear what processes, if any, the Panel had undertaken to satisfy itself that the other known factors had not attenuated the causal link between subsidies and their effects.

Additionally, the 'breaking the causal link' approach is potentially at odds with the guidance of the AB in *US—Large Civil Aircraft (2nd complaint)*, which said that it was not sufficient for a Panel simply to say that it had taken into account potentially mitigating factors in its causation analysis.[83] Instead, the AB held that a Panel must make an attempt to understand and take into account the interactions between the subsidies at issue and the various other known factors, as well as

[80] ibid.
[81] AB, *US—Large Civil Aircraft (2nd complaint)* (n 37) [914] and [1206].
[82] AB, *US—Upland Cotton* (n 7) [496].
[83] AB, *US—Large Civil Aircraft (2nd complaint)* (n 37) [1206].

their relative contributions to the alleged market phenomenon.[84] It would seem, then, that the kind of approach taken by the Panel in *US—Upland Cotton* may not satisfy the requirement of considering the interactions between subsidies and other known factors. Nonetheless, neither the AB nor any subsequent Panel have used any clear methodology for attempting to understand the interactions between subsidies and other known factors. Given the difficulty of conducting a non-attribution analysis, it is suggested that the second step of the Tripartite Non-attribution/Causal Link Analysis used in Chapter 2 may assist in providing guidance as to how to conduct the non-attribution stage of the analysis in this chapter.

It may be recalled that the second step of the Tripartite Non-attribution/Causal Link Analysis involves analysing whether an injurious effect that is necessary to the ultimate finding of a market phenomenon listed in Article 6.3 and the ensuing serious prejudice was caused by subsidies and/or other known factors. This has been called the 'Apportionment Analysis'. In the context of a serious prejudice analysis, it is suggested that the Apportionment Analysis ought to have three stages: (1) the amalgamation of the sub-effects of multiple subsidies, where necessary; (2) the 'identification of other known factors stage', which involves identifying the other known factors that may have contributed to the finding of serious prejudice; and (3) the 'Disentanglement stage', which involves disentangling the sub-effects brought about by subsidies from the sub-effects brought about by those other known factors. It may be observed that this chapter has suggested that an additional first stage to the Apportionment Analysis be included. That is, the idea of amalgamating sub-effects or sub-injuries was not raised in the context of Chapter 2. This additional stage takes account of the fact that sometimes subsidies are not independently sufficient to amount to a sub-effect but, when aggregated with other subsidies, may become sufficient to do so.

Once the sub-effects of the subsidies have been disentangled from the sub-effects of other known factors, the next step involves analysing the respective quantitative contributions of subsidies to producing those effects vis-à-vis other known factors. As with Chapter 2, this stage involves a process of apportioning responsibility for the identified sub-effects between the subsidies on the one hand and the other known factors on the other hand. Once the Apportionment Analysis is complete,

[84] ibid.

the next question is whether a specific sub-effect on the injured industry is sufficiently attributable to subsidies alone that it can pass the non-attribution limb and qualify for final analysis under the third step. As in Chapter 2, this second causation test will be called the 'Qualification Analysis'. This section now turns to give a more detailed examination of the Apportionment Analysis.

Apportionment Analysis

Amalgamation of the Sub-effects of Multiple Subsidies The non-attribution process may involve combining the effects of multiple subsidies to form a single sub-effect, where it is necessary to do so. The question of whether the effects of subsidies might be aggregated first arose in *US—Upland Cotton*, where the Panel considered whether a Panel must 'clinically isolate' each individual subsidy and its sub-effects, or whether a number of sub-effects might be aggregated.[85] The Panel decided that it believed that, for the purposes of Article 6.3(c), to the extent that 'a sufficient nexus with [prices and products] exists among the subsidies at issue so that the [sub-]effects manifest themselves collectively, we believe that we may legitimately treat them as a "subsidy" and group them and their [sub-] effects together'.[86] The Panel in *EC and certain member States—Large Civil Aircraft* determined that the possibility of considering subsidies and their sub-effects together for the purposes of making out a finding of serious prejudice also extends to Articles 6.3(a) and (b) of the SCM Agreement.[87] The AB in *US—Large Civil Aircraft (2nd complaint)* explained that the danger of a Panel unduly separating each sub-effect of a subsidy is that it will find that 'no subsidy is a substantial cause of the relevant adverse effects'.[88] In other words, the AB in *US—Large Civil Aircraft (2nd complaint)* was reflecting the logic that underpins Wright's NESS analysis of contributory duplicative over-determination cases.[89] It is important to note that, in some cases, the AB already amalgamates the sub-effects of subsidies through the processes of aggregation and cumulation. The methods of aggregation and cumulation might, therefore, be harnessed for the purposes of amalgamating the sub-effects of multiple subsidies.

85 Panel, *US—Upland Cotton* (n 4) [7.1192].
86 ibid.
87 Panel, *EC and Certain member States—Large Civil Aircraft* (n 1) [7.1960].
88 AB, *US—Large Civil Aircraft (2nd complaint)* (n 37) [1284].
89 For an explanation of the logic that underpins Wright's NESS analysis of contributory duplicative over-determination cases, see Chapter 1, Section 1.2.1.

In deciding whether to combine the injurious sub-effects of subsidies, a Panel must consider such matters as the design, structure, magnitude, and operation of the subsidy, as well as the nexus between the subsidy and the subsidised product.[90] Collecting subsidies that have a similar design, structure and operation is at once an acknowledgement that similar measures are likely to produce the same sub-effects, as well as a tool of efficiency, in the sense that such amalgamation means that a Panel does not need to repeat the same analysis for each subsidy.[91] As with the non-attribution and causal link analyses, the AB has found that a Panel has a certain amount of discretion as to the methodology that can be used to analyse the collective sub-effects of multiple subsidies for the purposes of assessing causation.[92] The question of whether subsidies and their sub-effects can be grouped together is one that must be answered in light of the particular facts and circumstances of the case at hand.[93] There may be cases where such a grouping together is inappropriate, in which case, there is no requirement that it be done.

The AB has explained the method of aggregation as follows:

> A Panel may group together subsidy measures that are sufficiently similar in their design, structure, and operation in order to ascertain their aggregated [sub-]effects in an integrated causation analysis and determine whether there is a genuine and substantial causal relationship between these multiple subsidies, taken together, and the relevant market phenomena identified in Article 6.3 of the *SCM Agreement* [. . .] In such circumstances, the Panel is not required to find that each subsidy measure is, individually, a genuine and substantial cause of the relevant phenomenon. Nor is it required to assess the relative contribution of each subsidy within the group to the resulting effects. When such an analysis is appropriate in the light of the design, structure, and operation of multiple subsidies, a Panel may also add together the *amounts* of the subsidies as part of its analysis of the collective [sub-]effects of that group of subsidies. Whether such an analysis is appropriate will depend upon the particular features of the subsidies at issue and the case presented by the complainant. The causal mechanism through which a subsidy produces [sub-]effects is one criterion that will be relevant to the issue of whether aggregation is appropriate in any given instance.[94]

[90] ibid [1292].
[91] ibid [1291].
[92] ibid [1284].
[93] ibid [1319].
[94] ibid [1285].

Returning to the case study of the cotton industry, aggregation might be used, for instance, in a case where Laurania has introduced a number of subsidies into its cotton industry, and this has resulted in diverse sub-effects to Ruritania's cotton industry. So, for example, imagine that Laurania has implemented a suite of measures to benefit its cotton industry, including tax reductions to cotton producers, sales tax abatements on sales of cotton, reduced prices for cotton pickers and harvesters and a one-off payment of £5 million to Laurania's local research centre for the research and development of cotton production methods. Ruritania might argue: (1) the tax reductions to cotton producers and sales tax abatements on sales of cotton, when aggregated, resulted in significant lost cotton sales within the meaning of Article 6.3(c); and (2) the reduced prices for cotton pickers and harvesters and the one-off payment of £5 million to Laurania's local research centre for the research and development of cotton production methods, when aggregated, resulted in displacement of imports of cotton within the meaning of Article 6.3(a).

The aggregation model is represented diagrammatically in Figure 3.2. Again, it is worth noting that, while each subsidy and each sub-effect is represented diagrammatically as being of equal size, in reality the size of the subsidies and effects may vary considerably. This aggregation model was used by the Panel in *US—Upland Cotton*, where the Panel held that, to the extent that there are interrelationships amongst the subsidies and 'their [sub-]effects manifest themselves collectively', those subsidies should be considered together.[95] In this way, the aggregation approach might be used to combine the injurious sub-effects of subsidies for the purposes of fulfilling the first step of the non-attribution process.

The method of cumulation is the inverse of aggregation. The AB described the process of cumulation as follows:

> A Panel may begin by analyzing the [sub-]effects of a single subsidy, or an aggregated group of subsidies, in order to determine whether it constitutes a genuine and substantial cause of adverse effects. Having reached that conclusion, a Panel may then assess whether other subsidies – either individually or in aggregated groups – have a genuine causal connection to the same [sub-]effects, and complement and supplement the [sub-]effects of the first subsidy (or group of subsidies) that was found, alone, to be a genuine and substantial cause of the alleged market phenomena. The other subsidies have to be a 'genuine' cause, but they need not, in themselves, amount to a

[95] Panel, *US—Upland Cotton* (n 4) [1286].

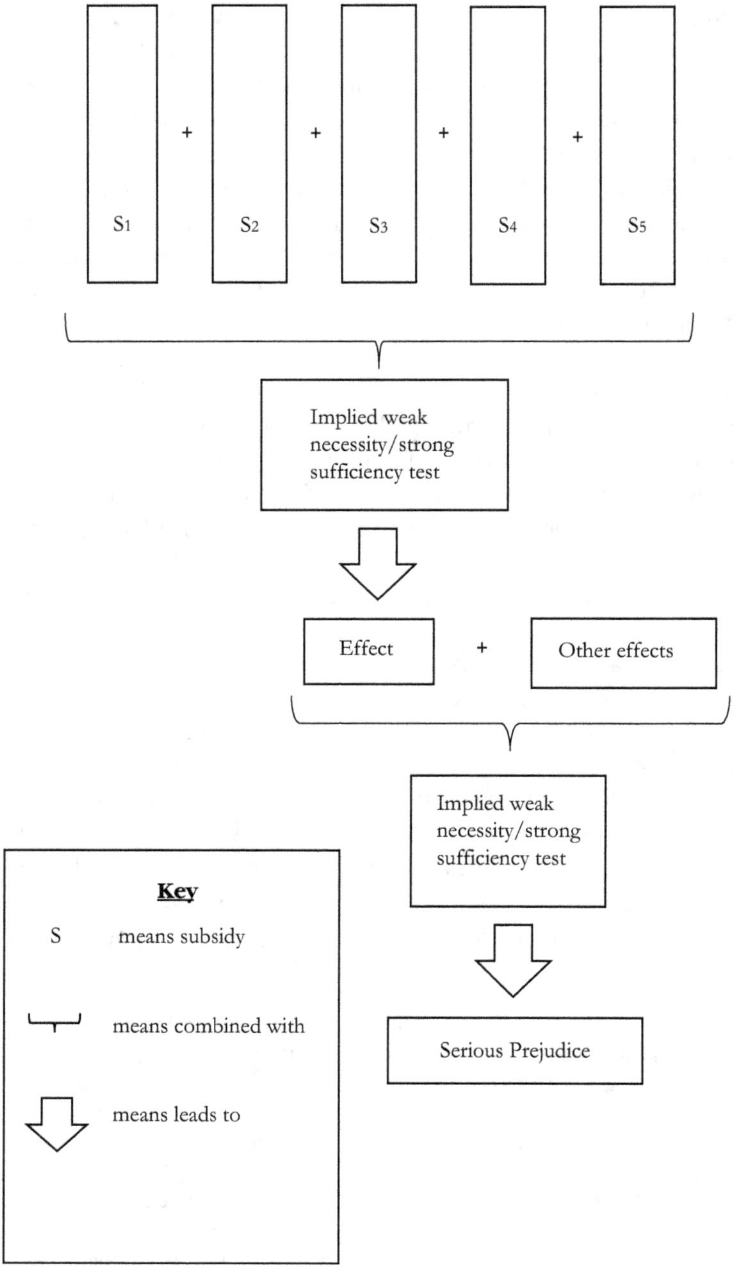

Figure 3.2 Representation of aggregation

> 'substantial' cause in order for their [sub-]effects to be combined with those of the first subsidy or group of subsidies that, alone, has been found to be a genuine and substantial cause of the adverse effects.[96]

In order to demonstrate the method of cumulation, this chapter will revert to the example of Ruritania's cotton industry. Under the cumulation method, a fact-finder would cumulate all of the sub-effects of Laurania's subsidy/ies and then make a determination as to whether their cumulative effect constitutes a genuine and substantial cause of adverse effects. So, for example, a fact-finder would cumulate: (1) displacement of imports of cotton within the meaning of Article 6.3(a); (2) displacement of exports of cotton within the meaning of Article 6.3(b); and (3) significant lost cotton sales within the meaning of Article 6.3(c) of the SCM Agreement. Based on this cumulation, a fact-finder would then weigh these sub-effects in order to decide whether they, together, constitute a genuine and substantial cause of adverse effects. The cumulation model is represented diagrammatically in Figure 3.3. Again, it is worth noting that, while each sub-effect is represented diagrammatically as being of equal size, in reality the size of each sub-effect may vary considerably. In its adverse effects analysis, the Panel in *EC and certain member States—Large Civil Aircraft*, considered the combined sub-effects of the LA/MSF subsidies and the non-LA/MSF subsidies, and found that the latter 'complemented and supplemented' the former in causing, inter alia, serious prejudice under Articles 6.3(a), (b) and (c).[97]

At present, the analysis in the jurisprudence performs a logical leap from grouping together the sub-effects of subsidies through the methods of cumulation and aggregation to determining whether the subsidies have caused the market phenomenon and the resulting serious prejudice. This tendency can be seen diagrammatically in Figures 3.2 and 3.3. The difficulty with this current approach is that it is premised on the assumption that a market phenomenon and the ensuing serious prejudice to the industry is caused solely by the effects of subsidies. In this sense, this approach does not allow for a genuine non-attribution analysis to be undertaken. This means, in turn, that if the methods of cumulation and aggregation are used, there is no possibility for a fact-finder to find that the market phenomenon and the ensuing serious prejudice was, in fact, caused by other known factors, as opposed to the effects of a subsidy.

[96] AB, *US—Large Civil Aircraft (2nd complaint)* (n 37) [1287].

[97] Panel, *EC and Certain member States—Large Civil Aircraft* (n 1) [7.1959]–[7.1960].

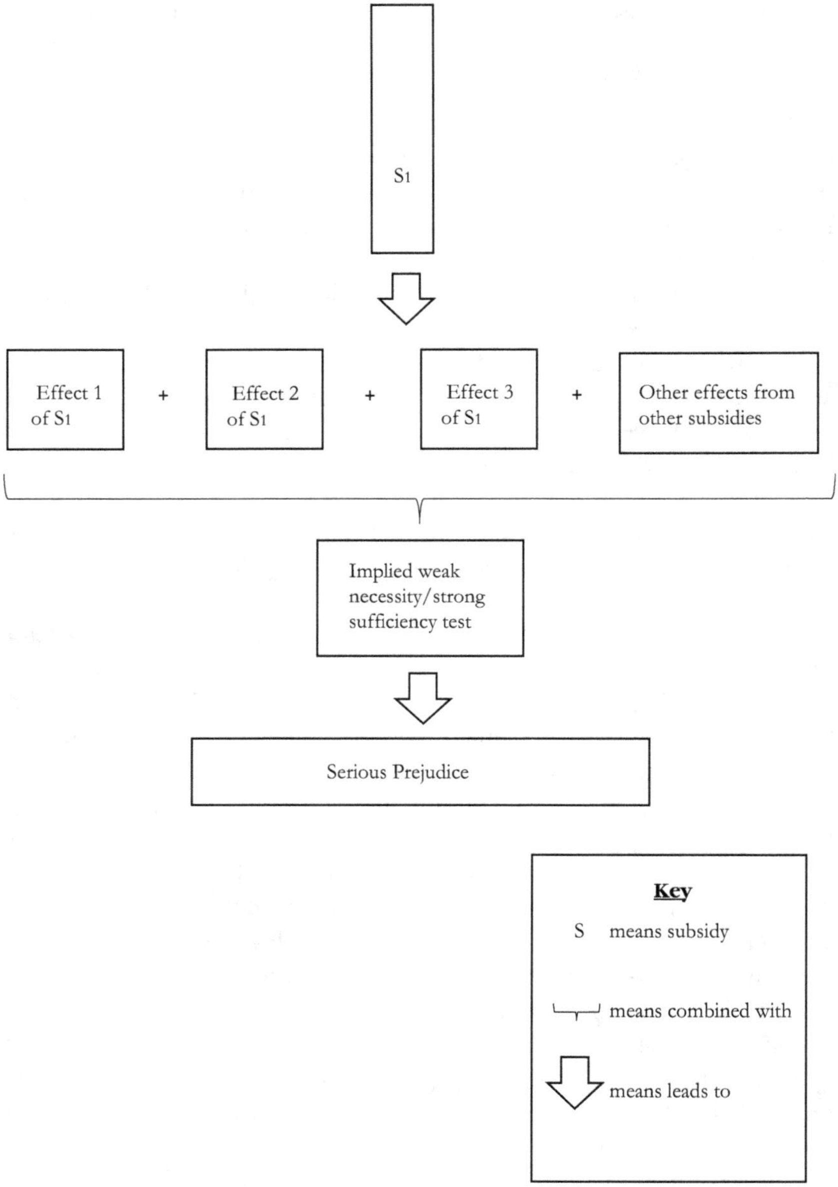

Figure 3.3 Representation of cumulation

Accordingly, it is suggested that the current aggregation and cumulation methods may be incorporated into the first step of the Tripartite Non-attribution/Causal Link Analysis. They are, however, only one part of the process required to make a serious prejudice determination, which must also include a non-attribution analysis.

Identification of Other Known Factors Stage As in the trade remedies context, the process of non-attribution in the SCM context first involves identifying what the other known factors are. In the safeguards context, the domestic competent authority must satisfy itself that all the other known factors have been identified. In the context of making a serious prejudice determination, however, the Panel does not need to identify any other known factors. This is because any other known factors are identified and raised by the Member whose subsidies have allegedly caused harm (in the cotton study example, this would be Ruritania). Accordingly, the Panel can simply adjudicate the matter based on those other known factors that are brought before it. Due to this fundamental difference, it is not necessary to set out the process of identifying other known factors in the context of serious prejudice, as it was in the context of safeguards in Chapter 2.

Disentanglement Stage There is nothing explicit in the text of the SCM Agreement or the jurisprudence to indicate that the non-attribution analysis should be performed by reference to the quantitative features of the subsidies or the other known factors. In fact, the Panel and AB in *US—Upland Cotton* explicitly held that a serious prejudice analysis does not require a subsidy to be quantified.[98] Further, where Brazil brought quantitative modelling before the Panel in *US—Upland Cotton*, the Panel:

> [took] note of the outcomes of the simulations . . . [but did not rely] upon the quantitative results of the modelling exercise – in terms of estimating any numerical value for the effects of the United States subsidies, nor, indirectly, in [the] examination of the causal link required under Articles 5 and 6.3(c) of the SCM Agreement.[99]

Moreover, none of the Panels or the AB have sought to use a quantitative approach for performing the non-attribution analysis. Nonetheless, the AB in *US—Large Civil Aircraft (2nd complaint)* held that:

> When confronted with multiple factors that may have contributed to the alleged adverse effects, a Panel must seek to understand the interactions between the subsidies at issue and the various other factors, and make

[98] Panel, *US—Upland Cotton* (n 4) [7.1171] and AB, *US—Upland Cotton* (n 7) [467].
[99] Panel, *US—Upland Cotton* (n 4) [7.1205].

> some assessment of their connection to, as well as the relative contribution of the subsidies and the other factors in bringing about, the relevant effect.[100]

It seems difficult to know how a Panel could assess the 'interaction' and 'the relative contribution' of the subsidies vis-à-vis the other known factors in any meaningful way without some form of quantitative analysis. Pablo Bentes reaches a similar conclusion in relation to the need for a quantitative approach when drawing a causal link in the law of serious prejudice.[101] Indeed, unless such quantitative analysis were used, it would seem that any attempt to set out 'the relative contribution' of the subsidies and the other known factors would be so approximate as not to be useful.

Given that the Panel and the AB have not found that a quantitative approach should be used to perform the non-attribution analysis, it is not surprising that there has been no commentary as to how any potential non-attribution analysis should be performed. Despite this lacuna, it is suggested that the basic conceptual similarities between the non-attribution analyses in the trade remedies context and those in the serious prejudice context are such that future Panels and the AB will be well-served by appropriating the econometric approaches used in the context of the former.[102] Alternatively, Article 13.2 of the DSU enables Panels to establish 'expert review groups'. Such a group could be convened and tasked with adapting the econometric approaches used to conduct non-attribution in the trade remedies context to the non-attribution analysis

[100] AB, *US—Large Civil Aircraft (2nd complaint)* (n 37) [1206].

[101] Pablo Bentes, 'In Search of a "Genuine and Substantial" Cause: The Analysis of Causation in Serious Prejudice Claims' in Marion Jansen, Joost Pauwelyn and Theresa Carpenter, *The Use of Economics in International Trade and Investment Disputes* (CUP 2017) 260.

[102] In particular, see Thomas J Prusa and David C Sharp, 'Simultaneous Equations in Antidumping Investigations' (2001) 14(1) JFE 63, 77; and JP Durling and MP McCullough, 'Teaching Old Laws New Tricks: The Legal Obligation of Non-Attribution and the Need for Economic Rigour in Injury Analyses under US Trade Law' in EK Choi and J Hartigan (eds), *Handbook of International Trade, Volume II* (OUP 2005) 80; Kenneth Kelly, 'The Analysis of Causality in Escape Clause Cases' (1988) 37(2) J Ind Econ 187; Douglas A Irwin, 'Causing Problems? The WTO Review of Causation and Injury Attribution in US Section 201 Cases' (2003) 2(3) WTR 297; and Dukgeun Ahn and William J Moon, 'Alternative Approach to Causation Analysis in Trade Remedy Investigations: "Cost of Production" Test' (2010) 44(5) JWT 1023, 1041–47.

required in order to conduct serious prejudice.[103] Indeed, Sapir and Trachtman have argued that an 'expert review group' formed under Article 13.2 of the DSU would be 'well-designed for use in cases where the Panel must make complex economic determinations'.[104] As with the non-attribution analyses under the Safeguards and Antidumping agreements as well as Part V of the SCM Agreement, the purpose of the non-attribution analysis for a finding of serious prejudice is to apportion responsibility between subsidies and other known factors in percentage terms. Once the responsibility for subsidies vis-à-vis other known factors has been apportioned, the Panel and the AB may then progress to the Qualification Analysis, to which this chapter now turns.

Qualification Analysis The aim of the Qualification Analysis is to determine whether a specific injurious effect is sufficiently attributable to subsidies alone that it can pass the non-attribution limb and qualify for final causal link analysis under Step Three. In order to perform the Qualification Analysis, it must be known whether only those effects that have been brought about by subsidies alone qualify for inclusion in the causal link analysis, or whether those effects that have been brought about by a combination of subsidies and other known factors might also be included. In other words, the question is whether the 'multi-factorial approach' might be used or whether only subsidies can qualify for inclusion in the causal link analysis.

On this point, Sapir and Trachtman say that 'the better answer' is that serious prejudice must be the result of subsidies alone.[105] There are two reasons that Sapir and Trachtman argue this. The first is economic in nature – namely:

> The 'prejudice' is not injury – it is impairment of the right to a market undistorted by subsidies. Even if it is permissible that injury (or more properly, 'prejudice') that is not serious without supplementation by other known factors can be the basis for a safeguards action, it seems impermissible that price suppression that is not significant without supplementation by other known factors could be actionable as serious prejudice.[106]

[103] Sapir and Trachtman say that an 'expert review group' formed under Article 13.2 of the DSU would be 'well-designed for use in cases where the Panel must make complex economic determinations': Andrew Sapir and Joel P Trachtman, 'Subsidization, Price Suppression, and Expertise: Causation and Precision in Upland Cotton' (2008) 7(1) WTR 183, 206.

[104] ibid.

[105] Sapir and Trachtman (n 103) 186.

[106] ibid.

The second reason is textual – that is, they note that the language of Article 6.3(c) provides that 'the effect of the subsidy' must be 'significant price suppression'. Prima facie, Sapir and Trachtman's arguments are sound and compelling, and at a purely theoretical level, they do seem to put forward the 'better answer'.

In practice, however, their argument overestimates the extent to which the effect of subsidies can be clinically separated from the effect of other known factors. That is, some of the cases indicate that the effects of both interact with each other. For example, in *US—Large Civil Aircraft (2nd complaint)*, the United States argued that the bulk of the research that led to the development and launch of the 787 was self-funded by Boeing, whereas the amount of research funded by The National Aeronautics and Space Administration (NASA) was relatively small.[107] It is difficult, therefore, to balkanise that research which was self-funded from that which was funded by NASA, since research tends to build on previous research in a cumulative fashion. In a case such as this one, then, it becomes particularly difficult to disentangle the effects of subsidies and other known factors. The AB appears to have recognised this when it said:

> As part of its assessment of the causal nexus between the subsidy at issue and the effect(s) that it is alleged to have had, a Panel must seek to understand the interactions between that subsidy and the various other known factors, and make an assessment of their connections to, as well as the relative importance of the subsidy, and of the other factors, in bringing about, the relevant effect(s). In order to find that the subsidy is a genuine and substantial cause, a Panel need not determine [a subsidy] to be the *sole* cause of that effect, or even that it is the *only* substantial cause of that effect. A Panel must, however, take care to ensure that it does not attribute the effects of those other known factors to the subsidies at issue, and that the other known factors do not dilute the causal link between those subsidies and the alleged adverse effects such that it is not possible to characterize that link as a genuine and substantial relationship of cause and effect.[108]

The AB's statement here would seem to suggest that those effects that are produced by a combination of subsidies and other known factors may be included in the final causal link stage of the analysis. Indeed, the AB's statement here is strikingly similar to its statement in *US—Wheat Gluten*, in which it proposed the 'multi-factorial approach' – namely, 'the language

[107] AB, *US—Large Civil Aircraft (2nd complaint)* (n 37) [982].
[108] ibid [984] (emphasis original). See also [914].

in the first sentence of Article 4.2(b) does *not* suggest that increased imports be *the sole* cause of the serious injury, or that "*other* factors" causing injury must be excluded from the determination of serious injury'.[109] This multi-factorial approach seems to be the more practical one, given the difficulty of separating the effects of subsidies from the effects of other known factors.

In sum, the statement by the AB in *US—Large Civil Aircraft (2nd complaint)* appears to support the 'multi-factorial approach'. As in Chapter 2, it is difficult to translate the AB's statement into a precise quantitative breakdown between subsidies and other known factors. That is, would a sub-effect caused by 90 per cent subsidies and 10 per cent other known factors be included in the causal link analysis in the third step? What about a sub-effect caused by 80 per cent subsidies and 20 per cent other known factors? Sapir and Trachtman are correct to point out that a serious prejudice finding would seem to demand less tolerance for other known factors than an injury finding in the case of, say, safeguards.[110] As such, it would seem logical that the percentage threshold for subsidies was very high – say, in the order of 90 per cent. That said, instead of prescribing a rigid quantitative breakdown between subsidies and other known factors, it would seem logical in the case of serious prejudice to allow some degree of flexibility depending on the case at hand. In particular, in cases where there is a particularly high degree of interaction between the effects of subsidies and other known factors (such as was the case in *US—Large Civil Aircraft (2nd complaint)*), the percentage threshold for the effects of subsidies would be lower than in cases where there is less interaction.

It has already been seen that the AB in *US—Large Civil Aircraft (2nd complaint)* found that it is not necessary for a market phenomenon listed in Article 6.3 and the ensuing serious prejudice determination to have been brought about by 100 per cent subsidies. In other words, the 'multi-factorial approach' applies to the Qualification Analysis, which means that those injurious effects that are brought about by a combination of subsidies and other known factors may possibly still qualify for inclusion in the causal link analysis in Step Three of the Tripartite Non-attribution/Causal Link Analysis. As in the trade remedies context discussed in Chapter 2, it will be up to a Panel or the AB to specify the threshold for the inclusion of injurious effects in the Qualification Analysis. If, for

[109] AB, *US—Wheat Gluten* (n 36) [67].
[110] Sapir and Trachtman (n 103) 186.

example, the threshold for the inclusion of injurious effects is 90 per cent, then those injurious effects caused by 95 per cent subsidies and 5 per cent other known factors will qualify for inclusion in the final causal link analysis. This can be seen at Effect B in Figure 3.1. Injurious effects that are caused by, say, 70 per cent subsidies and 30 per cent other known factors would be excluded from the causal link analysis in the tertiary stage of the Tripartite Non-attribution/Causal Link Analysis. Self-evidently, the lower the threshold is set, the more injurious sub-effects would qualify for inclusion in the causal link analysis and the easier it would be, in turn, to find a causal link between subsidies and 'serious injury or threat thereof'. It remains now to consider the process of drawing that causal link for the purposes of the tertiary stage of the Tripartite Non-attribution/Causal Link Analysis.

3.6 Causal Link: The Third Step of the Tripartite Process

The AB has said that the Panel is entitled to a certain amount of methodological discretion in the way in which it analyses the causal link between subsidies and the particular market phenomenon in question.[111] The only guidance is that, as in the trade remedies context, the causal link must involve a 'genuine and substantial relationship of cause and effect'.[112] This section will first look at the way in which the causal link between subsidies and the market phenomenon listed in Article 6.3 and the ensuing serious prejudice determination is currently drawn in the jurisprudence before turning to propose an alternative approach.

The Panel in *Korea—Commercial Vessels* said that the causal link analysis must be done on a case-by-case basis and be tailored to the particular circumstances of each individual dispute.[113] Nonetheless, all of the cases considering serious prejudice to date have used some form of counterfactual analysis in determining whether a causal link exists between subsidies and a market phenomenon. The first case, *US—Upland Cotton*, does not explicitly use the *sine qua non* test as such, but the Panel does say that 'the effect of the subsidies was to allow United States producers to sell upland cotton at a price lower than would otherwise have been necessary to

[111] AB, *US—Upland Cotton* (n 7) [436]-[437]; AB, *US—Large Civil Aircraft (2nd complaint)* (n 37) [1284].

[112] AB, *US—Upland Cotton* (n 7) [438] quoting AB, *US—Wheat Gluten* (n 36) [69].

[113] Panel, *Korea—Commercial Vessels* (n 2) [7.619].

cover their total costs'.[114] This is effectively a *sine qua non* test, in the sense that it is still comparing the effect of the subsidies with a hypothetical world in which the subsidies do not exist.[115] The AB in *US—Upland Cotton* makes this very point:

> The Panel's definition of price suppression [. . .] includes the notion that prices 'do not increase when they *otherwise* would have' or 'they do actually increase, but the increase is less than it *otherwise* would have been'. The word 'otherwise' in this context refers to the hypothetical situation in which the challenged subsidies are absent.[116]

The *sine qua non* test was used more explicitly as the basis of the causal link by the Panels in *US—Upland Cotton (Article 21.5—Brazil),*[117] *Korea—Commercial Vessels,*[118] *Indonesia—Autos,*[119] *EC and certain member States—Large Civil Aircraft*[120] and *US—Large Civil Aircraft (2nd complaint).*[121] The AB in *EC and certain member States—Large Civil Aircraft*[122] and *US—Large Civil Aircraft (2nd complaint)*[123] upheld the use of the counterfactual approach. Sapir and Trachtman, too, advocate for the use of the *sine qua non* test in this context.[124]

It is suggested that the *sine qua non* test or any counterfactual test is inappropriate as a causal test for interrogating the causal link between subsidies and market phenomena for a number of reasons. Indeed, even some of the Panels and the AB have expressed some reservations about the utility of the *sine qua non* test in making a determination as to whether there is a 'genuine and substantial relationship of cause and effect' between a subsidy and the particular market phenomena in question. These reservations go to the heart of the criticisms made about the *sine qua non* test more generally, as set out in Chapter 1 of this book.[125] That is, the AB remarked that the *sine qua non* test may find certain

[114] Panel, *US—Upland Cotton* (n 4) [7.1353].
[115] For an explanation of the *sine qua non* test, see Chapter 1, Section 1.2.1.
[116] AB, *US—Upland Cotton* (n 7) [433] (emphasis original; footnotes omitted).
[117] (n 25) [281].
[118] (n 2) [7.537].
[119] Panel, *Indonesia—Autos* (n 5) [14.218].
[120] (n 1) [7.1920], [7.1939], [7.1940], [7.1948], [7.1956], [7.1976], [7.1985], [7.1986], [7.1989], [7.1993], [7.2025] and [7.2154].
[121] (n 43) [7.1788], [7.1791] and [7.1794].
[122] (n 29) [1229]–[1300].
[123] (n 37) [1019] and [1182]–[1274].
[124] Sapir and Trachtman (n 103) 201.
[125] These criticisms were set out Chapter 1, Section 1.2.1.

factors to be causal that are necessary, but ultimately remote, to the final outcome.[126] For example, the AB in *US—Upland Cotton (Article 21.5)* acknowledged that '[a] subsidy may be necessary, but not sufficient, to bring about price suppression'.[127] Similarly, the AB in *EC and certain member States—Large Civil Aircraft* remarked on this possibility, holding that 'there are circumstances in which a "but for" approach does not suffice', observing that the *sine qua non* test may attribute causation to factors that are technically necessary but very remote.[128] This insight is important. It shows the danger of relying on a non-quantitative causal test that lacks a sufficiency criterion – which, again, is a criticism of the *sine qua non* test that was raised in Chapter 1.[129]

One of the ramifications of using a *sine qua non* test in this context is that the test is likely to generate a 'false positive' result – that is, to find that a subsidy or subsidies are the cause of the particular effect-based phenomena, even when they may have only played a minor role. This defect could be mitigated if the Panels and the AB repeated the *sine qua non* test with respect to each and every one of the other known factors that were raised. That is, the fact-finder would ask, 'But for this other causal factor, would the market phenomenon have occurred?' in respect of each and every potential other causal factor. The difficulty with this approach, however, is that the *sine qua non* test might return affirmative results in relation to a series of other known factors as well as subsidies. It would then follow from this that the fact-finder would have no way of adjudicating which of those factors was actually *sufficient* to have caused the market phenomenon if they relied on the *sine qua non* test alone. In sum, use of the *sine qua non* test may establish a causal link between a subsidy or subsidies and the market phenomenon in cases where the causal contribution of that subsidy or subsidies to the market phenomenon was actually only marginal.

Conversely, having just said that the *sine qua non* test could be overly inclusive in this context, it could actually be under-inclusive also. That is, the *sine qua non* test could be *under*-inclusive if it required that the subsidy be the only cause of the adverse effects to an industry. Indeed, the AB said in *US—Upland Cotton (Article 21.5—Brazil)* that the *sine qua non* text could be 'too rigorous' in this context by requiring that the

[126] See, for example, AB, *EC and certain member States—Large Civil Aircraft* (n 39) [1233].
[127] AB, *US—Upland Cotton (Article 21.5—Brazil)* (n 25) [374].
[128] (n 39) [1233].
[129] See Chapter 1, Section 1.2.1.

subsidy alone be responsible for the adverse effects,[130] rather than attributing partial responsibility to other known factors. Again, the under-inclusiveness of the *sine qua non* test is listed as a possible criticism of the test in Chapter 1 of this book.[131]

A third difficulty with the *sine qua non* test may be seen in a remark made by the AB in *EC and certain member States—Large Civil Aircraft*. In that case, the AB commented that:

> The use of a counterfactual analysis provides an adjudicator with a useful analytical framework to isolate and properly identify the effects of the challenged subsidies. In general terms, the counterfactual analysis entails comparing the actual market situation that is before the adjudicator with the market situation that would have existed in the absence of the challenged subsidies. This requires the adjudicator to undertake a modelling exercise as to what the market would look like in the absence of the subsidies.[132]

Whilst the AB does not raise this feature in a critical way, it is suggested that undertaking a 'modelling exercise' raises the same difficulty that has been seen in other contexts throughout this book – namely, the 'hypothetical world problem'.[133] That is, whilst the AB in *EC and certain member States—Large Civil Aircraft* said that the use of the *sine qua non* test in this context 'requires the adjudicator to undertake a modelling exercise as to what the market would look like in the absence of the subsidies',[134] it did not provide any clear sense of the way in which such a 'modelling exercise' should be performed. Even within the same case, the difficulty of creating these models is made clear, as the AB reviews four possible scenarios that the Panel had considered as to what the LCA industry would have looked like in the absence of the challenged subsidies.[135] The fact that there are four possible hypothetical scenarios underlines the degree to which the position of the LCA industry in the absence of the challenged subsidies is unknowable. Most of the subsidies only provide one hypothetical world as an alternative to the actual world – but, in fact, this world is as unknowable as each of the four hypothetical worlds in the *EC and certain member States—Large Civil Aircraft* case. It

130 AB, *US—Upland Cotton (Article 21.5—Brazil)* (n 25) [374].
131 See Chapter 1, Section 1.2.1.
132 AB, *EC and Certain member States—Large Civil Aircraft* (n 39) [1110].
133 For an explanation of the hypothetical world problem, see Chapter 1, Section 1.2.1.
134 ibid.
135 ibid [1261].

is important to emphasise that the position of an industry in the absence of subsidies is, in fact, unknowable with any precision. Therefore, the hypothetical world with which the actual world is compared is, in fact, nothing more than a 'guesstimate'.

Finally, it is argued that the *sine qua non* test is rendered otiose where a proper non-attribution analysis is conducted. That is, the very raison d'être of a non-attribution analysis in this context is to consider the interaction between subsidies and other known factors and to assess whether the market phenomenon is actually the result of other known factors, rather than a subsidy. The *sine qua non* test is unable to accommodate any interactions between subsidies and other known factors. Indeed, the incompatibility between the *sine qua non* test and a non-attribution analysis can be seen in the jurisprudence. For example, in *Korea—Commercial Vessels*, after having undertaken a *sine qua non* test to determine whether subsidies had caused price suppression or price depression under Article 6.3(c), the Panel then turned to perform a non-attribution analysis. The Panel found that it would 'bear in mind the need to take into account the effects of identified factors other than the subsidies, to determine whether such factors would attenuate any affirmative causal link that we may find, or render insignificant any price suppression or price depression effect of the subsidy that we may find'.[136] It is suggested that, not only is this a very methodologically questionable approach to conducting the non-attribution analysis, but it is also at odds with subsequent jurisprudence. That is, the AB remarked five years after the *Korea—Commercial Vessels* decision that it is not sufficient for a Panel simply to say that it had taken into account potentially mitigating factors in its causation analysis.[137] The implication of this is that the non-attribution analysis must be more rigorous than simply 'bear[ing] in mind' other known factors. Instead, it would seem that a fuller inquiry must be had as to the nature of the potentially mitigating factors and how they interact with the subsidy or subsidies.

Use of the *sine qua non* test becomes even more illogical where a fact-finder uses the Tripartite Non-attribution/Causal Link Analysis. This is because, as has been seen earlier, under the Tripartite Non-attribution/ Causal Link Analysis, only those subsidies and other known factors that have passed the threshold at the Qualification Analysis stage will qualify for the causal link analysis in the third step. The very fact that the

[136] Panel, *Korea—Commercial Vessels* (n 2) [7.618].

[137] AB, *US—Large Civil Aircraft (2nd complaint)* (n 37) [1206].

subsidies and other known factors have passed the Qualification Analysis stage means that they *must* be necessary. Accordingly, use of the *sine qua non* test – which only contains a necessity criterion – becomes redundant, as every single subsidy and other known factor that is interrogated at that stage must, ipso facto, pass the *sine qua non* test.

Given these fundamental drawbacks to the use of the *sine qua non* test, some of which have even been acknowledged by the AB, it is suggested that an alternative causal test should be used. Steinberg and Josling put forward regression analysis of the subsidy and trade data as well as simulation of the effect of subsidies by models as the best methods for finding causation between subsidies and the market phenomenon.[138] Steinberg and Josling, writing their article in 2003, were not able to take account of the fact that the subsequent jurisprudence would require that a non-attribution analysis be performed alongside the causal link analysis. Accordingly, the difficulty with their regression analysis and their proposal to simulate the effects of subsidies through the use of models is that it assumes that subsidies are responsible for the market phenomenon, without allowing for a non-attribution analysis.

It is contended, not only that the weak necessity/strong sufficiency test provides a viable alternative to the *sine qua non* test and the econometric models proposed by Steinberg and Josling, but also that the Panels and the AB have unwittingly been using an implied version of a weak necessity/strong sufficiency test in their use of aggregation and cumulation analyses already. That is, it is suggested that the aggregation and cumulation models that involve grouping subsidies and their effects together must actually implicitly rely on a weak necessity/strong sufficiency model of causation. The fact that the Panels and AB have already developed some kind of variant of the weak necessity/strong sufficiency model is strongly suggestive of its suitability in this context.

Turning first to the aggregation model, it is worth recalling that the aggregation model groups together subsidies that collectively produce the same effect. It is implicit in the aggregation model that each subsidy is a necessary element of a sufficient set to produce the relevant effect. This can be seen diagrammatically in Figure 3.2. Moreover, the finding of serious prejudice can only take place where the sub-effect is then combined with other sub-effects that are collectively sufficient to reach the

[138] See generally, Richard H Steinberg and Timothy E Josling, 'When the Peace Ends: The Vulnerability of EC and US Agricultural Subsidies to WTO Legal Challenge' (2003) 6(2) JIEL 369.

threshold of serious prejudice. In sum, there are two weak necessity/strong sufficiency tests implied in the aggregation model. Again, this idea can be seen diagrammatically in Figure 3.2.

Conversely, turning to the cumulation model, it may be recalled that the cumulation model separates out the diverse sub-effects of the one subsidy. Once the effects have been identified and separated, a weak necessity/strong sufficiency test is impliedly used in order to determine whether the effects might collectively be sufficient to result in a finding of serious prejudice. This can be seen diagrammatically in Figure 3.3. In sum, the aggregation and cumulation models are premised on the idea that the adverse effect would not have been identified except by grouping together a number of subsidies that would otherwise be independently insufficient to cause the adverse effect. This is confirmed by a statement made by the AB in *US—Large Civil Aircraft (2nd complaint)*, where the AB said that there is a risk that, by unduly separating each adverse effect of a subsidy, a Panel will find that 'no subsidy is a substantial cause of the relevant adverse effects'.[139]

Even where the methods of aggregation and cumulation are not used, a weak necessity/strong sufficiency test should still be used to make out a causal link between subsidies and serious prejudice. This is because the ultimate question should be whether those factors (subsidies and other known factors) that have qualified for the causal link stage are sufficient to reach the causal threshold of 'genuine and substantial relationship of cause and effect'. If the Tripartite Non-attribution/Causal Link Analysis is not used, then a Panel will need to adjudicate whether subsidies and/or other known factors were sufficient to have caused injury based on non-quantitative features. It is unclear how this might be done in any meaningful way.

It is instead suggested that the Tripartite Non-attribution/Causal Link Analysis offers an alternative approach to making a determination as to the existence of a causal link, as it involves making a quantitative assessment of the relative contributions of the subsidies vis-à-vis the other known factors. Once this is performed, only those factors that pass above the threshold can qualify for the causal link stage. Accordingly, at the causal link step, it is simply the role of the fact-finder to look at each of the factors that have qualified for the causal link stage and ask whether each is necessary to a set of factors that is collectively sufficient to cause the market phenomenon (and serious prejudice, in turn).

139 AB, *US—Large Civil Aircraft (2nd complaint)* (n 37) [1284].

To illustrate by returning to the case study of the cotton industry, at the third stage of the Tripartite Non-attribution/Causal Link Analysis, the fact-finder would group together all of the sub-effects that were sufficiently attributable to subsidies that they passed the Qualification Analysis. So, turning to Figure 3.1, if the threshold were 90 per cent, a fact-finder would include Sub-Effect B in the causal link analysis. The fact-finder would then use the weak necessity/strong sufficiency test to determine whether the sub-effects, once aggregated, were sufficiently significant to amount to a 'genuine and substantial relationship of cause and effect' between the subsidies and the market phenomenon in Article 6.3 and the concomitant serious prejudice.

The meaning of a 'genuine and substantial relationship of cause and effect' is not entirely clear. In Chapter 2, the AB's discussion of the term in *US—Large Civil Aircraft (2nd complaint)*[140] was extracted. Whilst the quote will not be set out in full here again, it is worth recalling that the AB in that case said that:

> The subsidy at issue may be found to exhibit the requisite causal link notwithstanding the existence of other causes that contribute to producing the relevant market phenomena if, having given proper consideration to all other relevant contributing factors and their effects, the Panel is satisfied that the contribution of the subsidy has been demonstrated to rise to that of a genuine and substantial cause.[141]

The extract is useful to the extent that it confirms that the multi-factorial approach is to be used. In terms of the meaning of the actual causal standard of 'genuine and substantial relationship of cause and effect', however, the way this is defined in the extract is almost tautological. The AB's statement in *US—Tyres (China)* is somewhat more helpful, in the sense that it said that the term 'genuine and substantial relationship of cause and effect' 'implies a higher degree of causality than subject imports being merely "a cause" of the requisite level of injury to the domestic industry'.[142] With this guidance in view, a fact-finder would determine whether the sub-effects, once aggregated, were sufficiently significant to amount to a 'genuine and substantial relationship of cause and effect' between the subsidies and the market phenomenon in Article 6.3 and the serious prejudice.

140 ibid [914] (emphasis original; footnotes omitted).

141 ibid (emphasis original; footnotes omitted).

142 AB, *US—Tyres (China)* (n 38) [181].

3.7 Conclusion

A finding of serious prejudice under Article 6.3 of the SCM Agreement has some similarities with an injury determination under the trade remedy agreements. Most obviously, both a serious prejudice finding and a finding of injury under the trade remedy agreements require non-attribution and causal link analyses to be performed. As was seen in Chapter 2, the non-attribution and causal link analyses are particularly difficult because they require a fact-finder to determine which factors are causative at the same time that they require a fact-finder to exclude non-causative factors. Moreover, the causal standard required to find serious prejudice is the same as under the trade remedy agreements – namely, a 'genuine and substantial relationship of cause and effect'.[143] The text of Article 6.3, however, provides far less detail as to how the non-attribution and causal link analyses should be performed than the text of the trade remedy agreements concerned with injury. This lack of detail in the text of Article 6.3 has given the Panel and the AB an even greater number of interpretative choices than in respect of the injury provisions in the trade remedy agreements.

One such interpretative choice is whether the causal relationship between the subsidy/ies and the market phenomenon ought to be drawn in one step (the unitary approach) or two steps (the bifurcated approach). Whilst the AB has indicated that the unitary approach is the preferred approach and that it has 'a sound conceptual foundation',[144] this chapter has argued in favour of the bifurcated approach instead. This is because the bifurcated approach supports a more coherent view of causation. It is also the only approach that would allow for a genuine non-attribution analysis to be conducted. A second interpretive choice that has dominated this chapter is the method of conducting a non-attribution analysis. It has been seen that the Panels and AB are yet to develop a coherent and consistent methodology for separating subsidies from other known factors. Indeed, it has been seen that some of the jurisprudence has used the 'breaking the causal link' approach, which does not truly interrogate the interaction between subsidies and other known factors. This chapter has argued that the Tripartite Non-attribution/Causal Link Analysis offers an alternative means for performing the required non-attribution and causal link analyses. Finally, another

[143] AB, *US—Upland Cotton* (n 7) [438], quoting AB, *US—Wheat Gluten* (n 36) [69].
[144] AB, *US—Upland Cotton (Article 21.5—Brazil)* (n 25) [354].

interpretive choice with which the jurisprudence must grapple relates to the causation test for determining the causal link between subsidies and the market phenomenon and the resulting serious prejudice. It has been seen that the jurisprudence has overwhelmingly preferred a counterfactual analysis for determining the causal link. This chapter has contended, however, that a weak necessity/strong sufficiency test is superior in this context. Moreover, those cases that use cumulation and aggregation to amass subsidies or their sub-effects already unwittingly rely on an implicit weak necessity/strong sufficiency test, which affirms its suitability here.

Finally, it is important to consider the policy implications of performing a genuine non-attribution analysis in the context of a serious prejudice analysis. The fact that the Tripartite Non-attribution/Causal Link Analysis provides a way of performing a genuine non-attribution analysis means that those sub-effects that were more the result of other known factors than subsidies will not falsely be attributed with causal responsibility. As a result, this genuine non-attribution analysis will mean that less sub-effects will go on to be considered at the causal link stage as compared to a tokenistic non-attribution analysis. If there are fewer sub-effects under consideration at the causal link stage of the analysis, it follows that it will be more difficult to draw a causal link between a subsidy/subsidies and the market phenomenon (and ensuing serious prejudice finding). From a policy perspective, it follows, in turn, that a genuine non-attribution analysis, such as that which the Tripartite Non-attribution/Causal Link Analysis affords, means that a serious prejudice determination will be more difficult to make out than if a tokenistic form of non-attribution is performed. Reverting to the cotton case study, a genuine non-attribution analysis will mean that Ruritania is less likely to be able to demonstrate that Laurania's subsidies are actionable. This means, in turn, that if Ruritania is less likely to find Laurania's subsidies are actionable, then Ruritania is also less likely to be able legally to bring countervailing duties against Laurania. From an economic perspective, some have argued that countervailing duties do 'more harm than good' and that global welfare would be improved if countervailing duties were reduced in number or even eliminated.[145] In this sense, there is an argument that the genuine non-attribution analysis that the Tripartite

[145] See generally Alan O Sykes, 'The Economics of WTO Rules on Subsidies and Countervailing Measures' (2003) University of Chicago John M Olin Law and Economics Working Paper No 186, 1.

Non-attribution/Causal Link Analysis is actually more in line with upholding global welfare than the current approach in the jurisprudence.

At the heart of each of the interpretive choices for which this chapter has advocated is an insistence on thinking through the consequences of having a genuine non-attribution analysis. That is, whilst the jurisprudence has consistently insisted that a non-attribution analysis must be undertaken, it has been seen that some of its analytical approaches are fundamentally at odds with a thorough non-attribution analysis. First, its unitary approach, with its focus on the effects of subsidies alone, does not allow for a true non-attribution analysis because the unitary analysis does not give any scope for the role of other known factors. Second, the 'breaking the causal link' approach, which has been used in some of the jurisprudence, does not allow for a non-attribution analysis that interrogates the interaction between subsidies and other known factors.[146] Moreover, in respect of the causal link analysis, it was seen earlier that the use of a counterfactual test to determine the causal link between a subsidy/ies and a market phenomenon actually makes no sense where a genuine non-attribution analysis has been undertaken. This is because if a true non-attribution analysis is conducted, all factors that have not been excluded by such an analysis would, ipso facto, be necessary. Accordingly, use of a causal test that relies on a necessity criterion is redundant.

Finally, the processes of cumulation and aggregation, as described by the AB, involve leaping straight from pooling subsidies or their effects together to then making a determination of serious prejudice. Yet again, such a tendency provides no scope for interrogating the role that may have been played by other known factors in bringing about serious prejudice to an industry. The overriding contribution of this chapter to the determination of causation with respect to serious prejudice, then, is to put forward a means by which a true non-attribution analysis might be undertaken and to argue in favour of those interpretive choices that must logically follow from it.

146 For a discussion of the importance of considering the interaction between injury and other known factors in the trade remedies context, see Chapter 2, Section 2.6.2.

4

Regulating for Non-trade Purposes

4.1 Introduction

The ability of Members to regulate for non-trade purposes is one of the most important issues in WTO law. Indeed, the importance of regulating for non-trade purposes is reflected in conditional exceptions to the disciplines of WTO law. These exceptions include: Article XX of the *General Agreement on Tariffs and Trade* (GATT 1994), Article XIV of the *General Agreement on Trade in Services* (GATS) (collectively, 'the General Exceptions') and Article 2.2 of the *Agreement on Technical Barriers to Trade* (TBT Agreement). Whilst Article 2.2 of the TBT Agreement is not as detailed as the General Exceptions, the criteria for the application of technical regulations under Article 2.2 is very similar to the General Exceptions.[1] Moreover, the sixth recital to the preamble of the TBT Agreement provides that a Member's right to regulate for non-trade purposes should not be constrained. This right, however, is qualified by the idea that technical measures taken must be necessary to fulfil certain legitimate policy objectives, and must not be applied in a manner that would constitute a means of arbitrary or unjustifiable discrimination or a disguised restriction on international trade, and must otherwise be in accordance with the provisions of the Agreement.[2]

Turning to the General Exceptions first, in order to avail itself of an exception, a Member must satisfy two analytical limbs – namely, that: (1) its measure may be prima facie exempted under one or more of the subparagraphs of the General Exceptions; and (2) the measure also fulfils the requirements of the introductory clause or 'chapeau' of the General

[1] WTO, *European Communities: Measures Affecting Asbestos and Asbestos Containing Products—Report of the Panel* (18 September 2000) WT/DS135/R (Panel, *EC—Asbestos*) [8.55].

[2] WTO, *European Communities: Measures Prohibiting the Importation and Marketing of Seal Products—Report of the Appellate Body* (22 May 2014) WT/DS400/AB/R; WT/DS401/AB/R (AB, *EC—Seal Products*) [5.124].

Exceptions.[3] This second analytical limb is beyond the scope of this chapter. The rationale underlying the General Exceptions is that the importance of the policy objectives set out in those provisions outweighs the importance of the trade values embedded in the disciplines of the GATT 1994 and the GATS.[4] The AB must consider a number of factors when determining whether a measure satisfies the first analytical limb. One of the most critical of these is the level of contribution that a measure must make to the realisation of its intended policy objective.[5] This chapter is principally concerned with the way in which a fact-finder can demonstrate that a measure made a causal contribution to a policy objective.

Similarly, Article 2.2 of the TBT Agreement provides that 'a technical regulation must: (1) pursue a "legitimate objective"; and (2) not be more trade-restrictive than "necessary" to fulfil that legitimate objective (taking

[3] The idea of approaching the analysis of the General Exceptions in this two-tiered manner has been called into question by Lorand Bartels, 'The Chapeau of the General Exceptions in the WTO GATT and GATS Agreements: A Reconstruction' (2015) 109(1) AJIL 95. A discussion of this approach is beyond the scope of this chapter.

[4] See WTO, *United States: Import Prohibition of Certain Shrimp and Shrimp Products—Report of the Appellate Body* (12 October 1998) WT/DS58/AB/R (AB, *US—Shrimp*) [121].

[5] The level of contribution that a measure makes to the realisation of its intended policy objective is an important factor to consider in relation to seeking exemption under each of the subparagraphs of the General Exceptions. The AB in *Korea—Various Measures on Beef* held that a determination of whether a measure is 'necessary' for the purposes of the General Exceptions involves 'weighing and balancing' a series of factors, including: (1) the contribution of a measure to a policy objective; (2) the relative importance of the policy objective; and (3) the trade-restrictiveness of the challenged measure ('WAB test'): WTO, *Korea: Measures Affecting Imports of Fresh, Chilled and Frozen Beef—Report of the Appellate Body* (11 December 2000) WT/DS161/R; WT/DS169/R (AB, *Korea—Various Measures on Beef*) [162]–[164]; and WTO, *Colombia: Measures Relating to the Importation of Textiles, Apparel and Footwear—Report of the Appellate Body* (7 June 2016) WT/DS461/AB/R [5.71]–[5.73] and [5.77]. Moreover, the contribution of a measure towards realising a policy objective is also important in relation to Article XX(g), where measures must be 'primarily aimed at' or have a 'direct connection' with the policy objective: WTO, *United States: Standards for Reformulated and Conventional Gasoline—Report of the Panel* (29 January 1996) WT/DS2/R (Panel, *US—Gasoline*) [6.40]; WTO, *United States: Standards for Reformulated and Conventional Gasoline—Report of the Appellate Body* (29 April 1996) WT/DS2/AB/R (AB, *US—Gasoline*) p 19. Finally, in relation to Article XX(j), the same 'WAB test' required in relation to those subparagraphs containing the word 'necessary' must also be undertaken in relation to measures seeking exemption under Article XX(j): WTO, *India: Certain Measures Relating to Solar Cells and Solar Modules—Report of the Appellate Body* (24 February 2016) WT/DS456/R (AB, *India—Solar Cells*) [5.63]. It seems that the threshold for contribution must be higher under Article XX(j) than that which is expected under subparagraphs containing the word 'necessary': AB, *India—Solar Cells* (n 5) [5.62].

into account the risks non-fulfilment would create)'.[6] As under the General Exceptions, the second limb is beyond the scope of this chapter, and the focus of this chapter is instead on the way in which the jurisprudence has analysed the relationship between a technical regulation and a policy objective. To this end, 'a panel adjudicating a claim under Article 2.2 of the TBT Agreement must seek to ascertain to what degree, or if at all, the challenged technical regulation, as written and applied, actually contributes to the legitimate objective pursued by the Member'.[7]

In respect of both the General Exceptions and Article 2.2 of the TBT Agreement, then, this chapter is concerned with the concept of causation for its *explanatory* power – that is, to see if a measure contributed to the intended policy outcome. This use of causation is different to the attributive use discussed in Chapters 2, 3 and 5. It will be argued that the relationship between a measure and its intended policy objective is impliedly a causal relationship. Indeed, this idea has been put forward by a number of Members in the jurisprudence. Moreover, the Panel in *Dominican Republic—Import and Sale of Cigarettes*[8] and the Panel in *Colombia—Ports of Entry*[9] even referred to the link between a measure and its policy objective as a 'causal link'. Nonetheless, despite the Panel's apparent acknowledgement of the role of causation in this relationship, the Panel and AB have so far refused to follow up this insight with the use of causal tests that interrogate causation. Moreover, whilst the AB has said that both quantitative and non-quantitative factors might be used to assist with determining the causal contribution of a measure,[10] in reality,

[6] WTO, *United States: Measures Affecting the Production and Sale of Clove Cigarettes—Report of the Panel* (2 September 2011) WT/DS406/R (Panel, *US—Clove Cigarettes)* [7.333].

[7] WTO, *United States: Measures Concerning the Importation, Marketing and Sale of Tuna and Tuna Products—Report of the Appellate Body* (16 May 2012) WT/DS381/AB/R [317] (AB, *US—Tuna II (Mexico)*) (footnotes omitted).

[8] WTO, *Dominican Republic: Measures Affecting the Importation and Internal Sale of Cigarettes—Report of the Panel* (26 November 2004) WT/DS302/R (Panel, *Dominican Republic—Import and Sale of Cigarettes*) [7.226].

[9] WTO, *Colombia: Indicative Prices and Restrictions on Ports of Entry—Report of the Panel* (27 April 2009) WT/DS366/R (Panel, *Colombia—Ports of Entry*) [7.581].

[10] In the Article XX GATT context, see: AB, *EC—Seal Products* (n 2) [5.215]; and WTO, *Brazil: Measures Affecting Imports of Retreaded Tyres—Report of the Appellate Body* (3 December 2007) WT/DS332/AB/R (AB, *Brazil—Retreaded Tyres*) [146]. In the Article 2.2 TBT context, see WTO, *United States: Certain Country of Origin Labelling (COOL) Requirements—Recourse to Article 21.5 of the DSU by Canada and Mexico—Report of the Appellate Body* (29 May 2015) WT/DS384/AB/RW; WT/DS386/AB/RW [5.211] and [5.268]; WTO, *Australia: Certain Measures Concerning Trademarks, Geographical*

they have largely relied on non-quantitative evidence.[11] In the majority of cases, the Panel and AB have tended to analyse the properties of the measure itself in an attempt to infer causation from those properties. It is suggested that this approach fundamentally misunderstands the nature of causation. It will be seen that this methodology is even more questionable in cases where the effects of a measure will not manifest themselves until the future.

The contribution of this chapter, then, is to set out the implications that must logically follow from regarding the relationship between a measure and its policy objective as causal in the context of the General Exceptions and Article 2.2 of the TBT Agreement. To that end, it will be suggested that Panels and the AB must draw on real-world data detailing the effects of a measure, since causation cannot be determined in the absence of an analysis of the effects of a measure. In cases where the effects of a measure do not materialise until the future, this chapter will set out some quantitative approaches that might be used to predict future effects based on past data. To this extent, in this context causation is used for its *predictive* potential – namely, trying to infer the future contribution of a condition to a future state of affairs. Again, this differs from the attributive use of causation discussed in Chapters 2, 3 and 5. Where such data is collected, the effects may well be the result of a combination of the measure as well as other known factors. Accordingly, it is important that a non-attribution and causal link analysis is undertaken; and, to this end, the Tripartite Non-attribution/Causal Link Analysis may again be applied in this context.

Indications and Other Plain Packaging Requirements Applicable to Tobacco Products and Packaging—Report of the Panel (29 June 2020) WT/DS435/R (Panel, *Australia—Tobacco Plain Packaging (Honduras)*) [7.500] and [7.982].

11 Exceptions include: Panel, *Australia—Tobacco Plain Packaging (Honduras)* (n 10), for example, [7.958] and [7.963] and WTO, *Australia: Certain Measures Concerning Trademarks, Geographical Indications and Other Plain Packaging Requirements Applicable to Tobacco Products and Packaging—Report of the Appellate Body* (9 June 2020) WT/DS435/AB/R; WT/DS441/AB/R (AB, *Australia—Tobacco Plain Packaging (Honduras)*), for example, [6.361]. To a lesser extent, WTO, *European Communities: Measures Prohibiting the Importation and Marketing of Seal Products—Report of the Panel* (25 November 2013) WT/DS400/R; WT/DS401/R (Panel, *EC—Seal Products*) [7.456]–[7.457], though the limitations of the data were openly acknowledged.

4.2 Jurisprudence Concerning the Relationship between a Measure and Its Policy Objective under the General Exceptions and Article 2.2 of the TBT Agreement

4.2.1 The Relationship between a Measure and a Policy Objective as Causal in Nature

The relationship between a measure and its intended policy objective may not appear, at first sight, to be a causal relationship. Indeed, so far, it has not been expressly treated as such by a Panel or by the AB, in the sense that they have never interrogated the relationship using formal causal tests. Nonetheless, the idea that a measure must causally contribute to a policy objective may easily be implied.

Indeed, Korea raised the idea of a causal relationship between a measure and a policy objective in *Korea—Various Measures on Beef.*[12] Specifically, Korea argued that there was an 'uninterrupted causal link' between the separation of its sales outlets and the objective of complying with laws or regulations that are not inconsistent with the GATT 1994.[13] Neither the Panel in that case nor the AB, however, addressed Korea's causation argument. Nonetheless, two Panels have referred to the link between a measure and its policy objective as a 'causal link'. First, the Panel in *Colombia—Ports of Entry*, in relation to Article XX(d), referred to a causal link between a measure and a policy objective, opining that '[t]he Panel therefore finds that there is no correlation, much less causal link, demonstrated between implicit prices and the ports of entry measure'.[14] Similarly, the Panel in *Dominican Republic—Import and Sale of Cigarettes* said:

> Even assuming *arguendo* that Exhibit DR-8 contains evidence that forgery of tax stamps may occur, the Panel finds no supporting evidence in Exhibits DR-8 and DR-29 to the Dominican Republic's assertion that there is a causal link between allowing stamps to be affixed abroad and the forgery of tax stamps. The fact that two events may occur simultaneously (affixation of tax stamps and forgery of tax stamps) does not necessarily imply that those two events are correlated, much less that they are causally linked.[15]

[12] WTO, *Korea: Measures Affecting Imports of Fresh, Chilled and Frozen Beef—Report of the Panel* (31 July 2000) WT/DS161/R; WT/DS169/R (Panel, *Korea—Various Measures on Beef*) [254].

[13] ibid.

[14] Panel, *Colombia—Ports of Entry* (n 9) [7.581].

[15] Panel, *Dominican Republic—Import and Sale of Cigarettes* (n 8) [7.226].

Moreover, it is notable that the words 'link',[16] 'connection',[17] 'nexus'[18] and 'relationship'[19] continually recur in the jurisprudence when describing the association between a measure and its intended policy objective for the purposes of the General Exceptions. These words have not arisen in the jurisprudence concerning Article 2.2 of the TBT Agreement, though the word 'correlation' has been used.[20] Nonetheless, the Panels in *US—Clove Cigarettes* and *US—COOL* have held that analysing the relationship between the measure at issue and the objective pursued is just as relevant an approach for Article 2.2 of the TBT Agreement as Article XX of the GATT 1994.[21] Moreover, the Panel in *EC—Seal Products* found that there was a need to interpret Article XX of the GATT 1994 and Article 2.2 of the TBT Agreement in 'a consistent and harmonious manner'.[22] Accordingly, it is contended that the conception

[16] Panel, *US—Gasoline* (n 5) [6.39]; WTO, *Brazil: Measures Affecting Imports of Retreaded Tyres—Report of the Panel* (12 June 2007) WT/DS332/R (Panel, *Brazil—Retreaded Tyres*) [7.45] and [7.132]; Panel, *EC—Seal Products* (n 11) [7.485]; WTO, *China: Measures Affecting Trading Rights and Distribution Services for Certain Publications and Audiovisual Entertainment Products—Report of the Appellate Body* (21 December 2009) WT/DS363/AB/R (AB, *China—Publications and Audiovisual Products*) [233]; WTO, *China: Measures Related to the Exportation of Rare Earths, Tungsten, and Molybdenum—Report of the Appellate Body* (7 August 2014) WT/DS/AB431/AB/R; WT/DS/432/AB/R; WT/DS433/AB/R (AB, *China—Rare Earths*) [7.290].

[17] AB, *US—Gasoline* (n 5) [17]–[18].

[18] AB, *US—Shrimp* (n 4) [133]; WTO, *United States: Measures Affecting the Cross-Border Supply of Gambling and Betting Services—Report of the Appellate Body* (7 April 2005) WT/DS285/AB/R (AB, *US—Gambling*) [292] cited with approval in AB, *EC—Seal Products* (n 2) [5.169]; WTO, *China: Measures Affecting Trading Rights and Distribution Services for Certain Publications and Audiovisual Entertainment Products—Report of the Panel* (12 August 2009) WT/DS363/R (Panel, *China—Publications and Audiovisual Products*) [4.319]; AB, *China—Rare Earths* (n 16) [5.112] and WTO, *United States: Tariff Measures on Certain Goods from China—Report of the Panel* (Panel, *US—Tariff Measures*) (15 September 2020) WT/DS543/R [7.177]–[7.179], [7.185] and [7.124].

[19] AB, *US—Gasoline* (n 5) [17]–[19]; WTO, *United States: Import Prohibition of Certain Shrimp and Shrimp Products—Report of the Panel* (15 May 1998) WT/DS58/R [7.119]; Panel, *Brazil—Retreaded Tyres* (n 16) [7.119]; AB, *US—Shrimp* (n 4) [136]; WTO, *United States: Measures Concerning the Importation, Marketing and Sale of Tuna and Tuna Products—Recourse to Arbitration by United States under Article 21.5 of the DSU and Second Recourse to Article 21.5 of the DSU by Mexico—Decision by Arbitrations* (14 December 2018) WT/DS381/AB/RW/USA; WT/DS381/AB/RW2 [6.287] and [6.289] and Panel, *US—Tariff Measures* (n 18) [7.214] and [7.222].

[20] Panel, *Australia—Tobacco Plain Packaging (Honduras)* (n 10) [7.1034].

[21] Panel, *US—Clove Cigarettes* (n 6) [7.379] and WTO, *United States: Certain Country of Origin Labelling (COOL) Requirements—Report of the Panel* (18 November 2011) WT/DS384/R; WT/DS386/R (Panel, *US—COOL*) [7.693].

[22] Panel, *EC—Seal Products* (n 11) [7.634].

of the association between a measure and its contribution to a policy objective as a causal relationship is just as relevant for Article 2.2 of the TBT Agreement as it is for the General Exceptions.

In sum, on the one hand, there is evidence that the Panels and the AB acknowledge that the relationship between a measure and a policy objective is a causal one. On the other hand, they have so far failed to follow up this insight by interrogating the relationship using formal causal tests. Accordingly, there is a disconnect between the classification of the relationship as causal and the methods by which they have interrogated the nature of that relationship. Indeed, instead of using traditional causal tests, the Panels and the AB have expressly resisted laying down a methodology to assess the contribution of a measure to its policy objective.[23] The AB has held on several occasions that a determination as to the effectiveness of a measure may be made using both 'qualitative' and quantitative evidence.[24] To date, all of the relevant Panels and the AB have relied on so-called qualitative evidence in making the determination. It is difficult to know, in practice, what the AB means by 'qualitative' evidence – except that it is non-quantitative. In the General Exceptions context, a number of cases have assessed the contribution of a measure to the policy objective by examining the 'design and structure' of the measure.[25] Similarly, in the context of Article 2.2 of the TBT Agreement, the AB has said that the degree to which a technical measure contributes to a particular objective 'may be discerned from the design, structure, and operation of the technical regulation, as well as from evidence relating to the application of the measure'.[26]

It is by no means clear what the 'design and structure' of a measure means. For example, it may be helpful to take the analogy of subsidies or trade remedies. It would be nonsensical to attempt to interrogate the causal contribution of a subsidy or import to causing serious prejudice or injuring another Member's industry simply by looking at the 'design and structure' of that particular subsidy or import, with no regard to its

[23] AB, *Brazil—Retreaded Tyres* (n 10) [145]. This was recalled with approval by the AB in *EC—Seal Products* (n 2) [5.210].

[24] AB, *Brazil—Retreaded Tyres* (n 10) [146]; AB, *EC—Seal Products* (n 2) [5.215].

[25] AB, *US—Shrimp* (n 4) [138]; WTO, *Argentina: Measures Affecting the Export of Bovine Hides and the Import of Finished Leather—Report of the Panel* (19 December 2000) WT/DS155/R [11.303].

[26] AB, *US—Tuna II (Mexico)* (n 7) [317]. See also WTO, *United States: Certain Country of Origin Labelling (COOL) Requirements—Report of the Appellate Body* (29 June 2012) WT/DS384/AB/R; WT/DS386/AB/R (AB, *US—COOL*) [373] and [461].

effects. This is not to say that qualitative or non-quantitative features cannot be used effectively to interrogate causation; but rather, that those features would need to relate to the qualities of necessity or sufficiency. Instead, the 'design and structure' test requires that a fact-finder interrogate causation by looking at the features of the alleged *cause*, instead of looking at the features of the *causal link*. In short, the 'design and structure' test aims to determine causation simply by looking at the properties of C, with no regard to the nature of E.

The Assumption That an Effect May Be Knowable A Priori

The 'design and structure' test, applied in both the context of the General Exceptions as well as Article 2.2 of the TBT Agreement, involves the same logical fallacy that was discussed in Chapter 3. That is, it involves falsely assuming that an effect may be knowable a priori simply by examining the nature of its cause. As was observed in Chapter 3, a cause and an effect are separate phenomena, and the former in and of itself can never be used to predict the latter. Chapter 3 excerpted an extended quotation from David Hume to the effect that '[t]he mind can never possibly find the effect in the supposed cause [. . .]'.[27] Hume's critique of deriving an effect simply by examining the cause is just as applicable here. In short, a Panel or the AB are no more capable of deriving a causal link between a measure and its policy objective through the process of examining the 'design and structure' of a measure than Hume was of predicting the motion of the second billiard-ball simply by examining the movement of the first. It surely follows from this that the 'design and structure' test, or indeed any other non-quantitative test that involves looking at the nature of the measure alone, cannot be relied upon accurately to interrogate causation and should be abandoned.

Indeed, the impossibility of accurately predicting the effect of a measure on a policy objective without actually quantifying its effects is reflected in the non-quantitative descriptors that Panels and the AB have given to describe the level of contribution of a measure to a policy objective. They have variously held that a measure: made 'a material contribution',[28]

[27] David Hume, *An Enquiry Concerning Human Understanding* (LA Selby-Bigge ed, 3rd edn, OUP 1975) s IV, pt I, 29 quoted in Chapter 3, Section 3.3.

[28] Panel, *China—Publications and Audiovisual Products* (n 18) [7.836]; AB, *Brazil—Retreaded Tyres* (n 10) [210].

'makes "some contribution",[29] 'contributed to a certain extent',[30] contributed 'at least to some extent',[31] or was 'capable of making a contribution'.[32] It is difficult to know whether the discrepancy between these labels is significant, and if so, in what way. Indeed, even the AB in *EC—Seal Products* expressed doubt as to whether the slightly different qualitative descriptions of the contribution of a measure to its policy objective were significant.[33] Specifically, the Panel in *EC—Seal Products* found that the measure contributed to the policy objective under Article XX(a) of the GATT 1994 'to a certain extent',[34] whilst it simply said that the same measure 'makes a contribution' under Article 2.2 of the TBT Agreement.[35] The AB in *EC—Seal Products* said '[a]lthough it is not apparent why the Panel framed its conclusion differently in these two sections, we do not see any appreciable difference between a finding that a measure "makes a contribution" and a finding that it "contributes to a certain extent"'.[36] In sum, it would appear that the variation between the ways in which the contribution of a measure to a policy objective are described is not significant.

Another source of confusion in the jurisprudence is whether the degree of contribution to a policy objective is different with regard to the General Exceptions vis-à-vis Article 2.2 of the TBT Agreement. The Panel in *EC—Seal Products* noted at footnote 977 that the AB in *US—Tuna II (Mexico)* and *US—COOL* did not consider that a certain threshold degree of contribution exists for the purposes of Article 2.2 of the TBT Agreement.[37] Specifically, the Panel in *EC—Seal Products* noted that the AB in *US—Tuna II (Mexico)* and *US—COOL* assessed 'the "degree of contribution" by a measure without necessarily determining whether the actual degree of contribution by the measure reaches a certain minimum threshold such as a material or significant contribution'.[38] To put it

29 WTO, *United States: Certain Country of Origin Labelling (COOL) Requirements—Recourse to Article 21.5 of the DSU by Canada and Mexico—Report of the Panel* (20 October 2014) WT/DS384/RW; WT/DS386/RW [7.352].

30 Panel, *EC—Seal Products* (n 11) [7.638].

31 WTO, *United States: Measures Affecting the Cross-Border Supply of Gambling and Betting Services—Report of the Panel* (10 November 2004) WT/DS285/R [6.494].

32 Panel, *Brazil—Retreaded Tyres* (n 16) [7.148].

33 AB, *EC—Seal Products* (n 2) [5.227].

34 Panel, *EC—Seal Products* (n 11) [7.638].

35 ibid [7.459].

36 AB, *EC—Seal Products* (n 2) [5.227].

37 Panel, *EC—Seal Products* (n 11) n 977.

38 ibid.

differently, the AB simply said that the measure made a contribution within the meaning of Article 2.2 of the TBT Agreement, but did not indicate the *extent* of that contribution. This insight might, in fact, explain the discrepancy in the descriptors of contribution to Article XX(a) of the GATT 1994 vis-à-vis Article 2.2 of the TBT Agreement applied by the *EC—Seal Products* Panel discussed in the previous paragraph. That is, it was just seen that the Panel in *EC—Seal Products* found that the measure contributed to the policy objective under Article XX(a) of the GATT 1994 'to a certain extent',[39] whilst it simply said that the same measure 'makes a contribution' under Article 2.2 of the TBT Agreement.[40] Regardless, just as the AB in *EC—Seal Products* found no 'appreciable difference' between classifying a measure as making 'a contribution' vis-à-vis making a contribution 'to a certain extent', it is unclear that there is any practical difference between the descriptors, and if there is, how and where the line between the two ought to be drawn. Once again, using a quantitative approach in order to determine the causal contribution of a measure to a policy objective could help to remedy this confusion.

One of the implications of relying on vague, non-quantitative descriptors, instead of interrogating causation using quantitative tests, is that Members face a lack of legal certainty about the process by which their measure will be adjudicated by a future Panel or the AB. That is, because adjudicating the impact of a measure on a policy objective without actually quantifying its effects is inherently arbitrary, it follows that it is very difficult for Members to predict whether a measure will be found to contribute to a policy objective, and if so, by how much. In short, at the heart of the problem with the 'design and structure' test (and any other tests that focus solely on the nature of the measure alone) is a failure to quantify the effects of that measure.

Indeed, this idea has been raised before Panels and the AB on a number of occasions. First, in *US—Gasoline*, Venezuela argued that the baseline establishment rules that were relevant to that case must not only 'reflect a conservation purpose' but also be shown to have had 'some positive conservation effect'.[41] In other words, Venezuela was arguing that the effects of the measure ought to be quantified and the impact of

[39] ibid [7.638].

[40] ibid [7.459].

[41] Venezuela's Appellee's Submission, dated 18 March 1996; Venezuela's Statement at the Oral Hearing, dated 27 March 1996, quoted in AB, *US—Gasoline* (n 5) n 39.

the measure must be analysed in light of the quantified effects. The AB rejected Venezuela's argument as follows:

> We do not believe, finally, that the clause 'if made effective in conjunction with restrictions on domestic production or consumption' was intended to establish an empirical 'effects test' for the availability of the Article XX (g) exception. In the first place, the problem of determining causation, well-known in both domestic and international law, is always a difficult one. In the second place, in the field of conservation of exhaustible natural resources, a substantial period of time, perhaps years, may have to elapse before the effects attributable to implementation of a given measure may be observable. The legal characterization of such a measure is not reasonably made contingent upon occurrence of subsequent events. We are not, however, suggesting that consideration of the predictable effects of a measure is never relevant. In a particular case, should it become clear that realistically, a specific measure cannot in any possible situation have any positive effect on conservation goals, it would very probably be because that measure was not designed as a conservation regulation to begin with. In other words, it would not have been 'primarily aimed at' conservation of natural resources at all.[42]

In sum, the AB in *US—Gasoline* gives two reasons against quantifying effects: (1) that it is 'always [. . .] difficult'; and (2) that the effect of a measure on a policy objective may not be known until sometime later. These reasons will be addressed in Sections 4.2.2 and 4.2.3, respectively.

Before proceeding to address these two reasons, it is worth noting that the AB's response to Venezuela's causal argument in *US—Gasoline* did not put an end to the issue of whether the effects of a measure ought to be quantified. The idea was also put forward by the EC in *Brazil—Retreaded Tyres*,[43] which the Panel rejected.[44] More recently, China argued that demonstrating the nexus between a measure and Article XX(g) should not only involve an examination of the text, structure and design of a measure, but also the effects of a measure.[45] The Panel in *China—Rare Earths* found that Panels are not required to consider the effects of a measure but are not precluded from doing so.[46] In sum, the idea that the empirical effects of a measure ought to be interrogated and analysed was

[42] AB, *US—Gasoline* (n 5) p 21.
[43] Panel, *Brazil—Retreaded Tyres* (n 16) [7.116].
[44] ibid [7.118].
[45] China's appellant's submission, para 208, cited at AB, *China—Rare Earths* (n 16) [5.102].
[46] WTO, *China: Measures Related to the Exportation of Rare Earths, Tungsten, and Molybdenum—Report of the Panel* (26 March 2014) WT/DS431/R; WT/DS432/R; WT/DS433/R [5.113].

rejected outright by a Panel the first time, and permitted but not considered necessary on the second occasion. It is contended, however, (1) that the Panels are yet to give a truly compelling reason for refusing to quantify the effect of a measure on a policy objective; and (2) that a genuine interrogation of the impact of a measure on a policy objective is impossible without doing so.

The Importance of a Non-attribution Analysis

A second problem with the current approach in the jurisprudence is that it provides no scope for performing a non-attribution analysis. That is, the current 'design and structure' test or variations thereon not only assume that causation can be deduced from the nature of the measure, but also that there are no other factors that confound the causal link between a measure and a policy objective. This seems unrealistic given that there are potentially numerous other known factors that may have contributed to a particular policy outcome.

Indeed, the AB in *Brazil—Retreaded Tyres* recognised the difficulty associated with distinguishing the contribution of one measure from a multiplicity of interacting measures, particularly in the short-term, saying:

> We recognize that certain complex public health or environmental problems may be tackled only with a comprehensive policy comprising a multiplicity of interacting measures. In the short-term, it may prove difficult to isolate the contribution to public health or environmental objectives of one specific measure from those attributable to the other measures that are part of the same comprehensive policy. Moreover, the results obtained from certain actions – for instance, measures adopted in order to attenuate global warming and climate change, or certain preventive actions to reduce the incidence of diseases that may manifest themselves only after a certain period of time – can only be evaluated with the benefit of time.[47]

In a similar vein, the Panel in *EC—Seal Products* said, in reference to the EU Seal Regime, that:

> The entry into force of the EU Seal Regime may not be the only factor explaining a reduction in the number of seals hunted; other factors may also have come into play, including weather conditions that may have contributed to reducing the duration of the hunting season and the adoption of legislation on trade in seal products in other countries.[48]

[47] AB, *Brazil—Retreaded Tyres* (n 10) [151].

[48] Panel, *EC—Seal Products* (n 11) [7.458].

Finally, in the context of Article 2.2 of the TBT Agreement, the Panel in *Australia—Tobacco Plain Packaging (Honduras)* found that:

> All parties recognize the inherent difficulty, in assessing the impact of the [Tobacco Plain Packaging] measures since their entry into force, of isolating their effect from that of other factors contributing to the outcomes of interest, both proximal and more distal. In particular, the simultaneous application of enlarged [Graphic Health Warnings], which came into effect at the same time as the [Tobacco Plain Packaging] measures, complicates an assessment of the actual effect of the [Tobacco Plain Packaging] measures.[49]

This recurring concern in the jurisprudence about isolating the causal contribution of one measure vis-à-vis other known factors is justified and ought to be taken seriously by performing a non-attribution analysis before a fact-finder makes an assessment as to causation. Again, it is suggested that the Tripartite Non-attribution/Causal Link Analysis is one possible approach to conducting a non-attribution and causal link analysis. Before setting out how the Tripartite Non-attribution/Causal Link Analysis might operate in this context, this chapter will first turn to address the two reasons that the AB gave for rejecting an effects test in *US—Gasoline* - namely: (1) the difficulty of determining causation; and (2) the problem of predicting future effects.

4.2.2 The Difficulty of Determining a Causal Link

The first reason that the AB gave for refusing to treat the relationship between a measure and its effect on a policy objective as causal in nature is that it is difficult to determine causation. Indeed, to repeat the quote from David Hume with which this book opened, '[t]here is no question, which on account of its importance, as well as difficulty, has caus'd more disputes both among antient and modern philosophers, than this concerning the efficacy of causes, or that quality which makes them be follow'd by their effects'.[50] Nonetheless, the difficulty inherent in performing a causal analysis is a poor reason for avoiding it. It would not, for example, be acceptable for a Panel or the AB to refuse to engage in a causal analysis in the context of trade remedies or subsidies simply because doing so was too difficult. By the same logic, it is unacceptable

[49] Panel, *Australia—Tobacco Plain Packaging (Honduras)* (n 10) [7.980].

[50] David Hume, *A Treatise of Human Nature* (LA Selby-Bigge ed, 1789; revised by PH Nidditch, 2nd edn, OUP 1975) Bk I, pt III, s xiv, 156.

to refuse to engage in a causal analysis in the face of a textual agreement where the causal relationship between a measure and its policy objective is easily implied.

Perhaps the most obvious means of assessing causation is to use the non-quantitative tests of necessity and sufficiency. This would involve using either the *sine qua non* test or the weak necessity/strong sufficiency test to determine the causal link between the measure and a policy objective. It is suggested, however, that non-quantitative causal tests are inappropriate in this context for three reasons. First, the effect of a measure tends to involve very precise measurements, which could not be captured using non-quantitative tests (e.g., an effect might be that there was a 22.5 per cent reduction in the number of turtles killed in nets in the wider Caribbean/western Atlantic region since the introduction of the measure). Second and relatedly, using quantitative causal tests helps to elucidate the exact *degree* of contribution that a measure makes to a policy objective. This clarity assists, in turn, when determining whether the policy objective was sufficiently the product of a measure that the measure could be labelled as 'causal'. The third reason that non-quantitative causal tests are more suited here is that, as was seen earlier, determining causation in this context requires a non-attribution analysis. In particular, the effect of a measure on its policy objective must be distinguished from the effect of other known factors. Non-quantitative causal tests are unable to separate causal factors in this way, thereby making quantitative causal tests more appropriate in this context.

In order for non-quantitative causal tests to be used, it means that real-world data about the nature of the effect of a measure on a policy objective must be collected over a series of years before and after the introduction of the measure. This was done, for example, in the case of *EC—Seal Products*, where Members collected data in relation to the decline in the volume of seal skins hunted[51] and imported into the EU.[52] Similarly, in *Australia—Tobacco Plain Packaging (Honduras)*, Australia collected data regarding the effect of Tobacco Plain Packaging on positive public health outcomes.[53] It is suggested that collecting data in relation to the effects of a measure ought to be done in every case, since determining causation is meaningless without doing so. This might involve a government agency of the Member who introduced the measure collecting the data and

[51] Panel, *EC—Seal Products* (n 11) [7.457].
[52] ibid [7.456].
[53] See appendices A–E in Panel, *Australia—Tobacco Plain Packaging (Honduras)* (n 10).

including it as evidence, as was done in *EC—Seal Products*[54] and in *Australia—Tobacco Plain Packaging (Honduras)*, where data was provided in the form of appendices.[55] Once the raw data on the effects of a measure is collected, this is not sufficient on its own to show that a measure caused the impact on the policy objective. Before causation can be determined, a non-attribution analysis must first be undertaken. The process of performing a non-attribution as well as a causal link analysis will be set out in Sections 4.3 and 4.4.

4.2.3 Predicting the Future Effect of a Measure on a Policy Objective

The second reason that the AB gave for avoiding the performance of a causal analysis here is that it is difficult to estimate the future effect of a measure on a policy objective. Accordingly, a Panel or the AB would be forced to make an adjudication about the contribution of a measure to a policy objective without the effect having yet manifested. Whilst the Panel's second argument is superior to its first, in practice, there have already been a number of cases where Panels and the AB have been required to assess the likely effect of a measure on its policy objective anyway,[56] to which this section now turns.

First, in the context of Article XX(b) of the GATT 1994, the Panel in *Brazil—Retreaded Tyres* was forced to consider the question of future effects in significant depth. In particular, the Panel was required to determine whether Brazil's import ban on retreaded tyres would, in the future, be 'necessary' to achieve the policy objective set out in Article XX (b) of the GATT 1994. In order to answer this question, the Panel examined the so-called qualitative evidence regarding the measure, particularly the fact that retreaded tyres have a shorter lifespan than new tyres and will become waste sooner and, therefore, add to Brazil's volume of wasted tyres.[57] As a result of limiting their analysis to qualitative considerations alone, the EC argued that the Panel had only examined whether Brazil's import ban *could* make a contribution to the protection of human life or health, rather than having determined *actual*

[54] See ibid [7.456] and [7.457].

[55] See ibid.

[56] See, for example, Panel, *Brazil—Retreaded Tyres* (n 16) [7.127]–[7.130]; AB, *Brazil—Retreaded Tyres* (n 10) [151]–[155]; Panel, *EC—Seal Products* (n 11) [7.459]; AB, *EC—Seal Products* (n 2) [5.228]. Also, see generally, Panel, *US—Gasoline* (n 5); AB, *US—Gasoline* (n 5) and AB, *US—Shrimp* (n 4).

[57] Panel, *Brazil—Retreaded Tyres* (n 16) [7.127]–[7.130].

contribution.[58] Again the EC's objection here goes back ultimately to the fallacy of making a priori judgments that was observed earlier – namely, attempting to assess causation by examining the nature of the cause, with no regard to its effect.

The AB in *Brazil—Retreaded Tyres*, citing *EC—Asbestos*,[59] upheld the Panel's reasoning and defended the right of the Panel and the AB to rely on qualitative, rather than quantitative, evidence in determining the likely future contribution of a measure to a policy objective.[60] The AB further held that:

> The results obtained from certain actions – for instance, measures adopted in order to attenuate global warming and climate change, or certain preventive actions to reduce the incidence of diseases that may manifest themselves only after a certain period of time – can only be evaluated with the benefit of time. In order to justify an import ban under Article XX(b), a Panel must be satisfied that it brings about a material contribution to the achievement of its objective. Such a demonstration can of course be made by resorting to evidence or data, pertaining to the past or the present, that establish that the import ban at issue makes a material contribution to the protection of public health or environmental objectives pursued. This is not, however, the only type of demonstration that could establish such a contribution. Thus, a Panel might conclude that an import ban is necessary on the basis of a demonstration that the import ban at issue is apt to produce a material contribution to the achievement of its objective. This demonstration could consist of quantitative projections in the future, or qualitative reasoning based on a set of hypotheses that are tested and supported by sufficient evidence.[61]

In other words, when confronted with a situation in which the AB is not in a position to assess the contribution of a measure to its policy objective, the AB may assess future contribution based simply on projection. The AB's reasoning is that it is possible not only to adjudicate whether a causal link exists based simply on the qualities of the measure itself (with no analysis of its effects), but also whether a causal link exists based simply on the qualities of the measure where the effects have not yet even materialised. Reverting to Hume's analogy of billiard balls, this

58 European Communities' appellant's submission, para 166, cited in AB, *Brazil—Retreaded Tyres* (n 10) n 33.

59 WTO, *European Communities: Measures Affecting Asbestos and Asbestos-Containing Products—Report of the Appellate Body* (12 March 2001) WT/DS135/AB/R [167] (original emphasis; footnote omitted).

60 AB, *Brazil—Retreaded Tyres* (n 10) [146]–[147].

61 ibid [151] (footnotes omitted).

might be compared to determining that the first billiard ball caused the second billiard ball to strike a third billiard ball based simply on the movement of the first billiard ball alone. This legal reasoning is highly specious.

The issue of assessing the future contribution of a measure to a policy objective under Article XX(a) based on minimal data arose again before the Panel in *EC—Seal Products*. Although the Panel in *EC—Seal Products* was provided with data in relation to the actual operation of the measure, it found that the data was inconclusive.[62] Accordingly, the Panel refrained from making any 'concrete conclusions' from the data – though it did note briefly that the general trajectory appeared to demonstrate that seal product imports from the complainants into the EU market decreased significantly over the few years following the introduction of the measure.[63] Finding the quantitative data inadequate, the Panel drew on the AB decisions in *US—Tuna II (Mexico)*[64] and *US—COOL*[65] as support for the view that the degree of contribution of the measure to the fulfilment of the objective might be ascertained from examining 'the design, structure, and operation of the technical regulation, as well as evidence relating to the application of the measure'.[66] Accordingly, the Panel based its decision about the contribution of the measure to the policy objective based on these non-quantitative features.[67]

The complainants in *EC—Seal Products* contended that the Panel had failed to make 'clear and precise' findings in relation to the contribution of the measure to the objective and that such precision was necessary in order to establish a benchmark against which alternative measures might be compared.[68] The AB defended the reasoning of the Panel on the basis that there was 'limited and uneven information relating to the *actual* operation of the measure on the Panel record', including the actual impact of the measure on trade.[69] As such, the Panel had made clear that it was focusing on 'the design and expected operation of the measure' and that this focus has implications for the way the Panel framed its

62 Panel, *EC—Seal Products* (n 11) [7.456].
63 ibid.
64 AB, *US—Tuna II (Mexico)* (n 7) [317].
65 AB, *US—COOL* (n 26) [373].
66 AB, *US—Tuna II (Mexico)* (n 7) [317] quoted in Panel, *EC—Seal Products* (n 11) [7.441].
67 Panel, *EC—Seal Products* (n 11) [7.459].
68 Canada's appellant's submission, para 158; and Norway's appellant's submission, para 257, cited in AB, *EC—Seal Products* (n 2) n 1308.
69 AB, *EC—Seal Products* (n 2) [5.228] (emphasis original).

findings.[70] The AB recalled the guidance in *Brazil—Retreaded Tyres* that a Panel has some 'latitude' in determining the particular methodology for determining contribution, and that this methodology may be either qualitative or quantitative[71] depending on 'the nature, quantity, and quality of evidence existing at the time the analysis is made'.[72]

Additionally, the complainants argued that the Panel in *EC—Seal Products* was in error for assessing the contribution of the measure based on possibility, rather than actual contribution.[73] The AB further defended the Panel's approach with regard to other reasoning used by the AB in *Brazil—Retreaded Tyres*, holding that:

> In these disputes, the Panel faced significant limitations in examining aspects of the measure other than through its design, structure, and *expected* operation. Principally, the Panel recognized, correctly in our view, that there was limited and uneven information relating to the *actual* operation of the measure on the Panel record, in particular relating to the *actual* operation of the exceptions, and the *actual* impact the measure had on the EU seal product market. Given the particular nature of the measure at issue, and the specific circumstances of these disputes, it is not clear that the Panel could have done more.[74]

The AB concluded, '[w]e therefore do not see that a Panel falls into error by projecting what contribution will be brought about by the measure.'[75]

The question of the future contribution of a measure to a policy objective arose yet again in *Australia—Plain Packaging Tobacco (Honduras)*, which concerned, inter alia, Article 2.2 of the TBT Agreement. In that case, the Panel was required to decide whether Australia's Tobacco Plain Packaging (TPP) (the measure) could influence smoking behaviour, resulting in reduced initiation and relapse of smoking as well as increased cessation of smoking, thereby bringing about positive public health outcomes (the policy outcome).[76] In particular, the Panel had to determine whether the packaging and appearance of tobacco products had this policy outcome as a result of reducing the appeal of tobacco products, increasing the

[70] ibid [5.223].
[71] ibid [5.221].
[72] AB, *Brazil—Retreaded Tyres* (n 10) [145].
[73] Canada's appellant's submission, para 166; and Norway's appellant's submission, para 284, cited in AB, *EC—Seal Products* (n 2) n 1307.
[74] AB, *EC—Seal Products* (n 2) [5.228] (emphasis original; footnotes omitted).
[75] ibid [5.224].
[76] Panel, *Australia—Tobacco Plain Packaging (Honduras)* (n 10) [7.490].

effectiveness of Graphic Health Warnings and decreasing the ability of the pack to mislead consumers about the harmfulness of tobacco products.[77]

As in *EC—Seal Products*, the respondent (namely, Australia) presented quantitative evidence about the contribution of the measure to the policy objective. Specifically, Australia presented evidence in the appendices regarding: (A) Post-implementation evidence on non-behavioural outcomes of the TPP measures; (B) Evidence on quitting-related outcomes and other distal outcomes since the entry into force of the TPP measures; (C) Evidence on smoking prevalence following the entry into force of the TPP measures; (D) Evidence relating to tobacco product sales and consumption following the entry into force of the TPP measures; and (E) Post-implementation evidence on downward substitution in the cigarette market.

Whilst the Panel took account of Australia's quantitative evidence regarding the contribution of the measure to the policy objective, it did not regard it as conclusive on its own. Specifically, the Panel said that:

> The overall impact of the TPP measures is difficult to quantify in terms of the magnitude of changes in smoking behaviours attributable to the measures, on the basis of the evidence available to us. In particular, this impact, as described above, is difficult to isolate empirically, on the basis of the evidence before us, from other factors that also affect the evolution of smoking behaviours, including other tobacco control measures applied simultaneously with the TPP measures.[78]

In other words, the lack of a non-attribution analysis (discussed at Section 4.2.1) was significant for the Panel in deciding not to rely exclusively on Australia's quantitative evidence about the contribution of TPP to the policy objective. Additionally, the Panel took into account that the measure had only been in effect for a limited period of time, and therefore its full effects on the policy objective may not yet have fully manifested.[79]

Instead, the Panel first assessed the anticipated effect of the TPP measures, based on their design, structure and expected operation.[80] The Panel then went on to examine evidence relating to the actual effects of the TPP measures following their entry into force. In particular, the Panel assessed the contribution of the TPP measures on: (1) 'proximal' or

[77] ibid [7.490]–[7.491].
[78] ibid [7.1040].
[79] ibid [7.1044].
[80] ibid s [7.2.5.3.5].

'non-behavioural' outcomes (i.e., the appeal of packaging, the effectiveness of graphic health warnings, and the ability of packaging to mislead consumers);[81] (2) 'distal' or 'behavioural' outcomes (i.e., intention and behavioural outcomes, such as increased intentions to quit and increased quit attempts);[82] and (3) smoking behaviour (i.e., prevalence and consumption).[83] Additionally, the Panel examined the impact of the TPP measures on illicit trade.[84] It was only after an examination of the totality of this evidence that the Panel concluded that the TPP measures 'are apt to, and do in fact, contribute to Australia's objective of reducing the use of, and exposure to, tobacco products'.[85]

On appeal, the appellants challenged, inter alia, the fact that the Panel had made its determination about the contribution of the TPP measures to Australia's objective based disproportionately on the predicted effects of the measure, instead of the actual effects.[86] Specifically, Honduras claimed that 'the Panel failed to provide a reasoned and adequate explanation of the quality and probative value of the pre-implementation evidence in light of the post-implementation evidence'.[87] Moreover, the Dominican Republic claimed that the Panel did not address:

> the[] 'discrepancies' between the predicted effects and the actual effects resulting from the operation of the TPP measures, or offer any justification for adopting a different approach to assessing those outcomes for which the predicted effects were discredited, rather than confirmed, by the evidence on the actual impact of the TPP measures.[88]

Nonetheless, the AB examined the Panel's two reasons for placing only limited reliance on the data – namely: (1) the difficulty of isolating the impact of the measure from other measures; and (2) the fact that the full impact of the measure 'may evolve over time'.[89] The AB considered that, in light of these reasons, the Panel 'was well within the bounds of its discretion, as the trier of fact, to accord greater probative weight to the evidence of the anticipated effects of the TPP measures than to the

81 ibid [7.491].
82 ibid [7.491].
83 ibid s [7.2.5.3.6].
84 ibid s [7.2.5.3.7].
85 ibid [7.1025].
86 AB, *Australia—Tobacco Plain Packaging (Honduras)* (n 11) [6.346]–[6.347].
87 ibid [6.346].
88 ibid [6.347].
89 Panel, *Australia—Tobacco Plain Packaging (Honduras)* (n 10) [7.1044].

evidence of the actual effects of the TPP measures'.[90] On this basis, the AB rejected the appellants' challenge of the Panel's decision to give more weight to the evidence of the anticipated effects of the TPP measures than to the evidence of the actual effects. In sum, in the instances where a Panel or the AB has been required to assess the likely future contribution of a measure to a policy objective under the General Exceptions or Article 2.2 of the TBT Agreement, it has made this assessment largely using non-quantitative data.

It is argued that an alternative approach in this context is to use what limited quantitative data is available in order to make inferences about future events. This approach might be called the Statistical Inference Approach. It is suggested that the most appropriate quantitative tests for the Statistical Inference Approach are: (1) the Statistical Significance Test; and (2) Linear Regression Analysis, both of which were introduced in Chapter 1 of this book. It may be recalled from Chapter 1 that the SST can be used to estimate the probability that a particular effect was produced by random chance. In this manner, the SST eradicates the need to use vague labels, such as 'a material contribution', as a means of determining the level of contribution. Additionally, the Linear Regression Analysis can be used to show the likely future trajectory of a phenomenon based on past data. This ability is particularly useful for a case involving limited data.

The Statistical Inference Approach will be explicated by drawing upon the case study of *EC—Seal Products*, since the data from that case is freely available. The first step in the Statistical Inference Approach is to separate the effects of the EU Seal Regime into sub-effects. In this case, the sub-effects under examination might include: (1) a reduction in the number of seal deaths; (2) a reduction in the number of commercial sealers; (3) a reduction in the corporate profits accruing to the sealing industry; and (4) consumer demand for seal furs. The separation of sub-effects can be seen diagrammatically at Figure 4.3. Taking the first sub-effect first, the SST can first be used in this context to indicate the degree of confidence that there is a causal relationship between the EU Seal Regime and a decline in the number of seal deaths. In order to demonstrate the way in which the SST would apply to the analysis required in the *EC—Seal Products* case, the following assumptions can be used:

[90] AB, *Australia—Tobacco Plain Packaging (Honduras)* (n 11) [6.361].

- that 1,000 seals are sampled across the total population of seals for any one country in a uniformly random way across geographical region;
- that a seal is equally likely to be hunted in one geographical region as in any other; and
- that the number of seals in the total population is much higher than the 1,000 sampled seals. Therefore, any variation in the number of seals is due to the relatively small number of seals in the sample, rather than uncertainty about the number of seals killed in the total population.

With these assumptions in view, imagine that the following data was collected:

- every year for the ten years prior to the introduction of the EU Seal Regime, 1,000 seals were sampled and, on average, 50 of those samples were killed, meaning that 5 per cent of the seals in the sample were killed; and
- in the one year following the introduction of the EU Seal Regime, 35 seals (k) were killed out of a sample size of 1,000 seals (n), meaning that 3.5 per cent of the seals in the sample were killed.

It is important to note that having more data prior to the introduction of the EU Seal Regime means that it is possible to have more confidence in the estimated 5 per cent.

Based on this data, it is possible to formulate the 'null hypothesis' and the 'alternative hypothesis' as follows:

- The *null hypothesis* is that there is no causal relationship between the introduction of the EU Seal Regime and the reduction in the number of seal deaths. This means that, even after the introduction of the EU Seal Regime, the probability of a seal dying within the sample size per year is $p = 5\%$.
- The *alternative hypothesis* is that the EU Seal Regime contributes to a reduction in seal deaths.

The distribution of the number of seals that must be killed in order for both the null hypothesis vis-à-vis the alternate hypothesis to be accepted may be seen graphically in Figure 4.1. The probability that the null hypothesis will be accepted is coloured dark grey, whilst the probability that the alternative hypothesis will be accepted is coloured light grey.

It may be recalled from Chapter 1 that it is customary to set a significance value (represented as α) and that α is traditionally 5 per cent

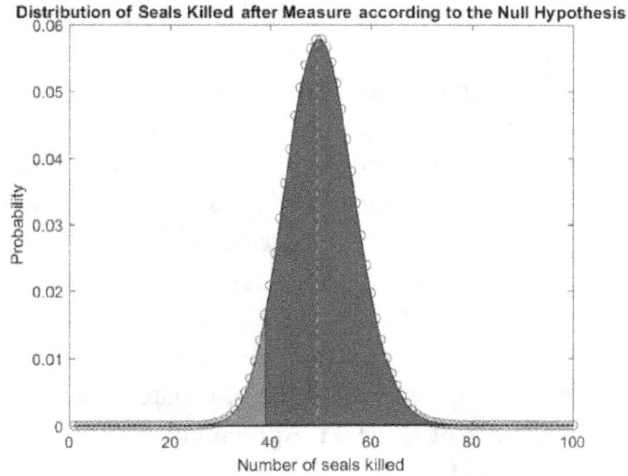

Figure 4.1 Probability distribution of seals killed per year according to the null hypothesis

or 0.05. In this case, α will be 5 per cent, meaning that if the result of the SST is less than or equal to 5 per cent, the null hypothesis will be rejected. The expectation value (η) is the size of the sample multiplied by the probability that a seal will be killed. Under the null hypothesis, the expectation value is 50 for a sample size of 1,000. This can be expressed mathematically as follows: Expectation value (η) = n ∗ p = 50.

In the sample set after the first year following the introduction of the EU Seal Regime, 35 out of 1,000 dead seals were counted. In order to test whether this fulfils the significance value, it is necessary to calculate the probability that 35 seals or less were killed after the introduction of the EU Seal Regime. In statistical terms, this can be written as follows:

$$P(x) = \binom{x}{x} p^x (1 - p)^{n-x}.$$

The probability of getting less than or equal to 35 dead seals per 1,000 seals sampled without the policy intervention may be calculated as follows:

$$P(x \leq 3|p = 1.2\%) = \sum_{a=0}^{3} P(x = a) = \sum_{a=0}^{3} \binom{n}{a} p^a (1 - p)^{n-a}$$

$$= \sum_{a=0}^{3} \binom{1,000}{a} 0.012^a 0.988^{1,000-a} = 0.2\%.$$

Given that the probability of 1.4 per cent is less than 5 per cent, the null hypothesis must be rejected. In other words, it is highly unlikely that the reduction in the number of seal deaths is due to random chance, and highly likely that there is a causal link between the introduction of the EU Seal Regime and the reduction in the number of seal deaths. As mentioned above, instead of relying on vague non-quantitative descriptors like, 'a material contribution', contributed 'at least to some extent' etc, the SST can actually quantify the likely degree of contribution. This ability has the benefit of offering Members additional legal certainty about the degree of contribution that a measure must make to its policy objective in order to be found to be consistent with the General Exceptions or Article 2.2 of the TBT Agreement.

Having established that it appears highly likely that there is a causal relationship between the EU Seal Regime and the reduction in the number of seal deaths, this section turns now to perform a Linear Regression Analysis, and to discuss how a Linear Regression Analysis might be used to predict future effects. It is useful to draw on the quantitative data reproduced by the Panel in *EC—Seal Products*,[91] which is set out as shown in Table 4.1.

The Panel in *EC—Seal Products* conceded that the data showed a general trend indicating that seal skins from the complainants into the EU market have decreased significantly since the introduction of the measure.[92] Nonetheless, the Panel observed that it is difficult to know whether the downward trajectory might be explained by other known factors, such as weather conditions and/or the adoption of legislation on trade in seal products in other countries.[93] The Linear Regression Analysis can be used to show whether the downward trend after the introduction of the EU Seal Measure in late 2009–10 is a continuation of the same downward trend that was taking place prior to the introduction of the EU Seal Measure, or if, in fact, the decline is much sharper. In this particular Linear Regression Analysis, the y-axis will use logarithmic data points because there is so much variation between the values in the data.

[91] Panel, *EC—Seal Products* (n 11) [7.456].
[92] ibid.
[93] ibid [7.458].

Table 4.1 *Data representing trade in seal skins from Canada and Norway to the EU from 2002–11, as taken from Panel,* EC—Seal Products *(n 11) [7.456]*

Year	Canada		Norway	
	Number of Seal Skins Imported into the EU	**Value of Seal Skins Imported (€)**	**Number of Seal Skins Imported into the EU**	**Value of Seal Skins Imported (€)**
2002	20,016	689	23,753	1,627
2003	11,594	455	10,996	400
2004	6,169	347	8,156	319
2005	5,964	396	9,046	300
2006	6,609	415	3,226	175
2007	551	44	5,437	448
2008	25,892	464	2,811	213
2009	549	48	3,225	234
2010	10	1	81	26
2011	5	1	36	2

The assumptions for this linear regression analysis are as follows:

- any uncertainties arising from other known factors in the data are the same for each value point;
- any uncertainties arising from other known factors are normally distributed once the log of the data has been taken;
- the uncertainties arising from other known factors for each value point must be independent of each other; and
- a linear fit to the logarithmic data is the most appropriate form of the fit.

The two central light grey and dark grey lines are 'least-square fit lines' – which means that they are lines that best optimise or 'fit' with the Canadian and Norwegian value points. If the EU Seal Measure had no influence on the trade of seal skins, it would be expected that the trade volumes in seal skins for both Canada and Norway would be close to the extrapolated lines in Figure 4.2. Instead, it can be seen from the above graph that, following the introduction of the EU Seal Measure in late 2009–10, there is a sudden and dramatic drop in the trade of seal skins in the EU. This drop represents a factor of approximately 100.

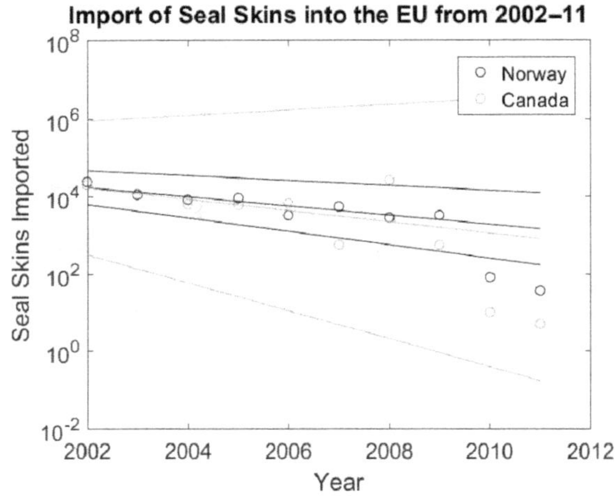

Figure 4.2 Linear regression analysis of the data represented in Table 4.1

The dark grey and light grey lines on either side of the 'least-square fit lines' indicate the range of statistical significance. As before, it is possible to formulate two hypotheses:

- a *null hypothesis*, which provides that there is no causal relationship between the EU Seal Measure and the reduction in the import of seal skins; and
- an *alternative hypothesis*, which is that the EU Seal Measure contributed to a reduction in the import of seal skins.

As above, the significance value (represented as α) will be set at 5 per cent or 0.05 – though it may be recalled from the above that the significance value may potentially be set at any value. Where a Member's data falls within the statistical significance lines, it must be said that the drop in data values is not considered statistically significant for the purpose of this model. Accordingly, for this reason, the null hypothesis must be accepted.

In relation to Norway's data, it can be seen that the Norwegian data values for 2010 and 2011 fall outside the statistical significance lines. This means that the null hypothesis should be rejected in relation to the Norwegian data. In contrast, the Canadian data values in relation to 2010 and 2011 fall within the range of statistical significance and therefore the alternative hypothesis must be rejected, and the null hypothesis accepted. It must be noted in relation to the Canadian data, however, that the data value for 2008 is an outlier that breaks the general linear pattern. This outlier to some extent distorts the 'fit' of the line as well as the SST lines on either side of it. Accordingly, the Canadian data and the concomitant acceptance of the null hypothesis must be approached with some caution.

The linear regression analysis and the SST were appropriate quantitative approaches for analysing the data reproduced by the Panel in *EC —Seal Products*, but they may not be the most appropriate quantitative tests in all cases. That is, the quantitative approach adopted depends upon the nature and quality of the data available. For example, where the data indicates that the trade flows were fairly constant until the introduction of a measure, it may not be necessary to perform a linear regression analysis. Instead, it may be sufficient to: (1) perform a non-attribution analysis; (2) take the average of the data prior to the introduction of a measure; (3) compare it with the average of the data after the measure; (4) and then apply the SST to determine if the difference is significant.

Self-evidently, the more data before and after the introduction of the measure, the more likely that the quantitative approaches will produce an accurate result. Nonetheless, even where a Member is only able to provide one year's worth of data – say, the one year between the introduction of the measure and the litigation – the SST is still able to provide Members with an approximate sense of how much difference the measure made to an outcome. This ability would be heightened in situations where Members are able to provide data on the policy area for a significant period of time prior to the introduction of the measure. That is, the greater the number of years provided prior to the introduction of the measure, the greater the sample size, and the greater the probability that the SST could demonstrate the difference produced by the measure. In this sense, the limited amount of data available after the introduction of the measure may, to some extent, be counteracted by providing fuller data about the state of the policy area prior to the introduction of the measure.

It may be objected that adopting such a quantitative approach requires particular expertise that is likely to be beyond the skills of a Panel or the AB. This objection, however, is by no means fatal to the use of quantitative methods. Indeed, the WTO Secretariat has itself said that 'quantitative economic analysis is bound to occur with most regularity in WTO arbitrations due to their specific mandate and the need to make a precise award that in most cases must be quantified, often with reference to the effects of the inconsistent measure'.[94] Moreover, under Article 13.2 of the DSU, Panels may 'consult experts to obtain their opinion on certain aspects of the matter'. Such consultation could certainly extend to the consultation of statisticians or econometricians.

Moreover, the Panels and the AB have already used econometric tests in analysing other parts of WTO law. For example, in *US—COOL*, in making its determination as to whether US country of origin labelling requirements provided 'less favourable treatment' to Canadian and Mexican meat imports as compared to US meat under Article 2.1 of the TBT Agreement, the Panel extensively reviewed the parties' quantitative data in relation to the import volume of Canadian and Mexican cattle in the United States over the previous five-to ten-year period.[95] The Panel commented that:

> There is no reason to consider economic or econometric evidence inappropriate per se, let alone exempt from Panels' review. The ultimate role of Panels is to conduct the necessary factual and legal review of the arguments and evidence advanced by the parties, and thus to carry out an objective assessment of the matter brought before the Panel. The basic function of Panels does not exclude – and may, in fact, necessitate – the review of economic and econometric evidence and arguments.[96]

Although the AB reversed part of the Panel's conclusions on other grounds, it did not express any disagreement with the Panel's reliance on quantitative data. Moreover, investigating authorities in the context of safeguards, antidumping and countervailing duties cases often rely on regression analysis in determining whether a subsidised or dumped import caused injury.[97] Indeed, the importance of quantitative analysis in the context of countervailing duties and antidumping cases was

[94] World Trade Organization, 'World Trade Report 2005: Exploring the Links between Trade, Standards and the WTO' (2005) <www.wto.org/english/res_e/booksp_e/anrep_e/world_trade_report05_e.pdf> accessed 15 October 2016.

[95] Panel, *US—COOL* (n 21) [7.455]–[7.564].

[96] ibid [7.452].

[97] See generally James Fetzer, 'Inference for Econometric Modelling in Antidumping, Countervailing Duty and Safeguard Investigations' (2009) 8(4) WTR 545.

emphasised in *EC—Countervailing Measures on DRAM Chips*.[98] Finally, there is precedent for domestic judiciaries using the SST in particular – for example, it has been frequently used by the judiciary in United States courts, including the United States Supreme Court.[99]

Once it has been established that it is likely that a measure has made a positive contribution to one of the sub-effects, it remains to attempt to divide responsibility for the sub-effect between the measure vis-à-vis other known factors, in the usual manner of the second step of the Tripartite Non-attribution/Causal Link Analysis. Obviously, it is also very difficult to predict the future effect of other known factors on a sub-effect. It is suggested, however, that data about the past and present effect of other known factors might be collected and extrapolated in order to gain a sense of the breakdown of responsibility for a sub-effect between the measure and other known factors. Once this is done, a fact-finder might follow the usual steps in the Tripartite Non-attribution/Causal Link Analysis, which will be detailed below. Obviously, this process would need to be repeated in relation to all of the sub-effects identified in the first step of the Tripartite Non-attribution/Causal Link Analysis.

4.3 Non-attribution: The First Two Steps of the Tripartite Process

4.3.1 Introduction

Once the effects (or projected effects) of a measure are identified, a fact-finder must be satisfied that the effects are purely the result of the measure and not confounded by other known factors. It was seen in Section 4.2.1 that the absence of a non-attribution analysis is one of the fundamental problems with the current approach in the jurisprudence. Similarly, there is a possibility that each of the sub-effects could be produced wholly or substantially by other known factors. It is important, therefore, to have some methodology in place for: (1) separating the causal impact of a measure vis-à-vis other known factors; and (2) establishing the existence of a causal link between the measure and the policy

[98] WTO, *European Communities: Countervailing Measures on Dynamic Random Access Memory Chips from Korea—Report of the Panel* (17 June 2005) WT/DS299/R (Panel, *EC—Countervailing Measures on DRAM Chips*) [7.405].

[99] See, for example, *Castaneda v Partida* 430 US 482 (1977) and *Hazelwood School District v United States* 433 US 299 (1977). See generally David H Kaye, 'Is Proof of Statistical Significance Relevant?' (1986) 61 Wash L Rev 1333.

objective. It is suggested that the Tripartite Non-attribution/Causal Link Analysis is a possible methodology for performing these two functions.

It will be recalled that the Tripartite Non-attribution/Causal Link Analysis was developed by the AB in *US—Wheat Gluten* in the context of analysing the injurious impact of safeguard measures. In this chapter, the Tripartite Non-attribution/Causal Link Analysis will be applied to assist with determining whether a policy outcome was achieved as a result of a measure (as opposed to some other known factor). It is worth recalling the analytical steps set out by the AB in *US–Wheat Gluten*[100] and how they can be adapted to this context of non-injury – namely: (1) authorities must separate the effects that the measure has had on various aspects pertaining to the policy objective; (2) authorities must then attribute to the measure the effects that it had on the policy objective vis-à-vis the effects that the other known factors had on the same policy objective; and (3) finally, authorities should determine whether there is a causal link between the measure and the policy objective. As in Chapters 2 and 3, the first two steps are directed at performing a non-attribution analysis, while the third step is aimed at determining a causal link. As in other chapters, this section will draw on a worked hypothetical example to illustrate how the Tripartite Non-attribution/Causal Link Analysis would operate in practice. This chapter will take the example of the EU Seal Measure from *EC—Seal Products* because this case set out real world data.

4.3.2 The First Step of the Non-attribution Process

The first step of the non-attribution process involves identifying the types of effects that the measure has had on the policy objective. As in Chapter 3, these effects will be called 'sub-effects' for the purpose of this chapter. Taking the example of the impact of the EU Seal Measure on improving seal welfare, the sub-effects of the measure might include – for example, (1) a reduction in the number of seal deaths; (2) a reduction in the number of commercial sealers; (3) a reduction in the corporate profits accruing to the sealing industry; and (4) a reduction in the amount of consumer demand for seal fur skins. Of course, it is possible that there may be more sub-effects than those identified here and in Figure 4.3. A representation of the separation of the sub-effects of a measure can be

[100] WTO, *United States: Definitive Safeguard Measures on Imports of Wheat Gluten from the European Communities—Report of the Appellate Body* (22 December 2000) WT/DS166/AB/R (AB, *US—Wheat Gluten*) [69].

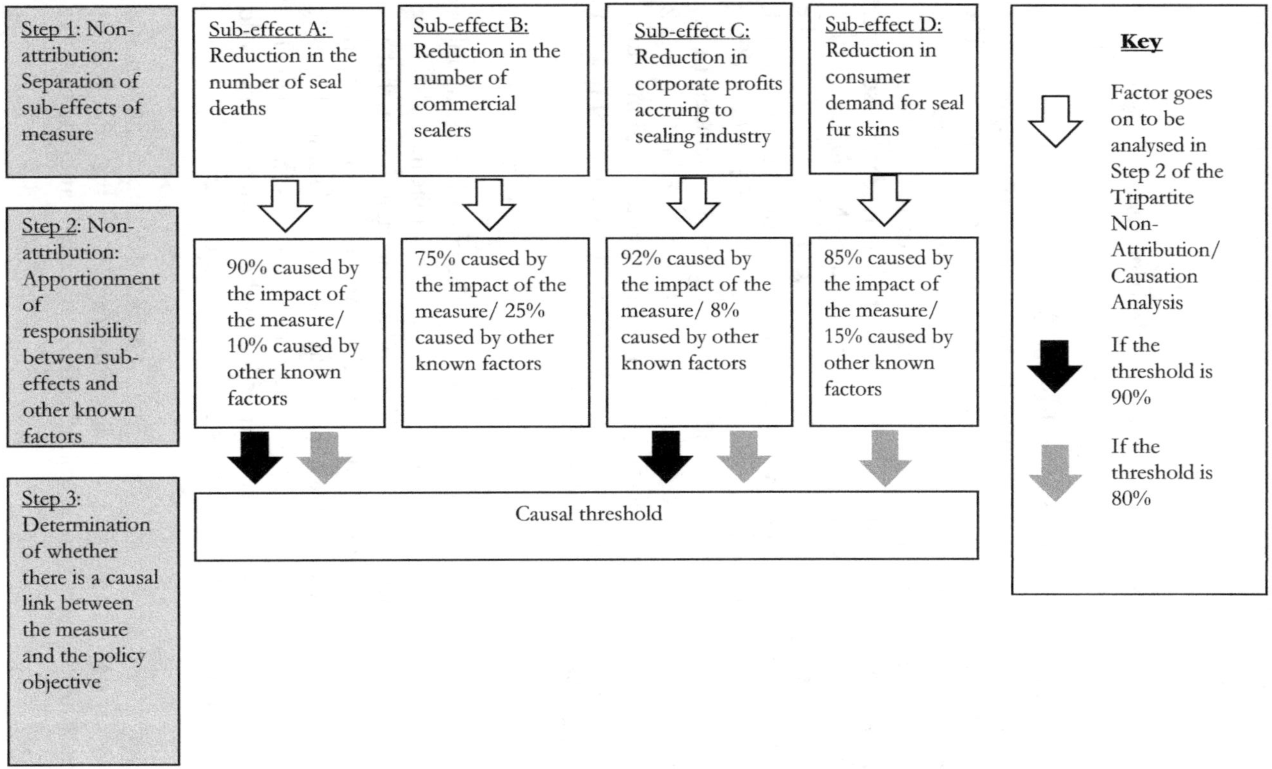

Figure 4.3 Overview of Steps One, Two and Three of the Tripartite Non-attribution/Causal Link Analysis with respect to Articles XX of the GATT, XIV of the GATS and Article 2.2 of the TBT Agreement

seen in Step One of Figure 4.3. As in Chapters 2 and 3, the size of the sub-effects in Figure 4.3 is not indicative of their importance to the overall effect of the measure.

4.3.3 The Second Step of the Non-attribution Process

Introduction

Once the sub-effects of the measure have been identified, the second step of the non-attribution process involves two broad types of analysis: (1) an Apportionment Analysis; and (2) a Qualification Analysis. The Apportionment Analysis is broadly aimed at apportioning causal responsibility for bringing about a policy objective to a measure vis-à-vis other known factors. To this end, a Panel must first consider those other known factors that are identified by the complaining Member, and then seek to disaggregate the effects of those other known factors from the effects of the measure. The Qualification Analysis, on the other hand, involves determining whether causal responsibility for a sub-effect exceeds a nominated threshold, and if it does, it will be included in the final causal link analysis to be discussed in Section 4.4. As in Chapters 2 and 3, a diagrammatic overview of the Tripartite Non-attribution/Causal Link Analysis, as it is applied to the relationship between a measure and a policy objective, is set out in Figure 4.3.

Apportionment Analysis

Identification of Other Known Factors Stage The complainant Member would be required to raise any other known factors that may also have contributed to the achievement of the policy objective. Given that the complainant Member may not necessarily be aware of all possible other known factors (particularly as they may pertain to some domestic matters of which a complainant Member may not have knowledge), it may be that Panels have a duty to investigate other known factors, as do the domestic competent authorities in the safeguards context.[101]

Disentanglement Stage It was seen in Section 4.2.2 that the AB has held on several occasions that a determination as to the effectiveness of a measure may be made using both 'qualitative' and quantitative

[101] ibid [52]–[56].

evidence.[102] It was also seen that the Panels and the AB have actually only used 'qualitative' (or non-quantitative) evidence in practice when making a determination as to the effectiveness of a measure, despite the fact that various Members have argued in favour of the importance of analysing real-world effects. It was argued in that section, and it will be argued again here, that drawing a causal link between a measure and a policy objective can more effectively be done by using quantitative data based on the effects of the measure. Indeed, the idea of drawing on quantitative data to measure the extent to which a measure contributes to its stated policy goal under the General Exceptions has also been suggested by other scholars, including Pauwelyn and Van Anken.[103]

An additional benefit of using quantitative data is that it is arguably the only way by which the effects of a measure vis-à-vis the effects of other known factors can meaningfully be separated. Obviously, there has not been any commentary about separating the effects of a measure from the effects of other known factors, but it is suggested that it would follow the same fundamental principles as those that have been used in the trade remedies contexts. As such, it is contended that the methodology for disaggregating effects used in the context of trade remedies might be adapted here.[104] Alternatively, as was suggested in Chapter 3, Panels have the ability, pursuant to Article 13.2 of the DSU, to establish 'expert review groups' for the purpose of adapting the econometric approaches used in the trade remedies context to the current context. As in Chapters 2 and 3, the overriding purpose of the disentanglement analysis is to be able to apportion a percentage of causal responsibility for the sub-effects to a

[102] AB, *Brazil—Retreaded Tyres* (n 10) [146]; AB, *EC—Seal Products* (n 2) [5.215].

[103] Joost Pauwelyn, 'The Use, Non-use and Abuse of Economics in WTO and Investment Litigation' in Jorge A Huerta-Goldman, Antoine Romanetti and Franz X Stirnimann (eds), *WTO Litigation, Investment Arbitration, and Commercial Arbitration* (Kluwer 2013) 179; Anne van Anken, 'Opportunities for and Limits to an Economic Analysis of International Law' (2001) Transnatl Corp Rev 3(1) 27, 40–43.

[104] In particular, see Thomas J Prusa and David C Sharp, 'Simultaneous Equations in Antidumping Investigations' (2001) 14(1) JFE 63, 77; and JP Durling and MP McCullough, 'Teaching Old Laws New Tricks: The Legal Obligation of Non-Attribution and the Need for Economic Rigour in Injury Analyses under US Trade Law' in EK Choi and J Hartigan (eds), *Handbook of International Trade, Volume II* (OUP 2005) 80; Kenneth Kelly, 'The Analysis of Causality in Escape Clause Cases' (1988) 37(2) J Ind Econ 187; Douglas A Irwin, 'Causing Problems? The WTO Review of Causation and Injury Attribution in US Section 201 Cases' (2003) 2(3) WTR 297; and Dukgeun Ahn and William J Moon, 'Alternative Approach to Causation Analysis in Trade Remedy Investigations: "Cost of Production" Test' (2010) 44(5) JWT 1023, 1041–47.

measure vis-à-vis other known factors. Once the causal responsibility for the sub-effects has been apportioned in this way, it remains to determine which factors qualify for consideration under the Qualification Analysis.

Qualification Analysis It will be recalled from Chapters 2 and 3 that the Qualification Analysis allows a fact-finder to assess which sub-effects qualify for inclusion in the causal link analysis that makes up Step Three of the Tripartite Non-attribution/Causal Link Analysis. To this end, the most foundational questions are: Can sub-effects only be included in the causal link analysis if they were 100 per cent caused by a measure? Alternatively, can sub-effects be included in the causal link analysis if they have been found to be caused by a combination of a measure and other known factors (i.e., what this book has termed the 'multi-factorial approach')? It is difficult to predict how a Panel or the AB would approach these basic questions. Nonetheless, the better approach would seem to be to use the 'multi-factorial approach' – that is, allowing sub-effects to be included in the causal link analysis where they have been caused by some combination of a measure and other known factors. This is because, with something as complex as a policy outcome, it is rarely the case that a sub-effect would be the result of one casual factor alone. Indeed, the idea that a sub-effect was caused by only one causal factor seems unrealistic. Accordingly, it would arguably be overly rigid to discount a sub-effect from inclusion in the causal link analysis because of a small causal contribution from another causal factor.

Having just said that it is difficult to choose between only allowing sub-effects caused by the measure and a 'multi-factorial approach' in the absence of any guidance from a Panel or the AB, it is even more difficult to nominate any threshold that a sub-effect must reach in order to be included in the causal link analysis. That is, the question is – as in Chapters 2 and 3 – should a sub-effect that is 90 per cent caused by the measure and 10 per cent caused by other known factors be included in the causal link analysis? What about a sub-effect that is 85 per cent the product of a measure and 15 per cent brought about by other known factors? It may be that a Panel or the AB would wish to hold off providing a precise percentage weighting in order to allow some degree of flexibility depending on the nature of the policy objective and the other known factors involved in the case in question.

In the context of the General Exceptions (as opposed to Article 2.2 of the TBT Agreement), it may also be that the threshold will vary depending on the paragraph of the General Exceptions under appraisal.

That is, the beginning of each paragraph of the General Exceptions contains a word (such as 'necessary') or a phrase (such as 'relating to') that indicates the level of contribution that a measure must make to its policy objective. The jurisprudence has consistently suggested that the degree of connection between the measure in question and the achievement of the policy objective varies with each paragraph of the General Exceptions. The Panel in *US—Gasoline* made this point:

> It does not seem reasonable to suppose that the WTO Members intended to require, in respect of each and every category, the same kind or degree of connection or relationship between the measure under appraisal and the state interest or policy sought to be promoted or realized.[105]

This statement, made in respect of Article XX of the GATT 1994, has also been extended to the interpretation of Article XIV of the GATS.[106] In *US—Gambling*, the AB similarly held that '[t]he required nexus – or "degree of connection" – between the measure and the interest is specified in the language of the paragraphs themselves, through the use of terms such as "relating to" and "necessary to"'.[107] Given this variation between the paragraphs of the General Exceptions, it would seem to make sense that the threshold may vary depending on the particular paragraph of the General Exceptions in question. The threshold in relation to Article 2.2 of the TBT Agreement may be more consistent. Indeed, it was seen previously that the Panel in *EC—Seal Products* took note of the fact that the AB in *US—Tuna II (Mexico)* and *US—COOL* assessed 'the "degree of contribution" by a measure without necessarily determining whether the actual degree of contribution by the measure reaches a certain minimum threshold such as a material or significant contribution'.[108] It is unclear at this point whether this trend in the jurisprudence will continue. If it does, it may be that the threshold might be lower in respect of Article 2.2 of the TBT Agreement than in respect of the General Exceptions.

The implication of having a lower threshold would, self-evidently, be that more sub-effects would qualify for the causal link analysis, and therefore the likelihood of making out a causal link would be increased. The more likely that a causal link would be made out, the greater the likelihood, in turn, that a responding Member's measure would be found to

105 AB, *US—Gasoline* (n 5) p 18.
106 AB, *US—Gambling* (n 18) [292].
107 ibid.
108 Panel, *EC—Seal Products* (n 11) n 977.

have been effective in producing the intended policy objective. That said, this is only one of a number of considerations that a Panel or the AB must have regard to in determining whether a measure ought to be exempted under the General Exceptions and Article 2.2 of the TBT Agreement. Accordingly, even if it is easier for a measure to be found to have caused a policy objective due to the use of the 'multi-factorial approach' and a lower threshold, it does not follow from this that the measure will be exempted under the General Exceptions or Article 2.2 of the TBT Agreement. In this sense, the analytical choices made here are important to one component of the decision about whether a measure ought to be exempted, but they are by no means determinative of the outcome.

4.4 Causal Link: The Third Step of the Tripartite Process

Given that the jurisprudence has not in any way advocated for the use of a causal test in this context, let alone use of the Tripartite Non-attribution/Causal Link Analysis, it follows that there is no jurisprudence on point that may assist with: (1) the causal standard that must be reached; or (2) how causation ought to be made out in this context. In the absence of any guidance from the jurisprudence, it is difficult to provide any very detailed discussion of how the causal link should be drawn. It is nonetheless suggested that the best approach for determining causation is to examine those factors that have passed the Qualification Analysis and, with the use of a weak necessity/strong sufficiency test, assess whether they are sufficient collectively to have caused the intended policy objective.

4.5 Conclusion

The Panels and the AB have sometimes referred to the relationship between a measure and its intended policy objective as if it were causal in nature. This would seem to make sense given that a causal link between the two is easily implied – and, indeed, it has been implied by several Members that have argued in favour of a causal analysis in this context. Nonetheless, the Panels and the AB have been reluctant to: (1) quantify the real-world effects of the challenged measure; and (2) use causal tests to interrogate the relationship between the measure and those real-world effects. Instead, they have attempted to assess causal contribution simply by looking at the nature of the measure, and sought, from these, to infer their likely effects.

This chapter has argued against this approach for two chief reasons. First, the current approach is premised on a misconception that causation can be inferred simply by looking at the nature of the cause. Second, even if one could infer causation simply by looking at the nature of the measure, this does not account for the possibility that other known factors could confound such a causal link. An alternative approach to determining the level of causal contribution that a measure makes to a policy objective is: (1) to collect real-world data about the effects of the measure; and (2) to subject that data to a non-attribution and causal link analysis through applying the Tripartite Non-attribution/Causal Link Analysis. It is conceded that gathering real-world data is particularly troublesome where the effects of a measure may not yet have manifested – which is one of the reasons that the AB in *US—Gasoline* gave for refusing to rely on effects when determining contribution. It is suggested, however, that this reason, whilst reasonable, is not insurmountable, as there are some quantitative approaches that can be used in order to predict future effects based on past data. The SST and LRA have been put forward as suitable in this chapter, but it is quite possible that different quantitative methods might be used depending on the nature of the data in question.

The contribution of this chapter, then, is to set out the implications that ought to follow from regarding the relationship between a measure and its intended policy objective as a causal relationship for the purposes of regulating for non-trade purposes under the General Exceptions and Article 2.2 of the TBT Agreement. It may well be objected that the approach to determining causation that has been detailed in this chapter is far more involved and more complex than the current approach taken by Panels and the AB. This complexity, however, is a direct reflection of the complexity of causation itself. The current approach in the jurisprudence may be simpler and more straightforward, but this is because it fails adequately to grapple with the implications of the link between a measure and its policy objective as being causal in nature and the concomitant need for a non-attribution analysis.

5

Retaliatory Measures

5.1 Introduction

The concept of reparation is an important principle in general international law,[1] and the concept of causation is fundamental to the way in which reparation is calculated.[2] Reparation as such does not exist in WTO law because remedies are prospective – that is, the objective of the dispute settlement mechanism is to bring about a mutually acceptable solution to the parties going forward,[3] and in the absence of that, to secure the withdrawal of the measures that are inconsistent with the covered agreements.[4] If both these primary aims fail, a Member may seek compensation from the other;[5] but, even then, compensation is only a voluntary remedy.[6] The last resort for Members of the WTO to resolve their dispute involves the possibility of retaliation. Retaliation may be used where a Member fails to bring its measure into compliance with the covered agreement(s) and the other Member 'suspend[s] the application of concessions or other obligations under the covered agreements on a

1 *Case Concerning the Factory at Chorzów (Germany v Poland)* (Jurisdiction) (26 July 1927) PCIJ Rep Series A No 9, p 21; Article 31, *Draft Articles on the Responsibility of States for Internationally Wrongful Acts*, Report of the International Law Commission on the Work of Its Fifty-Third Session, UN GAOR, 56th Sess, Supp No 10, p 43,UN Doc A/56/10 (2001).

2 Article 31(2), *Draft Articles on the Responsibility of States for Internationally Wrongful Acts* (n 1); International Law Commission, *Draft Articles on Responsibility of States for Internationally Wrongful Acts, with Commentaries*, UN GAOR, 56th Sess, Supp No 10, UN Doc A/56/10 (2001), para 9.

3 *Understanding on Rules and Procedures Governing the Settlement of Disputes*, LT/UR/A-2/DS/U/1 (signed 15 April 1994, entered into force 1 January 1995) (DSU) Article 3.7.

4 ibid.

5 ibid.

6 DSU (n 3) Article 22.1.

discriminatory basis vis-à-vis the other Member, subject to authorization by the DSB of such measures'[7] ('retaliatory measures').[8]

There is a considerable amount of academic debate about the precise policy goal of retaliatory measures.[9] Indeed, the Arbitrator in *US—Offset Act (Byrd Amendment) (Article 22.6)* said that 'it is not completely clear what role is to be played by the suspension of obligations in the DSU and a large part of the conceptual debate that took place in these proceedings could have been avoided if a clear "object and purpose" were identified'.[10] Some cases appear to conceive of retaliatory measures as serving a compensatory function,[11] some as a means of enforcing compliance with a DSB ruling,[12] and yet others as punitive in

[7] ibid Article 3.7.

[8] The suspension of concessions occurs when Member A denies a benefit to Member B that Member A is otherwise legally required to grant. For example, the DSB might authorise Member A to suspend its tariff concessions on products imported from Member B because of Member B's failure to implement its DSB ruling. The words 'retaliation' or 'retaliatory measures' are not used in the DSU, though they will be used throughout this chapter.

[9] See, for example, Gregory Shaffer and Daniel Ganin, 'Extrapolating Purpose from Practice: Rebalancing or Inducing Compliance' in Chad P Bown and Joost Pauwelyn, *The Law, Economics and Politics of Retaliation in WTO Dispute Settlement* (CUP 2010); Joost Pauwelyn, 'The Calculation and Design of Trade Retaliation in Context: What Is the Goal of Suspending WTO Obligations?' in Bown and Pauwelyn (ibid); Alan O Sykes, 'Optimal Sanctions in the WTO: The Case for Decoupling (and the Uneasy Case for the Status Quo)' in Bown and Pauwelyn (ibid); Steve Charnovitz, 'Rethinking WTO Trade Sanctions' (2001) 95 AJIL 792.

[10] WTO, *United States: Continued Dumping and Subsidy Offset Act of 2000—Recourse to Arbitration by the United States under Article 22.6 of the DSU—Decision by the Arbitrators* (31 August 2004) WT/DS217/ARB/BRA (*US—Offset Act (Byrd Amendment)*) [6.4].

[11] The Arbitrators in *US—Gambling (Article 22.6)* confirmed that it was difficult to calculate compensation accurately, given the limited information available: see WTO, *United States: Measures Affecting the Cross-Border Supply of Gambling and Betting Services—Recourse to Arbitration by the United States under Article 22.6 of the DSU—Decision by the Arbitrators* (21 December 2007) WT/DS285/ARB (*US—Gambling (Recourse to Arbitration—Article 22.6 DSU)*) [3.173]–[3.174].

[12] WTO, *European Communities: Regime for the Importation, Sale and Distribution of Bananas—Recourse to Arbitration by the European Communities under Article 22.6 of the DSU* (9 April 1999) WT/DS27/ARB (*EC—Bananas III (Recourse to Arbitration—Article 22.6 DSU—US)*) [6.3]; WTO, *European Communities: Regime for the Importation, Sale and Distribution of Bananas—Recourse to Arbitration by the European Communities under Article 22.6 of the DSU—Decision by the Arbitrators* (24 March 2000) WT/DS27/ARB/ECU (*EC—Bananas III (Recourse to Arbitration—Article 22.6 DSU—Ecuador)*) [76]; WTO, *Brazil: Export Financing Programme for Aircraft—Recourse to Arbitration by Brazil under Article 22.6 of the DSU and Article 4.11 of the SCM Agreement* (28 August 2000) WT/DS46/ARB (*Brazil—Aircraft (Recourse to Arbitration—Article 22.6 DSU)*) [3.44]; WTO, *United States: Tax Treatment for 'Foreign Sales Corporations'—Recourse*

nature.[13] A discussion of the policy goals underlying retaliatory measures is beyond the scope of this chapter, but it is fair to say that retaliatory measures have been variously aimed at each of these policy goals in different cases. Moreover, the jurisprudence appears to support the view that there has been a gradual evolution from compensation to enforcing compliance with the DSB ruling.[14]

Regardless of their policy goal, the value of the retaliatory measures suspended must be 'equivalent' to the nullification or impairment of benefits that the measure has caused,[15] except in the context of the SCM Agreement, where the retaliatory measures must be 'appropriate'.[16] The Arbitrator in *US—FSC (Article 22.6)* said that, for the purpose of Article 4.10 of the SCM Agreement, 'a Member is entitled to act with countermeasures that properly take into account the gravity of the breach and the nature of the upset in the balance of rights and obligations in question'.[17] Article 22.6 DSU and Article 4.10 SCM panels have discussed various methodologies by which the level of nullification or impairment

to Arbitration by the United States under Article 22.6 of the DSU and Article 4.11 of the SCM Agreement (30 August 2002) WT/DS108/ARB (*US—FSC (Recourse to Arbitration—Article 22.6 DSU)*) [5.52]; WTO, *Canada: Export Credits and Loan Guarantees for Regional Aircraft—Recourse to Arbitration by Canada under Article 22.6 DSU and Article 4.11 of the SCM Agreement* (17 February 2003) WT/DS222/ARB (*Canada—Aircraft Credits and Guarantees (Recourse to Arbitration—Article 22.6 DSU and Article 4.11 SCM)*) [3.48] and [3.107].

13 *Canada—Aircraft Credits and Guarantees (Recourse to Arbitration—Article 22.6 DSU and Article 4.11 SCM)* (n 12) [3.121] but cf *EC—Bananas III (Recourse to Arbitration—Article 22.6 DSU—US)* (n 12), where the Arbitrators stated that '[. . .] there is nothing in Article 22.1 of the DSU, [. . .], that could be read as a justification for counter-measures of a punitive nature': [6.3].

14 Pauwelyn (n 9).

15 DSU (n 3) Article 22.4.

16 *Agreement on Subsidies and Countervailing Measures*, LT/UR/A-1A/9 (signed 15 April 1994, entered into force 1 January 1995) (SCM Agreement) Article 4.10. Footnote 10 to Article 4.10 states that the wording 'appropriate' is 'not meant to allow countermeasures that are disproportionate in light of the fact that the subsidies dealt with under these provisions are prohibited'. In other words, the word 'appropriate' anticipates a certain degree of proportionality. In this sense, the requirement that countermeasures be 'equivalent' (DSU (n 3) Article 22.4) or 'appropriate' (SCM Agreement (ibid) Article 4.10) is consistent with the principle in general international law that countermeasures in response to an internationally wrongful act must be 'proportionate' to the injury suffered by the state taking the countermeasures: see Article 51, *Draft Articles on the Responsibility of States for Internationally Wrongful Acts* (n 1).

17 *US—FSC (Recourse to Arbitration—Article 22.6 DSU)* (n 12) [5.61].

might be identified.[18] In doing so, however, they have effectively overlooked the need to explicitly demonstrate, as an initial step, the causal link between a Member's failure to bring its measure into conformity with a DSB ruling and the level of nullification or impairment incurred (that is, a causal link analysis). In fact, a discussion of causation appears only to take place in the jurisprudence where it is *not* made out, which seems to lead to the conclusion that there is a presumption of a causal link. Moreover, retaliation arbitral panels have also neglected meaningfully to consider any approach by which other known factors might be separated from those causal factors that are related to a Member's failure to bring its measure into conformity with the covered agreement(s) (that is, a non-attribution analysis).

The jurisprudence consistently shows, however, that both a non-attribution and causal link analysis are in fact necessary in the context of Articles 22.6 DSU and 4.10 SCM Agreement ('retaliation arbitrations'). That is, there are a number of cases where the responding Member puts forward evidence that other known factors have confounded the causal link between a responding Member's failure to comply with a DSB ruling and the complainant Member's nullification and impairment. The jurisprudence has not dealt with these in any consistent way. This chapter argues that other known factors will always remain a feature of retaliation arbitrations; and, therefore, that they ought to be considered in a more systematic manner – namely, by using a more formalised non-attribution

[18] See, eg, *EC—Bananas III (Recourse to Arbitration—Article 22.6 DSU—Ecuador)* (n 12) [131]–[133]; *EC—Bananas III (Recourse to Arbitration—Article 22.6 DSU—US)* (n 12) [7.1] (regarding the use of counterfactuals); *US—Gambling (Recourse to Arbitration—Article 22.6 DSU)* (n 11) [3.136] and [3.178]; WTO, *United States: Continued Dumping and Subsidy Offset Act of 2000—Recourse to Arbitration by the United States under Article 22.6 of the DSU—Decision by the Arbitrators* (31 August 2004) WT/DS217/ARB/IND [3.114]–[3.151]; WTO, *United States: Continued Dumping and Subsidy Offset Act of 2000—Recourse to Arbitration by the United States under Article 22.6 of the DSU—Decision by the Arbitrators* (31 August 2004) WT/DS217/ARB/KOR [3.114]–[3.151]; WTO, *United States: Continued Dumping and Subsidy Offset Act of 2000—Recourse to Arbitration by the United States under Article 22.6 of the DSU—Decision by the Arbitrators* (31 August 2004) WT/DS217/ARB/JPN [3.114]–[3.151]; WTO, *United States: Certain Country of Origin Labelling (COOL) Requirements—Recourse to Arbitration by the United States under Article 22.6 of the DSU—Decision by the Arbitrators* (7 December 2015) WT/DS384/ARB; WT/DS386/ARB (*US—COOL (Recourse to Arbitration—Article 22.6 DSU)*) [6.27]–[6.32]; WTO, *United States: Measures Concerning the Importation, Marketing and Sale of Tuna and Tuna Products—Recourse to Arbitration by the United States under Article 22.6 of the DSU—Decision by the Arbitrators* (25 April 2017) WT/DS381/ARB (*US—Tuna II (Mexico) (Recourse to Arbitration—Article 22.6 DSU)*) [6.49]–[6.77].

analysis. It follows from this that a direct causal link between a responding Member's failure to comply with a DSB ruling and the complainant Member's nullification and impairment cannot be presumed. Instead, as a logical matter, Arbitrators must perform a non-attribution analysis before establishing a causal link and then turning, as a final step, to consider how nullification and impairment ought to be quantified.

One part of the analysis in which the Arbitrator does consistently use a causal test is in relation to the determination of nullification and impairment. In that part of the analysis, the Arbitrator uses a counterfactual test to interrogate the difference between the value of trade (if any) that took place with the WTO-inconsistent measure in place vis-à-vis the value of trade that would have taken place over the same period if the responding Member had complied with the DSB ruling. There are a number of insoluble difficulties with the use of a counterfactual test here. One obvious problem is that the use of a counterfactual here raises the hypothetical world problem, as it is difficult to reconstruct the likely trade flows that would have taken place if the responding Member had complied with the DSB ruling. A second problem is that use of a counterfactual is premised on the idea that no other known factors have confused the causal link between the responding Member's failure to comply with the DSB ruling and the nullification and impairment. The use of the Tripartite Non-attribution/Causal Link Analysis in this context would offer a possible solution to this second problem. An additional benefit of the Tripartite Non-attribution/Causal Link Analysis is that the results of its analysis might be used in order to inform the quantification of nullification and impairment.

5.2 Jurisprudence Concerning Non-attribution and Causal Link Analysis in Respect of the Retaliatory Measures

5.2.1 Causation in Retaliation Arbitrations

Once a Panel has found that a measure is inconsistent with the covered agreements, there is a presumption in place, pursuant to Article 3.8 DSU, that the inconsistency has caused nullification and impairment. For the purposes of determining whether a measure is inconsistent with the covered agreement, it is sufficient simply to make such a presumption, whilst the onus is on the opposing Member to rebut it. Arbitrators in the context of Articles 22.6 DSU and 4.10 SCM Agreement, however, are required to quantify the complainant Member's level of nullification and impairment. Article XXIII:1 of the GATT 1994 provides that the nullification or impairment must arise 'as a result of [. . .] the failure of another contracting party to carry out its obligations under this Agreement'. In other words, Article XXIII:1 of the GATT 1994 would seem to require an Arbitrator to quantify the level of nullification and impairment that was actually 'a result of [. . .]' or *caused by* the failure of a responding Member to bring its measure into conformity with the DSB ruling.

It logically follows that the first consideration for an Arbitrator must be whether there was a causal link between a responding Member's failure to bring its measure into conformity with a DSB ruling and the complainant Member's nullification and impairment. Only then, as a secondary step, would it be appropriate for an Arbitrator to attempt to estimate the level of nullification and impairment caused to a complainant Member's industry. The current jurisprudence demonstrates, however, that Arbitrators have not set out any clear, rigorous method for interrogating the causal link between a Member's failure to conform with a DSB ruling and a complainant Member's nullification and impairment. Indeed, the jurisprudence reflects a general paucity of discussion about the way in which the causal link should be drawn; and causation appears only to be discussed in those cases in which the causal link is *not* made out. The discussion now turns to two such cases.

The existence of a causal link was discussed explicitly and ultimately rejected in *Brazil—Aircraft (Article 22.6)*. In that case, Brazil argued that, but for Canada's failure to comply with the DSB ruling, Air Wisconsin would have changed suppliers from Canada's Bombardier aircraft to Brazil's Embraer aircraft.[19] The Arbitrator concluded that there was no causal link between Canada's failure to comply with the DSB ruling and the nullification and impairment caused to Brazil's industry.[20] This was because the Arbitrator believed that Canada's Bombardier aircraft would have had incentives to retain its relationship with Air Wisconsin and that the costs to retain the contract would not have been too great.[21] Indeed, Brazil even made this point elsewhere in its written submission.[22]

[19] *Canada—Aircraft Credits and Guarantees (Recourse to Arbitration—Article 22.6 DSU and Article 4.11 SCM)* (n 12) [3.22].

[20] ibid [3.22]–[23].

[21] ibid.

[22] Canada rebuttal submission [45], quoting Brazil's written submission in *Brazil—Aircraft (Recourse to Arbitration—Article 22.6 DSU)* (n 12) [56] quoted in *Canada—Aircraft Credits and Guarantees (Recourse to Arbitration—Article 22.6 DSU and Article 4.11 SCM)* (n 12) n 53.

In other words, the Arbitrator essentially looked at the commercial reality of the relationship between Air Wisconsin and Bombardier to infer that it was unlikely that Canada's failure to comply with the DSB ruling would have caused the relationship between Air Wisconsin and Bombardier to end. It concluded from this, then, that Canada's failure to comply with the DSB ruling did not cause the level of nullification and impairment to Brazil's industry that Brazil proposed. To put this in causal terms, Brazil used a *sine qua non* test to contend that Canada's failure to comply with its DSB ruling had meant that its industry did not receive a benefit that it otherwise would have received. The Arbitrator might also be said to have found against causation using the *sine qua non* test, in the sense that they established that the hypothetical world that Brazil proposed would not have come to pass anyway.

A causal link was also rejected in *EC—Hormones (Article 22.6)*. In that case, the United States argued that, but for the fact that the EC did not comply with its DSB ruling, US exporters would have engaged in marketing and promotional efforts that would, in turn, have led to increased exports of edible beef offal worth $20.1 million.[23] The Arbitrator, however, concluded that the increased exports that may have resulted from the greater marketing and promotional efforts were 'too speculative'.[24] That is, the United States' argument was based on what would have happened in a hypothetical world. Without any more tangible evidence regarding the effect that marketing and promotional efforts would have had, the Arbitrators could not make out causation.

In short, there are two cases in which the Arbitrator did *not* find a causal link. In both cases, the Arbitrator used a *sine qua non* test to interrogate the arguments of Members. That is, the Arbitrator set up a parallel hypothetical world in which it compared the current level of nullification and impairment with the level of nullification and impairment that would be expected if the responding Member had complied with the DSB ruling. In both cases, the reason that causation was not found related to the fact that the Arbitrator did not find the alternative hypothetical scenario put forward by the complainant Member to be plausible. The difficulty with the approach of the Arbitrator here is that it

[23] WTO, *European Communities: Measures Concerning Meat and Meat Products (Hormones)—Recourse to Arbitration by the European Communities under Article 22.6 DSU—Decision by the Arbitrators* (12 July 1999) WT/DS26/ARB (*EC—Hormones (US) (Recourse to Arbitration—Article 22.6 DSU)*) [76]–[77].

[24] ibid [77].

is impossible truly to know whether the scenario put forward by the complainant Member would have happened or not due to the intractable 'hypothetical world problem'.[25]

Whilst these two cases are examples of where the Arbitrator did *not* make out causation, as has been mentioned previously, causation tends not to be explicitly discussed in those cases where a causal link *is* found. Accordingly, it is difficult to discern the basis on which a positive causal link is found. This omission would seem to lead to the conclusion that there is some kind of presumption in place in this context that a causal link exists, unless found otherwise – that is, the presumption is rebutted.

Moreover, just as Arbitrators have failed to elucidate the basis on which causation may be made out, so, too, have they failed to engage in any formal non-attribution analysis. To put this in symbolic language, Arbitrators skip to quantify the effect of C, without first making a determination that C actually caused E, and that E was not partially caused by X, Y and/or Z. Accordingly, by skipping over any true non-attribution and causal link analysis, Arbitrators are just as guilty as ordinary Panels of presuming the causal link between a responding Member's failure to comply with its DSB ruling and the nullification and impairment to a complaining Member's industry.

Moreover, by making this presumption of nullification and impairment as a result of a Member's failure to comply with its DSB ruling, the Arbitrators are making the same logical fallacy as the AB was observed to have made in Chapters 3 and 4. That is, such a presumption is essentially a way of leaping from the existence of a supposed cause to an effect without demonstrating the causal link between the two. Yet again, the trouble with making such a logical leap is summarised in the extended quotation from Hume that was excerpted in Chapter 3 and has been repeated in each subsequent chapter – in short, 'the effect is totally different from the cause, and consequently can never be discovered in it'.[26] That is, nullification and impairment to a complaining Member's industry cannot be presumed simply from the responding Member's failure to comply with its DSB ruling. Instead of making such a presumption, the Arbitrators ought positively to draw the causal link between the two with the same rigour as they currently do to disprove the link

[25] For an explanation of 'the hypothetical world problem', see Chapter 1, Section 1.2.1.

[26] For the more extended quotation, see David Hume, *An Enquiry Concerning Human Understanding* (LA Selby-Bigge ed, 3rd edn, OUP 1975) s IV, pt I quoted in Chapter 3, Section 3.4.

between the two. Drawing an accurate causal link arguably also involves a non-attribution analysis, and it is to this that the chapter now turns.

5.2.2 *Non-attribution in Retaliation Arbitrations*

Despite the lack of a formal non-attribution analysis, the Arbitrators have, at several points, engaged in an informal process of disaggregating other known factors from causal factors. Moreover, the Arbitrator has even explicitly acknowledged the importance of considering the way in which other known factors might mitigate the causal link between the responding Member's failure to comply with the DSB ruling and a complainant Member's nullification and impairment. In *EC—Hormones (Article 22.6)*, the Arbitrator gave credence to this idea, saying:

> What would annual prospective US exports of hormone-treated beef and beef products to the EC be if the EC had withdrawn the ban on 13 May 1999? An answer to this question, like any question about future events, can only be a reasoned estimate. It is necessarily based on certain assumptions. In making those estimates and assumptions, we need to guard against claims of lost opportunities where the causal link with the inconsistent hormone ban is less than apparent, i.e., where exports are allegedly forgone not because of the ban but due to other circumstances.[27]

The jurisprudence indicates that responding Members have consistently put forward other known factors when contending that the causal link between the failure to bring its measure(s) into conformity with a DSB ruling and the resulting nullification and impairment may have been confused. Nonetheless, despite some level of receptiveness to the idea that other known factors might attenuate the causal link, Arbitrators are yet to develop any formalised non-attribution analysis or even a consistent approach to disaggregating other known factors. This can be seen from a survey of some of the jurisprudence.

To take the case of *US—Gambling (Article 22.6)* first, this case concerned the question of whether Antigua's proposed level of suspension was equivalent to the level of nullification or impairment of benefits accruing to Antigua as a result of the United States' failure to bring its GATS-inconsistent measure into conformity with its obligations; and, if not, what the correct level of nullification or impairment was. With respect to calculating the level of nullification or impairment, the

[27] *EC—Hormones (US) (Recourse to Arbitration—Article 22.6 DSU)* (n 23) [41].

United States argued that its failure to bring its measure into conformity did not cause the level of injury contended by Antigua. The United States contended that the level of nullification or impairment put forward by Antigua had to be mitigated by the fact that Antigua lost market share in other countries due to the low market entry barriers to internet gambling and the ensuing growth in competition from operators in other locations.[28] Antigua dismissed all of the United States' arguments,[29] and the Arbitrator was required to make their own assessment as to the level of nullification or impairment brought about by the United States' failure to bring its measure into conformity with the DSB ruling.

Finding the approach of both parties deficient,[30] the Arbitrator sought to calculate the level of nullification and impairment using its own approach.[31] To this end, the Arbitrator: (1) sought to establish Antigua's approximate revenues from remote gambling services exports to the United States; (2) adjusted the time series for the impact of competing suppliers; (3) determined what the likely proportion of betting services on horseracing derived from Antigua's total revenues from remote gambling; and (4) considered the demand for gambling services on horseracing in the United States.[32] Most importantly, for present purposes, the Arbitrator took into account the other known factors raised by the United States – namely, Antigua's lost market share due to low market entry barriers – and considered the mitigating impact this may have had on the level of nullification and impairment. To do this, the Arbitrator looked at data concerning countries in the region that compete with Antigua for the US market and, therefore, should have been similarly affected by the United States' measures.[33] When analysing this data, the Arbitrator concluded that Antigua underperformed in the relevant period 2002–06 relative to its main competitors.[34] The Arbitrator then reduced Antigua's proposed level of nullification and impairment on account of the fact that the data indicated that the nullification and impairment had not been caused by the United States' failure to comply with the DSB ruling alone. In sum, the Arbitrator did allow for the idea that other known factors – in this case, Antigua's loss of market share – could attenuate the causal link between

[28] *US—Gambling (Recourse to Arbitration—Article 22.6 DSU)* (n 11) [3.127]–[3.128].
[29] ibid [3.131].
[30] ibid [3.172].
[31] ibid [3.173].
[32] ibid [3.174].
[33] ibid [3.181]–[3.182].
[34] ibid.

the United States' failure to apply the DSB ruling and the nullification and impairment to Antigua.

The idea that other known factors might mitigate the causal link between a failure to comply with the DSB ruling and the ensuing nullification and impairment arose again in *US—Tuna II (Mexico) (Article 22.6)*.[35] In that case, the Arbitrator considered the level of nullification or impairment that Mexico suffered as a result of the United States' 2013 Tuna Measure. The United States argued that the nullification and impairment of Mexico's tuna industry as a result of the 2013 Tuna Measure must be mitigated by a change in consumer preferences in the US market. That is, the United States contended that there was a decline in the consumption of canned yellowfin at the same time as the 2013 Tuna Measure was taking effect.[36] The Arbitrator analysed the data provided and concluded that 'the sharpness of the decline in both imports of tuna from Mexico and purchases of yellowfin by US canneries following the adoption of the Tuna Measure in 1990 suggests that the adoption of the Tuna Measure was the main reason for the declining trend'.[37] The Arbitrator went on to say that it was not persuaded by the United States' argument that the sharp decline was brought about by a sharp change in consumer preferences.[38] The Arbitrator also pointed to the fact that the decline 'came on the heels of the adoption of the Tuna Measure'.[39] It concluded with respect to the United States' argument regarding the change in consumer preferences that '[a]lthough we do not rule out that this may be possible, in our view the United States has not submitted evidence sufficient to establish the existence of such a change in this case'.[40]

In short, the Arbitrator in this case made a decision about the cause of the decline in the purchase of yellowfin by US canneries based on the sharp change in the gradient of the graph and the proximity of that change to the introduction of the Tuna Measure. In so doing, the Arbitrator took an all-or-nothing approach based on the coincidence in time between the two phenomena, and did not interrogate the way in which the change in consumer preferences might have had the effect of attenuating the causal link between the United States' measure and

[35] *US—Tuna II (Mexico) (Recourse to Arbitration—Article 22.6 DSU)* (n 18).
[36] ibid [5.29].
[37] ibid [5.31].
[38] ibid [5.32].
[39] ibid.
[40] ibid.

Mexico's level of nullification and impairment. In other words, unlike in *US—Gambling (Article 22.6)*, the Arbitrator did not make any attempt to discern how the other known factors may have had the effect of reducing the level of nullification and impairment.

The Arbitrator in *US—COOL (Article 22.6)*[41] gave more scope to the idea that other known factors attenuate the causal link between a responding Member's failure to comply with a DSB ruling and the complainant Member's ultimate nullification and impairment. The Arbitrator in that case considered the proposed level of nullification and impairment by Canada and Mexico and then proposed its own determination, which took account of a number of other known factors. Whereas Mexico's proposed level of nullification and impairment relied on simulating the use of the COOL impact on export prices and a derived elasticity of export supply,[42] Canada's proposed level of nullification and impairment was based on the assumption that there was '[a] high level of integration between the Canadian and US markets'.[43] Canada argued that there was 'price arbitrage' between the Canadian export price of live cattle and hogs and the price of domestic cattle and hogs, and that '[t]here [were] no domestic factors that impede this mechanism'.[44] Canada argued that the result of this arbitrage mechanism was that there was:

> a direct causal link between the amended COOL measure and the domestic price suppression losses experienced in Canada. Because of this arbitrage between markets, the price impacts for the domestic price-suppression analysis are the same as those that are used in the calculation of export revenue losses.[45]

The United States, however, brought data showing volatility between the Canadian and United States' markets and showed that such volatility was caused by causal factors other than the COOL measure.[46] These other known factors included, according to the United States, economic fluctuations and recession; long-term unemployment; increased feed costs; shifts in Canadian and Mexican livestock and meat processing; shifting transportation costs; weather patterns and drought; impacts of animal disease such as bovine spongiform encephalopathy in the Canadian herd;

[41] *US—COOL (Recourse to Arbitration—Article 22.6 DSU)* (n 18).
[42] ibid [5.111].
[43] ibid Annex B-1, 39.
[44] ibid.
[45] ibid.
[46] ibid [5.40].

and increased demand for meat during US holidays.[47] The United States submitted that 'it is important to ensure that, in determining the level of nullification or impairment, trade effects attributable to a factor other than the measure at issue are not attributed to the measure at issue since that would result in an erroneous level of nullification or impairment'.[48] The Arbitrator reviewed the evidence brought by both Canada and the United States and concluded that Canada's econometric model failed to account for a number of variables or other known factors.[49] In so doing, the Arbitrator affirmed the importance of using a model that is able to disaggregate other known factors from the causal effect of the measure.[50] In other words, the Arbitrator essentially found fault with Canada's econometric model for failing to perform an adequate non-attribution analysis prior to its causal link analysis.

The importance that the Arbitrator placed on other known factors can be seen in the way in which it decided to calculate the level of nullification and impairment experienced by Canada and Mexico. That is, in formulating the linear regression equation that it ultimately used to estimate the effect of the COOL measure, the Arbitrator used 'monthly dummies' to control for seasonality; changes in the exchange rate; Canadian cattle-specific events (such as BSE) and for Canadian pigs; the closure of a hog-processing plant.[51] Additionally, the Arbitrator included variables to control for changes in transport costs, the recession, changes in feed costs and the level of competing imports, drought events as well as the spread of the porcine epidemic diarrhea virus.[52] Moreover, it also considered the impact of transport costs for Canada only.[53] In short, the Arbitrator recognised that, in calculating the level of nullification and impairment brought about by the United States' COOL measure, it also needed to take into account the effect of other known factors.

Whilst recognising the impact that other known factors might have on attenuating the causal link between the United States' failure to bring its measure into conformity with a DSB ruling and the impact on Canada and Mexico's economies, the *US—COOL (Article 22.6)* Arbitrator nonetheless

[47] ibid [5.65].
[48] United States' opening statement at the meeting of the Arbitrator, para 28 quoted in *US—COOL (Recourse to Arbitration—Article 22.6 DSU)* (n 18) [5.64].
[49] *US—COOL (Recourse to Arbitration—Article 22.6 DSU)* (n 18) [5.106]–[5.110].
[50] ibid [5.106]–[5.108].
[51] ibid [6.36].
[52] ibid [6.38].
[53] ibid [6.29].

did not perform a discreet causal analysis. Instead, the linear regression equation that it formulated sought simultaneously to: (1) establish a causal link; (2) make allowance for other known factors; and (3) quantify the level of nullification and impairment. Again, to express this symbolically, the linear regression equation would read as follows: 'Did C cause E? To what extent do X, Y and Z mitigate the causal link between C and E? And how much is E?' On the one hand, it is positive that the Arbitrator showed a willingness to consider the way in which other known factors have mitigated the causal link. On the other hand, it is suggested that the linear regression equation attempts to do too much in one step. Moreover, the very way in which the equation is formulated again reflects the presumption that a causal link exists. That is, the formula is calculating the level of the effect at the same time as it analyses the causal link, which implies that the existence of causation is a fait accompli. In this sense, this approach is similar to the unitary approach to determining serious prejudice under the SCM Agreement, discussed in Chapter 3. It is contended that an alternative approach might involve, first, performing a non-attribution analysis, then determining whether there was a causal link as a secondary step, before moving, lastly, to quantify the level of nullification and impairment.

Finally, in *US—Countervailing Measures (China) (Article 22.6)*,[54] the United States also argued that adjustments should be made to the two-step Armington model based on other known factors.[55] Specifically, the United States argued that the evolution of the market in the time between the imposition of the countervailing duties and the remedy year was affected by new market participants and third countries whose market shares grew disproportionately quickly 'as a result of "industry investments" or certain "government policies"' ('Rising Suppliers').[56] The Arbitrator found, however, that the USITC was not able to provide sufficient evidence to support its claim.[57] Moreover, the Arbitrator also held that the United States was not able to demonstrate that the Rising Suppliers were not actually a direct consequence of the introduction of the countervailing duties at issue.[58] In sum, the Arbitrator ultimately

54 WTO, *United States: Countervailing Duty Measures on Certain Products from China—Recourse to Arbitration by the United States under Article 22.6 DSU—Decision by the Arbitrator* (26 January 2022) WT/DS437/ARB (*US—Countervailing Measures (China) (Recourse to Arbitration—Article 22.6)*).

55 ibid [3.94].

56 ibid.

57 ibid [3.101]–[3.102].

58 ibid [3.103].

rejected the United States' arguments that other known factors should be considered when drawing the causal link between its failure to comply with the DSB ruling and the nullification and impairment suffered by China. Nonetheless, it is of note that the United States raised the possibility of other known factors as having a mitigating effect on the causal link.

Indeed, the fact that many Members have raised other known factors as possibly mitigating the causal link between its failure to comply with a DSB ruling and the nullification and impairment suffered by another Member is revealing. It indicates that it is too simplistic to draw a causal link between a responding Member's failure to comply with a DSB ruling and a declining industry or economy. It has been seen that the Arbitrator has been receptive to the idea that other known factors can complicate this causal link and that they must therefore take this possibility into account in their calculations. It has also been seen through this survey of the jurisprudence, however, that the Arbitrator is yet to develop any consistent methodology for accommodating other known factors. It is suggested that the Tripartite Non-attribution/Causal Link Analysis might be used to fill this lacuna. Before turning to consider the way in which the Tripartite Non-attribution/Causal Link Analysis might be used here, it remains first to consider the way in which the Arbitrator uses a kind of counterfactual analysis in order to determine the level of nullification and impairment caused to a Member's industry.

5.3 Causal Link Analysis in the Determination of Nullification and Impairment

Whilst the jurisprudence does not indicate any consistent methodology for making a determination of non-attribution or a causal link, the Arbitrator has consistently drawn on a counterfactual analysis as a means of determining the nullification and impairment of an industry. In *US—Anti-Dumping Methodologies (China) (Article 22.6)*, the Arbitrator said that a counterfactual in the context of Article 22.6 was 'an analytical tool that allows an [Arbitrator] acting under Article 22.6 of the DSU to determine the level of nullification or impairment caused by the WTO-inconsistent measures maintained by the original respondent'.[59] In *US—Tuna II (Mexico)*

[59] WTO, *United States: Certain Methodologies and Their Application to Anti-Dumping Proceedings Involving China—Recourse to Arbitration by the United States under Article 22.6—Decision by the Arbitrators* (1 November 2019) WT/DS471/ARB (*US—Anti-Dumping Methodologies (China) (Recourse to Arbitration—Article 22.6)*) [5.2].

(Article 22.6), moreover, the Arbitrator defined a 'counterfactual' in the context of Article 22.6 of the DSU as 'a hypothetical scenario that describes what would have happened in terms of trade flows had the responding party implemented the DSB recommendations and rulings'.[60] The Arbitrator went on to explain in the same case that 'the legal standard that a scenario must meet for it to constitute an appropriate counterfactual for purposes of Article 22.6 proceedings is that of *plausibility* and *reasonability*'.[61] These principles of plausibility and reasonability take precedence over simplicity or expediency. For example, in *US—Anti-Dumping Methodologies (China) (Article 22.6)*, the Arbitrator rejected China's counterfactual assessment even though it was 'undoubtedly more straightforward and easier to implement' because the assessment was not reasonable or plausible.[62] Moreover, the Arbitrator in *US—Gambling (Article 22.6)* further held that:

> . . . the considerations of plausibility and reasonableness are connected to the nature and scope of benefits that are nullified or impaired by the measure at issue: [T]o the extent that the estimation of the level of nullification or impairment requires certain assumptions to be made as to what benefits would have accrued, in a situation where compliance would have taken place, such assumptions should be reasonable, taking into account the circumstances of the dispute, in order for the proposed level of suspension to accurately reflect the benefits accruing to the complaining party that have actually been nullified or impaired.[63]

In sum, the Arbitrator estimated the level of nullification or impairment brought about by a responding Member's failure to comply with the DSB recommendations. It did so by calculating the difference between the value of trade (if any) that took place despite the WTO-inconsistent measure over a designated time period and the value of trade that would have occurred over the same period if the other responding Member had complied with the DSB recommendation.[64] In other words,

60 *US—Tuna II (Mexico) (Recourse to Arbitration—Article 22.6)* (n 18) [4.4].

61 ibid [4.5] (emphasis original).

62 *US—Anti-Dumping Methodologies (China) (Recourse to Arbitration—Article 22.6)* (n 59) [5.8].

63 *US—Gambling (Recourse to Arbitration—Article 22.6 DSU)* (n 11) [3.30]. This was quoted with approval in WTO, *United States: Anti-Dumping and Countervailing Measures on Large Residential Washers from Korea—Recourse to Arbitration by the United States under Article 22.6—Decision by the Arbitrations* (8 February 2019) WT/DS464/ARB (*US—Washing Machines (Recourse to Arbitration—Article 22.6)*) [3.10].

64 See, eg, *US—Tuna II (Mexico) (Recourse to Arbitration—Article 22.6)* (n 18) [4.3]; *EC—Bananas III (Recourse to Arbitration—Article 22.6 DSU—US)* (n 12) [7.1]; *Canada—Aircraft Credits and Guarantees (Recourse to Arbitration—Article 22.6 DSU and Article*

the Arbitrator effectively used a *sine qua non* test as a means of assessing what the value of a Member's exports would have been 'but for' the responding Member's failure to comply with the DSB ruling.

The most obvious difficulty with relying on a counterfactual in this context is the hypothetical world problem. That is, it is impossible to know with any degree of certainty what a Member's trade flows might have been had the other Member complied with the DSB ruling. This lack of certainty has a number of elements to it. First, if the responding Member were to have complied with the DSB ruling, it has a degree of choice about the way in which it implements the DSB recommendations.[65] That is, there is no one prescribed manner of complying; and it follows from this that it is difficult for an Arbitrator to reconstruct the manner in which the non-compliant Member would have implemented the DSB recommendations, had it done so.[66] Article 22.6 DSU simply requires that the Arbitrator 'determine whether the level of such suspension is equivalent to the level of nullification or impairment'. The jurisprudence consistently demonstrates, however, that the choice of counterfactual is somewhat arbitrary, even though the financial implications of the counterfactual that goes on to be chosen are significant.

The arbitrary nature of choosing a counterfactual can be seen in the variety of counterfactuals chosen by the Arbitrator in some of the cases. Typically, the Arbitrator has chosen a counterfactual based on the hypothetical world in which the challenged measure had been inexistent. This was the case, for example, in the *EC—Hormones (Article 22.6)* arbitration. That is, the original Panel proceedings involved a dispute about the EC's ban on imports of hormone-treated beef based on scientifically contentious beliefs. In order to determine the level of nullification and impairment caused by the ban, the Arbitrator compared the value of beef exports under the WTO-inconsistent EC regime with the value of beef

4.11 SCM) (n 12) [3.21]; WTO, *European Communities: Measures Concerning Meat and Meat Products (Hormones)—Recourse to Arbitration by the European Communities under Article 22.6—Decision by the Arbitrators* (12 July 1999) WT/DS48/ARB (*EC—Hormones (Canada) (Recourse to Arbitration—Article 22.6)*) [3.5]; [5.45]; [6.32].

65 See, eg, WTO, *United States: Sunset Review of Anti-Dumping Measures on Oil Country Tubular Goods from Argentina—Recourse to Arbitration by Argentina under Article 21.5—Decision by the Arbitrators* (12 April 2007) WT/DS268/AB/RW [184] and *US—Tuna II (Mexico) (Recourse to Arbitration—Article 22.6)* (n 18) [4.4].

66 *US—Tuna II (Mexico) (Recourse to Arbitration—Article 22.6)* (n 18) [4.4]. See also, Kym Anderson, 'Peculiarities of Retaliation in WTO Dispute Settlement' (2000) 1(2) WTR 123, 130.

exports that would have occurred in a WTO-consistent EC import regime.[67] The Arbitrator did not explicitly consider, however, that the EC might have been able to keep the import ban in place whilst imposing an adequate risk assessment. If this counterfactual had been chosen instead, it would have resulted in a different calculation as to the effect of the import ban.

In contrast, in *US—Washing Machines (Article 22.6)*, the Arbitrator went to some lengths to create its own counterfactual. That is, the counterfactual that the Arbitrator implemented was not based on the challenged measure being inexistent, nor on the counterfactual proposed by either party. Instead, the Arbitrator adopted a different counterfactual entirely. In so doing, the Arbitrator relied on the United States Department of Commerce (USDOC) investigation as the basis for its calculation of the new counterfactual.[68] Balistreri, Mavroidis and Prusa argue that, by relying on USDOC's calculations in order to use it as a benchmark for a new counterfactual actually constitutes a form of *de novo* review.[69] In this sense, the case indicates the lengths that an Arbitrator can go to in order to select a plausible and reasonable counterfactual. It also raises concerns about a lack of legal certainty over which counterfactual will be chosen, since the parties in that case were afforded little control over the final counterfactual assessment.

Additionally, in *EC—Bananas III (Article 22.6)*, the Arbitrator selected one counterfactual from amongst several possible alternatives without explaining the reason for the choice.[70] As Spamann noted, it is arguable that if another counterfactual were used, the level of impairment suffered by the United States could be calculated as being zero, as opposed to \$191.4 million per year.[71] In this sense, although the choice of counterfactual may appear somewhat arbitrary, it nonetheless has significant financial implications for the parties.

[67] *EC—Hormones (US) (Recourse to Arbitration—Article 22.6 DSU)* (n 23) [42]–[43].

[68] *US—Washing Machines (Recourse to Arbitration—Article 22.6)* (n 63) [3.31]–[3.32].

[69] Edward Balistreri, Petros C Mavroidis and Thomas J Prusa, 'What If? Tinkering with the Counterfactual: A Comment on *US—Washing Machines (Article 22.6—US)*' (2020) EUI Working Papers (RSCAs 2020/50) Robert Schuman Centre for Advanced Studies, Global Governance Programme-405, 12 <https://cadmus.eui.eu/handle/1814/67092> accessed 1 June 2022.

[70] *EC—Bananas III (US) (Recourse to Arbitration—Article 22.6)* (n 12) [7.4]–[7.7]; *EC—Bananas (Ecuador) (Recourse to Arbitration—Article 22.6 and Article 4.11)* (n 12) [166]–[167].

[71] Holger Spamann, 'The Myth of "Rebalancing" Retaliation in WTO Dispute Settlement Practice' (2006) 9 JIEL 31, 53.

Second, even if an Arbitrator were able accurately to predict how the responding Member would have implemented the DSB's recommendations, it is nonetheless difficult to reconstruct the complainant Member's flow of trade that would follow from that implementation. This difficulty may be seen, for example, in the *EC—Large Civil Aircraft (Article 22.6)* arbitration[72] and the *US—Large Civil Aircraft (2nd complaint) (Article 22.6)* arbitration.[73] Both of these cases involved hypothetical 'lost sales' within the selected counterfactual. Taking the *EC—Large Civil Aircraft (Article 22.6)* case first, in order to reconstruct the hypothetical lost sales, the United States needed to select comparator orders from the real world that it believed approximated the lost sales. One of the points of dispute in the arbitration concerned the choice of comparator orders selected by the United States in their counterfactual assessment. The EU argued that the United States' selected comparators were not 'representative, reliable, and robust approximations of the counterfactual lost sales'.[74] The Arbitrator was then required to examine the comparator orders in detail before settling on its own likely comparator orders as a means of reconstructing the hypothetical lost sales.[75] The need to do so reinforces the difficulty of reimagining the likely flow of trade that would have followed from implementing the DSB's ruling.

Similarly, one of the issues in *US—Large Civil Aircraft (2nd complaint) (Article 22.6)* concerned the EU's counterfactual assessment of its lost sales due to the Washington State B&O tax rate reduction. The compliance panel and the AB both found that Airbus would have won the five lost sales campaigns; and accordingly, winning these sales was consistent with the EU's counterfactual for the purposes of the arbitration. Given the uncertainty around the lost sales, however, the United States contended that the Arbitrator ought to include a probabilistic adjustment to the expected value of each of the sales campaigns in its valuation of the adverse effects.[76] The Arbitrator, however, rejected the United States'

[72] WTO, *European Communities and Certain Member States: Measures Affecting Trade in Large Civil Aircraft—Recourse to Arbitration by the European Communities under Article 22.6—Decision by the Arbitrators* (2 October 2019) WT/DS316/ARB (*EC—Large Civil Aircraft (Recourse to Arbitration—Article 22.6)*).

[73] *United States: Measures Affecting Trade in Large Civil Aircraft (Second Complaint)—Recourse to Arbitration by the United States under Article 22.6—Decision by the Arbitrators* (13 October 2020) WT/DS353/ARB (*US—Large Civil Aircraft (Recourse to Arbitration—Article 22.6)*).

[74] *EC—Large Civil Aircraft (Recourse to Arbitration—Article 22.6)* (n 72) [6.279].

[75] ibid [6.311], table 11.

[76] *US—Large Civil Aircraft (Recourse to Arbitration—Article 22.6)* (n 73) [6.10].

proposal, due to the fact that the AB had already upheld the compliance panel's assessment of the likelihood of the Airbus sales.[77] Nonetheless, both cases showcase the difficulty involved in reconstructing the flow of trade in a hypothetical world for the purposes of arbitrations under Article 22.6 DSU.

Yet another difficulty with selecting a hypothetical world in this context concerns the selection of a suitable time frame that the Arbitrator should consider when determining the level of nullification or impairment caused by a Member's failure to comply with a DSB ruling. There is no rule in the DSU prescribing the time frame for the determination of the level of nullification or impairment. As such, an Arbitrator has some degree of discretion as to whether to consider the impact of a failure to comply with the DSB ruling on a more short-term or long-term basis. The time period ultimately chosen has implications for the kinds of considerations to be factored into the causal link analysis, such as the reliability of the data for discerning a causal link and the possibility that other known factors might confound such a causal link.

Past arbitrations under Article 22.6 DSU suggest that the period of time for determining the level of nullification or impairment is usually the period that immediately follows the end of the 'Reasonable Period of Time'. That is, the period of time that is agreed upon by the parties for the responding Member to implement the DSB ruling. The *US—Tuna II (Mexico) (Article 22.6)*[78] raised difficult timing issues, however, because it concerned a measure (the 2013 Tuna Measure) that sought to implement the DSB ruling, but was found to do so inadequately. Accordingly, in that case, Mexico sought compensation for the nullification and impairment caused by the 2013 Tuna Measure. The Arbitrator then had to decide the time period over which to assess the impact of the withdrawal of the measure. Whilst the parties agreed that the time period should be short-term,[79] they disagreed on whether the time period should be immediately following the withdrawal of the measure or in the most recent year, where the United States argued that it was more appropriate to use the most recent data available.[80] Ultimately, the Arbitrator decided to select the time period immediately following the withdrawal of the measure.[81]

77 ibid [6.164]–[6.165].
78 *US—Tuna II (Mexico) (Recourse to Arbitration—Article 22.6)* (n 18).
79 ibid [4.14].
80 ibid [4.15].
81 ibid [4.17].

In doing so, however, the case brings attention to the fact that in some instances the time period selected is left to the Arbitrator's discretion, and in this sense, is somewhat arbitrary.

All of these aspects mean that the selection of a counterfactual can be very troublesome. That said, it would seem that, regrettably, there is no obvious alternative to the use of a counterfactual in this context. That is, it is difficult to conceive of a way of attempting to quantify the level of nullification or impairment in a manner that does not involve formulating a counterfactual,[82] and the hypothetical world problem that is inherent in the use of counterfactuals is insoluble.

A genuine non-attribution analysis goes a small way towards mitigating these difficulties, in the sense that it aims to disaggregate those factors that are irrelevant to drawing a causal link. This means that, in effect, the number of possible hypothetical worlds is somewhat reduced compared to where no non-attribution analysis is undertaken. Nonetheless, a non-attribution analysis is certainly not able to mitigate the problems associated with the hypothetical world problem completely. Therefore, all the Arbitrator can do is simply be mindful of the fact that the hypothetical world problem is methodologically problematic, and accordingly approach the choice of counterfactual with great caution.[83]

There is one aspect of the use of counterfactuals in this context, however, that might be remedied. This is the presumption that is currently in place in the jurisprudence that the level of the nullification and impairment was 100 per cent caused by the responding Member's failure to bring its measure(s) into conformity with the DSB ruling. That is, the way in which the test currently operates in the jurisprudence is essentially as follows: 'but for' the responding Member's failure to comply with the DSB ruling, what would the complainant Member's industry look like?

[82] The Arbitrator in *US—Washing Machines (Recourse to Arbitration—Article 22.6)* (n 63) footnote 42 lists nine disputes in which counterfactuals are used, which effectively omits three disputes adjudicated under Article 22.6. In practice, however, even the three cases that are omitted involve setting up an implicit counterfactual. This point is also made by Balistreri, Mavroidis and Prusa (n 69) 2.

[83] Some of the jurisprudence already evidences a degree of caution about the selection of counterfactuals; see, for example, the following: *US—Tuna II (Mexico) (Recourse to Arbitration—Article 22.6)* (n 18) [4.2]–[4.10]; *EC—Bananas III (Recourse to Arbitration—Article 22.6 DSU—Ecuador)* (n 12) [7.1]–[7.8]; *US—COOL (Recourse to Arbitration—Article 22.6 DSU)* (n 18) [3.10]–[3.12]; *US—Gambling (Recourse to Arbitration—Article 22.6 DSU)* (n 11) [3.16]–[3.73]; *EC—Large Civil Aircraft (Recourse to Arbitration—Article 22.6)* (n 72) [6.77]–[6.79]; and *US—Anti-Dumping Methodologies (China) (Recourse to Arbitration—Article 22.6)* (n 59) [5.4]–[5.63].

By using the counterfactual test in this way, the Arbitrator is presuming that no other known factors have confused the causal link. This presumption is not just flawed in a conceptual sense, in that it misunderstands the multi-dimensional nature of causation. It is also at odds with other aspects of the jurisprudence, in which it has been seen that the Arbitrator has conceded that other known factors have the potential to attenuate the causal link between a responding Member's failure to comply with a DSB ruling and a complainant Member's injured industry.

To put the current approach in symbolic terms, then, this would involve asking, 'How much is E?' before even establishing that C caused E. It might be counterargued that the Arbitrator could simply readjust the amount of nullification and impairment in light of the other known factors raised by the responding Member, as is currently done in the jurisprudence. This approach, however, continues to misunderstand causation, as it essentially asks, 'How much is E? Is the effect of E mitigated by X, Y and Z?' This is essentially similar to the 'breaking the causal link' approach discussed in Chapter 2. A superior approach would instead ask, 'To what extent must C be mitigated by X, Y and Z? With X, Y and Z accounted for, may it nonetheless be said that C caused E? If so, how much is E?' This sequence of logic underlies the Tripartite Non-attribution/Causal Link Analysis, which will be discussed in Sections 5.4 and 5.5. In short, the Tripartite Non-attribution/Causal Link Analysis still requires that a counterfactual be used as a point of comparison from which the nullification and impairment must be measured. It does not, however, presume that 100 per cent of the nullification and impairment was caused by a responding Member's failure to comply with a DSB ruling. Instead, it is open to the possibility that the causal link was attenuated by other known factors. The next two sections will discuss in greater detail how the Tripartite Non-attribution/Causal Link Analysis might work in this context.

5.4 Non-attribution: The First Two Steps of the Tripartite Process

5.4.1 *Introduction*

It has been seen in Chapters 2–4 that the Tripartite Non-attribution/Causal Link Analysis involves three analytical steps.[84] These steps can be

[84] These steps have been taken from WTO, *United States: Definitive Safeguard Measures on Imports of Wheat Gluten from the European Communities—Report of the Appellate Body* (22 December 2000) WT/DS166/AB/R (AB, *US—Wheat Gluten*) [69].

adapted to this context as follows: (1) the Arbitrator must identify the specific types of nullification and impairment that have been inflicted on the affected industry; (2) the Arbitrator must then disaggregate the harm brought about by the responding Member's failure to comply with the DSB ruling vis-à-vis the harm brought about by other known factors; and (3) finally, the Arbitrator should determine whether there is a causal link between a responding Member's failure to comply with a DSB ruling and the nullification and impairment. It may be recalled that the first two steps are directed at performing a non-attribution analysis, while the third step relates to the causal link analysis. It is suggested that it is only once these non-attribution and causal link analyses are complete that the Arbitrator should then turn to quantify the level of nullification and impairment incurred.

The use of the Tripartite Non-attribution/Causal Link Analysis in this context has three important benefits. The first is conceptual, in the sense that it reflects a clearer understanding of causation. That is, if an Arbitrator uses the Tripartite Non-attribution/Causal Link Analysis in this context, they are able to establish causation (instead of presuming it) before going on to then quantify the effects. To put this in symbolic language, if the Tripartite Non-attribution/Causal Link Analysis were used prior to the Arbitrator turning to quantify the level of nullification and impairment, the analysis would proceed as follows: 'To what extent must C be mitigated by X, Y and Z? With X, Y and Z accounted for, may it nonetheless be said that C caused E? If so, how much is E?' This is a more logical approach than skipping straight to quantifying effects before a causal link has even been properly established.

The second benefit of the Tripartite Non-attribution/Causal Link Analysis here is that it provides greater consistency to the analysis and, therefore, also greater legal certainty. It has been seen that the jurisprudence to date has a number of inconsistencies in it. First, it has been seen that the causal link analysis is only really explicitly performed when a causal link is *not* made out. Second, it has also been seen that the Arbitrator has not developed any consistent methodology for taking into account other known factors. The Tripartite Non-attribution/Causal Link Analysis can go a long way towards providing greater consistency to these analyses.

The third benefit of using the Tripartite Non-attribution/Causal Link Analysis in this context is a practical one. Due to the fact that the Tripartite Non-attribution/Causal Link Analysis takes a quantitative approach, it is able to provide a percentage approximation of the extent to which a responding Member's failure to comply with a DSB ruling is responsible for the harm in the complainant Member's industry. This percentage approximation can then be used by the Arbitrator to assist in quantifying the amount of compensation payable to the complainant Member. A worked example of this will be seen in Section 5.5.

Despite these important benefits, the AB has never considered the way in which non-attribution and causal link analyses might be applied in the context of Article 22.6 arbitrations. Self-evidently, this lack of consideration means that no Arbitrators have provided any guidance as to how non-attribution and causal link analyses might work in this context, in contrast to the trade remedies context discussed in Chapter 2 and the serious prejudice context discussed in Chapter 3. Some guidance in the context of Article 22.6 arbitrations would be useful at several points in the Tripartite Non-attribution/Causal Link Analysis, particularly in respect of the Qualification Analysis and the causal link parts of the analysis. In the absence of this guidance, it is unfortunately necessary to speculate to some degree about how the Tripartite Non-attribution/Causal Link Analysis might work.

As in Chapters 2–4, a worked hypothetical example will be used, given the abstract nature of the aforementioned three steps. In this case, imagine that Member A has failed to bring its measure into conformity with a DSB ruling. Member B attempted to negotiate with Member A in order to develop mutually acceptable compensation, pursuant to Article 22.2 of the DSU. These negotiations failed, and Member B now requests arbitration under Article 22.6 of the DSU so that the Arbitrator might determine the level of nullification and impairment caused to Member B's cotton industry.

5.4.2 *The First Step of the Non-attribution Process*

It may be recalled that the aim of the first step of the non-attribution process is to separate the injuries caused by a Member's failure to comply with a DSB ruling vis-à-vis the injuries caused by other known factors. In the present case study involving Member B's adversely affected cotton industry, the Arbitrator would be required to separate all of the injurious effects to Member B's cotton industry into smaller injuries. This chapter, as in Chapter 2, will call these 'sub-injuries'. In this context, sub-injuries inflicted on Member B's cotton industry might include: (1) loss of productivity; (2) suppressed utilisation of capacity; (3) injury to corporate profits; (4) negative effects on cash flow and so forth. Again, these sub-injuries are examples only, and the nature and number of sub-injuries will differ from case to case. Figure 5.1 sets out a representation of the separation of the sub-injuries. Whilst Figure 5.1 represents each sub-injury to the cotton industry as being of equal size, in reality, the impact on each sub-injury might vary significantly.

5.4.3 *The Second Step of the Non-attribution Process*

Introduction

As in Chapters 2–4, the purpose of the second step of the non-attribution analysis in the context of Article 22.6 disputes is ultimately to apportion responsibility for the sub-injuries inflicted on the complainant Member's industry between the responding Member's failure to comply with the DSB ruling on the one hand and other known factors on the other hand. As in the other contexts discussed in this book, causal responsibility could be attributed to: (1) the responding Member's failure to comply with the DSB ruling alone; (2) other known factors alone; or (3) some combination of the two. Once the Arbitrator has apportioned causal responsibility between these groups, it is then in a position to determine which factors would qualify for inclusion in the final causal link analysis.

Apportionment Analysis: Disentanglement Stage The disentanglement stage involves analysing and separating the sub-injuries of a responding Member's failure to comply with a DSB ruling vis-à-vis the effects of other known factors. In order to gain data on the effects of a Member's failure to comply with a DSB ruling and the effects of other known factors, a fact-finder would need to use the same kind of counterfactual analysis that was discussed under Section 5.3. Whilst this counterfactual analysis brings with it the attendant difficulties associated with the hypothetical world problem that were discussed in that section, these would appear to be unavoidable as a means of assessing effects.

Moreover, the disentanglement exercise would seem to require that these effects be assessed in quantitative terms. A quantitative approach is consistent with the insistence on a quantitative approach for the nullification and impairment analyses in the Article 22.6 context. Indeed, in *US—1916 Act (Article 22.6)*, the Arbitrator rejected the EC's request for suspension of 'qualitatively equivalent'[85] obligations.[86] The Arbitrator in

[85] WTO, *United States: Antidumping Act of 1916—Recourse to Arbitration by the United States under Article 22.6 of the DSU—Decision of the Arbitrators* (24 February 2004) WT/DS136/ARB [5.17].

[86] ibid [5.23].

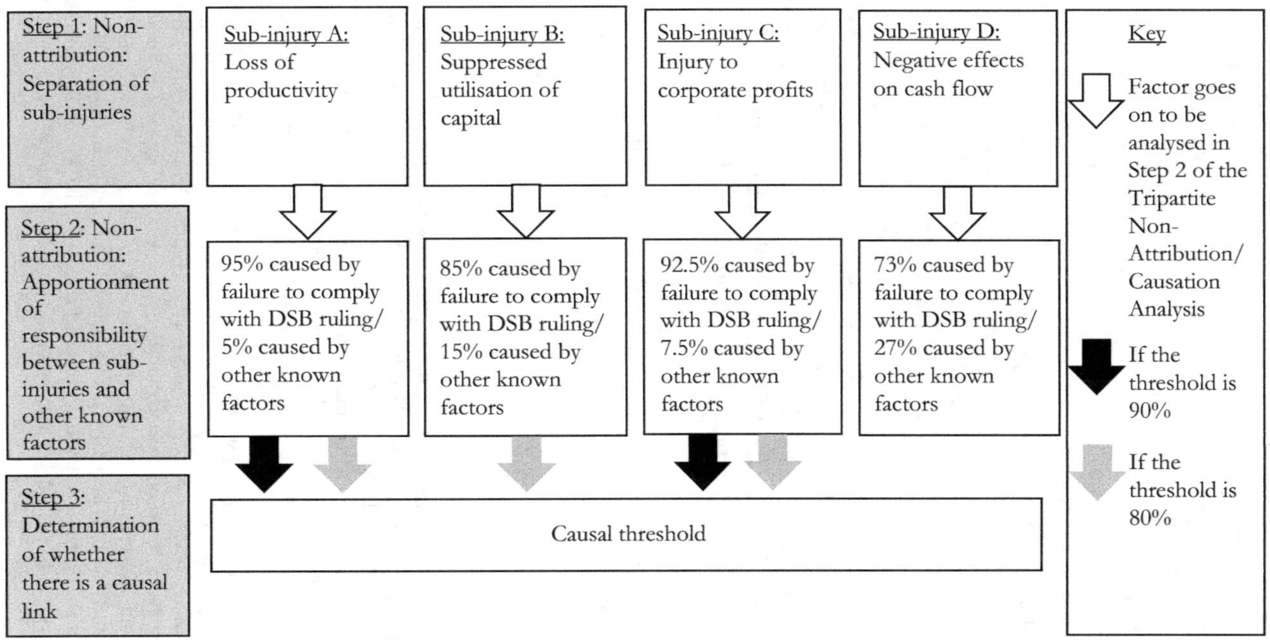

Figure 5.1 Overview of Steps One, Two and Three of the Tripartite Non-attribution/Causal Link Analysis with respect to Articles 22.6 DSU and 4.10 SCM Agreement

that case said that, in order to assess 'equivalence', it was necessary to determine the trade or economic effects of the measure in numerical or monetary terms.[87] This ruling is consistent with others, where a quantitative approach was also emphasised.[88] Just as a determination of 'equivalence' is difficult without the use of a quantitative analysis, so, too, is it difficult to perform a genuine disentanglement of the different types of effects on the complainant Member's industry. Moreover, Article 22.6 arbitrations have been identified as one area of WTO jurisprudence to which the use of economic analysis is particularly well-suited.[89] Using a quantitative approach would allow the Arbitrator to draw on those econometric approaches that have been used in the safeguards and antidumping contexts in order to separate injuries produced from trade measures vis-à-vis other known factors[90] or, alternatively, any other econometric approach developed by an 'expert review group' formed under Article 13.2 of the DSU. Once the effects of a responding Member's failure to comply with a DSB ruling are separated from the effects of other known factors, the Arbitrator can then turn to consider which effects should go on to be included in the final causal link analysis.

Qualification Analysis It may be recalled that the Qualification Analysis is required to determine which factors ought to qualify for consideration

[87] ibid.

[88] *EC—Hormones (US) (Recourse to Arbitration—Article 22.6 DSU)* (n 23) [20]; *EC—Hormones (Canada) (Recourse to Arbitration—Article 22.6)* (n 64) [20]; and *US—FSC (Recourse to Arbitration—Article 22.6 DSU)* (n 12) [5.46]–[5.47].

[89] Robert Teh and Alan Yanovich, 'Integrating Economic Analysis into WTO Dispute Settlement Practice: A View from the Trenches' in Marion Jansen, Joost Pauwelyn and Theresa Carpenter, *The Use of Economics in International Trade and Investment Disputes* (CUP 2017) 17.

[90] In particular, see Thomas J Prusa and David C Sharp, 'Simultaneous Equations in Antidumping Investigations' (2001) 14(1) JFE 63, 77; and JP Durling and MP McCullough, 'Teaching Old Laws New Tricks: The Legal Obligation of Non-Attribution and the Need for Economic Rigour in Injury Analyses under US Trade Law' in EK Choi and J Hartigan (eds), *Handbook of International Trade, Volume II* (OUP 2005) 80; Kenneth Kelly, 'The Analysis of Causality in Escape Clause Cases' (1988) 37(2) J Ind Econ 187; Douglas A Irwin, 'Causing Problems? The WTO Review of Causation and Injury Attribution in US Section 201 Cases' (2003) 2(3) WTR 297; and Dukgeun Ahn and William J Moon, 'Alternative Approach to Causation Analysis in Trade Remedy Investigations: "Cost of Production" Test' (2010) 44(5) JWT 1023, 1041–47.

under the causal link analysis in Step Three of the Tripartite Non-attribution/ Causal Link Analysis. It may also be recalled from Chapters 2–4 that the two questions that determine the way in which the Qualification Analysis is conducted are: (1) whether the 'multi-factorial approach' should be used; or if, instead, only sub-injuries produced from a responding Member's failure to comply with the DSB ruling should be included in the causal link analysis; and (2) the threshold that a sub-injury must reach in order to be included in the causal link analysis.

As in Chapter 4, there are no statements in the jurisprudence that may be drawn upon to guide how these questions should be answered. Nonetheless, it is suggested that the 'multi-factorial approach' is superior for similar reasons than those that were set out in Chapter 4 – namely, that economic effects are so complex that it is unlikely that a sub-injury would be the result of one causal factor alone. Moreover, as was mentioned in Chapter 3, there is a possibility that the effects of a failure to comply with the DSB ruling might actually interact with other known factors in the economy. Due to this possibility, it is perhaps artificial to insist solely that only those sub-injuries caused by a responding Member's failure to comply with a DSB ruling should qualify for inclusion in the causal link analysis.

In terms of the threshold that might be set, once again, there is no guidance in the jurisprudence to draw upon on this point. Moreover, it may be that the Arbitrator would wish to retain some flexibility on this point, depending on the nature of the case at hand. Obviously, the implication of having a lower threshold would be that more sub-injuries would qualify for the causal link analysis and therefore the likelihood of making out a causal link is increased. The more likely that a causal link will be made out, the greater the probability, in turn, that a responding Member will be required to provide compensation to the complainant Member for its failure to comply with the DSB ruling.

5.5 Causal Link Analysis: The Third Step of the Tripartite Process

The fact that the Arbitrator has so far simply presumed the causal link between a responding Member's failure to comply with a DSB ruling and the injury to the complainant Member's industry means that the Arbitrator has provided absolutely no guidance about the way in which this causal link should be drawn. Moreover, they have also failed to provide any kind of causal standard that must be reached, such as a 'genuine and substantial relationship of cause and effect' in the context of serious prejudice and trade remedies.[91] Accordingly, in the absence of any such guidance or case law that attempts to draw this causal link, it is difficult to provide any very detailed discussion of how the causal link should be drawn. It is suggested simply that the Arbitrator could examine those factors that have passed the Qualification Analysis and then assess whether those factors belong to a set of factors that is collectively sufficient to cause the overall injury to the complainant Member's industry.

5.6 Quantification of the Level of Nullification and Impairment

The Arbitrator has shown a lack of consistency in its approach to quantifying nullification and impairment. For example, the earlier Arbitrators sought to quantify the level of nullification or impairment by applying a counterfactual based on a relatively simple equation and simple parameters.[92] Later arbitrations have used more sophisticated models for quantifying the level of nullification or impairment, such as an economic model, in the case of *US—Offset Act (Byrd Amendment) (Article 22.6)*,[93] a partial equilibrium model in the case of *US—Tuna II (Mexico) (Article 22.6)*,[94] a linear regression analysis and a dynamic econometric model analysis in the *US—COOL (Article 22.6)* case[95] and a two-step Armington model in *US—Washing Machines (Article 22.6)*,[96] *US—Anti-Dumping Methodologies (China) (Article 22.6)*[97] and *US—Countervailing Duty Measures on Certain Products from China (Article 22.6)*.[98] It is suggested that the Tripartite Non-attribution/Causal Link Analysis offers an alternative approach that could result in greater consistency to the process of quantifying nullification and impairment.

It has already been seen that one of the benefits of using the Tripartite Non-attribution/Causal Link Analysis before turning to quantify the level of nullification and impairment is that the Disentanglement Stage and

[91] WTO, *United States: Subsidies on Upland Cotton—Report of the Appellate Body* (3 March 2005) WT/DS267/AB/R (AB, *US—Upland Cotton*) [438] quoting AB, *US—Wheat Gluten* (n 84) [69].

[92] See, eg, *EC—Bananas III (US) (Recourse to Arbitration—Article 22.6)* (n 12) [7.8]; *EC—Hormones (US) (Recourse to Arbitration—Article 22.6 DSU)* (n 23) [48]–[79]; *EC—Hormones (Canada) (Recourse to Arbitration—Article 22.6))* (n 64) [44]–[68].

[93] (n 10).

[94] (n 18).

[95] (n 18).

[96] (n 63).

[97] (n 59).

[98] (n 54).

Qualification Analysis should provide the Arbitrator with an approximate sense of the level of nullification and impairment caused by the responding Member's failure to comply with the DSB ruling. It is suggested that this information could then be used to assist with quantifying the level of nullification and impairment brought about to a complainant Member's industry as a result of the responding Member's failure to comply with the DSB ruling. It must be noted, however, that the idea that the Tripartite Non-attribution/Causal Link Analysis can assist with quantifying the level of nullification and impairment is premised on the idea that all of the sub-injuries have been captured. If not all of the sub-injuries have been captured, it is possible that use of the model will lead to an erroneous outcome.

Turning to how the model might be applied, imagine that, at the first stage of the Tripartite Non-attribution/Causal Link Analysis, the Arbitrator finds that the injury to the complainant Member's industry may be divided into six sub-injuries. Imagine, then, at the Disentanglement stage, the Arbitrator finds as follows:

1. Sub-injury 1, loss of productivity: 95 per cent caused by the responding Member's failure to comply with the DSB ruling, and 5 per cent caused by other known factors.
2. Sub-injury 2, suppressed utilisation of capacity: 85 per cent caused by the responding Member's failure to comply with the DSB ruling, and 15 per cent caused by other known factors.
3. Sub-injury 3, injury to corporate profits: 92.5 per cent caused by the responding Member's failure to comply with the DSB ruling, and 7.5 per cent caused by other known factors.
4. Sub-injury 4, negative effects on cash flow: 73 per cent caused by the responding Member's failure to comply with the DSB ruling, and 27 per cent caused by other known factors.
5. Sub-injury 5, suppressed ability to raise capital or investments: 91 per cent caused by the responding Member's failure to comply with the DSB ruling, and 9 per cent caused by other known factors.
6. Sub-injury 6, lower return on investments: 88 per cent caused by the responding Member's failure to comply with the DSB ruling, and 12 per cent caused by other known factors.

Say that the Arbitrator has set down a threshold of 80 per cent; five of the aforementioned six sub-injuries would therefore qualify for consideration in the causal link analysis. Depending on the causal standard that is chosen, it is likely that the aforementioned breakdown of sub-injuries would be sufficient to find a causal link between a responding Member's failure to comply with the DSB ruling and injury to the complainant Member's industry. This being the case, the Arbitrator then has the task of quantifying the level of nullification and impairment.

In order to make this quantification, the Arbitrator could proceed as follows:

1. Calculate the percentage contribution of harm that each sub-injury has made to the industry's overall injury. For instance, to take the example of Sub-injury 1, the Arbitrator would attempt to calculate the proportion of the overall harm that was caused by Sub-injury 1 and then multiply it by 100 per cent. This will be called 'Sub-Injury's Causal Contribution'. This step should then be repeated in relation to each sub-injury.

   Imagine that the Sub-Injury's Causal Contribution to the overall level of nullification and impairment in relation to the cotton case study is as follows for each of the aforementioned six sub-injuries:

   - Sub-injury 1: 16%
   - Sub-injury 2: 14%
   - Sub-injury 3: 19%
   - Sub-injury 4: 27%
   - Sub-injury 5: 8%
   - Sub-injury 6: 16%

   To view the breakdown of sub-injuries graphically, see Figure 5.2.
2. Multiply the Sub-Injury's Causal Contribution by the percentage of causal responsibility allocated to the responding Member's failure to comply with the DSB ruling. For example, in the case of Sub-injury 1, the Arbitrator would multiply the Sub-Injury's Causal Contribution found in Step One (i.e., 16 per cent) by 95 per cent. Accordingly, the calculation would be 95% × 16%, which equals 15.2%. This means that, on the basis of Sub-Injury 1 alone, it is known that 15.2 per cent of the ultimate nullification and impairment was caused by the responding Member's failure to comply with the DSB ruling. This new percentage will be called the 'Proportionate Contribution by Sub-Injury'. This step should be repeated in relation to each sub-injury. For the avoidance of doubt, those sub-injuries where the causal contribution to the sub-injury as a result of the failure to comply with the DSB ruling is less than the threshold of causation (in this case, say, 80 per cent) should still be included in the calculation.

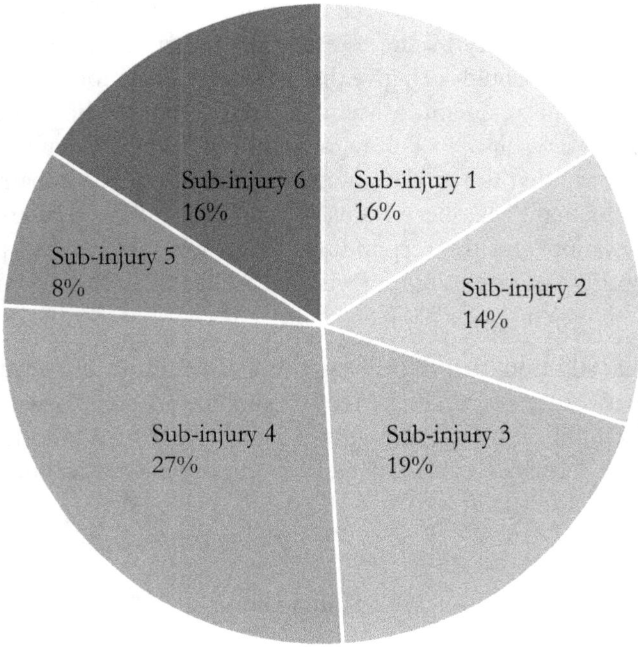

Figure 5.2 Sub-injury's causal contribution

The 'Proportionate Contribution by Sub-Injury' for each of the aforementioned sub-injuries is as follows:

- Sub-injury 1: 15.2%
- Sub-injury 2: 11.9%
- Sub-injury 3: 17.575%
- Sub-injury 4: 19.71%
- Sub-injury 5: 7.28%
- Sub-injury 6: 14.56%

3. Once Step Two has been repeated in relation to all of the sub-injuries, it is then possible to add together all of the percentages representing the 'Proportionate Contribution by Sub-Injury'. This will then give the Arbitrator the percentage contribution that the responding Member's failure to comply with the DSB ruling made to the overall injury. This percentage will be called the 'Percentage Contribution to the Overall Injury'. In this particular case study, the Percentage Contribution to the Overall Industry is 86.295 per cent.
4. Once the Arbitrator has calculated the 'Percentage Contribution to the Overall Injury', it is possible to calculate the amount of compensation

payable by multiplying the total amount of nullification and impairment to the industry by the 'Percentage Contribution to the Overall Industry'. This would then give the Arbitrator the amount of compensation that the responding Member should pay to the complainant Member as a result of its failure to comply with the DSB ruling. So, for example, say that the total amount of nullification and impairment to the complainant Member's industry was $300 million. The amount of compensation that the responding Member would need to pay as a result of its failure to comply with the DSB ruling is $300 million × 86.295%, which equals $258,885,000.

In sum, in addition to performing a non-attribution and causal link analysis between a responding Member's failure to comply with a DSB ruling and nullification and impairment, the Tripartite Non-attribution/Causal Link Analysis can also assist with the quantification of that nullification and impairment.

5.7 Conclusion

The concepts of retaliation and causation are inextricably linked. It has been seen that this linkage is envisaged in a number of the provisions of the WTO's covered agreements. Most obviously, Article XXIII:1 of the GATT 1994 directs the Arbitrator to quantify the complainant's level of nullification and impairment that was actually 'a result of [. . .]' the responding Member's failure to bring its measure into conformity with the DSB ruling, which clearly suggests causation. Article 22.4 DSU, moreover, provides that suspended retaliatory measures must be 'equivalent' to the nullification or impairment of benefits that the measure has caused, or 'appropriate', in the case of Article 4.10 SCM Agreement. These notions of 'equivalence' and what is 'appropriate' would also seem to require that any assessment must take into account the level of injury caused.

Despite these conceptual and textual linkages, the jurisprudence indicates that the Arbitrator has shown a consistent lack of engagement with the analysis of both non-attribution and a causal link. Instead, they have seemingly just presumed the existence of the causal link between a responding Member's failure to comply with a DSB ruling and the complainant Member's level of nullification and impairment. Indeed, it would seem that the existence of the causal link is only explicitly considered by Arbitrators when it *cannot* be made out. Whereas Article 3.8 DSU allows ordinary Panels to presume a causal link between a breach of the covered agreements and nullification and impairment, the Arbitrator is not entitled to continue to make such a presumption in the context of arbitrations concerning Articles 22.6 DSU and 4.10 SCM Agreement. Moreover, Arbitrators are yet to consider, in any systematic manner, the way in which other known factors might confuse the causal link, despite the fact that the jurisprudence indicates that responding Members have consistently raised the need to consider the impact of other known factors.

This chapter has proposed that the Tripartite Non-attribution/Causal Link Analysis might be used to address some of the analytical problems that currently exist in the jurisprudence. Using such a methodology arguably supports a more coherent vision of causation, in which causation is established prior to a calculation of nullification and impairment. Moreover, at a practical level, it has been seen that the data that is obtained from the Tripartite Non-attribution/Causal Link Analysis can be used to assist with the quantification of nullification and impairment. One of the final implications of conducting a more rigorous non-attribution analysis is that other known factors may be found to mitigate the causal link between the responding Member's failure to comply with the DSB ruling and the resulting nullification and impairment. It follows from this that it is likely that a responding Member would be required to pay less compensation to the complainant Member than it would if a non-attribution analysis had not been undertaken. This lesser amount, however, is more likely to be a more accurate reflection of the amount of nullification and impairment actually caused by the responding Member's failure to comply with the DSB ruling.

Conclusion

Restatement of Argument

This book opened with a quotation from David Hume, who said:

> There is no question, which on account of its importance, as well as difficulty, has caus'd more disputes both among antient and modern philosophers, than this concerning the efficacy of causes, or that quality which makes them be follow'd by their effects.[1]

Not only has this study confronted the question of determining causation in respect of certain provisions of WTO law, but also how to precede the determination of a causal link with an effective non-attribution analysis. In other words, the particular type of causal analysis that has been at the heart of this book has had a dual character – namely, the question of not only how to draw a causal link between two factors, but also the question of how to exclude causation between an effect and other known factors. In this sense, the causal analysis with which this book has been concerned has both positive and negative features to it.

This book has identified nine different parts of WTO law in which non-attribution and causal link analyses are explicitly required or in which they might be implied. These include: (1) safeguard measures (Articles 2.1 and 4.2(a) and (b) of the Safeguards Agreement); (2) antidumping measures (Articles 3.1 and 3.5 of the AD Agreement); (3) countervailing duties (Article 15.5 of the SCM Agreement); (4) serious prejudice (Articles 5(c) and 6.3 of the SCM Agreement); (5, 6 and 7) the relationship between a measure and its policy objective (Articles XX GATT, XIV GATS and Article 2.2 TBT Agreement); and (8 and 9) the relationship between a responding Member's failure to comply with a DSB ruling and the complainant Member's level of nullification and

[1] David Hume, *A Treatise of Human Nature* (LA Selby-Bigge ed, 1789; revised by PH Nidditch, 2nd edn, OUP 1975) B I, pt III, s xiv, 156.

impairment (Articles 22.6 DSU and 4.10 SCM Agreement). The Tripartite Non-attribution/Causal Link Analysis has been put forward as a possible methodology for performing the non-attribution and causal link analyses in these parts of WTO law.

Whilst the basic steps of the Tripartite Non-attribution/Causal Link Analysis are broadly applied in the same way across each of the chapters, the purpose of performing the non-attribution and causal link analyses varies with each chapter. In Chapter 2, the purpose is to make a determination as to whether Member B has injured the industry of Member A to such an extent that Member A is justified in implementing trade remedies. Chapter 3 is concerned with determining whether Member B's subsidised products have caused negative effects to Member A's trade interests. In Chapter 4, the objective of the analysis is to determine the effect of a measure on a policy objective. Finally, the aim of the non-attribution and causal link analyses in Chapter 5 is to determine the level of nullification and impairment that Member B has caused to Member A's industry. Chapters 2, 3 and 5 all involve some kind of economic harm to a Member (whether realised or potential), whereas Chapter 4 is the only chapter that is concerned with the causal contribution of a measure to a policy objective. This difference is reflected in the fact that Chapter 4 is the only chapter in this book that substantively draws on causation for its explanatory and even predictive potential, rather than its attributive qualities.

Current Jurisprudence

In the process of putting forward the Tripartite Non-attribution/Causal Link Analysis, this book has examined the current approach to analysing non-attribution and causal links in the jurisprudence in the nine identified areas of WTO law. In so doing, it has identified a number of conceptual problems in the current jurisprudence. One of the most fundamental problems with the current jurisprudence is that it consistently reflects a tendency to attempt to derive an effect from the nature of its supposed cause. Indeed, Hume's warning against doing so was repeated in Chapters 3–5, where the tendency manifested in each.

Taking Chapter 3 first, it was seen that there are two approaches to performing the non-attribution and causal link analyses in relation to a determination of serious prejudice under the SCM Agreement – namely, the unitary approach (which requires determining the cause and effect of a subsidy together in one step) and the bifurcated approach (which requires analysing the cause and effect of a subsidy separately in two steps). It was argued that the unitary approach is premised on a failure to recognise cause and effect as separate phenomena, and a misconception that an effect may be knowable a priori through analysing its cause. It is for this reason that this book preferred the bifurcated approach. Similarly, in Chapter 4, when tasked with interrogating the effect of a measure on a policy objective, Panels and the AB have tended to look at the design and structure of the supposed cause in order to make conclusions about its impact on a policy objective. In so doing, Panels and the AB have resisted the idea of quantifying the effects of a measure by using real-world data. Finally, in Chapter 5, arbitrators have tended to presume the causal link between a responding Member's failure to comply with its DSB ruling and a complainant Member's nullification and impairment. This presumption of a causal link, then, involves inferring the effect simply from examining the nature of its supposed cause.

In a related vein, another problematic feature of the current jurisprudence is a preference for non-quantitative data over quantitative data at several points. That is, the jurisprudence holds in several cases that a determination about injury or causation may be made using either quantitative or non-quantitative data, but then precedes only to use non-quantitative data. This can be seen, most obviously, in relation to analysing the relationship between a measure and its policy objective under the General Exceptions or in relation to Article 2.2 of the TBT Agreement. It was seen in Chapter 4 that the AB has held that a determination as to the effectiveness of a measure may be made using both quantitative and non-quantitative evidence.[2] To date, all of the relevant Panels and the AB have relied on non-quantitative evidence in making the determination. In effect, then, the jurisprudence has shown a reluctance to embrace the use of quantitative data for determining the impact of a measure on a policy objective, despite the fact that quantitative data would be more reliable.

Similarly, in the context of a determination of serious prejudice under Chapter 3, it was seen that the Panel and AB in *US—Upland Cotton* explicitly held that a serious prejudice analysis does not require a subsidy

[2] WTO, *Brazil: Measures Affecting Imports of Retreaded Tyres—Report of the Appellate Body* (3 December 2007) WT/DS332/AB/R (AB, *Brazil—Retreaded Tyres*) [146]; WTO, *European Communities: Measures Prohibiting the Importation and Marketing of Seal Products—Report of the Appellate Body* (22 May 2014) WT/DS400/AB/R; WT/DS401/AB/R (AB, *EC—Seal Products*) [5.215].

to be quantified.[3] Moreover, none of the Panels or the AB have sought to use a quantitative approach for performing the non-attribution analysis required in relation to a determination of serious prejudice. As was argued in Chapter 3, it would seem nonsensical to engage in a non-attribution analysis that does not use quantitative data because the use of non-quantitative data does not allow a fact-finder to determine the *interaction* between subsidies and other known factors in any meaningful way, leading to a non-attribution analysis that is somewhat tokenistic.

In sum, the jurisprudence reflects a reluctance to embrace quantitative data, even in situations that make little sense without it. In part, this may be because Panels and the AB feel uncomfortable with quantitative data and econometric methods. This would seem to be a weak reason, however, since it has been seen that the jurisprudence has used quantitative approaches in analysing other parts of WTO law.[4] Moreover, Panels have the authority under Article 13.2 DSU to establish 'expert review groups' which can be convened for the purpose of handling the quantitative data that is required for a genuine non-attribution analysis (in all of the forms that this book discusses), or establishing the impact of a measure on a policy objective, for the purposes of the General Exceptions or Article 2.2 of the TBT Agreement in Chapter 4. Finally, and most fundamentally, a reluctance to use quantitative data potentially results in an analysis that misconceives of the nature of causation, thereby defeating the purpose of the exercise.

Contribution of This Book

The contribution of this book to the field is threefold. First, it identifies those parts of WTO law in which non-attribution and causal link analyses are explicitly required, or in which they might be implied. Second, the book analyses the current approach in the jurisprudence to undertaking non-attribution and causal link analyses for the nine parts of WTO law identified earlier and observes some analytical flaws with the

[3] WTO, *United States: Subsidies on Upland Cotton—Report of the Panel* (8 September 2004) WT/DS267/R (Panel, *US—Upland Cotton*) [7.1171] and WTO, *United States: Subsidies on Upland Cotton—Report of the Appellate Body* (3 March 2005) WT/DS267/AB/R (AB, *US—Upland Cotton*) [467].

[4] See, for example, Robert Teh and Alan Yanovich, 'Integrating Economic Analysis into WTO Dispute Settlement Practice: A View from the Trenches' in Marion Jansen, Joost Pauwelyn and Theresa Carpenter, *The Use of Economics in International Trade and Investment Disputes* (CUP 2017) 17.

current approach in the jurisprudence. Finally, this book has taken up the three-step process for analysing non-attribution and causal links in respect of the Safeguards Agreement that was set out by the AB in one paragraph of *US—Wheat Gluten* and detailed how such a methodology might work in practice as an alternative to the current approach. The book then applied the methodology to each of the nine parts of WTO law that have been identified as benefitting from it.

Whilst the Tripartite Non-attribution/Causal Link Analysis is employed to a different end in each chapter, the benefits that it brings to each are the same – namely, a more systematic approach, a genuine non-attribution analysis and concomitant consistency and legal certainty. An examination of the jurisprudence throughout this book has shown that, in the absence of the Tripartite Non-attribution/Causal Link Analysis, the analysis of non-attribution and causal links is often ad hoc and inconsistent. In relation to Chapter 3, for example, the jurisprudence sometimes uses a unitary approach to causation (that is, where the cause and effect of a subsidy should be determined together in one step), and sometimes it takes a bifurcated approach (where cause and effect are determined separately). It was seen that the jurisprudence also engages in a non-attribution analysis that is frequently inadequate and tokenistic. Chapter 4, moreover, discussed the way in which the jurisprudence has not used any consistent approach to interrogating the effect of a measure on a policy objective under the General Exceptions or Article 2.2 of the TBT Agreement. Instead, a number of vague, non-quantitative descriptors have been used to describe the level of contribution that a measure makes to a policy objective, without any indication as to what the discrepancy between these descriptors signify. Finally, Chapter 5 considers the ad hoc way in which arbitrators have taken account of other known factors and their impact on the causal link between a failure to comply with a DSB ruling and the resulting nullification and impairment. It has been suggested that the Tripartite Non-attribution/Causal Link Analysis could assist with providing greater consistency in each of these cases, and such consistency would also bring greater legal certainty to Members.

Having just set out some key advantages of the Tripartite Non-attribution/Causal Link Analysis, it is important to recall some of the pitfalls using a methodology reliant on econometric analysis that were set out in the Introduction to this book. Specifically, despite their scientific appearance, methodologically unsound econometric models can often suggest correlations between two variables that are statistically related but not, in fact, causally linked. Accordingly, econometric models must be very carefully designed and analysed. Moreover, the Tripartite Non-attribution/Causal Link Analysis relies on Members being able to provide sufficient data for the econometric model, which may not always be forthcoming, particularly amongst developing countries. Third, lawyers often struggle with understanding and applying quantitative evidence, and therefore a greater effort must be made by lawyers and econometricians alike to translate the benefits of quantitative evidence to those with little expertise in it. In this sense, the Tripartite Non-attribution/Causal Link Analysis does not serve as a total panacea for dealing with the difficult causal questions that underlie the nine areas of WTO law that this book has discussed. Instead, its more modest aim is to serve as an alternative to the current jurisprudential approach, where the limitations of econometric analysis and data collection can be sufficiently managed.

The difficulty and complexity of causation has been acknowledged at several points throughout this book. Causation in WTO law is arguably even more complex than many other areas of law because it is interested in causation not only for its attributive potential, but also for its explanatory and predictive ones (as was seen in Chapter 4). Moreover, it requires grappling with something as difficult and complex as international trade flows and financial markets, which brings with them many other known factors, as well as the need to use quantitative approaches to assessing causation. For this reason, excluding irrelevant factors is just as important in determining causation as drawing positive links between factors.

The nine parts of WTO law that were discussed in this book are all diverse and varied in nature and purpose. Nonetheless, the Tripartite Non-attribution/Causal Link Analysis represents a means of systematising these otherwise very different parts of WTO law. It also provides a way of analysing them with a more rigorous, clearer and more consistent methodology than that which is currently present in the jurisprudence, provided that the limitations of econometric analysis can be judiciously managed.

BIBLIOGRAPHY

Books

Antolisei, Francesco, *Il Rapporto di Causalità nel Diritto Penale* (Padua 1934)

Beauchamp, Tom L and Alexander Rosenberg, *Hume and the Problem of Causation* (OUP 1981)

Becht, Arno C and Frank W Miller, *The Test of Factual Causation in Negligence and Strict Liability Cases* (Washington University Studies 1961)

Beebee, Helen, Christopher Hitchcock and Peter Menzies (eds), *The Oxford Handbook of Causation* (OUP 2009)

Benitah, Marc, *The Law of Subsidies under the GATT/WTO System* (Kluwer 2001)

Bhandari, Jagdeep S and Alan O Sykes (eds), *Antidumping and Countervailing Duty Cases: A Reply to Professor Sykes, Economic Dimensions in International Law: Comparative and Empirical Perspectives* (CUP 1997)

Bown, Chad P, *Self-Enforcing Trade: Developing Countries and WTO Dispute Settlement* (Brookings Institution Press 2009)

Bown, Chad P and Joost Pauwelyn, *The Law, Economics and Politics of Retaliation in WTO Dispute Settlement* (CUP 2010)

Cane, Peter, *Responsibility in Law and Morality* (OUP 1950)

Cartwright, Nancy, *The Dappled World: A Study of the Boundaries of Science* (CUP 1999)

Choi, EK and J Hartigan (eds), *Handbook of International Trade, Volume II* (Blackwell 2005)

Cumming, Geoff and Robert Calin-Jageman, *Introduction to the New Statistics: Estimation, Open Science, and Beyond* (Routledge 2017)

Engisch, Karl, *Die Kausalität als Merkmal der strafrechtlichen Tatbestände* (Tübingen 1931)

Field, Andy, Jeremy Miles and Zoë Field, *Discovering Statistics Using R* (Sage 2012)

Goldberg, Richard (ed), *Perspectives on Causation* (Hart 2011)

Gruszczynski, Lukasz, *Regulating Health and Environmental Risks under WTO Law: A Critical Analysis of the SPS Agreement* (OUP 2010)

Hart, HLA and Tony Honoré, *Causation in the Law* (2nd edn, OUP 1985)

Hinton, Perry, *Statistics Explained* (3rd edn, Routledge 2014)

Huerta-Goldman, Jorge A, Antoine Romaneti and Franz X Stirnimann (eds), *WTO Litigation, Investment Arbitration and Commercial Arbitration* (Kluwer 2013)

Hume, David, *An Enquiry Concerning Human Understanding* (LA Selby-Bigge ed, 3rd edn, OUP 1975)

A Treatise of Human Nature (1789) (LA Selby-Bigge ed, revised by PH Nidditch, 2nd edn, OUP 1975)

Jansen, Marion, Joost Pauwelyn and Theresa Carpenter, *The Use of Economics in International Trade and Investment Disputes* (CUP 2017)

Johnston Jr, CR (ed and comp), *Law and Practice of United States Regulation of International Trade* (Oceana Publications 1989)

Kahmen, Benedikt and Markus Stepanians (eds), *Critical Essays on Causation and Responsibility* (Walter de Gruyter 2013)

Kant, Immanuel, *Critique of Pure Reason* (Paul Guyer and Allen W Wood tr and ed, CUP 1998)

Prolegomena to Any Future Metaphysics That Will Be Able to Come Forward as Science: With Selections from the Critique of Pure Reason (Gary Hatfield tr and ed, CUP 1997)

Keeton, Robert, *Legal Cause in the Law of Torts* (Ohio State UP 1963)

Leonhard, Franz, *Die Kausalität als Erklärung durch Ergänzun* (W Schmitz 1946)

Lewis, David, *Counterfactuals* (Blackwell 1973)

On the Plurality of Worlds (Blackwell 1986)

Lexis, Wilhelm, *Zur theorie der massenerscheinungen in der menschlichen gesellschaft* (W Schmitz 1877)

Mackie, John L, *The Cement of the Universe* (OUP 1974)

Mavroidis, Petros C, Patrick A Messerlin and M Wauters, *The Law and Economics of Contingent Protection in the WTO* (Edward Elgar 2008)

Michotte, Albert, *La Perception de la causalité* (Louvain 1954)

Mill, JS, *A System of Logic Ratiocinative and Inductive* (JM Robson ed, Routledge 1973)

Moore, Michael S, *Causation and Responsibility: An Essay in Law, Morals, and Metaphysics* (OUP 2009)

Moosa, Imad, *Econometrics as a Con Art: Exposing the Limitations and Abuses of Econometrics* (Edward Elgar 2017)

Murphy, Kevin R, Brett Myors and Allen Wolach, *Statistical Power Analysis: A Simple and General Model for Traditional and Modern Hypothesis Tests* (4th edn, Routledge 2014)

Nedumpara, James J, *Injury and Causation in Trade Remedy Law: A Study of WTO Law and Country Practices* (Springer 2016)

Owen, David G (ed), *The Philosophical Foundations of Tort Law* (OUP 1997)

Pearl, Judea, *Causality, Models, Reasoning, and Inference* (CUP 2000)

Perkins, Rollin M, *Criminal Law* (2nd edn, Foundation Press 1969)

Piérola, Fernando, *The Challenge of Safeguards in the WTO* (CUP 2014)

Prosser, William Lloyd et al, *Prosser and Keeton on the Law of Torts* (5th edn, West Publishing 1984)

Stoll, Hans, *Kausalzusammenhang und Normzweck im Deliktsrecht* (Tubingen 1968)

Sykes, Alan O, *The WTO Safeguards Agreement: A Commentary* (OUP 2006)

Tharakan, PKM (ed), *Policy Implications of Antidumping Measures* (Elsevier Science Publishers 1991)

Trendelenburg, Friedrich Adolf, *Logische Untersuchungen* (S Hirzel 1870)

Van Bael & Bellis, *EU AD and Other Trade Defence Instruments* (6th edn, Wolters Kluwer 2019)

Vigen, Tyler, *Spurious Correlations* (Hachette Books 2015)

Williams, Glanville, *Joint Torts and Contributory Negligence* (Stevens 1951)

Yan, Xin and Xiao Gang Su, *Linear Regression Analysis: Theory and Computing* (World Scientific 2009)

Journal Articles

Ahn, Dukgeun and William J Moon, 'Alternative Approach to Causation Analysis in Trade Remedy Investigations: "Cost of Production" Test' (2010) 44(5) JWT 1023

Anderson, Kym, 'Peculiarities of Retaliation in WTO Dispute Settlement' (2000) 1 (2) WTR 123

van Anken, Anne, 'Opportunities for and Limits to an Economic Analysis of International Law' (2001) 3(1) Transnatl Corp Rev 27

Balistreri, Edward, Petros C Mavroidis and Thomas J Prusa, 'What If? Tinkering with the Counterfactual: A Comment on *US—Washing Machines (Article 22.6—US)*' (2020) EUI Working Papers (RSCAs 2020/50) Robert Schuman Centre for Advanced Studies, Global Governance Programme-405 <https://cadmus.eui.eu/handle/1814/67092> accessed 1 June 2022

Bartels, Lorand, 'The Chapeau of the General Exceptions in the WTO GATT and GATS Agreements: A Reconstruction' (2015) 109(1) AJIL 105

'Procedural Aspects of Shared Responsibility in the WTO Dispute Settlement System' (2013) 4(2) J Int Disput Settl 343

Benitah, Marc, 'From Economic Complexity to Legal Indeterminacy: Causality between Subsidy and Injury' (1999) 33(1) JWT 87

Boltuck, Richard D, 'An Economic Analysis of Dumping' (1987) 21(5) JWT 45

Bown, Chad P, 'Why Are Safeguards under the WTO So Unpopular?' (2002) 47 WTR 47

Calabresi, Guido, 'Concerning Cause and the Law of Torts' (1975–76) 43 U Chi L Rev 69

Cartwright, Nancy, 'One Word, Many Things' (2002) 71(5) Phil Sci 805

Charnovitz, Steve, 'Rethinking WTO Trade Sanctions' (2001) 95 AJIL 792

Fetzer, James J, 'Inference for Econometric Modelling in Antidumping, Countervailing Duty and Safeguard Investigations' (2009) 8(4) WTR 545

Gnutzmann-Mkrtchyan, Arevik and Isabelle Van Damme, 'Expired Measures, Excess Duty Drawbacks and Causation: The Appellate Body Report in *EU–PET (Pakistan)*' (2020) 19 WTR 232

Goertzel, Ted, 'Myths of Murder and Multiple Regression' (2002) 26(1) The Skeptical Inquirer 19

Green, Leon, 'The *Wagon Mound No. 2*: Foreseeability Revised' (1967) 2 Utah LR 197

Grossman, Gene, 'Imports as a Cause of Injury: The Case of the US Steel Industry' (1986) 20 J Int Econ 201

Hausman, Daniel M, 'Essay Review: Physical Causation' (2002) 33 Stud Hist Philos 717

Horn, Heinrik and Petros C Mavroidis, '*US – Lamb: United States – Safeguard Measures on Imports of Fresh, Chilled or Frozen Lamb Meat from New Zealand and Australia: What Should Be Required of a Safeguard Investigation?*' (2003) 2(3) WTR 395

Irwin, Douglas A, 'Causing Problems? The WTO Review of Causation and Injury Attribution in US Section 201 Cases' (2003) 2(3) WTR 297

Kaye, David H, 'Is Proof of Statistical Significance Relevant?' (1986) 61 Wash L Rev 1333

Kelly, Kenneth, 'The Analysis of Causality in Escape Clause Cases' (1988) 37(2) J Ind Econ 187

Lacey, Simon, 'Causal Link, Non-Attribution and Contingency Protection in the WTO' (December 2002) Working Paper, 37, <https://ssrn.com/abstract=1135133> accessed 3 November 2017

Lewis, David, 'Causation' (1973) 70 J Phil 556

Leys, David, 'Does a Theory of Causation Exist under the WTO Safeguards Agreement?' (2014) 9(1) GTCJ 10

Mackie, JL, 'Causes and Conditions' (1965) 2 Am Phil Q 245

Mah, Jai, 'Injury and Causation in the WTO Agreement on Safeguards' (2001) J World Intellect Prop 373

McAller, Michael, Adrian Pagan and Paul Volker, 'What Will Take the Con Out of Econometrics?' (1985) 75(3) Am Econ Rev 293

Messenger, Gregory, 'The Development of International Law and the Role of Causal Language' (2016) 36(1) Oxford J Legal Stud 110

Miranda, Jorge, 'Causal Link and Non-Attribution as Interpreted in WTO Trade Remedy Disputes' (2010) 44(4) JWT 729

Mitchell, Andrew and Thomas Prusa, 'China – Autos: Haven't We Danced This Dance Before?' (2016) 15(2) WTR 303

Moosa, Imad, 'Blaming Suicide on NASA and Divorce on Margarine: The Hazard of Using Cointegration to Derive Inference on Spurious Correlation' (2017) 49(15) Appl Econ 1483

Morke, ME and HE Kruth, 'Determining Whether Dumped or Subsidised Imports Injure Domestic Injuries' (1989) 7 Contemp Pol Issues 78

Narayanan, Prakash, 'Injury Investigations in "Material Retardation" Antidumping Cases' (2004) 25(1) Nw J Int'l L & Bus 37

Nedumpara, James J, 'Causation in Trade Remedy Actions: Problems with the "But For" Test' (2015) 10(11) GTCJ 402

Pindyck, Robert S and Julio J Rotemberg, 'Are Imports to Blame? Attribution of Injury under the 1974 Trade Act' (1987) 30 J Law & Econ 101

Prusa, Thomas J and David C Sharp, 'Simultaneous Equations in Antidumping Investigations' (2001) 14(1) JFE 63

Robinson, JA, 'Hume's Two Definitions of "Cause"' (1962) 12(47) Phil Q 162

Rue, John D, 'Returning to the Roots of Bramble Bush: The "But for" Test Regains Primacy in Causal Analysis in the American Law Institute's Proposed Restatement (Third) of Torts' (2003) 71(6) Fordham L Rev 2679

Sapir, Andrew and Joel P Trachtman, 'Subsidization, Price Suppression, and Expertise: Causation and Precision in Upland Cotton' (2008) 7(1) WTR 183

Schaffer, Jonathan, 'Contrastive Causation in the Law' (2010) 16 Legal Theory 259

Scheines, Richard, 'Causation, Truth and the Law' (2008) 73(2) Brooklyn L Rev 625

Sharp, David and Kenneth Zantow, 'Attribution of Injury in the Shrimp Antidumping Case: A Simultaneous Equations Approach' (2005) 6 Econ Bull 1

Sikes, Devin, 'The Need for New Causation Standards in Antidumping, Countervailing Duty and Safeguard Actions' (2010) 7(1) Manch J Int Econ Law 39

Smith, Jeremiah, 'Legal Cause in Actions in Tort' (1911–12) 25 Harvard L Rev 103

Spamann, Holger, 'The Myth of "Rebalancing" Retaliation in WTO Dispute Settlement Practice' (2006) 9 JIEL 31

Steinberg, Richard H and Timothy E Josling, 'When the Peace Ends: The Vulnerability of EC and US Agricultural Subsidies to WTO Legal Challenge' (2003) 6(2) JIEL 369

Sykes, Alan O, 'The Economics of Injury in Antidumping Countervailing Duty Investigations' (1996) 16(1) Int Rev Law Econ 5

'The Economics of WTO Rules on Subsidies and Countervailing Measures' (2003) University of Chicago John M Olin Program in Law and Economics Working Paper No 186 <https://chicagounbound.uchicago.edu/cgi/viewcontent.cgi?article=1515&context=law_and_economics> accessed 22 May 2019

'The Safeguards Mess: A Critique of WTO Jurisprudence' (2003) 2(3) WTR 261

Tayal, Pratik, 'A New World of Causation in Safeguards: Application of the "But for" Test' (2015) 10(1) GTCJ 355

Tintner, Gerhard, 'The Definition of Econometrics' (1953) 21(1) *Econometrica* 31

Williams, Glanville, 'Causation in the Law' (1961) 19(1) *Camb LJ* 62

Wright, Richard W, 'Causation in Tort Law' (1985) 73(6) California L Rev 1735

Websites

Honoré, Antony, 'Causation in the Law', *The Stanford Encyclopedia of Philosophy* (Winter edn, 2010) <http://plato.stanford.edu/archives/win2010/entries/causation-law/> accessed 26 September 2015

Moore, Michael, 'Causation in the Law', *The Stanford Encyclopedia of Philosophy* (Fall edn, 2019) <https://plato.stanford.edu/entries/causation-law/> accessed 10 August 2021

Vigen, Tyler, 'Spurious Correlations' Tyler Vigen <www.tylervigen.com/spurious-correlations> accessed 14 September 2021

INDEX

For EU product safety concerns, contact us at Calle de José Abascal, 56–1°,
28003 Madrid, Spain or eugpsr@cambridge.org.

www.ingramcontent.com/pod-product-compliance
Lightning Source LLC
LaVergne TN
LVHW011809200926
848484LV00005B/1118

* 9 7 8 1 3 1 6 5 1 1 3 0 5 *